T0054564

"The book is structured so that each chapter functions in isolation, but when read front to back *Sellout* presents a fluid timeline of events that follows punk on its conflicting journey through the mainstream."
—*Vice*

"Ozzi nails the balance of knowledge and appreciation in this fantastic read."
—*SPIN*

"An intriguing look at a pivotal time for the music industry."
—*NME*

"Lucid, engaging, and largely objective. . . . Ozzi's true strength as a writer and storyteller comes through in the meticulous construction of chapters, and how these seemingly personal stories gradually lock together to form the backbone of the book's larger subcultural chronology."
—*New Noise*

"In *Sellout,* Ozzi has written a detailed, inviting map of the complicated world of punk ethics wrestling with corporate interests."
—*Razorcake*

"Ozzi's crisp prose and vibrant storytelling colorfully capture a flamboyant chapter in music history. This accomplishes what the best music books do: drives readers back to listening."
—*Publishers Weekly*

"A forensic and uniquely sympathetic dive into one of the most uncouth actions for an artist—selling out, baby."
—**Jeff Rosenstock**

"*Sellout* perfectly encapsulates the musician's delicate dance between art and commerce."
—**Jonah Ray, *Mystery Science Theater 3000***

"A fascinating and entertaining look at punk bands signing to major labels to expand their audience and their careers. *Sellout* offers crucial insight into the way punk rock and big business have attempted to work together in the thirty years following Nirvana's *Nevermind.*"
—**Craig Finn, The Hold Steady**

"In *Sellout,* Dan Ozzi tackles the history of each band and what happened in their careers leading up to the ultimate decision with precision and care, and delivers it without an ounce of judgment. For a punk . . . that's pretty remarkable!"
—**Jeremy Bolm, Touché Amoré**

SELLOUT

SELLOUT

The Major-Label Feeding Frenzy
That Swept Punk, Emo, and Hardcore
(1994–2007)

DAN OZZI

DEYST.

An Imprint of WILLIAM MORROW

HarperCollins books may be purchased for educational, business, or sales promotional use. For information, please e-mail the Special Markets Department at SPsales@harpercollins.com.

A hardcover edition of this book was published in 2021 by Houghton Mifflin Harcourt.

FIRST DEY STREET PAPERBACK EDITION PUBLISHED 2022.

Book design by Chrissy Kurpeski

The Library of Congress has cataloged a hardcover edition of this book as follows:

Names: Ozzi, Dan, author.
Title: Sellout : the major label feeding frenzy that swept punk, emo, and hardcore (1994–2007) / Dan Ozzi.
Description: Boston : Houghton Mifflin Harcourt, 2021. | Includes bibliographical references and index.
Identifiers: LCCN 2021014652 (print) | LCCN 2021014653 (ebook) | ISBN 9780358244301 (hardback) | ISBN 9780358450276 | ISBN 9780358450450 | ISBN 9780358239963(ebook)
Subjects: LCSH: Punk rock music—United States—History and criticism. | Rock music—United States—1991–2000—History and criticism. | Rock music—United States—2001–2010—History and criticism. | Rock groups—United States. | BISAC: MUSIC / Essays | MUSIC / Genres & Styles / Punk
Classification: LCC ML3534.3 (ebook) | LCC ML3534.3 .O99 2021 (print) | DDC 781.660973—dc23

ISBN 978-0-06-326914-9 (pbk.)

23 24 25 26 27 LBC 8 7 6 5 4

*For Matt Siblo and Tami Lynn Andrew,
and all the Saturday nights we spent in record stores
while everyone else was doing whatever normal kids do.*

CONTENTS

Rock and roll's a sacrifice.

— SINGLE MOTHERS, "WOMB"

INTRODUCTION

THEY ARRIVED WITH their business cards and with their check-books. They descended on dingy rock clubs and dimly lit bars. They talked a smooth game and their shirts were tucked into their jeans. They were major-label A&R scouts and, by 1993, they were every-where.

The punk scene had names for these sorts of people. They were the corporate villains mocked in song lyrics and torn apart in fan-zines. They were called vampires and leeches, and their sole mission was to suck the life out of independent bands and leave them dry. They were the enemy. And now here they were in the flesh, on the lookout for fresh meat.

This wasn't the first time that the majors had tried to sink their teeth into the genre. A&R reps had first come sniffing around punk rock during its birth in the mid-seventies, making unlikely stars of rock 'n' roll's antiheroes. Warner nabbed the Ramones, Virgin picked up the Sex Pistols, and CBS had the Clash. Punk infiltrated the system and planted its flag in pop culture. As it grew more popular, its countercultural ethos became part of the mainstream. But the moment was fleeting. After the punk explosion died out toward the end of the decade, due to dwindling cultural cachet and the deaths of some of its figureheads, major labels largely left the underground alone. Once there was no more money to be wrung out of punk, they turned their focus to emerging genres like new wave, R&B, and glam metal.

Throughout the eighties, few bands from the punk, hardcore, and alternative rock realms were even blips on the radars of major-label A&R reps, and with good reason. Much of the music lacked commercial appeal, often deliberately so. Of the handful of bands that were palatable enough to get called up to the majors—Hüsker Dü, the Replacements, Sonic Youth—none of them exactly proved themselves to be winning financial investments. Most were viewed internally at labels as prestige signings—a way for a company to buy themselves some cred and win the respect of critics.

And so, mainstream music and underground rock existed independently of each other for more than a decade without much overlap. On one end was the lucrative establishment, which helped artists dominate *Billboard* charts, MTV, and national press, and on the other, an autonomous network of small clubs, indie labels, promoters, and distributors struggling to get by. Aside from the anomalies of R.E.M. and U2, who successfully transitioned from college radio to Top 40 stations, there was little crossover between factions. The lines were drawn in crisp black and white.

Then a band from Aberdeen, Washington, came along and wrote an album that flipped the world upside down.

$ $ $

No one saw Nirvana coming. When Geffen/DGC Records took a chance on the band's sophomore album, *Nevermind,* in September 1991, expectations were modest, with only 46,000 copies shipping to stores in the United States. But thanks to the trio's small but rabid cult following on the indie rock circuit, the album quickly caught on with young listeners. Aided by minimal marketing, it debuted on the Billboard 200 chart at number 144 and climbed steadily over that month—to 109, then 65, then 35. Once MTV started airing their video for "Smells Like Teen Spirit," its momentum couldn't be contained. After just eight weeks, *Nevermind* had gone platinum.

Following a decade of bombastic, sex-crazed hair metal bands and shiny, mass-market pop acts, the raw and unpretentious Nirvana was the perfect candidate to usher in the fresh look, sound, and attitude of the 1990s. With his dirty Converse sneakers, the band's greasy frontman, Kurt Cobain, kicked the door open on a new era of rock that prided itself on authenticity and anti-commercialism. As a nation of despondent Gen Xers latched on to *Nevermind,* Nirvana's major-label debut organically took on a life of its own. When asked by the *New York Times* how DGC had created a phenomenon that was soon to unseat King of Pop Michael Jackson at the top of the *Billboard* charts, label president Eddie Rosenblatt shrugged. "We didn't do anything," he admitted. "It was just one of those get-out-of-the-way-and-duck records."

Nevermind's meteoric rise put the last nail in the coffin of the 1980s and torched any lingering hair metal popularity. Leather pants and teased hair gave way to ripped jeans and flannel shirts. "Cum On Feel the Noize" was out; "Come as You Are" was in. Radio stations, MTV, and record labels had a newfound interest in guitar bands that were grittier and edgier. Tastemakers ravenously combed local scenes for the next Nirvana, the next Kurt Cobain, the next Seattle. Ten years of DIY culture and its entire movement had finally hit a tipping point and fundamentally changed the world. "Grunge" was now the hot new industry term, and everything in its orbit was in demand. Suddenly, the underground was financially viable, and the lines that had been black and white turned gray. Or, more accurately, green, as money started flowing into the underground from the corporations trying to buy it all up.

What followed in the wake of *Nevermind* has been described as a major-label feeding frenzy, an A&R gold rush, and an indie rock signing blitz. A&R reps raced one another to mine previously untapped scenes where rock music was thriving, in hopes of discovering the next breakout stars. After they'd fully pillaged Nirvana's stomping grounds in Seattle, they searched elsewhere—D.C., San

Diego, Chapel Hill—and eventually landed in San Francisco. That's where this book begins—with a catchy punk trio from the East Bay called Green Day, who inked a deal with Reprise Records in the summer of '93 for the release of their third album, *Dookie*.

$ $ $

After Green Day left the indie world for the mainstream, a flood of other punk bands were given the chance to follow. A&Rs tried winning them over with fancy dinners and hefty bar tabs charged to the company card. Blue hair and piercings could be spotted in meeting rooms at label offices in New York and Los Angeles. The support system these bands were being offered was enticing—proper studio accommodations, budgets to make music videos, and placement in malls and chain stores like Sam Goody and Tower Records. For bands that considered themselves lucky to earn enough gas money to drive their Econoline vans to the next town each night, these luxuries were often well beyond the ceiling of their modest imaginations.

But with this opportunity came a catch. The insular underground communities that had incubated these musicians were not about to let their scene be ransacked again without a fight. After a decade of carving out their own space, punks grew protective of the DIY network they'd built. As they fought to secure their independence, fists were raised and spikes were drawn. Punk imposed an unofficial set of rules on itself and was unkind to those who broke them. A line was drawn in the sand: any band signing with the Big Six—Sony Music, EMI, MCA/Universal, BMG, PolyGram, and Warner Music Group—was doing business with the devil. They risked being banished, ostracized, or forever branded as sellouts.

For more than a decade, punk's second brush with mainstream interest bitterly divided the scene. The most ardent defenders of the underground grew militant toward those bold enough to break out of the communities that had birthed them. To toe the line, longtime fans found themselves turning their backs on bands to which they'd once been so devoted. Some "sellouts" got off light, with backlash that amounted to disgruntled columns in fanzines or snarky comments on the internet. For others, it meant being barred from their favorite clubs and being threatened with physical violence.

The notion of selling out didn't originate in the nineties, of course, nor was it relegated to punk rock or even music, for that matter. For as long as people have been offered the chance to profit in exchange for compromising their ideals and morals, cynics have been there to call them out for it. But the loaded term gained traction during this period as major labels began waving dollar signs in the faces of young musicians. Whether a band had gone major or stayed true to their indie roots became a defining characteristic in how they were perceived by their peers.

This book captures the stories of eleven bands at the pivotal moment in each of their careers when they signed with a major label—how they arrived there, why they decided to go for it, and what it did to their career. Each chapter chronicles one band's history around the release of their major-label debut album, a crucial and often tumultuous period that could make or break them. A few of these bands saw their gamble pay off and were rewarded with Grammy statues and platinum records. But for every success story, there were dozens of bands that collapsed under the pressure, leaving members beating the shit out of each other on the side of the highway. This is not an attempt to pick winners and losers, though. Too often, when art is viewed through the lens of capitalism, it is reduced to a gamble that either pays off or doesn't. Quite the contrary. Some bands released their best and most fully realized work through major labels, even if it didn't immediately translate into sales.

In no way is this book a comprehensive history of every punk band that made the jump. Plenty of bands with interesting major-label experiences had to be omitted. Sadly, Cave In didn't make the cut, despite a winding career during which they transformed from a gnarling hardcore band to a polished rock group making an overblown studio album for RCA Records. Anti-Flag is another interesting case, in which a mohawked political punk band with songs like "Kill the Rich" triggered a major-label bidding war after landing on the radar of Svengali producer Rick Rubin. Hell, Chumbawamba was a group of anarcho-punks who signed to EMI and wrote an accidental pub hit with their sing-along track "Tubthumping." Once they were in the spotlight, they used their platform to espouse feminism, animal rights, and class warfare in interviews. Singer Alice Nutter advised people to steal their albums from chain stores and once sparked outrage when she told *Melody Maker,* "Nothing can change the fact that we like it when cops get killed." That's a story worthy of its own book.

The eleven bands documented here were chosen because they were integral in shaping the trends that propelled the post-Nirvana alternative music boom forward. Each of them helped drive commercial interest into new territories, and thanks to their efforts, the genre had room to adapt and broaden its scope, far surpassing the limits it had reached in the seventies. Punk mutated and took on new forms as the sonics and geography of it shifted, from the Bay Area pop-punk sound to the hardcore screams emanating from the basements of New Brunswick, New Jersey, to a new wave of emo that existed not so much in any regional location as on the internet.

Punk's great sellout divide fostered one of the most heated and antagonistic eras of rock history. This is a book that explores the gray areas found where finance and artistry clash, and where opportunity and integrity collide. It's a story in which a few distorted power chords turned into a multi-million-dollar cultural phenomenon. And it all started as the sun was setting over San Francisco one evening and three punk kids turned up at the office of their independent record label, ready to take a leap of faith.

CHAPTER 1

GREEN DAY

Dookie

Reprise Records (1994)

A PEBBLE STRUCK THE window of the Lookout Records office one spring night in 1993. There was no doorbell, so this was how visitors made their presence known. Larry Livermore, co-founder of the Berkeley, California–based independent punk label, stuck his head out and peered down onto the sidewalk of Berkeley Way. The label's most popular band, Green Day, had arrived for a meeting and, unlike on past visits, they'd brought company this time.

Livermore and his two teenage employees were soon joined upstairs by the three members of Green Day. Following closely behind were two unfamiliar faces, those of Elliot Cahn and Jeff Saltzman, who collectively made up the band's legal team at Cahn-Man Management, a professional operation with a self-aware name. Guitarist/singer Billie Joe Armstrong, bassist Mike Dirnt, and drummer Tré Cool typically wore mischievous smirks, like they'd just gotten away with a prank, but when they stepped through Lookout's doorway with lawyers in tow, they more closely resembled students who'd been called into the principal's office.

As the group crammed in among the toppling boxes of records and cinder-block shelves, it became obvious there were too many bodies in the room. It wasn't unusual for so many people to be gathered in the Lookout office. Local teenage punks and bands associated with the label sometimes dropped by to help pack outgoing shipments or just hang out and talk a little shit. But the mood seemed more tense this evening because of the foreign presence. For the first time, the office felt cramped.

To call it an office is actually a bit of a stretch. It wasn't much more than a twelve-by-fifteen-foot room that doubled as a living space for Livermore, who paid $98 in rent. He slept on a pile of blankets, which he rolled up in the morning, freeing up floor space to operate his business. Piles of demo submissions were stacked on the stained tan carpet, and a flimsy accordion door concealed the tiny bathroom in the corner.

To call Lookout Records a business is also a bit of a stretch. Since its inception in 1987, the label had been little more than an excuse for Livermore to avoid getting a real job. It was a means for him to release records by bands he liked, many of which were based right in the Bay Area. As long as the bands were good people and their releases sold enough copies to recoup their initial investment, Livermore was happy. For a 1960s hippie turned punk like him, breaking even was a success.

But Green Day had been doing better than breaking even lately. The band's two records on Lookout, *39/Smooth* and *Kerplunk,* had each sold more than fifty thousand copies, making them the label's most successful active band. Their growing popularity was impressive enough to raise eyebrows among A&R reps at major labels like Geffen and Warner Bros., leading the trio to hire Cahn-Man to corral the interest and find them a more suitable home than Lookout.

Livermore was worried that the band wasn't ready for the big time. At forty-five, he was a full generation older than the members of Green Day, and he feared the young band would be eaten alive in the music industry without the familial support of Lookout. On a more selfish level, he worried that his label would take a huge finan-

cial hit with the loss of its bestselling band. But he wasn't their dad
and Lookout didn't own them, so all he could do once they'd made
up their minds was wish them well.

There were only three chairs in the office, so Livermore sat with
Cahn and Saltzman while everyone else awkwardly crouched or
leaned against the walls, watching the adults conduct business. Livermore was never one for formal contracts. Most of the agreements
he made with Lookout bands were based on friendly handshakes.
But in the case of Green Day, he was dealing with two albums that
were selling thousands of copies a month, so he thought it best to
get something in writing. He pulled out a contract he'd drafted himself and laid it on the table, which was just a wooden door propped
up on some filing cabinets. The paperwork didn't amount to much
more than two pages of bullet points outlining the basic terms of the
departure.

The agreement stipulated that both *39/Smooth* and *Kerplunk*
would remain exclusively on Lookout Records forever. No matter
where Green Day ended up in the future, those two records would
always belong to the independent label that birthed them, as long as
Lookout paid royalties on time. But the most important bullet point
in the agreement, as Livermore saw it, was the final one, which read:

"Lookout Records and Green Day agree to treat each other
with respect and openness at all times, and recognize that while this
agreement provides specific guidelines as to what is expected of each
other, the truest contract is one based out of trust and friendship."

Cahn and Saltzman got a bit of a chuckle out of that line, but
Livermore didn't see what was so funny. As for the band members,
they signed their names without so much as a second glance, with
Armstrong doodling a little amp next to his signature.

"I sure hope you know what you're doing," Livermore told Armstrong as the two shook hands.

"Don't worry," the frontman assured him. "We're gonna be fine."

The band and their managers then filed out of the office and back
onto the streets of Berkeley. And with that, Green Day was freed
from Lookout Records and unleashed upon the world.

$ $ $

In the 1980s, Larry Livermore moved into a solar-paneled cabin in the Spy Rock community, a remote area four hours north of San Francisco in the Mendocino Range, where residents lived off the land and off the grid. He spent his days writing a small publication, *Lookout* magazine, and annoying his neighbors with his loud guitar playing.

Although Spy Rock was home to a number of artists, musicians, and hippies, most of them were devoted Deadheads with no interest in the kind of music Livermore wanted to play, which was punk rock. "Nobody over the age of sixteen was going to play punk rock there," he says. "They all thought I was a complete nut." Unable to find bandmates his age, Livermore made musicians out of a couple of local kids. He taught the basics of bass guitar to Kain Hanschke, a friend's fourteen-year-old son. As for drummers, Livermore was willing to take anyone able to hold a pair of sticks.

"I didn't realize yet how important drummers were," he says. "I thought they were just some rowdy, crazy person that banged on things. So I was looking around for someone who would bang on things." He immediately thought of Frank Edwin Wright III, a hyperactive twelve-year-old neighbor who lived a mile away. Wright had no drumming experience, but as an uncontrollable wild child he possessed the right temperament for the instrument. "He was a rowdy and energetic kid," Livermore remembers. "He was a loudmouth and a show-off, so I figured he'd be perfect." As predicted, Wright had a natural gift for banging on things and took to the instrument quickly.

Livermore called the band the Lookouts and gave the boys nicknames—Hanschke became Kain Kong and Wright was dubbed Tré Cool. It might have seemed odd that, at thirty-seven, Livermore was older than both of his bandmates combined, but in a thinly populated wilderness community like Spy Rock, the musical-talent pickings were slim. For a guy who had wasted his own teenage years on alcohol, crime, and greaser gangs, it was also perhaps Livermore's attempt at a redo on youth.

The Lookouts practiced regularly, and wrote quick and sloppy songs like "Why Don't You Die," "Fuck Religion," and "I Wanna Love You (But You Make Me Sick)." They soon amassed enough material to record a primitive album, *One Planet One People,* which squeezed twenty-two songs into twenty-seven minutes and was the impetus for Livermore to start his own label, Lookout Records.

The band booked their first gig in 1985, playing to a smattering of people in the parking lot of a lodge off Highway 101. They took opportunities wherever they could get them over the next few years, rocking makeshift shows in middle-of-nowhere backyards or parks. In November 1988, Cool got the band booked for a party at a classmate's cabin in the woods thirty miles away. Wintry weather hindered the attendance, though, and only five kids came. "The kid whose parents' cabin it was didn't even show up," remembers Livermore, "so we had to break in and use a generator."

The low temperatures and freezing rain didn't deter the opening band, Sweet Children, from driving three hours from Rodeo, a run-down industrial town on the outskirts of San Francisco. Rodeo was the kind of place worth driving three hours away from under any circumstances. The Bay Area Air Quality Management District once deemed it the region's "most odoriferous community" because of the smells emanating from the oil refineries located in the five-square-mile suburb, leading to a *San Francisco Chronicle* headline: "Rodeo 'Stinks' Worst in Bay Area."

The five audience members sat on the floor and watched as Sweet Children set up by candlelight. The band didn't look like much—three goofy teenagers in desperate need of haircuts and clothes that fit properly. But as soon as they started to play, the hair on Livermore's arms stood up. Sweet Children took the poppy melodies of bands like the Who, the Kinks, and the Monkees and slapped enough distortion on top of them to give them a fast, punky edge. For a guy raised on the Motown and rock 'n' roll sounds of his native Detroit, Sweet Children was music to Livermore's ears.

He was especially impressed with their poise. The band might have only been playing for five people, but they performed like they were onstage at a sold-out Shea Stadium. Drummer John Kiffmeyer, the oldest of the group at nineteen, played with an effortlessly loose style in which he hardly ever looked at his drum kit. Bassist Mike Dirnt's head didn't stop bobbing for the entire performance, except when he dutifully sang backing harmonies.

Sixteen-year-old frontman Billie Joe Armstrong was the clear focal point, though. He had a shy demeanor that melted away as soon as he began strumming and singing, unveiling an undeniable rock star glow. He was a born performer who'd grown up on his siblings' Beatles and Elvis records and entertained the locals of Rodeo with his musical gift. At five, he cut his first record, "Look for Love." The B-side of the record featured an interview in which his music teacher asked him if he'd like to one day sing for people in other countries. "Yes," the young Armstrong responded. "I love people everywhere!"

The Lookouts never ended up playing that night—the crowd filed out after Sweet Children—but Livermore was too moved by what he'd just witnessed to care. After the set, he talked to the band and offered to release their first EP on Lookout Records, which they accepted on the spot. Whether or not anyone would buy a record by three teenagers from a shithole town was irrelevant. There was clearly something special about Sweet Children that Livermore found worthy of documenting. "The very first time I saw them," he recalls, "within minutes I thought they could be the next Beatles."

$ $ $

On the last day of 1986, a new punk club opened at 924 Gilman Street, an unremarkable brick building that sat at the corner on an industrial street in San Francisco's East Bay. Tim Yohannan, punk scene elder statesman and founder of the influential zine *Maximum Rocknroll,* had put up the money and resources needed to get the hangar-like space up and running, and intended it to be a haven for punks who didn't fit in. Of course, punk is inherently meant to cater to people who don't fit in, but Gilman Street was a place for the misfits among misfits—kids who weren't old enough to get into shows at bars and weren't tough enough to survive shows at violent punk venues.

Gilman didn't foster the unruly culture of slam dancing, spitting, and punching that had marked punk's early days in the 1970s. If anything, it was a playful mockery of it. Attendees would sometimes ride toy tricycles through the crowd or choreograph goofy dance routines while bands played. It heralded the return of an element that had faded from punk rock over the years: fun. To prevent bullies and boneheads from ruining their little slice of punk paradise, the Gilman board established a set of rules and spray-painted them in big letters right on the wall:

NO RACISM
NO SEXISM
NO HOMOPHOBIA
NO ALCOHOL
NO DRUGS
NO FIGHTING
NO STAGEDIVING

The long list of regulations might have made Gilman more puritanical than most punk clubs, but organizers knew that most punk clubs had very short life spans before being shuttered by police or lawsuits. "The East Bay scene had turned super violent in the mideighties," says Blatz singer and longtime Gilman organizer Jesse Luscious. "You had places like the Farm, which had great shows but also had bloody fights with mayhem and violence. And the DIY places and the house shows—sometimes it just takes one show that goes haywire and the place gets shut down. So you had some punks who wanted a utopian scene that was more tolerant and could last."

Word of the vibrant DIY clubhouse spread around town, and a community formed around it as more and more local weirdos found refuge there. Admission was cheap and operations were entirely volunteer-run, with performers and attendees doing everything from working the door to scrubbing the toilets. Gilman's stage became a proving ground for a diverse group of homegrown startups like the lightning-fast Stikky, the apocalyptically heavy Neurosis, and the unofficial Gilman house band, Isocracy, whose performances typically devolved into a mess of trash and shredded paper strewn about. The group that quickly rose to the top was Operation Ivy, whose exuberant fusion of fast-paced punk and upbeat ska tempos was the talk of the scene, with shows reliably drawing a couple hundred fans.

"Operation Ivy was above all else. There was no challenger," says Livermore, who pressed the band's debut EP, *Hectic,* as Lookout Records' third release. As more bands honed their sound at Gilman, Lookout provided a means of releasing their records while also capturing an audio document of an exciting time in the East Bay. In addition to Op Ivy, Livermore added to the fledgling label's catalog with releases from other bands from the prolific Gilman scene, like Corrupted Morals, Sewer Trout, and the feminist rap trio Yeastie Girlz.

Tales of Gilman soon reached neighboring towns like Pinole, El Sobrante, and San Pablo, attracting suburban outcasts who hitched rides, biked, or skateboarded to reach the fabled punk mecca. Eventually, word made its way up to Rodeo, leading Billie Joe Armstrong and Mike Dirnt to trek south to see bands like No Dogs and Christ on Parade. Once inside, the two sixteen-year-olds were introduced to a world beyond their small-town imaginations.

Armstrong's introduction to live music had come at twelve, when he attended a Van Halen concert, an experience that saw him gawking at larger-than-life rock stars. Gilman was the opposite—a place where the line between performer and audience was torn down. Anyone could play music, regardless of age, race, gender, or ability. All voices were heard and all ideas were welcome. So it was frustrating, then, when Armstrong submitted Sweet Children's demo tape to Yohannan and was told their sound was too poppy to play there. It was only because the band's drum seat was filled by John Kiffmeyer, who also played in Isocracy, that they earned their first show there on November 26, 1988. Their poppiness didn't offend the Gilman crowd as Yohannan had predicted, and the band went over well enough to get invited back a few times throughout the spring.

By April, a thousand copies of Sweet Children's four-song debut EP, *1,000 Hours,* were being pressed for release by Lookout, but there was a problem: the band no longer wanted to be called Sweet

Children. To distinguish themselves from another Gilman band, Sweet Baby Jesus, they decided on a new name, Green Day, a reference to an afternoon spent smoking pot. Livermore protested, partly because people were starting to recognize the name Sweet Children and partly, he says, because "Green Day was just about the dumbest name I'd ever heard." Despite Livermore's objections, the name change was made and record sleeves were printed with their new moniker. Scribbled inside were the band's mailing address and phone number, with a note: "We'll play anywhere!"

The band played their first show as Green Day on May 28, 1989, opening for Operation Ivy at Gilman. Op Ivy were celebrating the release of their first album, *Energy,* but they were also closing the door behind them, putting a cap on their brief but exciting two-year run. Nearly a thousand people tried to cram into the 249-capacity club for a final glimpse of the local legends at what would be their last official show. By the end of the set, most of them were piled onstage in a tangled mess of bodies and limbs, hugging and singing about unity.

As Operation Ivy was fading away, Green Day was revving up. They released their own debut album for Lookout, *39/Smooth,* in the spring of 1990. Recorded over a few days for $750 at Art of Ears Studio in San Francisco, the LP was an imperfect snapshot of a still developing band. But even through the muffled sound of the hasty recordings, the band's innate gift for addictive, bubblegum melodies shined through. Tracks like "Don't Leave Me" and "Going to Pasalacqua" were like sixties garage rock songs turned up to punk rock velocities.

Green Day jumped at any chance to play their growing repertoire of songs around town, performing at warehouses, garages, pizzerias, high schools, and coffeehouses for little or no money. Armstrong became consumed by two goals: playing music and getting out of Rodeo. He completely lost interest in school and dropped out in the middle of twelfth grade. Dirnt, feeling obligated to complete his education, stuck it out and got his diploma. The day he graduated, his bandmates were waiting outside of school with a Ford Econoline van, and the three sped off for a summer-long tour of the U.S. Playing basements and halls across the country sharpened their skills, and the band sounded better than ever by the time they returned to Gilman.

"They were the acorn that fell off the oak tree of the mighty Operation Ivy," Livermore says. "By 1990 or so, they were the new big thing." But right as Green Day were making a name for themselves, Kiffmeyer left the band at the end of the year to attend college. With the future of Green Day in jeopardy, Armstrong and Dirnt enlisted Livermore's bandmate Tré Cool, who had filled in for Kiffmeyer on a few shows. Cool's hyperactive energy proved to be the missing piece that rounded out Green Day. The new lineup spent nearly every week of 1991 on the road, with more than a hundred shows in the U.S. and a sixty-five-show debut in Europe.

"Once Tré joined the band, it was like somebody put a skyrocket on their rear end," says Livermore. "They were definitely a better band. All through 1991, they were doing a lot of touring. A lot of people were excited about them." Livermore noticed something distinct about the crowds Green Day attracted that set them apart from the other bands on his label. They were larger, sure, but they were also predominantly female. "There'd be a lot of girls up front, dancing. That was not the case with most punk bands, where it was 80 percent boys running around in circles, banging into each other. Based on my experience, I thought that was a pretty good sign they were gonna be popular. Half the human race is female."

Girls flocked to Green Day in part because girls were who their songs were about. Armstrong's lyrics weren't preachy, pretentious, or overtly political, like those of some of his peers. He instead documented his own experiences with romance and heartbreak. "I couldn't really sing about destroying the government or anything like that, because I don't know much about it," Armstrong told the L.A. fanzine *Flipside* in 1990. "That's my frustration in life—girls." Green Day had so many thoughts about girls that they quickly churned out a second album's worth of material in 1991 and returned to Art of Ears Studios for another tightly budgeted session.

The album, *Kerplunk,* saw Green Day taking a giant step forward. The addition of Cool, plus all the time on the road, had made their sound more muscular. Songs like "2000 Light Years Away," "Welcome to Paradise," and "One of My Lies" contained choruses that were utterly simple yet could stick in a listener's head for days. The album even had a ballad, "Christie Rd.," a slower, more sentimental tune about a quiet street near the railroad tracks where Armstrong would go to smoke weed. It became a fan favorite and assured that a street sign in Martinez, California, would be stolen forever.

The album was scheduled for release at the end of the year by Lookout, which had also been taking steps forward and could invest more resources into it. Livermore had relocated from the mountains and set up shop in a single-room apartment not far from Gilman, hiring two teenage employees at five bucks an hour to help ship mail orders.

Livermore took the *Kerplunk* recordings to L.A. for mastering, and on his flight back to Oakland he gave the finished cassette a first listen. "I put it in my Walkman just as we were going down the runway," he remembers. "We were rolling away, and when I heard the first chord of '2000 Light Years' it was like a whole different level. Whether I put out the record or not, it was gonna be big. I knew that things would never be the same again."

$ $ $

By the time Lookout released *Kerplunk* in December of 1991, Nirvana's *Nevermind* was an unstoppable *Billboard* chart wrecking ball, mercilessly knocking lesser albums out of its path to number one and changing the landscape of pop music. Chasing the high of the new rock craze kicked off by the grunge trio, major-label A&R scouts were on a quest to find other emerging rock acts.

In D.C. they found a clique of post-hardcore bands attached to the reputable label Dischord Records, most of which were too idealistic to consider corporate offers. The label's most popular band, Fugazi, prided themselves on their independent ethos and wanted nothing to do with it. Two Dischord bands were talked into the jump,

however, with Shudder to Think heading to Epic and Jawbox joining Atlantic. San Diego, poised to be the next Seattle, was home to a
diverse scene. Local favorites Rocket from the Crypt had a loud and
straightforward rock 'n' roll sound that seemed like a perfect fit for
rock radio. The band's guitarist, John Reis, bartered a deal with Interscope, not only to release Rocket's next album but to include his
other project, Drive Like Jehu, in the deal as well.

It was only a matter of time before the Bay Area, with its fertile crop of young bands, became a major-label target. Naturally,
the scene's fastest-rising band, Green Day, seemed like the top candidate. "You had that interesting scene coming out of Gilman that
fostered a lot of individualistic bands and real artists," remembers
Atlantic Records A&R rep Mike Gitter. "Green Day were the ones
who wrote the best songs, and whoever writes the best songs wins.
They were already selling a lot of records on Lookout, and they had
done the legwork throughout America."

Kerplunk may not have shaken the earth the way *Nevermind* was
doing, but by Lookout Records standards, it was a smash hit. On
the day of its release, the label sold through its entire pressing of ten
thousand copies. "I remember we pulled up to Gilman a few hours
before *Kerplunk*'s release party," says Lookout employee Chris Appelgren, "and there was already a line around the block."

Kerplunk caught on quickly among Green Day's growing fan
base, and word of their live show spread nationally. Crowds got
bigger with each tour; in some cities, the band was playing to more
than a thousand people. But just about everywhere Green Day went,
they'd hear complaints that their record was hard to find in stores. It
seemed there were more dubbed copies of *Kerplunk* floating around
than official ones. By 1993 the album had sold fifty thousand copies,
but it might have been able to sell much more had their label been
able to meet the demand. Green Day loved Lookout, but clearly the
band was growing at a pace that was too fast for a three-person operation to handle.

"For much of the nineties, it was about chain stores and getting
into the mall, not just into the cool indie record stores," Appelgren

says. "It was those bigger retail chains that were really selling copies. Initially, we didn't have bar codes on our records. That was a huge barrier to getting into retail stores. They just wouldn't take it if it didn't have a bar code, because they couldn't manage it in their inventory system."

Lookout was also ill-equipped to handle new opportunities that required industry know-how of things like publishing rights and licensing. "The Jerky Boys movie was the first to ask to use a song from *Kerplunk* on their soundtrack," remembers Appelgren. "They needed the master tapes to remix it, and we didn't know that we had the right to. We had a refrigerator that was unplugged that we used to store master tapes in."

Livermore was hopeful that his most popular band would start working on a follow-up for the label, but he was unaware that Green Day had other plans. "I'd been hearing rumors that maybe Green Day wouldn't want to do their next record with Lookout," he remembers. "But it made no sense, because we had such success for a punk band. They were making a lot of money, because we paid really generously. We did everything so cheaply, so it added up to quite a bit—two or three bucks a record sold. Back then, with a major label, a lot of bands were lucky to get more than a dollar."

When Livermore approached Cool about the possibility of a new Green Day record, the drummer let it slip that they were maybe thinking of hiring management to shop them around to bigger labels. Livermore had known him long enough to understand that when he said "maybe," he meant they'd already done it. "I was quite shocked," Livermore says. "I assumed they were making a big mistake. So I said, 'Get the band together, we've got to have a conference about this.' The three of them and me sat at Café Hell in downtown Berkeley and at that point it became very clear that I probably was not going to be able to talk them out of it."

When it became obvious that Green Day couldn't be convinced to stay with Lookout, Livermore asked the band to sign a retroactive contract to keep *39/Smooth* and *Kerplunk* on the label permanently. "They didn't have any hesitation. They said, 'Sure, write it up,'" he remembers. "They made it clear they had no desire to take the old records from Lookout. I didn't have any reason to doubt that, but I did feel like it should be written down, because I'd already seen other independent labels destroyed."

Livermore felt a bit of relief after his meeting with the Cahn-Man Management team at the Lookout office. "Most of their experience was working with metal bands. They were naming off all these big metal bands, most of which I'd never heard of," Livermore remembers. "But overall, my conclusion was that they could've done worse."

Cahn-Man had recently branched out from their metal roster in the wake of Nirvana's success, signing indie rock darlings Mudhoney and Melvins. They'd also ventured into punk with the SoCal newcomers the Muffs, whom they'd helped land a deal with Warner Bros. Records for the release of their first album. Their roster would also soon encompass up-and-comers like the Offspring, Pennywise, and Rancid.

"We were concerned about [Green Day]," says Appelgren. "But they reassured us—'We're gonna be fine. We'll be all right.' They were so confident, but we weren't. We didn't have that vision. It's like they just knew."

$ $ $

It was after midnight at Devonshire Studios, in North Hollywood, and Rob Cavallo was sitting at his desk with his head in his hands. For several hours he'd been mixing the Muffs' debut album for Warner Bros. Records, and he was hitting a wall. The twenty-nine-year-old producer was exhausted.

For six years, Cavallo had been employed at Warner Bros. in a dual role that allowed him to produce albums in the studio as well as discover and sign new talent to the label. But after six years there, he had little to show for himself. He'd worked with a mix of southern-fried rock bands and hair metal acts but had failed to land any grunge stars during the genre's boom. He needed a hit, or else, he feared, it would be a matter of time before the ax fell on him.

He took his glasses off and rubbed his eyes with his fingertips. When he opened them, there was a cassette sitting in front of him. "Rob, you gotta listen to this demo," the Muffs' manager, Jeff Saltzman, told him. "It's by this band called Green Day. They're underground heroes from the Bay Area. They think they're ready to sign to a major. Give it a listen?"

Cavallo looked at the cassette and then at Saltzman and muttered the first words his stressed-out brain could conjure: "Are you kidding me? You're asking me to do *more* listening? Can't you see my eyeballs are falling out of my fucking head trying to mix this song?" Cavallo considered throwing the tape in the trash, but instead he swept it to the side of the desk in frustration and returned to his mixing duties.

When Cavallo was finally ready to head home after a couple more hours of work, he spotted the Green Day cassette on the corner of his desk. He relented and stuffed it into his pocket. "Don't be a lazy prick," he grumbled to himself. "You never know, right? It might actually be good."

As he merged onto the 101, he slid the tape into his car's stereo. Green Day's rough, four-track recordings of songs like "She" and "Basket Case" blasted out of the speakers on the twenty-minute drive to Woodland Hills. "By the time I got there," he remembers, "I'd lost my fucking mind."

The band was everything Cavallo had been searching for. It was up-tempo punk rock that had melody. "It reminded me of the Beatles meets the Buzzcocks, with a little of the Sex Pistols' snotty attitude," he says. "I also felt this working-class anti-establishment thing about them like the Clash had." But most important, it was decidedly not grunge, a genre his label colleagues had mined for all it was worth over the past two years. This sound was completely new and fresh.

Eager to throw his name into the competition to sign Green Day, Cavallo soon arranged a trip up to Berkeley to meet them. In the summer of '93, he pulled up to Ashby Avenue, where the band lived together in the basement of a gray Victorian house. He wasn't the first A&R guy to make the pilgrimage. Rumors had been circulating around town that record-label limousines were sometimes parked out front of the coveted band's house.

The apartment looked and smelled as might be expected from a place inhabited by a bunch of young musicians—cheap second-hand furniture, empty pizza boxes and weed paraphernalia scattered about, mattresses on the floor. But despite their slovenly living quarters, Cavallo was impressed by the band members' professional approach to their music. "They were very businesslike," he remembers. "They were checking me out just as much as I was checking them out. Their vibe was so thick that they were going to make it. Most bands come to you and say, 'We want to be on a major label so you'll make us huge.' The Green Day guys were more like, 'We wanna be on a major label because we're *gonna* make it, and if you help us, it might go faster.'"

The band showed Cavallo to their practice room and gave him a bucket to sit on. The three plugged in and belted out songs they'd written for their new album. The college girls who lived upstairs may have grown sick of hearing the songs through Green Day's endless late-night practice sessions, but to Cavallo they sounded exhilarating. They were even more dynamic than what he'd heard on the demo, which had failed to capture the youthful intensity each of the members pounded into every note.

Dirnt was a reliable straight man, his noodling basslines steadily anchoring Cool's blazing drum assaults. Armstrong was a consummate punk rock showman, every lyric emphasized by contorted facial expressions and bug-eyed sneers. Much like the Clash's frontman John Mellor had adopted the name Joe Strummer because he could "only play all six strings at once, or none at all," Armstrong did away with fancy solos. He was all about chords, largely of the power variety. His sticker-covered guitar hung so low off his shoulder that it was practically at his knees, and he hit the instrument with such downward force that it looked as if he was trying to punch it through the floor.

After Green Day finished playing their songs, it was Cavallo's turn. "They'd heard this rumor that I could play all the Beatles' songs," he says. "They started quizzing me. *How do you play this? How do you play that?* We went into Billie's bedroom and I sat on the bed. They rolled me a joint and gave me an acoustic guitar and told me to play songs. The thing they were most impressed with was that I could play the descending line in 'Help!'" After strumming through a repertoire of Fab Four songs while the band sized up his chops, Cavallo left to catch his flight home. "I went to the Oakland airport and I got to my gate early. I was reading my book and by the time I looked up, I had missed my plane and the airport was empty. I was so stoned."

Although there were five or six labels in pursuit of Green Day, Cavallo's main competitor was Geffen Records, the label that had nabbed Nirvana. Green Day wielded much of the same appeal that had made Nirvana an enticing signing, specifically that they had built a national following, all on their own. "The Green Day guys were really smart. They took huge advantage of all their interest," says Geffen's Mark Kates. "Those guys were building a network, pre-internet, and doing it extremely effectively. They'd talk about playing shows in offbeat places like Allentown or somewhere like that. The stuff they were telling me was really hard to believe, except there was no way they could make it up."

But while Geffen's Nirvana boast was impressive, and although the band had milked the label for a free trip to Disneyland, Cavallo had left a better impression on them. "He was from L.A. and stuff, but he's married and thinking about having kids, and that made him seem like more of a genuine person," Armstrong told journalist Gina Arnold. "Whereas a lot of those fuckers are just like hipsters. Some of them just wanted to get laid, to tell you the truth."

That Cavallo had musical chops earned him some cred, as did the fact that he'd worked with a reputable band like the Muffs. "They told me later that they liked the other companies but they'd made missteps," he says. "I think Geffen was talking about Kurt Cobain. And Billie was like, 'Well, I love Kurt Cobain, but what does that have to do with me? I'm always gonna play second fiddle to Kurt Cobain.'"

With a mouthful of burrito, Armstrong joked to an interviewer a few weeks later that "it was either Geffen and heroin or Warner Brothers and cocaine. So we chose the coke." And so the band inked a modest deal that summer with Reprise Records, a Warner Bros. subsidiary founded by Frank Sinatra in 1960, which had since become home to everything from Eric Clapton to Depeche Mode.

"I think we signed 'em for something like two hundred grand, and I knew we could sell 100,000 albums and at least make enough money to break even," says Cavallo. In addition to their six-figure advance, Green Day talked their new label into paying for a bookmobile truck that they'd converted into a touring machine, decked out with sleeping bunks and video games. "It's not as crowded as a Ford Econoline van, which we did for years," Dirnt told one interviewer. "This is like being in a mansion."

The deal was closed and Cavallo took the band out to celebrate. "I brought my wife up to San Francisco and we took them out to a seafood dinner near the Bay," he remembers. "Then, a couple weeks later, I came down to San Diego to see them play a show at SOMA. I think they went on at seven or eight o'clock, and there were a thousand people wrapped around the building to get in. I remember thinking, *Wow, I wonder who the headliner is tonight.* [Green Day] blew me away and were amazing, but after they played, the entire club emptied out. Those thousand people were all there for Green Day. I said to Billie, 'You guys must play this place a lot.' And he said, 'No, it's like our third time.' That was the night I knew I was the luckiest motherfucker on the planet."

$ $ $

Shortly after Green Day signed to Reprise, the organizers at Gilman convened a meeting and decided that a new rule needed to be instituted at the club: NO MAJOR-LABEL BANDS. Any act affiliated with one of the Big Six was no longer permitted on the Gilman stage. It was nothing personal, but to protect the sanctity of the club, a line had to be drawn.

"Green Day were the reason why the major-label ban was put into effect," says Luscious, who pushed for the new rule's instatement. "They were our friends, they grew up there, they played there all the time. But we didn't want Gilman to be the farm league for the majors. Fuck that."

Luscious remembers Green Day reacting to the ban with a mix of emotions. "On one hand, they were really pissed off and upset," he says. "But on the other, they were from the scene: they understood exactly why. We'd already seen Nirvana blow up, and that was jaw-dropping. We'd seen the Seattle scene go crazy. We didn't want to see that happen to punk rock."

Green Day played at Gilman Street on September 3, 1993, under the name Blair Hess, their final show there before their major-label affiliation got them eighty-sixed. Livermore remembers it being a "bittersweet occasion"—joyous because everyone in attendance had a blast singing along to every song, but sad because it would be the last time they'd all get to do so there.

The crowd gave the band some light ribbing for committing the crime of selling out, though they carried it out in the most Gilman way possible. "I went to that show when Green Day played Gilman, the last time they played after they had signed," recalls Sergie Loobkoff of Sweet Baby Jesus. "When Billie was singing, some kid had a handful of uncooked beans and threw them in his face and hit his teeth and stuff." For their part, Blair Hess took it with a smile and cracked a few self-aware jokes. While singing a new song, "Burnout," Armstrong changed the lyric "I'm not growing up, I'm just burning out" to "I'm not being punk, I'm just selling out."

Leaving Gilman in their rearview, the band got to work on their next chapter, recording their Reprise debut, *Dookie*, with Rob Cavallo at Fantasy Studios in Berkeley—the same studio where Armstrong had recorded his childhood single "Look for Love." Green Day's previous rush-job recording sessions on shoestring budgets had primed them to be model clients for Cavallo, who was dumbfounded by their efficiency. "Billie sang the whole record in something like three days. I'd never seen anything like it," he says. "He'd do a take and say, 'What do you think?' And I'd say, 'I can't fucking believe it, but you nailed it. I guess . . . do another one, just in case?'"

The sessions lasted a month, during which Cavallo's meticulous production made Green Day sound light-years better than they ever had. Every instrument popped through the speakers with a strik-ing clarity, particularly Armstrong's guitar, which packed relentlessly mean punches of thick distortion. They cut a new version of "Wel-come to Paradise" whose surround-sound fullness added a new di-mension to the tin-can *Kerplunk* version, making it sound flat by comparison. There weren't any fancy studio frills on *Dookie*. It just sounded clean, crisp, and loud as hell, striking the perfect balance for a snotty punk band with a gift for catchy melodies. "It was a re-cord that'd be real easy to fuck up," Cavallo says. "You could make it sound too glossy or too rough."

The album kicked off with two machine-gun snare drum blasts from Cool, followed by Armstrong distilling the entire experience of adolescent frustration into a single lyric: "I declare I don't care no more." Armstrong's songwriting was at a personal peak, with each of the album's fifteen songs touting one perfectly crafted hook af-ter another. Leaving behind the love tunes he'd written in his teen-age years, he was now grappling with the confusion that came with entering adulthood—confronting his mental health, his bisexuality, and the ugliness of the world in front of him. It was a coming-of-age record for a slacker generation. Armstrong brought another "Chris-tie Rd."–style ballad about his girlfriend moving to Ecuador to the sessions, but it didn't fit thematically. The song wouldn't be released until three years later and would be called "Good Riddance (Time of Your Life)."

To help sculpt a distinct aesthetic for their first music video, the band hired director Mark Kohr, who had caught their attention through his work with another Bay Area group, Primus. While Pri-mus's funky jam-rock had little in common with Green Day's pop-punk sound, it was Kohr's visually striking style, which relied heavily on oversaturated colors and invasively bright lighting, that landed him the gig. "I wanted to create a new look for a new sound," Kohr says. "When filming them playing, it's just front, hard light. I went with that because I wanted it to not be grunge or metal. I wanted to give it this punk feel and for the look of it to support that vibe."

Wanting to capture the band in their natural state, he filmed the entire video for their first single, "Longview," in their Ashby Avenue apartment. They painted the walls of the practice space bright red, blue, and purple, but otherwise kept its bland bachelor pad charm. The scenes shifted abruptly between shots of the band rocking out and Armstrong demolishing their living room couch. Feathers and cushion stuffing flew through the air, soundtracked by lyrics about suburban boredom—getting high, watching TV, and masturbating to the point of blindness.

After Cavallo saw how much fun Kohr's video was, it started to dawn on him that *Dookie* could be bigger than he'd imagined. But still, he played a cool hand at the office, not wanting to oversell it. "I'd seen other industry people make this mistake: You can't hype your shit too much or you'll jinx it," he says. "Don't run around and tell everybody you have the next big thing. So I tried to be understated."

The day *Dookie*'s potential really sunk in for Cavallo was when he was talking to Wendy Griffiths, who ran video promotion for the label. "She said she had been hearing from MTV that for the past two or three years they'd been playing a lot of grunge," he remembers. "And they were starting to get feedback from their viewers that there was a sameness going on, that it was all very serious and black-and-white videos. MTV was looking for something a little more colorful and a little faster. When she said that, I almost fell over. Because I was like, *Oh my God, I'm holding exactly that!*"

Dookie was released on the first day of February 1994 and sold only nine thousand copies in its first week, hindered greatly by a brutally cold winter that prevented many shipments from reaching stores on time. It debuted on the Billboard 200 chart a couple of weeks later at number 127 but dropped off immediately after. But "Longview" was a radio slow burn that got more airplay as listeners called stations to request it, many of which, Cavallo admits, were him using a phony voice. Once MTV started giving more airtime to "Longview," the album steadily clawed its way up the charts until it cracked into the top 100 in April. The video struck a chord with MTV's angsty young viewers. Here was a band that looked just like them—three small-town weirdos who lived in a basement and had pimples and crooked teeth. The video had destruction, it had the word "fuck," it had the approval of the unofficial voices of a delinquent generation, Beavis and Butt-Head. "You know what they should do? They should, like, break that couch. They should like just rip it up," said Beavis, who was delighted to have his suggestion fulfilled by Armstrong seconds later. "Yeah, like that! Yeah! Rip it! Break it!"

The "Longview" video went over so well that Green Day signed on with Kohr to film two more videos, for "Basket Case" and "When I Come Around." "Basket Case" leaned in even further to their synthetically colorful look, which Kohr achieved by filming the video in black-and-white and colorizing it later. Set in a psychedelic mental hospital, the setting's obnoxiously bright blues and yellows popped out of the screen and made the band members resemble cartoon characters. Armstrong's maniacal eyes, which didn't blink for the entirety of the video, shined as green as two traffic lights.

Early one morning in April when Kohr was preparing for a day of filming with Green Day, a somber mood descended on the set. News had started to spread that the body of Kurt Cobain had been found in his Seattle home with a self-inflicted shotgun wound to the head.

"Billie came into the room and said, 'Oh my God, did you hear?'" remembers Kohr. The director watched the members of Green Day process the news that the world's most famous rock star had taken his own life. Through the shock and grief, a strange sense of clarity came to Kohr then, and for a brief moment he saw the future. "Talking to Billie, I had this weird notion in my head," he says, "where I thought, *Oh my God. I wonder if the universe is making space for these three guys right in front of me.*"

$ $ $

Maximum Rocknroll was known for its provocative covers, whether they were taking aim at Nazi punks or corrupt political leaders. The zine's inaugural issue, released in the summer of 1982, depicted President Ronald Reagan wearing a Ku Klux Klan hood. But the cover of the "Major Labels" issue in June 1994 really pushed the envelope. Featuring a close-up shot of a person jamming a handgun into their own mouth, the headline read: "Some of your friends are already this fucked." The message to all bands was loud and clear: Signing to a major label was punk suicide.

The timing was in poor taste, given that Kurt Cobain's death was still fresh in everyone's minds. But the issue wasn't so much about Cobain and Nirvana as it was a warning directed at any bands that were thinking of following in their path. Since it was a Bay Area publication, the issue's ire frequently turned to Green Day.

Founder Tim Yohannan set the tone of the issue up front by penning its first page and leaving little room for nuance, likening major labels to the violent Nazi skinheads who had infested the punk scene and wreaked havoc on clubs like Gilman years earlier. "The punk/indie/underground scene is under attack, just as it was back then," the screed declared, with "under attack" in bold. "No difference, except this time the thugs are smarter and richer. Their motivation is just about the same—control, power, dominance." Sections of it were so militant that they read like war propaganda: "There can be no middle ground or grey area when you're under attack by forces alien to the fundamental principles of a community or society."

"The place was famously didactic," says former *MRR* writer Kyle Ryan. "They're basically the scene police. Tim had this reputation for being super self-righteous. It was a confrontational approach to bands. It was a place where making a living off of music was selling out, and that wasn't allowed. They had very strict rules and wouldn't write about any bands on major labels."

The zine's columnists followed Yohannan's lead on the issue's subsequent pages—maybe not going to the extreme of comparing A&R departments to the Third Reich, but certainly major labels were a subject on which no writer had a lack of opinions and gripes. One writer, Brian Zero, was invited to write about the unethical business practices of major labels after he staged a protest outside Green Day's show in Petaluma, California, passing out flyers that advised fans to "walk out on Green Day." The protest hadn't amounted to more than a handful of folks holding anti–Green Day signs, but it was enough to make anyone entering the theater feel like a scab crossing a picket line.

Other columnists, like Lee Diamond, dumped a bucket of ice water on indie bands thinking of making the jump to a major, dispelling the three most common attractions: Those big fat advance checks and generous studio budgets seem impressive until you realize they come out of your royalties; A&R reps often seem young, cool, and relatable, but ultimately they're label employees and not your friends; and lastly, "NO person or band in the industry has a contract that allows them complete artistic control. NO ONE."

In a reprinting of his infamous article "The Problem with Music," producer and Shellac frontman Steve Albini broke down the dollars and cents of major-label deals, outlining in sobering detail how much more money went to producers, lawyers, and managers than the band members. He concluded that an artist that made $3 million for their label would earn "about 1/3 as much as they would working at a 7-11."

Not every writer went on the attack. Screeching Weasel's antagonistic frontman, Ben Weasel, took a surprisingly laissez-faire approach, advising ambitious bands to have realistic expectations and to own up to their choices. "I'm not going to condemn anyone who signs to a major. Their business is their own," he wrote. "But if you're going to sell out, at least do it smart. Admit you've sold out." He praised bands that proudly made music on their own terms, like his friends in the staunchly independent Bay Area trio Jawbreaker, who he claimed had been "approached by just about every major label and they've turned them down."

Larry Livermore, in his final column for the zine, was one of the lone voices defending Green Day's decision to go to Warner Bros. "If you're just going to sit there whining about how so-and-so sold out," he wrote, "pretty soon nobody is going to be listening."

As for Green Day themselves, being barred from playing at Gilman to preserve the club's independent identity was one thing, but reading personally spiteful words from the scene that had birthed them was a hard pill to swallow. Three months later, Armstrong fired back in the pages of *SPIN:* "Tim Yohannon can go and suck his own dick for all I care. He doesn't know what the fuck he's talking about. I've never waved a punk-rock flag in my life."

"They were very young and felt they were being rejected by the scene that had been so vital and important to them. It's got to hurt a lot," says Livermore. "On one hand, you've got everybody, sometimes even famous people you've looked up to all your life, telling you, 'Oh, you guys are geniuses, you're wonderful, you're amazing!' And on the other hand, you're thinking, *Yeah, but all my old friends hate me*. I think it came very close to destroying them."

$ $ $

It rained all morning on Sunday, August 14, the third and final day of Woodstock '94. Aside from the dreary weather, though, the upstate New York music festival aimed at Generation X music fans had little in common with the spirit of its legendary free-love predecessor of 1969. "There were two stages instead of one, the production values were much better, and the sound was much better," remembers Elliot Cahn, who himself had performed at the original Woodstock as a founding member of the doo-wop group Sha Na Na. "The ethos in the audience was also much different. It wasn't the 1960s anymore. It was much more of a commercial enterprise." Ticket prices had also risen considerably in the twenty-five-year interim, with weekend passes jumping from $18 to $135, plus Ticketmaster fees. Corporations had dug their claws into the festival, which was no longer a unique hippie paradise, but another big-business venture.

Originally billed as "2 More Days of Peace and Music," a third day was added to accommodate the high demand for tickets. More than 180,000 tickets were sold in advance and, with many thousands more people paying upon entry or simply sneaking in, the estimated attendance reached 400,000. The festival was also being broadcast on television via pay-per-view, pushing the worldwide audience into the millions.

Green Day had added a last-minute Woodstock set into their schedule, hopping off Lollapalooza in Atlanta to take a midday slot on the smaller stage in New York, across from main-stage acts like Spin Doctors, Bob Dylan, and the Red Hot Chili Peppers. It was a gig they took partly as a lark and partly because, as Dirnt explained to the *Washington Post*, "They're paying us a lot of money."

While Green Day waited backstage before going on, a reporter in a rain poncho pointed her microphone at Dirnt and posed a question about the corporate festival: "Some people are saying that the alternative bands that are playing here are selling out. What do you have to say to them?" Without missing a beat, Dirnt shrugged and said, "They're probably right."

A few minutes later, Dirnt, repping his Lookout Records roots in a Screeching Weasel T-shirt, was stomping toward the microphone stand. He grabbed it, bashed it into his head three times, and yelled at the massive crowd, "How you doin', all you rich muthafuckas?"

Billie Joe Armstrong soon emerged, blue hair and red necktie, and planted his feet at the front of the stage in a power stance. He ripped through the opening chords of "Welcome to Paradise" as the crowd bounced up and down. For the first fifteen minutes of their set, Armstrong struggled to connect with the audience. Unlike in the clubs they were used to playing, where the crowd was close enough to reach out and touch the performers, the perimeter of the Woodstock audience began a good twenty feet away, beyond several layers of barricades, security guards, and camera crews.

After three songs, though, Armstrong finally started connecting with the crowd. Or, more precisely, the crowd started connecting with him. People began reaching down, digging huge chunks of mud and grass out of the ground, and hurling them at the band. In the middle of "When I Come Around," one clump skimmed off the top of one of Cool's cymbals, followed immediately by another that clobbered Armstrong's strumming hand, and neither musician missed a beat. Mud projectiles splattered onstage as crew members scrambled to cover amps with towels and made desperate attempts to shield the TV cameras with plastic tarps.

While the crew was occupied with protecting the equipment, a couple of kids hopped the barricade and made a run for the stage, one of them making it all the way to the band and giving Armstrong a muddy hug. After another two songs, Armstrong took off his guitar and declared a friendly war on the crowd. He stood at the edge of the stage with his arms out and welcomed the barrage of mud clumps. He caught a few, took a bite out of one, and threw the rest back at the crowd. He taunted the audience, calling them "mud hippies" and "fucking idiots," and they ate it up. He pulled down his pants and mooned the crowd, which only made them love him more. At one point, Armstrong picked up a young boy—"a future idiot"—and carried him across the entire stage. "This isn't love and peace," the frontman said, "it's fucking anarchy!"

After ten minutes of an uncontainable mud brawl between Green Day and the Woodstock crowd, not an inch of clean stage remained. Mud was dripping from the speakers and smeared across the camera lenses trying to capture the mayhem. Finally, Armstrong decided it was time to put an end to the pandemonium. "Everybody say 'Shut the fuck up' and we'll stop playing," he told the mud hippies and the idiots. And on the count of three, they all obliged him. "Okay, we're gone," he said, dropping the microphone. "Goodbye." And just like that, the wildest set in the history of Woodstock came to an abrupt and unceremonious end.

Sensing their last chance to charge the stage, many shirtless men came running toward the band. As soon as Dirnt took his bass off, a burly guard, mistaking the bassist for a crazed fan, charged directly at him, put a shoulder into his gut, and tackled him to the ground. Dirnt went down on his elbow and felt an immediate pain. He felt around in his mouth with his tongue and realized a couple of teeth had been knocked out.

The situation was turning from fun to dangerous, and stage crashers outnumbered the security guards. "Hey, calm down, man," an announcer pleaded over the speakers. "Look, we're just trying to have a little fun. Rock and roll. All right, easy, guys. Easy, people! *Easy!*" As the mud hippies started to chase the members of Green Day and grab at their clothes, the band and their team quickly realized they needed to get out of there before it got much worse.

"It was chaos, but the kids were so into it," remembers Cavallo. "I was on the side of the stage and we saw all these kids running at us, and we had to run and not eat shit. Somebody rushed us into a white van with windows. We thought, *Oh, good, we made it to the van*. But even though it was in an area where other people couldn't get to, suddenly a thousand fucking kids were now smashing their hands on the windows and shaking the van and trying to get in. I remember looking at Mike and Tré and their eyes were bugging out."

A swarm of crazed mud people hopped fences and surrounded the van from every direction, pounding their fists against the glass. The driver threw the van into neutral and hit the gas, scaring some people away with engine noises just long enough to inch forward and then speed off. "We got to this other safety area where they opened a gate that had barbed wire on it, like they had it for just such emergencies," says Cavallo. "They took us in there and Mike got first aid treatment. He really cracked his elbow and his tooth. He was fucked up. Then they got us into a different kind of van with no windows."

From there, the band and their crew were ushered to a helicopter to transport them away. As the chopper carried them off through overcast skies, they looked down onto what was left of Woodstock, and it was nothing but an endless sea of brown. As far as promotion for an anarchic punk album named after excrement went, Green Day couldn't have asked for a more beautiful sight. Hovering above the demolished field, a thought hit Cavallo: "This is gonna make the news."

$ $ $

After their Woodstock melee, Green Day had a hard time showing up anywhere without attracting enough trouble to make the news. Three weeks later, on September 9, they were booked to play a free, all-ages gig at the Hatch Shell, an outdoor venue in Boston. Organizers anticipated a crowd of thirty thousand people. Despite afternoon downpours, the space filled up early in the day, and then another ten thousand people filed in, and then another, and then another. By the time the band took the stage just after 8 p.m., an estimated seventy thousand people had flooded the area, many of whom, the *Boston Globe* reported, "had tattoos and nose rings, were dressed in 'grunge' clothing, and appeared to be on drugs."

Not long into Green Day's set, the oversize crowd overwhelmed the security guards, collapsed the barricades, and rushed the stage.

Green Day had no choice but to pull the plug after twenty minutes. WFNX, the radio station promoting the event, had landed Snapple as a sponsor, resulting in hundreds of glass bottles being hurled as they left. "When this band was booked eight weeks ago, they were in relative obscurity," an incredulous WFNX president, Barry Morris, told the *Globe*. "All of a sudden they are the hottest band in the country."

The rowdy crowd lingered for several hours after the concert was shut down, taking their energy out on the streets of Boston and clashing with police, chanting "Pigs suck!" A reported 250 cops made more than sixty arrests, with dozens of people requiring medical attention. "They have been called punk rock's hyperactive problem children," WBZ reporter Joyce Kuhlhawik said of Green Day on that evening's news, "and tonight they lived up to that moniker."

Backstage, a calm and collected Armstrong talked to reporters about the riot they'd just incited. "Punk rock has become mainstream again, and a lot of the people in the public don't know how to grasp it," he said. "A band like us is basically a disaster waiting to happen a lot of times."

After Boston and Woodstock, the phones at the Reprise offices wouldn't stop ringing with requests to interview "America's hottest band," as they were called on the cover of *Kerrang!* magazine. Green Day's mugs also graced the covers of *Rolling Stone, SPIN,* and *NME*.

Not only did *Dookie* easily sell through the 100,000 copies Cavallo had hoped for; it proceeded to sell more than 100,000 copies a week. It went gold (500,000 albums sold) in June and platinum (one million) in August, and by the time the band played Madison Square Garden in December—at which Armstrong performed completely naked—it had sold more than three million copies in the United States alone. The overwhelming interest in Green Day also led their first two records on Lookout to go gold, netting Livermore's bedroom label $10 million in profits in a single year.

Over the second half of 1994, *Dookie* tore through the *Billboard* charts like a hot knife through butter. It broke into the top ten right after their Woodstock performance, and into the top five after the

Boston riot. It kept climbing through the holidays, and on January 28, 1995, the album hit its peak at number two, surpassing Pearl Jam, the Eagles, and Boyz II Men, getting edged out at the top only by Garth Brooks.

Armstrong's power chords blared out of radios everywhere that year. The album spawned five hit singles—one more than even *Nevermind*. Even the revamped "Welcome to Paradise," a song Green Day had in their arsenal for more than three years, hit number seven on the Billboard Alternative Airplay chart. Videos for "Longview," "When I Come Around," and "Basket Case" were on constant MTV rotation, and the channel named "Basket Case" its number one video of 1994.

Green Day was the musical guest on *Saturday Night Live* in December, getting an introduction from Roseanne Barr, who donned the band's shirt. They performed that year on *Late Night with Conan O'Brien, The Jon Stewart Show,* MTV's *120 Minutes,* and the *Late Show with David Letterman.* "Our next guests' most recent album was named the best rock CD of the year by *Time* magazine," Letterman said, holding up a copy of *Dookie.* They played "Basket Case," which Armstrong dedicated to his girlfriend, Adrienne, whom he married three days later.

But beyond spreadsheet data about radio plays and chart positions, Green Day's impact on a new generation of music fans was immeasurable. Newly indoctrinated punks around the world dyed their hair blue, and aspiring guitarists lowered their guitar straps by a few inches. If there was any question as to who would be the successor to Nirvana as the biggest rock band in the world, Green Day raised their muddy hands.

By the time the band returned to *The Late Show* the following year, Letterman's intro made mention of another impressive achievement. "The first time they were on our program, they scared the hell out of me," he said. "But they since have gone on to sell millions of albums and they've also won a Grammy." The band performed "86," a new song wherein Armstrong lamented how, despite all the accolades, playing sold-out arenas around the world and landing on numerous magazine covers, he was still heartbroken about their ban from Gilman Street. "We've played in front of 20,000, 30,000 people," the frontman told *SPIN*, "and I still haven't felt the same thing that I felt playing in that place."

$ $ $

Green Day's international superstardom split the punk scene in two. "Some bands went deeper into the underground to eschew ambitions, and some bands went the other way," says Appelgren. "Unfortunately, there was still this notion that being ambitious was radioactive. Either you pretended you didn't have any ambitions, or you had them but you wouldn't admit it."

Punk clubs like Gilman were bombarded with newcomers, a rapid growth that had its pros and cons. "We had an influx of crowds that really helped keep us in the black. It really, really helped our finances. We used that to pay our rent and survive," says Luscious. But on the other hand, it also sometimes attracted unwanted attention. "We had tourist buses passing by, pointing out the home of Green Day. We had newscasters ask to film inside and we wouldn't let them. We took a page from the riot grrrls: *No press, go fuck yourself.*"

Feeling a bit of guilt for shining an unsolicited spotlight on their local scene, Green Day did their best to safeguard those who didn't seek the exposure. When asked about Gilman or other Bay Area bands in interviews, they typically kept a tight lip or changed the subject—avoiding "punksploitation," as they called it. "I always thought of that Germs song, 'What We Do Is Secret,'" Armstrong later explained to *Rolling Stone*. "I can't really talk about that."

For those bands adventurous enough to branch out and brush off accusations of selling out, though, opportunities that had never seemed possible were suddenly presenting themselves. MTV and radio stations were more prone to giving chances to smaller rock bands, and independent labels had an easier time getting their releases into chain stores and malls. "There was a trickle-down effect to other bands," says Livermore. "Almost any band on our label could call up somebody on the other side of the country and say, 'Hey, we're on Lookout and we wanna come to your town,' and they'd get a gig.'"

Dookie was the rising tide that raised all boats in 1994, which became a breakout year for punk. Most notably, Epitaph Records, the Los Angeles–based independent label founded by Bad Religion guitarist Brett Gurewitz, enjoyed an overnight outburst of gains. Their most popular band, Orange County four-piece the Offspring, had a mega-seller with their April release, *Smash,* which went platinum that year and sold more copies than any independent album in history—more copies than could even fit in the Epitaph office. "We had Offspring records filling my entire building on Santa Monica Boulevard, from the floor to the ceiling," Gurewitz told *Rolling Stone.* "The inside of the building looked like a Rubik's Cube of pallets of Offspring vinyl, cassettes, and CDs. Then we had another building downtown that was also filled, and rental space in external buildings."

Epitaph also benefited from smaller-scale hits that year, with Rancid's *Let's Go* and NOFX's *Punk in Drublic* both of which would end up going gold. Rancid, which featured Tim Armstrong and Matt Freeman of Operation Ivy, became MTV favorites with their studded leather jackets and foot-high mohawks, introducing a new generation of music fans to punk rock aesthetics. Punk veterans Bad Religion, who'd made the jump from Epitaph to Atlantic, hit number 87 on the *Billboard* chart that September with their major-label debut, *Stranger Than Fiction.*

Epitaph wasn't the only independent punk label receiving *Dookie* windfalls. Fat Wreck Chords, the San Francisco label co-founded by NOFX frontman Fat Mike Burkett, had an arsenal of pop-punk bands like Lagwagon, No Use for a Name, and Face to Face, who saw their crowd sizes swell and could now sell a couple hundred thousand records. A slew of new indie labels began cropping up or expanding their operations to cater to the country's newfound interest in poppy punk bands—Hopeless, Go-Kart, Fearless, Nitro, SideOneDummy, Vagrant.

Sensing the undeniable dawn of a new rock movement, major labels started throwing huge piles of money at bands of Green Day's ilk, in hopes of landing the next punk rock stars. The Big Six were on the hunt, snatching up four-chord wonders left and right. "The signing blitz is on," the September 1994 issue of *SPIN* declared. "So for the punk community, Green Day really is the next Nirvana—harbinger of dramatic changes to come."

Punk was profitable again, and major labels wanted in on it. Every smart A&R rep was now on the lookout for worthy successors. "After *Dookie,* another facet of the underground became commercially viable," says Gitter. "So . . . who would be the next Green Day?"

CHAPTER 2

JAWBREAKER

Dear You

DGC (1995)

THE EAST BAY was such an unwelcoming place for Green Day after they signed to a major label that Billie Joe Armstrong sometimes disguised himself with a beard when he went out in public. Once the band was barred from the stage at Gilman Street, the frontman drew icy glares and furtive whispers when he walked into certain venues and hangout spots around town. Even something as mundane as taking a piss was robbed of its simple joy when he'd look straight ahead while standing at the urinal and see unkind words about his band scrawled on the wall.

One night in early 1994, Armstrong tried his best to blend into a dense crowd to watch one of his favorite local bands, Jawbreaker. Fortunately, all eyes in the room were fixed on the band's captivating frontman, Blake Schwarzenbach. Between songs, Schwarzenbach told the crowd he needed to take a minute to address some rumors about the band that had been going around. Gossip had been circulating in the punk scene that Jawbreaker had signed to a major label, and he wanted to set the record straight.

The rumors weren't far-fetched. The band had just done a stretch of dates opening for Nirvana, in support of their number one album, *In Utero*. Nirvana wielded the Midas touch in rock music, and any band that breathed the same air as them stood a good chance of being heralded as their successors. Plus, plenty of bands Jawbreaker had played shows with had already been swept up in the major-label feeding frenzy, from Samiam to Jawbox. It seemed as if Jawbreaker were the last indie holdouts among their peers.

So here it was, the truth, straight from the horse's mouth: those rumors, Schwarzenbach emphatically declared, were bullshit. Yes, Jawbreaker had been approached by major labels, but no, they didn't have any interest in selling out, now or ever.

Schwarzenbach had taken to giving this soapbox spiel at shows lately. It was a reliable way of getting the crowd on his side, but also, he really meant it. Major labels had taken an interest in his band, but Jawbreaker didn't have plans to sign with any of them. For them, it was DIY or die. Frankly, he was sick of repeating it.

The audience cheered at the confirmation that one of their scene's most beloved acts was holding firm to its place in the underground. But while everyone around him was clapping, Armstrong found himself shaking his head. He immediately felt very alone, knowing everyone there probably considered him a traitor. More than that, Armstrong worried about Jawbreaker. To stand in front of a few hundred witnesses and promise you'll never do something is to set them up for eventual disappointment. No band ever thinks they're going to sell out. Until, one day, they do.

$ $ $

The three members of Jawbreaker shared an apartment on the top floor of a syringe-littered building on Sycamore Street, in San Francisco's Mission District, in the early nineties, though they would never claim the city as their home. "We were identified as a San Francisco band but were always just a bit off to the side," says Schwarzenbach. "I think that was helpful to our identity and how we worked."

This disconnect was partly the result of an age gap between the band members and the punks that made up the core of the Bay Area scene. Though the three were barely out of college themselves, they felt ancient compared with the teenaged regulars who frequented punk gigs in the area. "We were too old for Gilman and the East Bay scene, socially. We were aged out," says Schwarzenbach. "It was *young*. There were a lot of kids—runaways—taking refuge in the underground."

The other reason they never waved the Bay Area flag was that, simply, they weren't from there. Although Schwarzenbach was born in Berkeley, he spent his adolescence in Venice, California, where he attended Crossroads School for Arts & Sciences, a private institution that catered to artsy teens. A *Vanity Fair* article about the exclusive Santa Monica school described it as the "elite, anti-prep mecca for entertainment-industry offspring"; among its star-studded alumni are Gwyneth Paltrow, Jonah Hill, and Zooey Deschanel. The magazine dubbed it the "school for cool," and the young Schwarzenbach fit right in.

Schwarzenbach describes his high school self as an acne-faced geek, but others remember him as boyishly handsome, charismatic, and smart—maybe too smart for his own good. He had spiky, bleached blond hair, a lean frame, and a razor-sharp jawline to match his razor-sharp wit. The school nurtured its students' creativity, and Schwarzenbach had an innate flair for everything he tried his hand at, whether it was drawing, writing, skateboarding, or music.

In tenth grade, Schwarzenbach was smoking cigarettes in an alley after class when he met Adam Pfahler, a troublemaker who'd just transferred to Crossroads. The two became fast friends and bonded over their love of punk, specifically Los Angeles products like Fear, X, and Circle Jerks, as well as SST Records bands like Black Flag, Meat Puppets, and Hüsker Dü. They soon started hitting up punk gigs around L.A. and playing together in a gothy instrumental band called Red Harvest, with Schwarzenbach on guitar, Pfahler on drums, and their friend Rich on bass.

After graduating in 1985, the two left Red Harvest and Crossroads behind to move across the country together and attend NYU, where they split a dorm room near Washington Square Park. The building's greatest advantage was that it was located just two blocks from CBGB, and the two freshmen immersed themselves in the New York hardcore scene.

Itching to play music again and searching for a third person to round them out, they called the phone number listed on a hand-drawn flyer pinned to the wall of the cafeteria. It read BASS PLAYER LOOKING FOR BAND, above a list of noisy influences like Scratch Acid, Naked Raygun, and Hüsker Dü. When they met the Chris whose name was on the flyer, Schwarzenbach and Pfahler recognized him instantly. There was no missing Chris Bauermeister on campus. His daily uniform was a black leather jacket spray-painted with colorful punk insignia. He had matted ginger hair, intense green eyes, and a wily, high-pitched voice. Everything about Bauermeister was eccentric, including the way he played bass. He used a traditional four-string but squeezed twice as many notes out of it as most players by relying heavily on chords or by hooking a thumb onto the E string to add deeper backing tones.

The three began practicing together at a nearby rehearsal studio largely occupied by intimidating hardcore bands. Schwarzenbach would later describe the situation in an interview as "total Cali wusses amongst the burliest Lower East Side guys." The next two years would be full of starts and stops as the group went through name changes, additional members, college transfers, and cross-country moves. They originally went by Terminal Island, then switched to Thump, and later, after relocating to Los Angeles after their junior year, they called themselves Rise.

Pfahler recruited his friend Jon Liu to sing for Rise, and the four-piece wrote songs together that sounded like the logical sum of their eighties punk influences. One day, Schwarzenbach showed up to practice with a song he'd written called "Shield Your Eyes" and took a crack at singing it. Not only did the lyrics read like something ripped from a poetry book, but Schwarzenbach's earnest voice was the perfect vehicle to deliver them. By the end of the first run-through of the song, Liu realized his services would no longer be needed.

The band continued on as a trio, with Schwarzenbach now adding vocals to his guitar duties. They put their heads together, jotted down a list of potential names for their newly minted lineup, and threw them into a hat. As they pulled out each one and tried it on for size, one name stood out, particularly because no one could remember who among them had suggested it. And so they settled on Jawbreaker, not only for its uniqueness but also because it belonged equally to none of them.

Jawbreaker released rough versions of "Shield Your Eyes" and other singles across a smattering of short-run demo tapes, compilations, and EPs, with the help of a few very small record labels, one of which was even called Very Small Records. It wasn't until 1990 that they found time between semesters to record their first full-length album, *Unfun,* which was released by Shredder Records, a small California label founded by *Maximum Rocknroll* contributor Mel Cheplowitz. Schwarzenbach later described it as being written "with limited abilities and unlimited enthusiasm."

While much of *Unfun* was dense and scattershot, its opener, "Want," proved that Jawbreaker also had a knack for penning catchy earworms when they wanted to. Its poppy chorus didn't kick in until after the song's midpoint, but it was unforgettable once it finally did. Schwarzenbach begged the listener to "yell it out before it kills you now / let it all out" and then hit them with the chaser: "I! Want! You!" His syllables were highly exaggerated, to the point that his delivery sounded vaguely cockneyed, while his nasally, repetitive whine took a bite-size lyric and made a meal of it: "Aye-aye-aye, aye-aye-aye, ayyye wantchew!" And with that, Jawbreaker had written their first bona fide sing-along. Even if the person standing in the back of the venue didn't know Jawbreaker, they'd leave with "Want" stuck in their head.

With his copy of *Maximum Rocknroll*'s touring guidebook *Book Your Own Fucking Life* and a phone card from his father, intended for emergencies, Schwarzenbach organized the "Fuck '90" tour, Jawbreaker's first conquest of the United States. It was a wildly ambitious summer-long loop around the country that was full of engine troubles, nights spent sleeping on dingy floors, and sparsely attended gigs in the middle of nowhere. A handful of good shows came out of it, too, but the positive experiences were overshadowed by the tension that quickly arose between the members. Two weeks into the tour, it became obvious that the three were not meant to be locked in a steel box with one another for ten hours a day. The oppressive summer heat only brought the strain to a boiling point.

Schwarzenbach and Bauermeister, in particular, had clashing personalities, which led to tense communication problems. Bauermeister, who was also privately grappling with undiagnosed depression, often felt like the third wheel tagging along for the ride with two best friends. Long stretches would go by without him saying more than a few words; by the last week of the tour, he was desperate to return home.

When asked about the meaning of the *Unfun* title in an interview with *Maximum Rocknroll* that summer, Bauermeister griped, "We just have shit luck. We seem to be building up litanies of disaster. Unfortunately, it's getting worse each time. One band's breaking point is basically our day-to-day."

By the time most readers saw the interview, though, Jawbreaker was no more. The day the "Fuck '90" tour hobbled home, the band members had grown sick of one another's faces and called it quits. It seemed the *Maximum Rocknroll* feature would be the last will and testament of a short-lived college project. Buried in the eulogy was a hypothetical question the zine's writers were fond of inflicting on their subjects: "If you had the opportunity to sign with a major label, would you accept?"

"No," replied Schwarzenbach. "All the majors are sweating right now, trying to pick up on the alternative thing. That's the only reason we'd even have an opportunity—because the indies are kicking major ass."

Pfahler drove the point home with a hammer: "It will never happen."

$ $ $

After avoiding one another for a few months while finishing school, the guys eventually agreed to put their differences aside and give

Jawbreaker the old post-college try. In the summer of '91, with degrees in hand, they moved to the San Francisco Bay Area, where rent was cheap and they could be surrounded by fellow musicians and artists. Bauermeister shared an apartment with their roadie Raul Reyes and Cringer guitarist Lance Hahn. Across the hall were Schwarzenbach and Pfahler.

After clocking out at their day jobs, they held long practices and wrote songs at a more dedicated pace than they had in their college days. Unencumbered by the additional burden of schoolwork, the members were even starting to have fun with one another. Their repertoire was sharpened at venues around town like Chameleon, Covered Wagon, and Gilman Street, where they shared stages with locals like Econochrist, Samiam, and Green Day. Even though *Unfun* was still finding its audience, the prolific Jawbreaker was already testing fresh material out on crowds. "We were always that band," says Schwarzenbach. "We were always playing the record that hadn't come out yet."

At first, Jawbreaker took slots shoved into the middle of six-band bills, but as their fan base grew in size and devotion, they soon started headlining shows in Berkeley and nearby cities like Los Angeles, Sacramento, and Seattle. "We're running this town now," Schwarzenbach joked in a fanzine interview. "If you're planning on visiting San Francisco in the near future, you should probably clear it with us first."

Although the band was adopted by the Bay Area scene—ingratiating themselves with the *Maximum Rocknroll* crowd and becoming regulars at local punk haunts—they had their own distinct air about them. "We were never really joiners," says Schwarzenbach. None of their records were released by Berkeley linchpin label Lookout Records, nor did their music share much DNA with the roster of swift and sloppy pop-punk acts associated with it. Jawbreaker were a little older, a little more collegiate. They had degrees in philosophy, history, and English literature, whereas many in the scene were high school students or dropouts. Schwarzenbach worked as a librarian and could usually be found walking around with a book tucked under his arm. The guys didn't even look all that punk. Schwarzenbach had ditched the bleached spikes of his youth in favor of a standard Supercuts special. Unless Bauermeister had his sleeves rolled up to reveal his forearm tattoos, the band could pass on the street without much notice.

"Jawbreaker moved to San Francisco and made their own scene, separate from the East Bay scene, by being really good, having a lot of friends, and being social," says Samiam guitarist Sergie Loobkoff. "They were outliers from DIY-minded people, but they could still fill up Gilman. Other DIY bands there were considered cool, but when they'd play, only fifty people would show up. [Jawbreaker] also played twenty-one-and-up clubs in San Francisco. That was weird for Gilman people."

Jawbreaker's first summer in the Bay would mark the end of an age of innocence for independent rock music. In September, Nirvana's *Nevermind* hit stores and became an instant success, intensifying the music industry's interest in independent rock bands. "The major labels started coming around in '91," says Pfahler. "We got letters from a couple majors, and they were easy to dismiss, because the letters were along the lines of 'send us your demo.' It was easy to say, 'Go fuck yourself.' They didn't know us. They were just casting a wide net after the success of *Nevermind*."

A one-page feature on the thriving San Francisco punk scene in the August '92 issue of *SPIN* put a spotlight on a handful of bands there. Samiam was deemed "the answer to critics' darlings Pavement and Urge Overkill." Green Day was likened to "R.E.M. in combat boots." Jawbreaker, the only act to get an accompanying photo, was praised as sounding like "a band that was—and is—ahead of its time" on its soon-to-be released sophomore album, *Bivouac*.

But just as their city was heating up, Jawbreaker was speeding away. They moved out of their apartments, put their belongings in storage, and took off for another tour. On August 19, 1992, the band played their first date of a ten-week stretch they dubbed the "Hell Is on the Way" tour, and hell was indeed close behind. Schwarzenbach quickly recognized that something was wrong with his voice; his throat felt hot and itchy when he sang. Every time he stepped up to the microphone, he was gambling on whether his ailing vocal cords were going to cooperate. Six dates into the tour, a night they were scheduled to play Kalamazoo, Michigan, Schwarzenbach knew that show wasn't going to be one of the good ones.

"You'll have to yell for me, because I lost my voice a couple days ago," he told the crowd at the start of their set, which prompted a person in the front to laugh. Schwarzenbach snapped back: "You think it's funny? I am in pain."

After the song, Schwarzenbach said, "I'm sorry for my voice. It's worse than I thought." He let out a nervous chuckle that sounded like it had scraped the lining of his throat to escape. "But we are gonna persevere." Six songs later, though, it was obvious that they could do no such thing. The frontman struggled through "Want," garbling the typically lively verses as if he were doing an unintentional Tom Waits impression. When he got to the line that begged listeners to "let it all out," he realized he couldn't heed his own advice. He skipped the "*aye-aye-ayes*" and rushed through the remainder of the song. When it was done, he took off his guitar, turned to Pfahler, and said, "I quit." But nothing came out.

Schwarzenbach couldn't actually quit, of course. That was just something the members of Jawbreaker said to—or, more often, screamed at—one another from time to time. In reality, they still had to gig their way east for another week to arrive in New York, where they would fly to Europe for a two-month tour. The next day, a doctor informed him that "a polyp the size of a grape" had developed on his vocal cords. Removing it would mean a $2,500 surgery and a two-week silent recovery. The band weighed their options that night at a Bob's Big Boy. Amazingly, canceling the tour never crossed anyone's mind. Instead, they decided to give their roadie a crash course in lyrics and see how he fared on the microphone.

Two weeks later, they were in Europe, where they hoped the health problem would resolve itself. Instead, Schwarzenbach left a trail of coughed-up blood through France and Spain, and when they got to Dublin he hacked up a red wad the size of his fist. He was taken to a hospital in London, where a surgeon removed the polyp. Schwarzenbach was instructed to give his voice ten days of rest, but he was back to singing within a week and powered through the remainder of the dates in Germany. If nothing else, the band got a song out of it, "Outpatient," and a lesson that they were hardheaded enough to persevere, even through discomfort and misery.

When asked in an interview for a European fanzine what the best and worst parts about being in Jawbreaker were, Pfahler quipped, "It's all the same to Jawbreaker."

$ $ $

One afternoon in October of 1993, Schwarzenbach came home to find a message from one of his roommates on the coffee table: "Tour with Nirvana next week? Yeah, right."

He called the number on the note and was patched through to John Silva, an artist manager at Gold Mountain Management, who was responsible for handling Nirvana through the release of their new album, *In Utero*. Schwarzenbach's recollection of the call went like this:

"Oh yeah, Blake, well, here's the long and short of it: Greg of the Wipers just fired his bassist in Europe, making it impossible for them to work the next leg of Nirvana's tour, so we're talking about six shows. You'd open, followed by Mudhoney . . ."

Schwarzenbach asked Silva a very reasonable question: "Why us?"

"Look, I just do what Kurt asks me to. He says, 'Get Jawbreaker.' So it's my job to get you and here we are. You've been on the band's list for a while. This is real, Blake. This isn't a joke."

It turned out that Kurt Cobain's nanny, a twenty-year-old Jawbreaker fan named Cali DeWitt, had turned Cobain on to *Bivouac* by playing it around their house in Seattle. Schwarzenbach relayed the request to the rest of the band, and they all agreed that the opportunity seemed like a no-brainer. Schwarzenbach and Pfahler had seen Nirvana blow the roof off the L.A. coffee bar Jabberjaw in '91 and had been hooked ever since.

Fast-forward a week and Jawbreaker's humble '78 Dodge van was tailing three buses carrying the members of Nirvana. The first show took place on October 19 at the Albuquerque Convention Center, in front of five thousand people. As the attendees trickled into the venue, Jawbreaker nervously took the stage for their twenty-five-minute set. Schwarzenbach looked out onto the biggest crowd he'd ever played for, turned to Pfahler, and said, "Well, here goes absolutely everything."

Very few in the audience were familiar with Jawbreaker; in fact, most of that week's tour posters and newspaper notices still listed the Wipers as the opening act. But to the band's surprise, they played well enough to rake in solid post-show business at the makeshift merch stands they had set up in the parking lots, a sneaky method of bypassing the venues' egregious sales cuts. T-shirts sold for eight bucks apiece or two for fifteen, and the extra cash helped cover nightly motel stays.

Jawbreaker blinked and the week passed them by. After the Milwaukee show on October 26, their time on the tour came to an end. "You guys were great, you totally went over," said Cobain, who had made a habit of watching the band from the side of the stage. He thanked them for coming and asked if they could swap band shirts. Pfahler grabbed an *In Utero* tee and Cobain took a black Jawbreaker shirt with the band's name emblazoned in big yellow block letters above their logo: the Morton Salt girl and the phrase WHEN IT PAINS IT ROARS. The two bands went their separate ways, Jawbreaker's van sputtering back to the West Coast and Nirvana's three buses soldiering on to Ohio. For the next several nights of the tour, the Boredoms and Meat Puppets filled the opening slots, but Jawbreaker was there in spirit, with Cobain proudly wearing their shirt onstage.

Jawbreaker's heads were still swirling as they drove home from their first experience with high-production arena touring. Their takeaway was that it was fun, overwhelming, and a glimpse into a world they enjoyed observing from a distance but would never feel comfortable inhabiting themselves. Schwarzenbach wrote in his tour diary that week that he felt like "a meddlesome ghost who really didn't have much business in this business." The six days only reinforced his anti-corporate rock stance. He wrote, "It has been my official platform since last year (when major labels began expressing an interest in us—oh, those foolish magnates!) to never sign to a major label. I stand firmer in this belief today than ever."

The trio returned to San Francisco to find that rumors about them had beaten them there. The band expected they'd be taking some shit around town for tagging along with the MTV darlings, but they were surprised by how willing people were to believe the wildest fabrications. One of the most ridiculous pieces of gossip claimed they'd received a $500-per-day food budget, when in actuality they were paid $500 to play each show, plus a free meal.

"I remember someone from that *MRR* scene said something to me, speculating something like 'Well, how much money did you make last year, $50,000?' And I was like, 'Are you fucking kidding me?'" says Pfahler. "At the time he said that to me, I had no money in the bank, I was living in an apartment for $650. I think people really thought, because we were a beloved cult band, we were selling hundreds of thousands of records. Any band on Fat Wreck Chords was selling ten times the records we were."

A preemptive backlash was building, fueled by fans' fears that Jawbreaker had gotten a taste of rock stardom and were hungry for more. There was a line in the sand, and the band got an unfriendly preview of what would happen if they crossed it. "I think it started —I *know* it started—when we went on tour with Nirvana," says Schwarzenbach. "People just assumed that because we did that, we were gonna be on Geffen or something."

$ $ $

As major-label interest in the East Bay intensified, punk purity was turning violent. That became clear one night at Gilman Street when one of punk rock's most recognizable figureheads was curled up on the floor while half a dozen punks stood over him, kicking and stomping his head and rib cage. After an apparent verbal altercation, Dead Kennedys frontman Jello Biafra was allegedly assaulted by an attendee who went by the name Cretin and a few of his friends. "[Biafra] was being kicked in the head by Cretin while being held down by several others, and people were yelling 'rich rock star' and 'sellout,'" *Maximum Rocknroll* founder Tim Yohannan wrote of the incident in the July 1994 issue. Biafra claimed he suffered a broken bone and torn ligaments in his leg, plus a hospital bill that amounted to five figures.

"I never went to Gilman Street, and once I heard about Jello Biafra being beaten up there, I decided I was not gonna go to Gilman Street," says Mark Kates. "It was ridiculous. It's like the most hypocritical thing that's ever happened in punk rock."

Kates had been doing A&R for DGC, a subsidiary of Geffen Records, since 1987, working with bands like Teenage Fanclub and White Zombie. He'd also accomplished the unthinkable by pulling the staunchly indie art rockers Sonic Youth into the major-label system for the release of their 1990 album, *Goo.* Upon signing to DGC, bassist Kim Gordon told him, "The next thing you should sign is Nirvana." A little more than a year later, Nirvana was talked into coming aboard as well.

Kates's introduction to Jawbreaker was their first night opening for his clients Nirvana, a show that, by Schwarzenbach's account, was one of the best of the tour. Kates liked what he saw from them onstage and appreciated them even more backstage. "Generally, the last thing they wanted to talk about is music," he remembers. It was a quality he found refreshing.

Jawbreaker saw Kates as surprisingly relatable for a suit, too, and was impressed with his punk rock bona fides. "Mark was an old DJ from Boston who was friends with Mission of Burma, and he had great taste," says Pfahler.

Always on the hunt for potential new signings, Kates wondered how interested they might be in taking a meeting with Geffen, but once he learned that Jawbreaker had a reputation as one of those devoutly anti-major-label bands, he knew that broaching the topic would be an A&R faux pas. "If that's what you heard about a band, then it wasn't cool to pursue them, like it was disrespectful," he says. "Knowing that scene from a distance, you could make a fool of yourself by pursuing a band that had no interest in signing."

Kates kept tabs on the band, though, in hopes that their position might eventually soften. "I was staying in touch," he says, "because if the day ever came when Jawbreaker suddenly might be open to making a deal, I would be in a strong position."

$ $ $

When Green Day released their major-label debut, *Dookie,* on the first day of February 1994, the album's cover, depicting a bomb being dropped on a city, became a good metaphor for its impact on the Bay Area. The Berkeley trio proved there was a national market for West Coast punk rock, and the music industry's spotlight on San Francisco shined brighter than ever.

"I remember pretty distinctly when 'Longview' became a single, because I lived with Bill Schneider, who ended up being Green Day's tour manager and plays in Pinhead Gunpowder with Billie," says Schwarzenbach. "He came into the apartment one day and said, 'They're playing this song all the time on the radio.' And then the video was on TV. We thought it was really cool but didn't know it was going to gain the traction and momentum that it did." When Jawbreaker hit the road for their "Come Get Some" tour, the single was inescapable. He laughs, "We were haunted by the success of Green Day."

"After Green Day hit, then things got more intense," says Pfahler. "Labels descended on the Bay Area, looking for whatever else is big up here, because they have no imagination. Wherever something hits, they paratrooper into the town, like they did in Seattle. They throw it all against the wall and see what sticks. More A&R people started showing up to the shows. There were a lot of invitations to tour the label offices, go get lunch. A lot of fancy business cards were passed to us at the shows."

It was in this fertile climate, a week after *Dookie*'s release, that Jawbreaker dropped their third album, *24 Hour Revenge Therapy,* their most accessible collection of songs to date. The album had been recorded over just three economical days at the Chicago home studio of producer Steve Albini for the cost of $1,032. In addition to his work as a respected audio engineer, Albini had played in a number of provocative and influential groups the Jawbreaker members were fond of, like Big Black, Rapeman, and Shellac. Although he was a fierce defender of the indie scene, he had recently helped Nirvana record *In Utero*. He justified the decision by turning down royalties and instead accepting a flat rate of $100,000.

Co-released by local indies Tupelo Recording Company and Communion Records, *24 Hour* saw the twenty-six-year-old Schwarzenbach hitting his stride as a songwriter. As a *Rock Candy* review put it, the lyrics centered around the frontman's "recent hardships— a throat operation and breakups with three different girls." But unlike his juvenile pop-punk peers who were content to rhyme "heart" with "fart," Schwarzenbach weaved wit, metaphors, and introspection through his tales of torment. His sharp narrative songwriting style had more in common with great American writers like Kerouac, Salinger, and Ginsberg, whose works he'd studied at his library job. An author trapped inside the body of a punk singer, he once described his songs as being about desperation, empty bottles, and ashtrays.

His confessional style of songwriting was sometimes saccharine, but this emotional vulnerability helped build upon the band's cult-like following among those who wore hearts on sleeves and romanticized the lonely nights and lovelorn pain he sang about on songs like "Ache": "I believe in desperate acts / The kind that make you look stupid."

"It's a very personal band for people," Schwarzenbach notes. "It's always been that way. Those who identify with it identify with it as *theirs*, and sacred, and truthful in some way."

Although *24 Hour* positioned Schwarzenbach as punk's poet laureate, there was one song on the record whose simplicity stood out as the sonic outlier. With its playfully seesawing melody, the two-minute "Boxcar" was the closest thing to a traditional punk song in Jawbreaker's catalog, in that it featured the three core elements of one: its three-chord verse could be learned by any novice guitar player in under a minute; it leaned on a singable count of "One, two, three, four," a device on which the Ramones had built an entire career; and lastly, it pulled the classic punk songwriting move of name-dropping the genre right in the first line: "You're not punk, and I'm telling everyone."

There was more to "Boxcar" than met the eye, though. Schwarzenbach was taking digs at the closed-mindedness of the cutthroat punk rock scene, prone to devouring its own, with lines like "My enemies are all too familiar / They're the ones who used to call me friend." It was punk cynicism disguised as punk celebration. But to the average listener oblivious to insular punk politics, it just sounded like a catchy song they could pogo along to.

The songs of *24 Hour Revenge Therapy* further deepened the band's relationship with their audience and intensified their live show. The album helped give Jawbreaker something that appealed to A&R reps—shows that were packed with a few hundred fans who knew every word to every song. It was always easier for a label to keep a fire going than to build one from scratch, and Jawbreaker had clearly established their own kindling. "You could feel the energy of anticipation in a room when Jawbreaker was about to go onstage," says Loobkoff. "That's the kind of feeling that you can't manufacture."

Although the band wasn't punk's biggest seller, with *24 Hour* selling around twenty thousand copies off little besides acclaim in *MRR* and *Flipside,* their vocal anti-majors stance made them the scene's forbidden fruit. *Magnet* magazine crowned them "the least likely to jump ship."

But with intense passion came intense scrutiny. The members of Jawbreaker were asked the same questions daily, and they came up in almost every interview: *Did you sign? Are you gonna sign? Would you ever sign?* Friends posed these questions with a whisper while fans shouted them from crowds, and not always in the politest of ways.

"Not that we're going to, but even if we were complete sellouts, whatever, that doesn't justify someone in Albuquerque spitting on Blake while we play. Spitting in his mouth because we allegedly signed to a major label," Pfahler told the zine *Rubberband* that year. "Why did they pay six dollars to spit in Blake's mouth and possibly give him hepatitis or something, you know?"

In an attempt to prevent more flying saliva, Schwarzenbach made a nightly habit of prefacing "Indictment," a song about the commodification of music and companies "selling kids to other kids," with a reminder about which side of the label wars Jawbreaker was on. "I didn't like the poacher aspect of shows becoming a little thick with industry people and jokers from the outside," he recalls. "I was emboldened by our place, foremost in the independent category."

Before playing the song at Emo's, in Austin, Texas, he clarified, "You may have read that we're on a major label. That's bullshit. Although we've been courted by a lot of major labels, we're not interested in that."

Among the cheers the proclamation elicited, two words came hurtling from a mouth in the crowd and landed squarely in Schwarzenbach's ears: "Yeah, right!" It stung, but at least it wasn't spit.

$ $ $

"This song is called 'Accident Prone.' You've never heard it. You're gonna hate it," Schwarzenbach assured a roomful of people in Leeds, England. The British audience dutifully nodded along through all six and a half minutes of a gloomy, unfamiliar tune that consisted of what felt like a dozen different slow-moving sections. The band had been testing out a handful of new songs, but they were doubtful they'd ever get a chance to record them, being flush with new material but thin on patience with one another.

"The place we were at as a band was that we had an album's worth of songs, but we were also talking about breaking up," says Schwarzenbach. "We'd just come back from a pretty hard European tour, just not getting along, and feeling not too inspired."

The issue of money, or lack thereof, had become a problem, too. They typically returned from tour with a few thousand bucks in their pockets, which was enough to pay rent but paled in comparison with their more financially solvent friends who were cashing in on the alternative gold rush. "We were making okay money but not set-for-life money, which a lot of people around us seemed to be making," says Bauermeister. "One of the people I knew from college was the guitarist from White Zombie. At one point he called me up and he told me he had two houses. And I was like, 'Wait, what?'" The stack of fancy business cards they'd accumulated over the years started to seem like tickets to a more profitable future. "There were tensions going on within the band, and maybe it was a way to save things. There was a certain degree of—I don't know if I'd call it greed, but recognition that [signing to a major] was an alternative."

"We decided: 'We're gonna either break up or do another record,'" says Schwarzenbach. "Maybe we should just do a record and get a really good deal. We wanted really good money and complete control. We wanted the money to be an amount that you'd say, 'Why not? Why wouldn't you?'"

With some trepidation, they contacted their friend Dave Hawkins, drummer for the band Engine 88, who also worked with Elliot Cahn and Jeff Saltzman at Cahn-Man Management, the firm that represented Green Day. "They were all very smart guys. They just didn't want to be in business with big business, is the best way to describe it," remembers Cahn.

"I think, in a way, it became a bit of a lark. Like, 'Let's just see what we would get, what we would be offered if we did,'" says Schwarzenbach. "We consulted Jeff Saltzman, who was Green Day's manager, and said, 'Would you see what the interest is?' And he said, 'I can tell you: I'll get you ten offers next week if you say go, but be prepared for it, because then it's gonna be *on*.'"

It took a bit longer than a week, but the interest in Jawbreaker was as strong as Saltzman had predicted. They soon had meetings lined up with MCA, Warner Bros., American, and Capitol. "They were exactly what you'd expect—certain people who had never heard you before telling you they're your biggest fan. Some blowhards, some very genuine people," remembers Schwarzenbach.

"It was a goof to go take those meetings," says Pfahler. "We thought we'd get a free trip to Los Angeles and go down there and bust balls and it'd be funny. And if someone makes us an offer we can't refuse, maybe we'll do that, maybe not. But we weren't necessarily agonizing over it. It was silly."

"I think we knew we could walk away from the table at any time with those people," says Schwarzenbach. "We were just entertaining their offer. We were a little surly. We were definitely a hermetic unit and had a very jaundiced view of Hollywood, having come from

L.A. and seeing hair metal and pay-to-play and all this shit that happened there. We weren't expecting a fairytale." Bauermeister adds: "I was a dick to every industry person we came across."

If the band had been hoping to pick up anecdotes about clueless label suits with which they could regale their friends back home, they got their share. Pfahler and Schwarzenbach remember being toured around a swanky Bel-Air country club by a rude label rep who berated and humiliated his assistant at every opportunity. "There was this other guy in a three-piece suit and cowboy boots," remembers Bauermeister. "He very prominently put his cowboy boots on his desk and said, 'I'm a fuckin' maniac and I hate to lose!'" They also got a private tour of Universal Studios and ate lunch from the porch of a fake house on the set of the *Jaws* ride, watching as a new boatful of tourists was terrorized by a mechanical shark every ten minutes.

The band racked up the funny wine-and-dine stories they'd wanted, but all they really cared about was the final offer. "It was a little bit of a challenge. Like, 'Well, everyone's talking big, let's see how far we can push it,'" says Schwarzenbach. "Adam's a real bargainer. I don't know how to do it, but he has no qualms about saying, 'You're a corporation. I'm gonna ask you for the moon.'"

"I read the Passman book, *All You Need to Know About the Music Business*. I read it cover to cover and took notes to figure out the best thing to do in that situation," says Pfahler. "What I'd determined was that the more money you make them invest in you, the more likely they are to fight to see a return on that investment."

One of the top offers came courtesy of Mark Kates at DGC/Geffen, who had been eagerly awaiting the opportunity to work with Jawbreaker since their Nirvana tour. As soon as he got the call from Saltzman, he was ready to pounce with the company checkbook. "I don't know if I can say I was on a plane that night, but I got on the first flight I could," says Kates. They were soon dining at Zuni Café, in San Francisco, where Kates tried to sell them on his thriving label. "I had the confidence of what was behind me. The company was so strong and significant in that genre."

And indeed, Jawbreaker was impressed with Kates's roster. "Mark was doing Hole and had worked with Nirvana, XTC, Sonic

Youth—they were all good bands. It felt like we'd be lucky to be part of this family," says Schwarzenbach. "We knew his interest was authentic. He'd come see our band and was really interested. So he was the standout all along."

Kates was so anxious to close the deal that the band nearly gave him a panic attack. "There was this one day where we'd brought them to L.A. for a meeting and I couldn't reach them," remembers Kates. "This was pre-cellphone, and I got super paranoid. Like, 'Oh fuck, those guys got kidnapped or something.' They weren't at their hotel. I assumed they were being wined and dined by another label trying to get them to sign a contract on the spot. Nothing of the sort was happening. They were at a movie and then they saw Andrew Dice Clay on the street and got totally freaked out."

For all the controversy that had long surrounded Jawbreaker's label status, their decision to pull the trigger on a major was rather unceremonious. Pfahler recalls walking with Schwarzenbach down Valencia, a street that had changed drastically in the years since they settled into the neighborhood after college. The sidewalks that had once been a popular gathering spot for strung-out junkies were now overrun with well-off hipsters patronizing restaurants and coffee shops. The two stopped at the corner and Pfahler shrugged, "You wanna sign?" Schwarzenbach said flatly, "Yeah, let's go with Geffen." They turned the corner onto 20th Street, and that was that.

The band members soon inked their names on a stack of paper that gave them just shy of a million dollars as part of a three-record deal. They got a hefty recording budget and some money to buy gear and a van, and, most important, they negotiated for total artistic control over whatever they were to make for the label. "They knew we weren't a fucking boy band," says Pfahler. "They knew we'd have a lot to say about the cover, the sound, the producer, the single, all that shit."

Immediately after signing, the weight of their decision started to sink in. What had started as a lark suddenly became real and turned into a source of paranoia. From then on, they'd no longer be able to stand onstage and preach their anti-major rhetoric to a round of applause. A feature in the *San Francisco Chronicle* reported that they were "so paranoid that at a gig at the Great American Music Hall right after signing the deal, Schwarzenbach wore a shirt emblazoned with 'zero cred.'"

$ $ $

Over the course of a year, Rob Cavallo had transformed from a rookie producer nervously awaiting a pink slip to a celebrated industry hotshot. His studio magic on Green Day's *Dookie* had netted the band an astounding five hit singles. Cavallo had accomplished something previously unheard of: he'd plucked a punk band from relative obscurity and polished their rough edges with enough radio-friendly sheen to catapult them into rock stardom. So when Mark Kates needed a producer to capture his newest signing, Jawbreaker, Cavallo's name immediately came to mind. "Cavallo is unique in that he doesn't have a cool factor," says Kates. "He just makes the biggest records he can."

"Mark Kates called me and said, 'Do you want to meet with Jawbreaker? They're a really cool band. They're one of Kurt Cobain's favorite bands and they opened for Nirvana on a leg of their tour,'" remembers Cavallo. "I heard their demos and thought to myself, *Oh jeez, this is a whole new kind of rock. I don't even know what the fuck to call this!* I don't know if they'd called it emo yet, but that was part of the birth of emo right there."

Cavallo ventured to San Francisco to meet with Jawbreaker over dinner and found their personalities as intriguing as their music. "Blake was this deep philosopher—a Hunter S. Thompson type, a New York artisan smoking cigs. And then Adam was just a fucking rock star. Chris was this great bass player who was also like a *Dungeons & Dragons* guy. Together, there was a heaviness to what they were doing," he says.

They all hit it off and were soon making plans to craft songs together over the winter. Cavallo recalls, "They got us this rehearsal space in San Francisco. I went up there for a couple weeks and it was so cold. We were in this place that had a cement floor. It was almost like we were in a prison. It was this weird, industrial building down by the train tracks. There was broken glass on the ground, with steel and concrete everywhere. It felt like we were doing grunt work, like we were going to war every night."

In February of '95, Cavallo returned to the familiar Fantasy Studios, in Berkeley, where he'd recorded *Dookie* a little more than a year prior, to take a crack at Jawbreaker's fourth album, *Dear You*. The grim, frigid conditions in which the album's songs had been incubated were reflected in their tone. Schwarzenbach describes *Dear You* as a "fractured, personal record," largely marked by rage, frustration, loneliness, and remorse over relationships gone bad.

Opener "Save Your Generation" saw Schwarzenbach evading suicide attempts by telling himself to "keep passing these open windows," a reference to John Irving's *The Hotel New Hampshire*. On "Fireman," he wallowed in sociopathic vindictiveness with lines like "Dreamed I was a fireman / I just smoked and watched you burn." "Accident Prone" and "Jet Black" were slow burners that took winding, cathartic journeys through the darkest caverns of his psyche. They distinguished themselves as not only the bleakest songs on the album, but the bleakest in Jawbreaker's entire catalog. The latter, in particular, was true to its noir title, with Schwarzenbach describing himself in the chorus as "funny like a funeral."

To break up the gloominess, Cavallo had the band cut a new version of their fan favorite "Boxcar" for fun. Its pace and structure remained identical to what had appeared on *24 Hour Revenge Therapy,* but Cavallo's rendition subtly buffed out its jagged texture and made Schwarzenbach's voice and guitar pop with a warm lucidity. It captured a version of Jawbreaker that wouldn't feel out of place following Green Day's "Basket Case" on the radio. When Kates heard it, he liked it so much that he thought it should be included on *Dear You*.

"I sent my assistant to have a conversation with the band to ask if there was any way they could put 'Boxcar' on the album," he says. "You go to see the band live and there's one song that stands out based on audience reaction. It's a perfectly legitimate question to ask, but it was just an impossible question to deal with at that moment."

Jawbreaker shot the idea down, feeling it would be a betrayal to their loyal fans who had earned some ownership of the song as well. So Kates tried asking again, this time through Cavallo. "The label called me and said, 'You've got to do us a favor and see if you can talk them into putting it on the record,'" says Cavallo, who also saw the merit in including it as an ideal entry point for new listeners. "To me, that song made Blake a star. When you're an artist and you're singing a lyric, it reflects back on who the artist is. That's the hero you then become to the fans. I believed that 'Boxcar' would have done that."

Cavallo suggested it to the band and they said no. He brought it up a second time and they again declined. Finally, he took the band out to lunch and pleaded his case. *Dear You*, he told them, was like a suitcase—it was a very heavy thing to ask audiences to lift, but putting a sturdy handle on it might help them better grasp it. He mentioned that Green Day had repurposed an older song, "Welcome to Paradise," for *Dookie*, and it was now booming out of every radio in America. The members of Jawbreaker considered everything Cavallo said and took the night to sleep on it. "The next day they said, 'We really heard you, we thought about it, but we decided we just can't put "Boxcar" on the record,'" says Cavallo. He trusted Jawbreaker's artistic vision enough to let the matter go after that.

Although Cavallo possessed a savant-like grasp of the musical dynamic that made Jawbreaker special, he was blind to the strained personal relationships bubbling just below the surface. Their sudden influx of cash had done nothing to improve communication between band members, and their rapport was colder than ever. Schwarzenbach had totally commandeered the writing process and Bauermeister grew more distant as he felt increasingly pushed to the sidelines.

"As far as recording it, that was the record I was least involved in, by my own choice," says Bauermeister. "There was a lot of unspoken tension going on. I have a bad tendency not to voice concerns. I don't like conflict. So I was just doing my job. I went in, recorded it, and left."

Bauermeister and Pfahler finished laying down bass and drum tracks within the first week, standard turnaround for Jawbreaker, and spent the remainder of the session taking advantage of their free time at home. Schwarzenbach kept coming in every day, though, working with Cavallo to hone vocal and guitar tracks.

"I wanted to make it really sound like if you were standing right in front of Blake's amplifier," says Cavallo. Through painstaking trial and error, he developed a recording technique he called the White Hot Sound that captured Schwarzenbach's unique guitar concepts, which leaned heavily on ominous, open-string riffs. By layering three contrasting guitar tones, Cavallo created a patchwork of sound designed to be so thick and rich that it would knock the listener over and carry them off on a tsunami wave of distortion.

"On a song like 'Accident Prone,' we said, 'Okay, we're gonna have a clean sound into a dirty sound into a fucking insane, smash-your-face sound,'" he says. One amp they employed to achieve this was Schwarzenbach's trusty Marshall JCM800. Another was a 1970s Hiwatt amp Cavallo had inherited from a member of Earth, Wind & Fire. "It's a clean amplifier and you can barely make it distort unless you turn it all the way up, and then it's so fucking loud that it'll break your eardrums. It will kill you," he says.

February rolled into March and Schwarzenbach was still spending fourteen-hour days with Cavallo, fine-tuning tracks and spending every penny of the album's $200,000 budget. The frontman felt like "a nocturnal factory worker," crossing the Bay Bridge and punching in to work for a month of late nights in the studio. *Dear You* being his second post-surgery album, he was still learning to utilize his voice in a way that didn't rely on high-volume shouting. Much of his approach on the microphone was now understated and subdued, replacing the occasional bark with a brooding rumble that was more Morrissey than MacKaye.

Every so often during his vocal sessions, the loud, unruly band in the next studio over would knock on the door and ask to borrow equipment. It was the East Bay's reigning punk kings, Rancid, recording their bombastic third album, . . . *And Out Come the Wolves*. Cavallo lent them a few amps, one of which had been used on *Dookie* and would make an appearance on Rancid's ska-infused "Time Bomb."

Schwarzenbach got a glimpse into the mohawked punks' studio

one night and was struck by the difference in their approach. All at once, the future of Jawbreaker crystallized in his mind. "Our session, which was basically just me at that point, was a dark, candlelit room, very austere," he says. "I went next door to see someone in the Rancid camp, and it was like this fraternity party with Brett [Gurewitz] from Epitaph and eighteen other people, and they were having such a good time. I work furtively in the shadows, and try to get an honest take when no one's looking. They had a showbiz attitude, they were so confident and in their zone, and we were trembling and melting down. It was pretty clear to me in that moment that I was totally not geared for this kind of business. I just thought: 'We are never, ever going to succeed in this world.'"

$ $ $

Since one of Jawbreaker's reliable set openers was a song about a boat doomed never to realize its dream of setting sail, it seemed appropriate that the release party for *Dear You* should take place at sea. On September 12, 1995, the band boarded a ferry that journeyed through the Sausalito harbor and under the Golden Gate Bridge to debut new material for 250 friends, associates, and radio contest winners.

"It was right after work and everyone showed up and they hadn't had a chance to eat dinner," remembers Bauermeister. "There was a huge open bar and some snack foods that vanished in five seconds. So it was a bunch of people with no food in their stomach, riding around in a boat, completely drunk."

After the Heinekens, Cheez Doodles, and candy jawbreakers were claimed, the band ran through a set that leaned heavily on *Dear You* songs. Aside from some technical issues that cut their performance short and the eight-foot ceiling that prevented excited fans from leaping too high, the positive energy in the air felt like a resounding success. The online music magazine *Addicted to Noise* reported, "Whether *Dear You* rocks the country the way *Dookie* did (nine-plus million copies sold!) remains to be seen, but Jawbreaker proved they can rock the boat."

The evening seemed like a triumph, but when the ferry returned to the harbor three hours later, Bauermeister noticed that few attendees were leaving with their free promotional copies of the album. "After everyone left, there were boxes of them left—easily a hundred records sitting there. A bunch of people didn't take them. So I loaded up my backpack and took as many as I could," he says.

The release show was a preview of the reactions toward *Dear You* that would follow, most of which swung between indifference and hostility. "It was shortly thereafter that we headed out on tour with Jawbox—the 'Monsters of Jaw' tour. That's when we started getting the blowback," says Bauermeister. "We were starting to get the negative reaction from people. The crowds seemed smaller than they had before. It didn't feel as familial. There was something weird going on. I remember hearing people were unhappy and weren't going to come see us again."

"It was weird," says Jawbox's J. Robbins. "For us, when we signed [to Atlantic Records], we went through pains to explain our thought process to people and worked very hard to bring our DIY ethos with us. I think people who liked our band understood that. They cut us slack. But Jawbreaker fans did not cut them that same slack."

Jawbreaker fans didn't much care about the technical wizardry Cavallo had poured into the songs or the intricacies behind the White Hot Sound. To devotees of the band's previous work, the overwhelming consensus was that *Dear You* sounded too clean, too slick, too overproduced. It had too much pop and not enough grit. The vocals were too soft and the guitars too heavy. Tall tales circulated about how many guitar tracks were crammed into each song —some folks had heard dozens; others, hundreds. *Dear You* divided Jawbreaker fans into two camps: those who hated it and those who hadn't heard it yet.

"It's funny, we always elicited that kind of response—the betrayed lover. That was familiar, because every record we put out was so different than the last one that we'd already kind of been hearing pushback from fans," says Schwarzenbach. "But I was hurt by the people who didn't like it as a record and said the songs were crap and the singing was crap. That part stung me."

At first, the band couldn't tell if the chilly reception to the *Dear*

You material in their set list was a result of its still being new and un-familiar or if people flat out hated it. Once concertgoers started turning their backs to the band, sitting on the floor, or shouting "MTV!" at them whenever they played songs from the album, that cleared the matter up fairly conclusively. Brian Zero, the activist who had passed out anti–Green Day flyers in front of the band's shows in Petaluma, did the same to Jawbreaker. "Just how much does Jawbreaker really care?" asked the sheet of paper, covered in photocopied dollar bills. "We are asking you to consider walking out on Jawbreaker tonight in solidarity with those in the punk scene who feel that their trust has been walked all over by this band."

In a review of the tour's October 27 date at New York City's Irving Plaza, a night that would end in the band's equipment being stolen, the *New York Times* reported fans' continuing attempts to land a loogie on Schwarzenbach: "As Mr. Schwarzenbach sang, one audience member in front of the stage kept trying to spit upward into his open mouth. Another leapt onstage during the encore and started violently slam dancing into Mr. Schwarzenbach as he tried to play guitar. Somehow, during the chaos of the night, Mr. Schwarzenbach ended up with somebody's blood on his face, most likely his own."

Two weeks later, the band swung through Emo's, the Austin venue where Schwarzenbach had forcefully assured fans the year prior that Jawbreaker wasn't interested in signing to a major label. The frontman no longer had a leg to stand on when introducing "Indictment," so he instead said nothing. Immediately after the song, the audience started to get rowdy. People called out song requests over one another until it blended into a singular, boisterous roar. Schwarzenbach pleaded a request into the microphone that seemed more metaphoric than literal: "Don't yell at us. We're under bright lights and we're liable to explode." A beer bottle then flew from the crowd and shattered against the bass drum. Pfahler came charging out from behind the kit and Bauermeister threw his bass down with a crash. The two identified the culprit and pointed him to the door. Bauermeister scolded, "Out! Out of the fucking bar, now! Get the fuck out!"

Back home in the Bay Area, Jawbreaker's label affiliation had earned them a ban from Gilman's stage, a distinction they shared with Green Day. As for *Maximum Rocknroll,* the influential zine was primed to trash *Dear You* before even hearing a note. "I ran into Tim Yohannan at Epicenter one day and he said, 'We're gonna give you what-for for this. You know that, right?'" says Pfahler. "And I said, 'Absolutely, have at it.' It didn't affect my rapport with Tim."

True to his word, Yohannan wrote in one issue, "Jawbreaker have signed to a major, contradicting everything they've been saying for years. The lesson here is watch for the telltale signs of a band undergoing a change in principles when the money and fame gets waved in front of them." In another issue, he named and shamed the *MRR* staffers who had enjoyed themselves at *Dear You*'s "celebrity cruise" release party, writing, "Can you imagine how cool it woulda been if this supposedly conscious crew had thrown the booze or amps overboard a la Boston Tea Party?"

"They had a stance and a philosophy, so of course they were gonna support that. I don't begrudge them for that. It helps them maintain their own integrity. I still had a fine time playing the monthly Risk game with Tim Yohannan, but we didn't talk about music," Bauermeister laughs.

One of their most vocal critics was also one of their closest friends. Ben Weasel, the outspoken *MRR* columnist and Screeching Weasel frontman, had once promised to eat his own hat if Jawbreaker ever signed to a major label. "I knew Ben was gonna bat us around. That's what he does," says Schwarzenbach. "Most of the people I was friends with, I was still friends with. It was just that, professionally, they had to scorn me. And I get that."

True to his word, Weasel appeared in the March 1995 issue, photographed with a fork and knife in his hands, about to dine on a hearty meal of a fedora. His accompanying column read, "When everybody was giving them shit for selling out even though they hadn't sold a thing and didn't plan to, I stood behind them 100 fucking percent. They made me look stupid, and for that, I'm kinda pissed. But the guys in Jawbreaker are my friends and I have few friends so I have to cut 'em some slack. And truthfully, I'm more disappointed than pissed. They coulda done it their way. They coulda been the biggest indie band EVER. They coulda talked the talk and walked the walk. It sucks. It's probably going to mean their band will end a lot quicker than it should."

$ $ $

Mark Kates was sitting in his office on Sunset Boulevard when he got a phone call from Jawbreaker's tour manager, Christy Colcord, with an unusual tour support request. "She called me and said, 'This isn't gonna make sense to you, but we need two vans,'" Kates remembers. His brain started doing calculations, wondering why a crew of just six people would necessitate two vans. "I was like, 'But it's the three of them, Anthony, Scott, and you. So how is that two vans?' And she was like, 'Trust me.'" This was what Kates describes as "alarm bell number one."

Since Jawbreaker was not playing venues large enough to justify a two-van operation, the request was a hard sell to his bosses, but the Geffen staff had high hopes for Jawbreaker and were confident in *Dear You*'s potential. Kates had first listened to the finished product while driving down the Maine Turnpike, and when the immense flood of distortion poured out of his car's stereo on opener "Save Your Generation," he turned the volume knob all the way up, and only wished it could go louder.

"I thought the album was so overwhelmingly great that it couldn't fail. It was the worst possible point of view to have," he says. "I had friends at the label telling me that there was an arrogant vibe about it. I remember sitting in the conference room with that record blasting and, the point where the break ends in 'Accident Prone,' looking at Eddie Rosenblatt's face, who ran the company, and he puffed his cheeks. It worked. It was so undeniable; it was that great."

To capture their first music video, for the single "Fireman," Saltzman tapped Mark Kohr, the director who had established Green Day's distinct visual identity on the videos for "Longview" and "Basket Case." Filmed at the Fox Theater, in Oakland, "Fireman" shared similar elements with Green Day's videos, namely that it depicted three guys performing their song in a cramped space through the brightness of highly saturated colors. But Jawbreaker didn't bleed through the screen with the same wild energy or youthful magnetism of their East Bay counterparts.

"I think the problem with the video was that it was a little slick," says Kates. "It wasn't what they were. They weren't a brightly colored band."

"Mark Kohr was a hot video director at the time. I didn't think our video was particularly great. No fault of Mark's, it was just ill-conceived," says Pfahler.

"I did my best to come up with a good idea. It was a tricky song," admits Kohr. "I just felt like I didn't do a very good job." Viewers agreed, and the video failed to garner much MTV rotation outside of a few showings on *120 Minutes*.

"Fireman" didn't catch a spark on the radio, either. "'Fireman' was the first single, 'Save Your Generation' was second. When 'Fireman' didn't hit, they gave up really quickly. They were on to the next thing," says Pfahler. "We had a radio edit of 'Accident Prone' where they just butchered that whole breakdown section. That was gonna be the third single, and I don't think it even went out."

"My general memory is that it came out to silence and it persisted that way. It was a non-event," says Schwarzenbach. "There was a lot of buildup to the release, but then when it went out to the marketplace, nothing. The local papers did their one story and that was it." In just about every one of those stories, Green Day's name was invoked, and the headlines were largely unkind: "Energized Jawbreaker Lacks Emotional Focus" (*Los Angeles Times*), "Soft Jawbreaker" (the *Washington Post*), "Big-Label Production Turns Jawbreaker to Mush" (the *Spokesman-Review*), to name a few.

Sales of *Dear You* fell far short of expectations, ultimately maxing out at around forty thousand copies. The band spent most of the year on the road, trying to sell records the old-fashioned way. After their two months with Jawbox, they played a handful of large festivals in Australia to close out the year, and in April of 1996 they hopped on a few dates opening for Nirvana drummer Dave Grohl's new project, Foo Fighters. "I thought they were good tours, but obviously we weren't getting along," says Pfahler. "I couldn't say how much of that was stress from not selling records. I'm sure it had something to do with it."

"We felt kind of pointless," says Schwarzenbach. "We were watching the Foo Fighters take off into the heavens and we were lingering in this remaindered section. No one seemed to care that much that we were playing. We were feeling degraded."

Bauermeister was growing especially detached because Jawbreaker was increasingly being positioned as the Blake Schwarzenbach Show. The frontman was featured prominently in promo photos, as well as the "Fireman" video, while the rest of the band faded into the background. After he made a few snide remarks in interviews, Bauermeister was asked to stop doing press altogether. "I wasn't happy with what was happening. I felt marginalized," he says. "I think part of the way the record company was pushing stuff was: Blake is this virtuoso singer-songwriter and we were the backup band. I was just becoming disengaged."

While driving through Eugene, Oregon, at the end of a tour, Bauermeister, who was at the wheel, and Schwarzenbach, who was drunk in the back, were bickering. On its surface, it was an argument over what time they'd agreed to start the drive, but really it was an argument about everything—a passive-aggressive airing of grievances that had been piling up between them over the years.

All of a sudden, Bauermeister felt something hit the back of his head. It was gum. When he turned back to find the source, Schwarzenbach was wearing a mischievous grin. Bauermeister pulled to the side of the road, threw the van into park, and charged into the back seat. He gripped his hands around Schwarzenbach's throat and screamed inches from his face, "You fucking prima donna!"

The van door opened and the two tumbled out in a tangled ball of flying limbs; it was like a brawl between a cartoon cat and mouse. Bauermeister had Schwarzenbach by the shirt, trying to smother him into the sidewalk. Schwarzenbach swung his fists wildly, looking to land punches on his bassist's skull, and yelled, "You've been ruining my fucking life since the day I met you!"

While their tour manager and roadie dodged flying hands and feet in their efforts to pull the two apart, they heard voices approaching from a nearby house. The group had apparently rolled onto the lawn of a house hosting a keg party and were soon surrounded by a gang of frat guys barking at them to leave before the cops showed up. The absurdity of the situation snapped Schwarzenbach and Bauermeister out of their rage-filled delirium and as they surveyed each other's torn shirts and shaken faces, they thought, "What the hell are we doing?"

After some uncomfortable silence, the two used the long drive to talk things out and work through the issues that had built up between them. Schwarzenbach chalks the fight up to "a combination of pettiness and fatigue," but clearly the pressure the band was under was wreaking havoc on their mental states. They were about to turn thirty and had dedicated their entire adult lives to Jawbreaker. It was time to take a breather.

Not long after returning home, the band gathered at Pfahler's house and Schwarzenbach put it plainly: "I can't do this anymore." To spare themselves further misery, Jawbreaker needed to be put to a merciful end. Bauermeister agreed. Pfahler, being the mediator of the group, tried to negotiate a solution that would allow them to continue, but his efforts were for naught. The three had reached the end of their journey together. "It was something," Schwarzenbach says, "you couldn't really argue with."

In the months following Jawbreaker's implosion, those on their team scratched their heads over what had gone wrong. Nirvana and Green Day had kicked the door open for the band; seemingly all they had to do was walk through it. "I think we were all kind of disappointed that it didn't do better than it did," says Cahn. "We had very high hopes for how ["Fireman"] was going to do, but sometimes you just have no control over what the public is going to jump on."

"It was our failure. I'm at least as responsible as everyone else, if not more," says Kates. "We thought we knew how to do this transition, but no career is transferable. I wish I knew that then. We were presumptive and arrogant."

"We had the same producer as Green Day, we had the same engi-

neer as Green Day, we had the same video guy as Green Day. And . . .
nothing! Music just doesn't work that way. You can't create a for-
mula," says Bauermeister.

"Blake is not Billie. Their songs aren't the same. Blake is someone who expresses himself in a really lyric-based way. Billie is someone who is able to mold his influences into something more melodic
and commercial," says Kates. "The other thing is, Jawbreaker was
a great live band; Green Day is one of the greatest live bands of all
time. It's also really hard to not mention the fact that they were not
functional. Everyone did a really good job of keeping that relatively
well hidden."

Schwarzenbach believes the comparison to Green Day, as well
as the attempt to ride in the slipstream of their success, hindered
the reception of *Dear You* in the long run. The towering presence of
Dookie cast a long shadow from which Jawbreaker's record couldn't
escape. "I felt that when it came out there was already this writer's
narrative constructed around us," he hypothesizes. "There was a reaction to it that was very much like 'We've been hearing this is the
next Green Day or Rancid or Nirvana, and it's not.' I felt like a lot
of the reviews tried to contextualize it so much that the record itself
didn't get listened to."

Geffen let *Dear You* go out of print, chalked it up as a loss, and
promptly moved on. But within punk circles, the album became the
genre's severed head on a pike—a notorious, cautionary tale about
what happens when a band breaks its promise never to sell out. For
the better part of a decade, Jawbreaker had been a beloved indie fix-
ture with a devoted following. Then they released one album with a
major label, and within a year there was nothing left of them but a
hole in the heart of the punk scene.

But even though most fans held Geffen responsible for Jawbreaker's death, the truth was, the label was more like the graveyard that
happened to serve as their final resting place. *Dear You* wasn't the
reason the band could no longer persevere; it was their last-ditch
effort to become the rock giants so many had known, or perhaps
feared, they could become.

In the end, Schwarzenbach is most grateful that just before Jaw-breaker collapsed, they were able to capture their final songs together, whether fans were ready for them or not. "Ultimately, I think you can only really sell yourself out, and that's if you're changing your work or your intensity in seeking a larger audience," he says. "As big and as produced as *Dear You* sounded, that was the best record we could've made."

CHAPTER 3

JIMMY EAT WORLD

Static Prevails

Capitol Records (1996)

IN THE CIRCULAR tower that houses Capitol Records' Los Angeles office, a talent scout named Loren Israel cringed in his cubicle whenever he heard Beck's oddball folk-rap single "Loser" played on KROQ. Israel had recently been promoted to his position after grinding it out for three years as an unpaid intern while also working gigs at a surf shop and bartending at a roller disco. Eager to get his first signing under his belt, he had spent weeks desperately courting the young virtuoso, having instantly recognized his potential star power. When Beck slipped through his fingers to Geffen's Mark Kates and became an overnight star, Israel took it as a personal failure.

Determined not to miss out on the next musical wunderkind, Israel voraciously hunted for new talent. During the day he spent hours combing through bins of mail submissions and demo tapes. Most nights he could be found leaning against the walls of local underground venues like Jabberjaw and the Cobalt Cafe. Every week he stopped by Aaron's Records, in Hollywood, and dropped a couple hundred bucks on records and cassettes that looked intriguing.

One of the records atop his ever-growing pile was a seven-inch EP by a band from Denver he'd been trading phone calls with called Christie Front Drive. It was a two-song split with a new band from the Southwest that went by the name Jimmy Eat World. There were only five hundred copies of it floating around, and he had gone to great lengths to track one down.

Israel listened to the Christie Front Drive side of the record and liked what he heard. The song shifted frequently between cathartic buildups and long, winding instrumental sections. Then he flipped the record over and dropped his turntable's needle on the Jimmy Eat World song, entitled "Digits." He had just sat back in his chair and eased into the track's noodling two-minute crescendo when suddenly the song stopped dead, then exploded.

"Pay attention! Stop paying for regret!" the singer pleaded as the band went full throttle behind him. Israel shot up straight and his eyes went wide. For another two and a half minutes, he sat there entranced by what he was hearing. The recording was rough, but the musicianship was there, he thought. These guys knew the difference between a verse and a chorus, which was more than he could say for most young bands he encountered. He also recognized something in the song that bands couldn't buy for all the money in the world: sincerity.

"Digits" ended and Israel immediately played it again, and then again. He scoured the record's sleeve for more information about this Jimmy Eat World band, but it was nothing more than a manilla envelope cut in half, with the two bands' names inked on its front. The only other markings were the words "Wooden Blue Records," stamped on the back, leading him to ask a very reasonable question: *What the fuck is Wooden Blue Records?* Below this was an address:

P.O. Box 1147
Tempe, AZ 85281-1147

For the next week, Israel talked Jimmy Eat World up to anyone in the office who would listen. "These guys have great voices and they know how to write a fuckin' song!" he stressed to his colleagues. "If we give them enough time, I guarantee they *will* find their hit."

But, as was often the case when Israel was excited about an artist, none of his co-workers shared his enthusiasm. The only person whose interest he immediately piqued was a fellow A&R rookie named Craig Aaronson, a wiry colleague with a big, toothy smile and an insatiable passion for discovering new music. Like Israel, Aaronson was also trying to cut his teeth at Capitol by landing a young artist the label could be proud to develop, and the two worked well as a team.

They devised a plan of attack and split up duties. Israel got on the phone and started making calls to track down someone—anyone—who knew Jimmy Eat World. Aaronson made a call as well, phoning the label's travel department:

"Get me a flight to Arizona."

$ $ $

There's not a lot for teenage boys to do in Mesa, Arizona, except attend Mormon church or get into trouble. Thirteen-year-old Jeremy Yocum was not raised Mormon, so trouble it was. His friend's father owned an orange grove in town, and the two boys often killed time after school by making the sprawling property their playground for destruction. "We'd buy gas and be little pyros," Yocum recalls. "Just boys being morons."

On November 28, 1988, after a drizzly afternoon spent lighting various things ablaze, the boys were killing off a five-gallon can of gasoline so they could head inside and play Nintendo. Yocum's friend flicked a match as the can was tossed into the air and, through a freak stroke of misfortune, the container doused Yocum in gas. The next thing Yocum knew, he was engulfed in flames. He screamed in panic as he stopped, dropped, and rolled on the damp grass until the fire was extinguished. Still smoldering, he ran into the house, rushed to the bathroom, got in the bathtub, and threw open the cold water.

"Dude, call my mom!" Yocum pleaded with his friend. But the boy was so paralyzed by the sight of charred flesh that he just stood there, white-faced and frozen. Eventually Yocum made the call himself and was rushed to the hospital, where he was treated for burns that covered 20 percent of his body, primarily his chest and right arm, which he'd used to shield his face from the flames. Yocum's parents had insurance that would cover most of the hospital costs, and a settlement paid out through a lawsuit covered the rest. They put any remaining money in an annuity for him that would start paying out once he turned eighteen.

Yocum spent two weeks recovering in the burn unit and missed more than a month of classes. When he finally returned to Poston Junior High School in January, he was welcomed back by friends who asked to check out his gnarly skin grafts. One of them was a boy named Jim Adkins, whom Yocum had known since second grade. His family lived one street over, and both of their moms were Cub Scout den mothers. Adkins was a year younger, but Yocum thought he was cool because he was the first kid in the neighborhood to own a guitar.

"He was the only ten-year-old I knew who played guitar," Yocum remembers. "Then at thirteen there was maybe one other kid who played, and by high school there's maybe three or four kids playing guitar. And he was leaps and bounds above all of them. We were weird, goofy kids, so he didn't look that cool, but this kid could shred."

Adkins could rip solos in the style of Def Leppard, Mötley Crüe, and other hair metal bands that were prominent in the eighties, but it was his work ethic and dedication to learning eclectic techniques that impressed Yocum the most. "Jim later took a classical guitar class and he had to buy a specific acoustic guitar, which God knows how much that thing cost," says Yocum. "He grew his nails out and would paint them with clear nail polish. He prided himself on a pick never touching this guitar. He'd pluck for four hours a day. That's homework. No one wants to do that as a teenager."

Adkins started forming bands with other burgeoning musicians once he got to Mountain View High School. The 1992 edition of the school's yearbook featured a photo of the sophomore, a mop of brown hair obscuring his entire face, jamming on an Ibanez guitar with his first band, the unfortunately named Sonic Pudding. They were practicing, as the caption noted, "in hopes of achieving fame."

"He had a band with some friends called Sonic Pudding, and they became I Ate the Sandbox, and then they ended up being Schon Theory," says Yocum. Most of what these groups were playing sounded like reflections of the boys' music collections, which skewed heavily to alternative rock and pop-punk, particularly the West Coast sound that was gaining in popularity at the time. There were two San Diego bands in particular that played a big part in their musical development. "At the time, Jim was super into Rocket from the Crypt and Drive Like Jehu," says Yocum. "I always thought he was a lot like John Reis, the guitarist in both of those bands."

In his senior year, Adkins was invited to join yet another band, this time by a friend at Mountain View he'd known since preschool named Zach Lind. Lind was a baseball player with an athletic build who played drums and, like Adkins, had started learning his instrument at an early age. Lind and Tom Linton, a guitarist and recent graduate of the nearby high school, Westwood, were in need of a bassist. The two had already invited their friend Rick Burch, another Westwood graduate, but Burch was busy with his band Carrier and turned them down.

Adkins played bass with them a few times before bringing his guitar to one practice and realizing that was a better fit. The three jammed together as two guitarists and a drummer, and eventually filled their empty bassist slot with Mitch Porter. "If you were to ask twenty people, half of them would say Mitch was the raddest dude ever and half would say, 'I couldn't stand that kid,'" says Yocum. "He was real snarky, real funny, and wouldn't back down. He wasn't aggro, but he would just talk mad shit."

The solidified lineup began writing songs and practicing them in Lind's parents' garage. They adopted the moniker Jimmy Eat World, a reference to a funny thing that happened in the Linton household when Tom's brother Jim beat up his other brother, Ed. Ed ran into his bedroom, locked the door, and reemerged later with his retaliation: a picture he'd drawn of Jim swallowing the entire earth, captioned JIMMY EAT WORLD.

Jimmy Eat World played with a speed that only the combined energy of four teenagers could produce. "The music was so fast," Yocum remembers. "It was like Propagandhi's first record, or NOFX's

Ribbed, or Green Day's early records—all that Lookout Records stuff." In addition to his rhythm guitar duties, Linton did most of the singing, with Adkins occasionally contributing vocals. "Jim sang like three songs. The rest were Tom's. Tom's lyrics were kind of hokey and silly, I thought, but also there was a childhood innocence to them."

Once the four had scraped together enough songs to fill a set list, they started playing around town. But unlike Berkeley's Gilman Street or New York's CBGB, Mesa was a sports-driven town that lacked a central hub for punk kids. So, where there was no scene, the band and their pals created one. "There would be venues that popped up for a month or three months or six months," says Yocum. "It would be a warehouse that somebody rented or a storage space that happened to have air-conditioning, and after 10 p.m. we could have shows there. You had to be innovative."

Jimmy Eat World typically found themselves playing to small crowds composed of members of the other bands on the bill and a handful of friends. It was often a last-minute struggle to borrow a working PA or find a spot where they wouldn't elicit noise complaints from neighbors. One friend in the scene was the son of a pastor whose church was located in a strip mall. Bands were allowed to play there on Saturday nights, as long as they had the place cleaned up before Sunday service. "We were trying to set up punk rock shows anywhere we could, really," Adkins says. "I'd like to apologize to any band we booked a show for, because it probably sucked."

Hoping to lure more touring bands to Mesa, Adkins teamed up with a schoolmate named Joel Leibow, and they got their mailing address and phone number listed in *Book Your Own Fucking Life.* "We listed ourselves as a promotion company," Adkins says. "In those days it was like, *Poof, I'm a promoter.*"

Jimmy Eat World soon set their sights on nearby cities like Tempe and Phoenix for gig opportunities, but those offered their own problems. "There was a Tempe bar band scene that the Gin Blossoms and the Meat Puppets and the Refreshments came out of, but we didn't play with those bands because we were all underage," says Lind.

"In Phoenix, you had the Silver Dollar Club and a few semi-legit venues where people could play," remembers Adkins. "Then there was a constant string of art spaces that would last a few months before getting shut down. At that point we didn't even have a van. If we were going out of town, we would rent something at the only location that would rent to a not-yet-twenty-one-year-old." Linton laughs that "the insurance would be like three thousand dollars a day."

Although the band had to hustle in their first few months to get heard, the more shows they played, the more connections they made. Eventually, Leibow was approached about an opportunity to get the band's songs recorded. "I ended up crossing paths with this guy named Steve Naughton, who worked out of a studio called the Groove Factory," he remembers. "We had put Jimmy Eat World on a show and Steve saw them and said, 'Hey, these guys are pretty good. If you have any interest in putting out a record, I'd record it for free.'"

A complimentary studio session sounded nice, sure, but who would put up the money to release the recordings into the world? They didn't have an in at any record labels, and they were far detached from the hip coastal music scenes. Yocum mentioned that he had some money in a savings account that he'd received from his burn injury a few years earlier, and Leibow figured his parents might lend him a few bucks if he asked. Maybe, the teenagers thought, they could pool enough cash together to do it themselves. "We really just wanted to get music out there and find other people who liked what we were into," says Leibow, "just to see what would happen."

So they decided that night that they would start their own record label. "It was another one of those things where it was like, *Poof, we're a record label*," says Adkins.

Yocum and Leibow named their new endeavor Wooden Blue Records, a reference to a joke from the MTV sketch comedy show *The State*. Besides Jimmy Eat World, the two offered to put out records by other bands in town and never expected any return on investment. "It was just like *I'm gonna burn money*," says Yocum—a funny way of putting it, given where it had come from. "We never had a business plan, we never had contracts, we never balanced books. I was just down six or seven thousand dollars."

Yocum and Leibow invested their money into pressing records by their friends' bands, like Safehouse, Aquanaut Drinks Coffee, and Carrier, but Jimmy Eat World was the most prolific. Within the span of six months, the band and Wooden Blue put out two releases together—a four-song seven-inch entitled *One, Two, Three, Four* and a self-titled, eleven-song LP. "It was sort of surreal when the box of five hundred records showed up at my mom and dad's house," Leibow says of the EP. "I remember taking a box of twenty-five and just handing them out to people before we even had artwork pressed, just because we were so excited about it."

The LP's cover featured a photo of a boy wincing in pain as he is held in a headlock by a larger boy. As anyone involved with making the record would attest, the experience of listening to it is similarly agonizing. It was recorded in three days, a tight turnaround that only intensified the speed of the band's bouncy melodies. Each song sounded like a race among members to see who could finish their part first. Levels were shaky and tempos were uneven. But for Leibow and Yocum, it wasn't about the quality. They weren't looking to change the world, just leave Mesa's small mark on it. It was their humble way of connecting the scene in their little southwestern town to the larger punk community.

"I didn't think that much of it," Yocum says of the album. "I always enjoyed seeing the band more than listening to them. I think it was just the wide-eyed excitement of being eighteen and nineteen, not being jaded, feeling like the world is our oyster."

$ $ $

Thirteen hours northeast of Mesa in Denver, Colorado, Christie Front Drive had their own angel investor funding the release of their self-titled debut twelve-inch in 1994.

"There was a guy in Colorado who had gotten money from a sort of trust fund," remembers frontman Eric Richter. "He was a punk kid and started putting out records by local bands. We had a box full of records, and that would help us with booking tours."

A box of promo records was a luxury in the DIY world, and Christie Front Drive took advantage of it by mailing copies to the promoters in *Book Your Own Fucking Life* in hopes of getting help with out-of-town gigs and reviews in fanzines. It was working, too. *HeartattaCk,* a recently launched national zine from a former *Maximum Rocknroll* contributor, lauded the record in its second issue. The reviewer called it "really beautiful music" and "a collision of Moss Icon and Samiam." The high praise more than made up for the fact that the review misspelled the band's name ("Christi Front Drive").

After the record's release, Christie Front Drive was scheduled to play a show in Los Angeles, opening for a band called Sense Field that was on the radar of some A&R reps. Looking to string together a tour from Colorado to California, Richter sought local help in Arizona, where he knew no one. He flipped through the pages of *Book Your Own Fucking Life* and found a listing for Adkins and Leibow's new promotion company, Bring Me the Head Of Productions, which described itself as "a non-profit collective dedicated to putting on all-ages, low-door and no alcohol punk shows." It even made an enticing promise: "We also promote all shows heavily."

"We got a message from Eric Richter saying that his band was touring and wanted to come through Phoenix, and [asking] if I was willing to take a few of their recently released twelve-inch records and take them around to record stores and also set up a show," says Leibow. "I called him and said I'd be interested, and he sent me maybe six copies of that record. I remember Jim and I listening to it and being like, 'Holy shit, this is amazing!' I talked to Eric on the phone for an hour, telling him we were blown away by it."

"The LP was awesome, so we were like, 'Yeah, we'll totally help you out!'" remembers Adkins. "So they came to town for this show we set up for them and it was horrible. It was just bad."

"It was awkward," says Leibow. "It was a weird venue that had just opened up. They gave us this weird stage inside a tiny little room and nobody really knew who Christie Front Drive were. The only people who came were Jimmy Eat World and their friends."

After the show, Leibow told Richter that if Christie Front Drive had any interest in recording a split seven-inch with Jimmy Eat World, Wooden Blue would be glad to put it out. "I'd never even heard them at the time," Richter recalls of Jimmy Eat World. "They gave us a copy of that first CD they did, with the two kids on the cover. I remember listening to it later and thinking, 'Uh-oh, this is, uh, *a different style* than us.' It felt more like an L.A. punk band—definitely more pop-punk. But we told them we'd do it, so we kept our word."

After gigging their way west, Christie Front Drive arrived in Los Angeles a few nights later. Their show there with Sense Field was different from the one they'd played in Arizona—namely, people actually showed up. One of those people introduced himself to Richter as Loren Israel, said he was impressed with his band's set, and asked for his phone number. In the bustle of loading out, Richter wasn't even sure he caught that the guy had mentioned he was from Capitol Records, but he gave him his info regardless.

When Richter returned home to Colorado after the tour, there were two things waiting for him. One was a cassette from Adkins with a new Jimmy Eat World song on it. But this wasn't like the CD that had made Richter cringe—Adkins and the rest of the band had clearly made an effort to step up their songwriting to impress their new Colorado friends. No longer leaning on up-tempo pop-punk, Jimmy Eat World was now experimenting with a more expansive sound.

"I think Christie Front Drive was the band that we started listening to where we loved the power and the melody of it. Even though it was slower, it had this weight to it," says Lind. "All of that informed a shift. We thought we could slow it down a little bit and explore more melodic ways of expressing ourselves. I think our first real attempt at that was our split with Christie Front Drive."

"Jim sent me a version of this song 'Digits,' and it sounded like a totally different band to me," says Richter. "I was like, 'Wow, this is really good!'" It might have been too good, in fact. Christie Front

Drive had decided that their contribution to the record would be a song called "Slide," which they hadn't been in a huge rush to release, but they figured it would be a good fit for a split EP with a relatively unknown pop-punk band. "It was a song we liked, but it wasn't our favorite song," Richter admits. "But that was before I heard 'Digits.' That's when we realized we'd fucked up, because their song was so good."

The other thing waiting for Richter at home was a message from Loren Israel. "At that point I was living with my parents because I was in between places to live," Richer says. "I got home from tour and my mom was like, 'Capitol Records called!'" Richter was skeptical but gave Israel a call back to hear him out.

"I talked to him and was like, 'You know, we're not really looking to get on a major label,'" says Richter. "We were very punk at the time. I was pretty adamant that we weren't really interested. I don't really know why. I look back and wonder if I was crazy or not. But I was young and idealistic. We just wanted to be punk like Fugazi."

But Israel was persistent. He or Aaronson called every so often to see if the band's anti-major-label position still stood. Richter remembers one call with Israel: "He asked, 'Well, what are you guys doing? You putting out records? What's your plan?' And I was like, 'Actually, we're gonna do a split seven-inch with this band from Arizona called Jimmy Eat World.' I could hear him writing it down. *Jimmy . . . Eat . . . World . . .* 'They're really good. You should check 'em out.' He said, 'Okay, cool. I will.'"

$ $ $

Jim Adkins and Jeremy Yocum wound up sharing an apartment in Flagstaff during Adkins's freshman year at Northern Arizona University. Their complex overlooked a graveyard, and every day he'd jump the fence and take a shortcut through the tombstones to get to class. One morning, while Adkins was out and about on campus, the phone rang and Yocum answered.

"Hey, I'm looking for Jim from Jimmy Eat World. Is he home?" the voice on the other end asked.

"Nah, he's in class or something," Yocum replied. He could tell by the tone of the man's voice that he was a serious businessperson, not another punk kid.

"All right, well, this is Craig Aaronson from Capitol Records and I'm trying to reach him. Will you take my information down and tell him I called?"

Yocum jotted down the caller's name and number, and right as the two were about to end the call, he thought of one more thing to mention. "Oh, by the way, next Saturday they're playing at the Nile in Mesa." He hung up, and by the time Adkins returned home hours later, Yocum had already forgotten about the call and failed to deliver the message.

"Fast-forward a week, I'm sitting at the merch table with my girlfriend, selling Wooden Blue shit at the Nile," remembers Yocum. "This older guy in a baseball cap that looks totally square comes over and says, 'Are you Jeremy?' He wasn't old, probably close to thirty, but old to a twenty-year-old. He says, 'Hey, I'm Craig Aaronson from Capitol Records.' Then it became real."

Yocum pointed Adkins out, and after the show, Aaronson introduced himself to the band. He told them that he'd heard about them through Christie Front Drive and had been listening to their seven-inch a lot at the office. "It was kind of awkward because it was like, *Who is this guy? Why is he here? And why is his shirt tucked into his jeans?*" remembers Leibow.

"We hung out with him after the show and thought it was crazy. We were just young kids and a major label was coming to see us," says Lind. "We met with him the next morning at some airport hotel for breakfast. He was just enthusiastic, and it felt like he wanted to pursue something."

"I thought that they were cool," Linton remembers of Aaronson and Israel. "You could tell they really loved music, but still, I think we were a little cautious because we were in a scene where you have to be careful what you do with labels."

"The *Maximum Rocknroll* issue, 'Some of Your Friends Are Already This Fucked,' that was on everybody's minds—the horror stories of getting screwed," says Adkins. "The worst-case scenario is you'd hear about some group going into the red making their record, the label hates it, they won't even give it back to release it, and they own the songs, so you can't even do anything with them. We were cautious of things like that going down."

Still, to a group of small-town teenagers fresh out of high school, the attention was flattering. So they exchanged information and the phone calls began. Over the next few weeks, Aaronson and Israel called regularly to check in. Unlike Israel's experience with Beck, who was heavily sought after by Warner Bros. and Geffen, the pursuit of Jimmy Eat World was not a competitive one. In fact, as far as he could tell, Capitol was the only label that had even heard of them.

Jimmy Eat World had been a band for only about seven months and didn't have a manager or a lawyer. They didn't even have a tour manager, because they weren't making enough money to pay one. Paul Drake, a friend from Denver they'd met through Christie Front Drive, eventually started accompanying Jimmy Eat World on short tours as an extra person to drive, sell merch, and take photos.

"The Jimmy guys, I think they thought, 'These guys are cheese-balls. Let's get free dinners off of 'em and see what happens,'" Drake remembers of the band's dealings with Capitol. "Craig was the cheesiest guy ever—a very nice guy, but he was your typical A&R yes-man that you'd think was a dork. Craig would bullshit you till you agreed. He meant well, but he was all business."

The band went to Los Angeles a few times, and Aaronson and Israel always made sure the guys were fed, were entertained, and had a place to stay. They weren't exactly putting the band up at the Four Seasons and charging nights at the strip club to the company card. They didn't have to, really. The band admits to being such suburban rubes that they were dazzled by L.A.'s simplest amenities. Even the concept of valet parking was foreign and impressive to them. Typically, Israel offered up his brother's place way out in West Hills as a place to crash, and Aaronson showed them whatever Los Angeles had to offer a group of guys who were under twenty-one.

"I was still underage, so there was no official 'wining' in the 'wining and dining,'" says Adkins. "Craig took us to Shakey's Pizza once. I also remember going to Barney's Beanery and getting my ass kicked at pool by some hustler there."

"Craig took us to the Viper Room to see Adam Ant," remembers Yocum, who accompanied the band on their first L.A. trip. "I turned and looked over my shoulder and Leonardo DiCaprio was standing right there. At the time he was just known for *Gilbert Grape;* he wasn't *Titanic* famous yet. But to some green kids from Phoenix, it was super crazy."

The most alluring Los Angeles attraction was the Capitol Records office, where the band and their friends raided the closets and pocketed their weight in the truest form of currency among music fans in the mid-nineties: compact discs.

"We'd go to all these different floors and raid their cupboards," remembers Drake. "We'd walk out of there with thirty CDs each and then just sell them all. Capitol didn't give a shit. They didn't even know who we were." Then, once they returned to Arizona with their hauls, Adkins says, "it was a rush to see who could get to the record store first." Whoever beat the pack to Zia Records raked in the most cash.

As the weeks and months went by and their stacks of free CDs piled higher, Jimmy Eat World got to know Aaronson and Israel better. They grew to see them as real people instead of the faceless, corporate suits *Maximum Rocknroll* made guys like them out to be. Capitol Records seemed less like a shady corporation and more like a place in Los Angeles where they could drop by to hang out and pocket some free stuff.

Any inborn punk skepticism the band members might have harbored about dealing with a major label started to wash away as Aaronson and Israel talked about what Capitol Records could offer them—studio time, a decent recording budget, a professional producer. Plus, the band realized they had no other options. "It was either continue putting records out with my roommate's label or with Capitol Records," laughs Adkins. "No one else was knocking on our door."

Jimmy Eat World knew that if they were going to take this band thing seriously, Wooden Blue Records was not a sustainable home, and they were right. One morning soon, Yocum would wake up to a phone call that would put an end to his shoestring operation. "It was the Arizona Department of Revenue," he says. "They were say-ing, 'Where are your taxes? Where's this, where's that?' They said there were going to be fines and penalties unless we shut it down, so we said, 'Fuck this, let's shut it down.' I was too scared of them."

Just as haphazardly as the label had been created, *poof*, it was gone.

$ $ $

Capitol Records appeared to be thriving in the mid-nineties. In 1992, the legendary label celebrated its fiftieth anniversary with the release of an eight-CD box set featuring its landmark artists past and pres-ent, like Tina Turner, Dean Martin, Iron Maiden, and Garth Brooks. The following year, Capitol got some fresh blood with the hiring of a new president, thirty-seven-year-old industry executive Gary Gersh, who had made a name for himself by helping sign Nirvana to Gef-fen Records. In 1994, the label was praised as a digital pioneer when it launched the first-ever website for a band, to promote the release of Megadeth's *Youthanasia*. And the company had a cash cow in its back catalog of legacy acts like the Beatles, Nat King Cole, and Frank Sinatra.

Capitol had also kicked off the decade with the release of MC Hammer's *Please Hammer Don't Hurt 'Em*, in February 1990, an album whose crossover success set the tone for a new era of pop music and topped the *Billboard* album charts for twenty-one weeks, selling more than ten million copies. But as the industry saying goes, you're only as good as your last hit, and the way Loren Israel saw it, by 1995 Capitol needed to find its next big thing.

"The heyday of money had passed us. It stopped with MC Ham-mer," he says. "After MC Hammer, it kind of started its downhill roll. Alterna-rock never sold that many records. If you really evalu-ated the alt-rock bands that sold records, it was very few, and not nearly as many as the butt-rock stuff and the pop stuff that came be-fore it. Sure, Green Day sold a lot, but how many Green Days were there? Very few. It started to get segmented, and the crazy money—the kind of money people were literally bathing in—was slowly go-ing down."

Israel wasn't sure what kinds of artists his fellow scouts at Capitol were on the hunt for, but he knew what he wanted. Plain and simple: he wanted a band that could write hits. He looked for bands that sang catchy choruses he could imagine hearing on the radio and had faces he could picture seeing on magazine covers.

"Most of the A&R people that were at Capitol weren't hip to what was going on on the streets, and if they were, it was more collegiate," he says. "One of the guys liked this band Skeleton Key. I remember seeing these motherfuckers and the singer got onstage and started hitting a fucking trash can. I was looking at everyone there and thinking, *Are you all serious?* Because I recognized the fuel of a major label are songs for the radio. That is the absolute truth. If you're not signing artists with great voices who want to write a hit song, you're going to fail."

He saw the potential in Jimmy Eat World to deliver something the label could develop and sell, even through the roughness of the band's early recordings. "It was very rudimentary, but I could tell they knew the difference between a verse and a chorus," Israel says. "And they were young and good-looking. Sorry, but that's part of it."

But his excitement about Jimmy Eat World largely fell on deaf ears among his colleagues. Whenever he brought the band up in conversation, he could feel everyone's eyes glazing over. On paper, the band looked like a bunch of well-mannered, clean-cut Boy Scouts who lacked the dangerous edge of the amplifier-smashing Nirvana and didn't pack the same power-chord punch as Green Day.

"I knew no one at the label would like it. You have to understand that most people at the executive level at a label, they're usually rich kids who don't need the job," Israel explains. "You're talking about a boys' club and a history of a record label signing 50 to 150 bands and focusing on one or two. But I always believed that Jimmy Eat World would get their shot if they stuck in long enough."

Fortunately, Israel's lone ally in the crusade for Jimmy Eat World at the Capitol office was Craig Aaronson, whose mentor in the music industry happened to be Gary Gersh. Gersh had met Aaronson years earlier, when Aaronson was working in the mailroom at Geffen Records. Aaronson pestered Gersh relentlessly for an opportunity to work under him in the A&R department. Gersh, who had begun his career many years prior in the Capitol mailroom, perhaps saw a bit of himself in the young Aaronson and finally agreed to take him under his wing.

"Craig trusted me, God bless him, and he had a very good relationship with the president of the record company, Gary Gersh," says Israel. "So he campaigned for Gary Gersh to give him the opportunity to sign the band."

"Gary Gersh was telling Craig, 'You shouldn't sign this band.' And he probably wasn't wrong," says Lind. "There was no bidding war around us or anything like that."

Gersh ultimately relented and let Aaronson test the waters with a development deal, whereby Capitol could stake a claim in Jimmy Eat World without fully committing to release an album. "It was like a 'Let's sort of date and see how this goes' type of thing," Lind explains. "It was basically us signing away our rights to them in case they want to pick up an option for us to put out an album."

The band was presented with a short stack of paperwork to sign and, having no management to look it over, they did the next best thing: they showed it to their parents. "It was so sketchy. Zach's family lawyer looked over our contract," says Linton. "He was not an entertainment lawyer!"

"He kept saying, 'I'm not an entertainment lawyer, but here's what I *think* it says,'" adds Adkins.

Some of the band members' parents expressed concern that it was not worth sacrificing an education to pursue a music career that seemed like a tenuous career path at best. But the way the band saw it, school would always be there next year. "It seemed odd, but it also seemed like an opportunity," says Lind. "It was an open door, so we're gonna walk through it and see where it leads." Adkins decided to drop out of college to focus on the band.

But bassist Mitch Porter's family situation was a bit more complicated, and signing the contract became a line in the sand. Porter was raised Mormon, and at the age of nineteen, Mormon men are encouraged to pursue a mission call. Missionaries travel at their own expense for a period of two years, knocking on doors to spread the word of their religion and seek potential converts.

"Capitol wanted to sign 'em, and Mitch's parents told him to go on a mission like a good Mormon," says Yocum. "When you're told that at seventeen or eighteen it's like, 'Well, shit, I don't wanna turn my life upside down on a gamble.'"

"When it came time to sign this development deal, Mitch had this dilemma, because he was keeping the deal a secret from his parents," says Lind. "When it was finally time to sign, he had to quit the band."

Porter's departure left the contract short a signature and Jimmy Eat World short a member. Scrambling to find someone to fill in on bass, the guys once again turned to Rick Burch, and this time he was in. For Burch, the decision was a simple one. Not only was he skipping college to play music with friends he'd known for years; the band was also about to sign a deal with a huge record label. "One of the reasons I joined the band was it had just become a viable thing," says Burch. "Like, 'Maybe this thing could really happen.'"

The deal was signed and, armed with a new lineup—Jim Adkins, Zach Lind, Tom Linton, and Rick Burch—Jimmy Eat World was officially on Capitol Records.

$ $ $

Jim Adkins sighs deeply as he recalls this about Jimmy Eat World's deal with Capitol: "We didn't pocket any money."

"When we signed Jimmy Eat World, it was a small deal and nobody liked 'em," Loren Israel remembers. The band's monetary offer was relatively tiny compared with bands like Green Day and Jawbreaker. The members had to keep their side gigs working for temp agencies and art supply stores to scrape enough money together to afford the rent for their crowded apartments. "Tom and I shared a room in a house in Tempe—a five-bedroom house with seven dudes," laughs Burch. "Having a record deal definitely doesn't mean you've made it."

But while they may not have struck it rich, there were definitely benefits to having a corporate machine behind them. "They did give us tour support, and for us, any amount of money was great. Like, 'Oh, cool, we got a thousand bucks!'" says Lind. Capitol also did something else for Jimmy Eat World that gave them a leg up on their peers. "They bought us a $20,000 used Ford Econoline van. That was the best thing they ever did for us, because we could go on tour and not worry about breaking down."

Aaronson and Israel were eager to book their new band studio time to see what they could accomplish with better recording resources. Aaronson asked them if there were any producers they might like to be paired with, and the first name that came to Adkins's mind was Mark Trombino. Trombino had been the drummer for one of his favorite bands, the recently disbanded Drive Like Jehu, a San Diego punk outfit that had stumbled into their own major-label deal with Interscope a year earlier for the release of their 1994 album *Yank Crime*.

"Jim had shown us Drive Like Jehu because he was really into them," says Lind. "Mark had also done some recordings of other bands we knew, like Boys Life and Boilermaker. We thought he was really cool. So Craig arranged for us to work with Mark at Big Fish Studios, in Encinitas."

"I think Jim was a fan of Drive Like Jehu and some of the records I'd made," says Trombino. "They reached out to me and I got an opportunity to do a seven-inch with them, just to see how it goes." In Trombino, Jimmy Eat World found an instant kinship. The twenty-nine-year-old producer immediately took to the young Arizonans and appreciated their lack of pretension. "I remember really liking them as people," he says. "They were super-good guys and I loved their music. We had a lot of fun when we made that seven-inch."

The two-day session with Trombino went so well that when Capitol gave Jimmy Eat World the green light to make a full-length studio album at the end of the summer of '95, the band wanted to work with him again. But Trombino's production experience was limited, and he had yet to work on a commercially successful album. Aaronson was concerned that he was not a big enough name for his label bosses to get excited about. So, in an effort to piggyback off one of

Capitol's darlings, he roped in Wes Kidd to produce the record. Kidd was the frontman of the Chicago-based band Triple Fast Action, a promising new addition to the Capitol roster. And to make Jimmy Eat World feel more comfortable, Trombino was brought in to work alongside Kidd.

"Triple Fast Action had just signed with Capitol, and they were a legitimate signing in Capitol's eyes—a bigger band that was bringing more to the table," says Lind. "So bringing Wes in was an attempt to appease the label and have someone with more of a songwriting sensibility."

"I think Craig, as a smart A&R person, knew that the two bands the president likes are the ones that are gonna get any kind of attention," says Adkins, "and Triple Fast Action was one of those two bands at Capitol."

Unlike Jimmy Eat World's first album, which they had recorded in a couple of days by playing in a room together and hitting the "record" button, the band was introduced to multitrack recording and had weeks to experiment. They initially did days of pre-production work with Kidd, who helped them sharpen sketches of new songs and make them as tight as possible. They also spent a week tracking drums at Sound City, the legendary recording studio in Van Nuys, made famous by the A-list artists it had hosted, including Elton John, Neil Young, Slayer, and REO Speedwagon, as well as punk favorites Rancid. It was also where producer Butch Vig recorded Nirvana's *Nevermind*.

"We tracked in the same room where Tom Petty did *Wildflowers* and Rage Against the Machine made their self-titled album and Fleetwood Mac made *Rumours*," says Lind. "We recorded in that space and we got to learn how records are made. That was huge. That totally informed who we'd become."

The new batch of songs saw Jimmy Eat World continuing their musical evolution, taking cues from more mid-tempo rock bands like Seam, Low, and Sunny Day Real Estate. They were landing somewhere between the band they wanted to sound like and the band they thought their record label wanted them to be.

The most noticeable difference in their approach was that Adkins was stepping up to handle more vocal duties, so much so that it initially confused Trombino. "When I first met them, I thought Tom was the lead singer and Jim sang occasionally," he says. "But they were in a sort of transition where Jim was taking over more singing responsibilities. It was to the point that when we were doing the album, I was like, 'Wait, why isn't Tom singing more?'"

Adkins's voice is the first one heard on the album's opener, "Thinking, That's All," and the last one heard on closer "Anderson Mesa," as the song's final words pay homage to his old college apartment: "Run around or jump the fence / Graveyard."

His delivery took a turn, too. No longer struggling to cram a full page of lyrics into lightning-fast punk verses, he could now stretch out a bit and occupy the space the band created for themselves. His voice became more earnest and had a bite of passion to it, a youthful exuberance bleeding through in the frequent cracks and squeaks in his still-developing singing voice.

To accommodate the band members who were still in semesters at college, the album had to be recorded in two sessions, one in August and another in December. It included a revamped version of "Digits" that featured new sections and expanded the track by three minutes. Needing some additional vocal work to fill the space, or perhaps just wanting to see a familiar face while making their first record away from home, the band used a portion of their budget to fly Christie Front Drive's Eric Richter out to sing on the track.

"At the time, it was awesome," says Richter. "I was getting flown out to L.A. for free and hanging out with Mark Trombino, who was a hero of mine. I was only in the studio for a very little time. Behind the studio there was a basketball court, and Tom, Jim, and I would mostly just hang out there and play basketball."

Jimmy Eat World titled their major-label debut *Static Prevails,* and the album signaled that the band was evolving beyond their sloppy early days. Even the CD's cover, a photo taken by Paul Drake of a snow-covered Denver rooftop, hinted at a decidedly artsier direction for the band—or at least a more mature one than the shot of two boys beating the crap out of each other.

"I think when you start out as a group, especially when you're younger, you're gonna end up playing music that sounds like your record collection," Adkins explains. "When we started, our record collection was lopsided towards the pop-punk things. Then each of us built up our record collections in more diverse ways. It was a combination of everyone's interests and tastes expanding, mixed with us figuring out our own voice. It made for a much different record than we were probably on the path to make."

$ $ $

The debate over "selling out" had become such a mainstream topic by the time *Static Prevails* was released, in July 1996, that three weeks later the Orange County ska band Reel Big Fish released a song about it, bluntly entitled "Sell Out." Ironically, it found radio success thanks to its catchy, satirical chorus, "Sell out with me tonight / The record company's gonna give me lots of money and everything's gonna be all right."

The record company hadn't given Jimmy Eat World lots of money, but the band did have a record they were proud of. The Capitol Records logo on the front of *Static Prevails* didn't put Jimmy Eat World at odds with their fans, mainly because they hardly had any at this point. When the album was released, they'd barely been a band for two years and hadn't played all that much outside of Arizona. They couldn't really sell out because, as Burch puts it, "the band was so young that there wasn't anything to sell."

"We didn't have a fan base that was gonna be like, 'Aw fuck, man. They sold out!'" says Lind. "And honestly, I'm so fucking glad we didn't. I'm glad we were able to make our decisions based on what we felt was best, and not this bullshit, made-up, fake ethic."

Locally, the Arizona scene proved more accepting of Jimmy Eat World's rock star pursuits than the Berkeley scene was with its hostile treatment of homegrown bands who made the major-label jump. In fact, when word got around Arizona that some local boys had struck it big with a record deal in Los Angeles, it became a point of hometown pride.

"They've got like four hundred brothers and sisters," Yocum says of the band members. "So all their siblings' friends and everyone they've ever shared a class with, now they're like, 'Hey, I know Jimmy Eat World!' All of a sudden, it's the coolest thing to be part of. People would brag that Jim's dad was their dog's vet. Phoenix is six million people, but it's a very small town. If anything, it only benefited them in popularity."

The local weekly paper, the *Phoenix New Times,* ran a feature about the band and likened them to the Replacements: "Adkins sings with an obvious Westerberg-inspired urgency, and the rest of the band grinds out the kind of controlled noise that defined the pre-grunge, postpunk sounds of American bands in the Reagan years."

"The very local scene in Arizona was more concerned that we don't get screwed over rather than selling out," explains Adkins. "It was a supportive skepticism rather than thinking we'd abandon our creative ideals."

There was only one time the band recalls feeling the sting of angry punk fervor. The same year *Static Prevails* was released, one of its songs, "Seventeen," appeared on a promotional compilation CD for a new citrus soda from the Coca-Cola Company called Surge, alongside other Capitol artists like Luscious Jackson, Five for Fighting, and Loren Israel's least favorite band, Skeleton Key. The packaging read, "Yeah, yeah, we know. This is a corporate manipulation coupon to get you to try Surge. But that's okay because Surge tastes great and it's free with this coupon. Redeem and feed the rush." Lind says the band got more pushback for this cheesy corporate placement than for their Capitol deal, and remembers it drawing a few punk loudmouths outside their show in Little Rock, Arkansas.

But while Jimmy Eat World maintained a good standing with their local punk community, their relationship with their new label got off to a rocky start. The band quickly found that Capitol Records had no clue what to do with them. "Our situation was different than Jawbreaker or Green Day, because people knew who they were before they made the jump. No one knew who we were," says Adkins. "I discovered later on that major labels know exactly what to do with a band that's selling thirty thousand records a week.

They've got that. They had no idea what to do with us, who, for our combined releases, probably sold two thousand copies of everything put together."

Static Prevails didn't offer much in the way of singles, since it lacked a catchy standout track, so radio promotion was largely abandoned. Unlike the downtrodden alterna-rock hits that were enabling teenage MTV viewers at the time to wallow in suburban ennui, Jimmy Eat World encouraged listeners to get the hell out of their hometown. On "Call It in the Air," Adkins begged, "Leave home today, escape your region!" It was an album that saw four guys standing at the edge of adulthood, waving goodbye to their adolescence as they left it behind.

It was also an uphill battle to get *Static Prevails* press reviews and magazine features, as Jimmy Eat World slipped into an unfortunate middle ground. They were too small to get mainstream press to pay much attention, and the influential punk zines wouldn't touch anything released by a major label—though that didn't stop Israel from making underhanded attempts. He admits, "We couldn't get them any press, so you know what I did? I wrote their press reviews and sent them to *Maximum Rocknroll* and *Razorcake* or whatever these fucking fanzines were called."

"This was in the era when these fancy writers were talking about Jawbox and Texas Is the Reason, or Rites of Spring, Cap'n Jazz, Jawbreaker, Knapsack—all of these bands," he continues. "I'm sorry, but Jim and Tom had better voices than all these guys and they knew how to write a hook."

Israel and Aaronson were banging their heads against the wall in the Capitol offices, trying to get attention for their emerging band, to no avail. Gersh was not interested in loosening the purse strings for a band nobody had heard of. Jimmy Eat World tried to create their own promotional opportunities, but even those were often dead ends. Their friends Richard and Stefanie Reines, siblings who had recently launched an indie label called Drive-Thru Records, knew of an aspiring filmmaker who wanted to help the band. "Richard and Stefanie had this friend who really liked our music. I guess he was a kid with rich parents or whatever, and he wanted to help us make a video for 'Rockstar.' This kid basically fronted a lot of money to shoot a video," says Lind.

"I remember we had a fight in a meeting," remembers Israel. "Some kid said he wanted to do a video for 'Rockstar' and would pay for half the video. The video cost five or ten grand or something, and this fan was willing to pay for half, and Gary Gersh said no." Ultimately, the video got made with no backing from the label and it didn't get any pickup.

Conversely, any promotional ideas that were coming from the label's end didn't go over well with the band. Drake remembers being dragged into one meeting at Capitol where the marketing team pitched an idea to the band that made their skin crawl. "These label guys were like, 'Okay, we're gonna give you a PA, and every day you're gonna go to a 7-Eleven parking lot close to a high school and play in the parking lot of 7-Elevens all around the U.S.'," he remembers. "We just looked at each other like, 'These guys are fucking morons!' A, where are we gonna put the PA in the van? And B, that's the cheesiest idea ever. And they really, really pushed it. But we were like, 'We're not doing it. That's gonna ruin us. We'd be a joke.'"

The band could feel that most of the Capitol employees were content to let *Static Prevails* get lost in the deluge of 1996 releases, and they even had a man on the inside telling them as much. That summer, Joel Leibow got an internship at Capitol doing college promotion and saw it firsthand. "The people I was working with there didn't push the record too hard," he says. "It just seemed like they didn't know what to do with it and didn't understand the audience for it. There was a sense that nobody there really cared. The big record I was told to be pushing that summer was a Butthole Surfers record."

It was a tough pill for the aspiring rockers to swallow. For Jimmy Eat World, there was a part of them that recognized the whole situation had been a fluke and they had no business being on a major label as a group of punk teenagers with no following. But another part was heartbroken to watch their rock 'n' roll dreams go up in flames, slowly realizing they weren't going to be playing big stages or seeing themselves on MTV, even if they might have publicly shrugged those things off. "If any band signs to a major label and they tell you they're not interested in selling a million records, they're fucking lying to you," says Israel. "They might not even know it. Any kid who picks up a guitar has dreams of being a rock star."

The band continued to operate as usual. Lind was still booking their tours, and Adkins's mother would bake cookies for them to take on the road. They'd spend a few weeks playing people's living rooms or showing up to gigs that wound up falling through, or playing punk festivals with more bands on the lineup than attendees. They'd share bills with hardcore bands and ska bands. They'd have nights where it felt like they were playing for nobody but the sound guy. They'd visit record stores in whatever town they were in and struggle to find copies of *Static Prevails*.

Even at their label, traces of *Static Prevails* were scarce. Adkins remembers swinging by Capitol Records' New York offices once and entering through double doors adorned with gigantic posters showcasing the debut album by P, the new band that featured actor Johnny Depp and Butthole Surfers frontman Gibby Haynes. Adkins wandered the office, looking for any signs for *Static Prevails*, and not only found none but was asked by a label employee if he was lost, as if he were a student on a class trip who'd strayed from a tour of the building.

"I didn't get the feeling they were getting huge in the way you'd plan if you were on a major label," remembers Richter. "I had conversations with Jim where it felt like he was kind of bummed out and was wondering if he should do something else."

Being the polite southwesterners they were, though, Jimmy Eat World were still appreciative of the progress they were making on the road, particularly when grinding it out with their contemporaries like Mineral, Braid, and Jejune. A tour opening for the Promise Ring and Burning Airlines in the spring of 1998 saw them playing to six hundred people a night. The tour's final stop, in Philadelphia, featured the debut of Jets to Brazil, a new band formed by Blake Schwarzenbach after the demise of Jawbreaker.

Jimmy Eat World even agreed to release split EPs with some of these bands through independent labels. This was prohibited by their contract with Capitol, but they figured that one of the benefits of flying under their label's radar was that no one would even notice. "We were putting out seven-inches illegally," says Lind. "Technically we could get sued, but because no one at Capitol knew who we were, we just did it."

They were starting to fit in among a crop of bands across the country that were being described within the scene as "emo-core," or "emo," punk rock's more thoughtful and introspective offshoot. The only difference was, when all these emo bands displayed their records and cassettes on the merch tables, Jimmy Eat World was the only one that had an album that had cost $100,000 to make. "We didn't think big. If we sold thirty CDs a night, that was huge," says Drake. "Everywhere we went, though, the second time, there were more people there. *Static Prevails* sounded so good compared to all their contemporaries, because the recording was so much better. If you play a Promise Ring record against *Static Prevails*, it was totally different, so they stood out."

$ $ $

In its first year, *Static Prevails* sold fewer than ten thousand copies —a tremendous flop by all measures. Jimmy Eat World had already begun considering what indie labels might want to sign them once Capitol inevitably showed them the door. It came as a surprise, then, when Craig Aarsonson informed the band that Capitol was interested in picking up a second record.

Jimmy Eat World wasn't sure why, exactly, they were being afforded another shot, and they didn't stop to question it. In the back of their minds, though, they recognized that in all likelihood, this would be the last chance they'd ever get to release an album through a major label. So, as Lind puts it, they loaded up their plate like it was last call at the buffet.

"We viewed it as our last opportunity to do this, because we'd probably get dropped," he says. "Our mentality coming out of *Static Prevails* was: 'Okay, we're gonna use everything we've learned and we're gonna throw the kitchen sink at it, because it might be our last chance to have a budget to make a big studio album.'"

They again tapped Mark Trombino to produce, and over two months of California recording sessions, one again at Sound City and one at Clear Lake Audio, in Burbank, the group swung for the fences. They brought in additional musicians and rented instruments they'd never imagined themselves using. The four-piece rock band that had never employed much more than guitars, bass, and drums suddenly found themselves experimenting in a studio full of cellos, violins, chimes, bells, temple blocks, triangles, pianos, organs, and Minimoogs.

There was also a drastic difference in Adkins's approach in the studio this time around. In the early days of the band, both he and Linton had brought ideas to practice and traded off singing duties. But Adkins was now more prolific than ever, doing the majority of the writing and all of the lead vocals, save for one song, "Blister."

"Jim was on a trajectory that was really exciting," says Lind. "There was this clear development that Jim was going through. It was becoming obvious. I feel like Jim was hungry to develop and explore that more, and Tom was acknowledging that."

Adkins's passion also seeped into their live show. He had always stood stage right during their performances, until one day the band's friend Rama Mayo made a fairly obvious suggestion: "Why doesn't Jim stand in the middle?" Adkins immediately morphed from energetic wingman to full-on show-stealer, and from then on he was the frontman of Jimmy Eat World. He was able to shift from hushed lullaby melodies to sweaty, bombastic choruses that he made feel larger than life. He looked the part, too. Any lingering teenage gawkiness had washed away, revealing his leading-man good looks.

"Watching Jim Adkins is one of the most thrilling things I have ever seen," says Israel. "Performing a song in the studio, performing it live, he constantly strives to connect the emotion, the music, the meaning of the lyrics, everything. He's absolutely mesmerizing."

The result of Jimmy Eat World's go-for-broke efforts was *Clarity,* a sweeping epic of an album that fused textured orchestral compositions with whimsical rock arrangements. Its opener, "Table for

Glasses," was a slow burner that flooded open midway through with a thundering boom of Lind's concert bass drum. From there, the band seamlessly weaved together the fully realized version of a driving rock sound they'd been chasing for three years with delicate string sections and twinkling bells. Its final track, "Goodbye Sky Harbor," was a looping, sixteen-minute sendoff full of references to John Irving's 1989 novel *A Prayer for Owen Meany.*

Clarity didn't sound like anything on the radio, nor did it sound like anything in the underground emo scene. It didn't sound much like *Static Prevails*, and it certainly didn't sound like a punk record. It didn't sound like anything else, really. After the album's completion that summer, Adkins cracked an unintentionally prophetic joke to a *Phoenix New Times* reporter: "We're out to redefine emo." Then he added, "Don't quote me on that, please."

Not surprisingly, Capitol was unsure how to market a revolutionary emo record eons ahead of its time. For a while, the band sat on the finished product, artwork and all, waiting for the label to assign it a release date. As the months dragged on, the band started to suspect that Aaronson was hiding the fact that Capitol had no intention of releasing it. They foresaw a grim future for themselves, doomed to be one of the major-label horror stories they'd read about in *Maximum Rocknroll*, a band with a masterpiece record forever cursed to collect dust on an office shelf in Hollywood.

But then, for a brief moment, it seemed as though Jimmy Eat World might finally be getting their shot. The most accessible single from the album, "Lucky Denver Mint," was released via an EP on independent label Fueled by Ramen and started getting airplay on KROQ. The song was also pitched for a new Drew Barrymore romcom, *Never Been Kissed.* Capitol was suddenly moved to schedule *Clarity* for a release date.

By the time *Clarity* hit the streets in February 1999, though, KROQ DJs had lost interest in "Lucky Denver Mint," and it fell out of rotation. A video for the song failed to garner much play on MTV. *Never Been Kissed* did well at the box office but didn't make a household name out of Jimmy Eat World, though the band could at least brag that they'd met Drew Barrymore.

The recently launched and increasingly influential music website Pitchfork was unimpressed, giving the album an abysmal 3.5 out of 10. The critic wrote of Jimmy Eat World, "They sound like sensitive white American boys. I imagine if one of the photos in those vaguely homo-erotic Abercrombie and Fitch catalogs came to life and start[ed] playing music, it would sound like this."

But on the ground, Jimmy Eat World's contemporaries were floored by *Clarity*. Texas Is the Reason guitarist Norman Brannon heard an early copy through the album's graphic designer, Jason Gnewikow. "I remember listening to it and saying out loud, 'Well, *that's* ambitious.' Even the way it started—you don't hear a distorted guitar until five minutes into the record. You hear a fucking violin before you hear a distorted guitar!" Brannon says. "No one from our scene was really using the studio as an instrument in 1998."

Braid heard an early copy of *Clarity* on a European tour with their shared roadie, Paul Drake. "The songwriting and production choices were so audacious," remembers frontman Bob Nanna. "Honestly, it was inspiring that a band of our peers were using their time, energy, and budget to make such a bold statement."

Capitol's hands-off approach with *Static Prevails* had taught Jimmy Eat World how to operate autonomously, so by the time *Clarity* was finally released, they were a self-sufficient machine on an upward trajectory. They were opening for bigger bands and headlining larger venues. They were booking their first European tour that fall, an opportunity that came about largely because Paul Drake had lugged a box of *Static Prevails* CDs with him on a European tour with Braid and the Get Up Kids and sold them at shows. Sensing interest overseas, Jimmy Eat World started buying copies of their own records from their label at cost and shipping them to an international distributor who got them placed in stores. By the time the band arrived at their first gig in Germany, there were six hundred eager fans singing along to their songs.

"We were getting our wildest dreams fulfilled. We were on tour, we were able to make records we were proud of. The whole thing felt like we were getting away with something," says Adkins. "We saw more people at our gigs. Every time we'd come to a town we'd see new people, we'd be on better opening slots. Things seemed like they were progressing from our perspective, so if Capitol went away, it wouldn't be the end of the world because we knew what to do."

Ultimately, their relationship with Capitol did go away. Gary Gersh left the label and would soon head up the music imprint of a new tech company, Digital Entertainment Network, with Aaronson following him there soon after. Not long after the release cycle for *Clarity* ended, the new guard at Capitol informed the band they would be dropping them from their roster. "They were horrified, and rightfully so," remembers Israel. "But they got through it, and that's what made them so special. They had the indomitable spirit to find their artistry in the face of defeat. Jimmy Eat World opened every door individually. They earned every single one of their fans, one by one, for years."

For Jimmy Eat World, four Arizona teenagers who had stumbled onto the same record label as the Beatles and the Beach Boys, it felt like the jig was finally up, and they were content to be on their way. They'd already started plotting their next album with some leftover ideas and material that didn't make the cut for *Clarity*. Most notably, they had a song with a dynamic hook they'd been testing at shows, called "Sweetness." They had a newfound confidence in their abilities in the studio, too. Mark Trombino recognized it, and told the band he'd record their next album for free. *Clarity* was netting him so much new work from bands that wanted to make records that sounded like it that he figured another record with them would only further benefit his career.

As the 1990s ended and Jimmy Eat World treaded into the new millennium, they found themselves at a turning point—too ambitious to go back through the indie-label route but too worn down by the major-label system to try again. What they decided was that they were going to forge ahead by funding their next album themselves, with money they earned touring Europe and working odd jobs back home. Maybe, they hoped, they could find success in the middle.

nywise—all these West Coast poppy punk rock bands. We were already finishing off each other's musical sentences from the very beginning."

Both self-taught musicians, they got comfortable with each other's styles by covering songs from punk bands they both loved, like NOFX, and alternative rock groups, like Dinosaur Jr., and then moved up to writing their own material, which landed somewhere in the middle. They wrote songs primarily centered around money and girls, specifically their struggles maintaining both. Neither was the captain of the ship. The two traded off vocal duties equally, and their distinct singing styles complemented each other. Hoppus had a flat, monotone delivery, which was offset by DeLonge's nasally whine.

Beyond their natural musical kinship, they formed an instant bond over their love of irreverent humor. They'd grown up on Chevy Chase movies, *The Kids in the Hall,* video games, fast food, and prank phone calls. The two were immediately cracking each other up with jokes about genitals and butt sex, usually at the expense of one another, and they had a quick-witted comedic timing that a professional improv team would envy. If one of them set up a gag, they could trust the other to ad-lib a raunchy punch line on the spot.

The two roped in a fourteen-year-old friend of DeLonge's named Scott Raynor to play drums. He was more reserved and didn't share his bandmates' passion for the perverted comedic arts, but he was a decent enough drummer and proved to be the glue that kept them from falling apart musically. After deeming their first band name, Duck Tape, too silly, the trio started calling themselves Blink (often stylized as "blink"), a name as simple and flippant as their music.

Blink tried their hand at playing their first handful of songs in public and got the reception they more or less expected. "The very first show we ever played was a bar called the Gorilla Pit," says Hoppus. "It was a weeknight, and we drove in and it was me, Tom, Scott, and Cam, who was a friend of ours that we skated with. We loaded in and there was literally the bartender and one patron sitting at the bar. He said we could set up on the stage. We set up and started playing the first song. After the first song the bartender said, 'Hey, please turn it down.' So we turned it down. We played another song and he said, 'Please turn it down some more.' So we turned it down some more. We played a third song and the bartender said, 'Hey, guys, can you just stop playing? We'll give you guys some Snapple.' So that was our first show—we played three songs and got free Snapple."

Through 1993 and 1994, Blink got themselves booked around San Diego at venues like the Spirit Club, the Soul Kitchen, and the YMCA skate park. Sometimes they'd even get paid in real money —usually only fifty or a hundred bucks, but still, a better deal than free iced tea. They passed out cassette recordings of their early songs and dropped them off at stores in the area. "We started calling clubs asking if we could get on shows, playing friends' parties, building a very small following," says Hoppus. "We recorded a demo tape and took it to a duplication place. I'd pick up the tapes, go to Kinko's, print out the artwork we made ourselves, cut out the inserts, fold them all on my mom's living room floor with my mom, my sister, and my stepdad. And I would drive the demos around to all the record shops in San Diego County on consignment. I'd go back every week or so and was surprised that copies were sold. I didn't know who bought them. It wasn't my family or friends. Once that started happening, I was really blown away that people were buying our demo tape."

They were so enamored with the experience of reaching unknown listeners with their music that they quickly put together another, slightly higher-quality demo tape. The cover featured a photo of a Buddha statue, leading most people to refer to it as the Buddha tape. On the inside, their long list of acknowledgments thanked everyone from the adult film industry to Snapple to "the guys who made fun of Tom's dick in the second grade."

Dubbed copies of the Buddha tape made their way around San Diego, and songs like "Carousel" and "Fentoozler" stuck with local skate rats. Blink became regulars at SOMA, San Diego's premier venue, which housed two stages. On the large stage, they opened for more established acts like Face to Face, Unwritten Law, and the Muffs. And on the side stage, they played five-dollar weeknights gigs with other unremarkably named locals like Product and Grip. By the end of 1994, Blink had enough of a following that they could head-line these shows and pack the place with two hundred friends and fans from around town.

Most bands reputable enough to fill SOMA were bound to even-tually wind up on Cargo, the area's main indie label, which was home to acts like Three Mile Pilot, fluf, and Deadbolt. "Back then, Cargo was a phenomenally successful independent label out of San Diego," says Hoppus. "At that time, San Diego was being billed as the new Seattle. There was a new wave of grunge coming in and there was a big scene for it in San Diego—bands like Rocket from the Crypt and Drive Like Jehu. Cargo had their finger on the pulse of that scene that was really starting to pop off."

But Blink's amateur style of bouncy skate punk didn't exactly win over the snobbier employees at Cargo. It was only through a persis-tent push from a man on the inside that they got noticed. "The son of the owner of Cargo Records somehow became a fan of Blink," remembers Hoppus. "Every day he'd put the *Buddha* demo in his dad's car stereo so that when his dad got in the car to go to work, he'd hear Blink. Finally, the owner acquiesced and said, 'Fine, fine, fine, we'll put out this thing, but I don't want it to be on Cargo Re-cords, because we're building our brand with nouveau grunge. But I'll make it this side thing called Grilled Cheese and it'll be a pop-punk thing.'"

The result of their Cargo collaboration was the band's debut al-bum, *Cheshire Cat*. Recorded over a few days at Westbeach Record-ers, the Los Angeles studio opened by Bad Religion guitarist and Epitaph Records founder Brett Gurewitz, the album is a rough jum-ble with a few bright spots peeking through. The kindest praise for it would be that it could fittingly soundtrack a skateboard video. Many of its tracks were just revamped versions of their rough demo songs. The standout addition was "M+M's," Hoppus's most sincere attempt at a punk rock love song, which only made one mention of masturbation ("There are only so many ways I can make love with my hand"). Tacked onto the end of the album were three tracks the band would refer to as joke songs, but given the immaturity and sexual metaphors prevalent throughout the record, it was hard to understand what distinguished them from the serious material.

Cheshire Cat was released in February 1995, and to say that Cargo's expectations for its first printing were low is an understatement. "The owner actually bet people that worked at the label that we would not sell more than a thousand copies," laughs Hoppus. "Even the owner didn't believe in us enough. But he put out our record anyway and we blew through it pretty quickly. I think the label was surprised. Some of the people who worked at the record label were really cool to us, and some people, we'd walk in and they thought we were juvenile asses. We were playing fast music that wasn't cool enough for them. To their credit, we were kinda shitty."

$ $ $

With their first album in hand, Blink did mini-tours as far as weekend excursions allowed, traveling either in a borrowed van or a two-vehicle convoy—Raynor's pickup truck and Hoppus's Toyota Corolla. "We worked our asses off," says Hoppus. "We'd tour and play shows everywhere. We'd play a show in San Diego, we'd play a show in Los Angeles, we'd play a show in San Francisco. Then a week later we'd play San Diego, San Francisco, Vegas. I was in college at the time and I scheduled my classes so that I'd only have classes on Tuesdays and Thursdays so I could leave and play Friday, Saturday, Sunday, Monday. But I was blowing myself out. There were more touring opportunities coming in. I went to my mom and I was like, 'I'm at a crossroads here. I can either drop the band and focus on college and get my degree, or I have to drop college, because the band is overtaking all my time.' She said, 'You can go back to college anytime. You only get one chance at being in a band, so go do that.' So I dropped out of college and we started pursuing touring full-time."

To expand their touring capacities outside the West Coast, Blink added two Ricks and a Millennium Falcon to their operation in 1995. Rick DeVoe was a twenty-seven-year-old San Diego promoter whom DeLonge talked into managing the band. Rick Bonde was the owner of the Tahoe Agency, who agreed to book them more gigs. And the Millennium Falcon was what they called their first Chevy Beauville tour van, an homage to their love of *Star Wars*.

Blink made another major change in 1995, one that was forced upon them. A funky pop rock group from Dublin contacted the band, informing them that they'd already claimed the name Blink and they had proof, in the form of their appearance on a promo CD, *CMJ Seminar 1992*. And while the Irish Blink's "Is God Really Groovy?" was unlikely to be mistaken for the California Blink's "Does My Breath Smell?," they were insistent that California Blink stop using the moniker. "We got a cease-and-desist letter mailed to us from this techno band, these old dudes in Ireland," remembers DeVoe. "It was just such a pain that wouldn't go away. It was a thorn in our side. So, finally, we caved."

Hoppus was pushed for a new name for weeks before finally blurting out "Blink-182" off the top of his head. The added number was meaningless, but lore grew among fans about its origins, which the band fueled by giving various decoy explanations in interviews. The 182 would be cited as a reference to Hoppus's goal weight or the number of times Al Pacino says the word "fuck" in *Scarface*. But really, Hoppus swears, it means nothing.

DeVoe used his connections in the surf and skate worlds to get the band booked on their first proper tour, a run of shows promoting the Taylor Steele–directed surf movie *Good Times,* which featured a number of bands from its soundtrack, like 7 Seconds, Unwritten Law, and Sprung Monkey. Blink-182 took to the heavy-partying tour life too hard, too soon. On the very first stop, at the Milk Bar, in Jacksonville, Florida, DeLonge got himself arrested. "He was drinking outside the club and a cop rolled up and he got caught. He was nineteen, I think," says DeVoe. "I remember going to bail Tom out. I saw him sitting in the room all by himself and I said, 'You idiot.' We took a picture of Tom in the police car and, funny enough, I think he was even wearing a Down by Law shirt."

Following that run of North American shows, Blink-182 was offered the opportunity to join one of their favorite bands, Pennywise, on tours through Australia and then Alaska. Pennywise even covered Blink's costly airfare out of their own pockets, and Blink repaid them by waiting until they fell asleep on the plane and leaving signs on them that read, I'M DREAMING ABOUT NAKED MEN. "Pennywise kindly put us on their tour and I have no idea why," says Hoppus. "We were worth zero tickets in Australia."

"We took them because they were friends with Rick DeVoe," says Pennywise guitarist Fletcher Dragge. "Rick talked us into it, and we training-wheeled them through Australia. They had a good crowd response and they were just funny youngsters."

Pennywise took Blink-182 under their wing and gave them an education, not only in how to travel internationally as a band, but how to survive punk-tour chaos. For several weeks, the troupe was a hotel manager's worst nightmare—a roaming destruction unit of Roman candle wars and drunken, naked debauchery. "Pennywise brings mayhem with them everywhere they go," says Hoppus. "There were broken hotel room doors, there were BB guns being shot off in hotels. It was the mid-nineties, and we were punk rock bands on tour. Things got broken."

In particular, Blink learned not to pull pranks on Pennywise, specifically their gargantuan guitarist. "They'd try to fuck with me," says the six-foot-five Dragge. "One night in Alaska, they piled up four feet of snow in front of my hotel door. But they were stupid, because the door opened in, so it didn't block me in. I opened the door while they were doing it and I was like, 'Oh, you're all fucked now.' The last night of that tour, I got five people and bought spray bottles full of Tabasco and a twenty-foot extension cord with the ends of it stripped so there were hot wires on the end. So basically it was a 120-volt cattle prod, which is pretty bad. So we kicked their door down, fire-extinguishered them, disabled them by squirting them with Tabasco sauce in the eyes, and electrocuted them. I think Mark jumped out of the second-story hotel window into the snowbank in his underwear just to get out of the room."

The aftermath was so bad that the police showed up and questioned Blink-182 about how their room had gotten torn up and why a man had been seen running through the parking lot in his underwear. Not wanting to return to jail, DeLonge and the others kept their mouths shut. "To their credit, the guys didn't crack," says Dragge. "But I think I had to pay a $2,000 damage bill for the room."

Somewhere between the arrests and the electric shocks, Blink-182 sold around fifty thousand copies of *Cheshire Cat* and caught on heavily in Australia, even hitting the ARIA charts there. Much to the surprise of Cargo, the album became the label's top seller, thanks to their devoted California following. The band even had a regional hit with "M+M's," off of pickup on popular San Diego station 91X. They filmed a music video for the single that was full of amusement park antics. They even pitched it to executives at MTV, they told skate magazine *Thrasher* that year, but midway through the first viewing, the network's response was "Why are you showing us this shit?"

$ $ $

As alternative music grew in popularity through the early nineties, a few entrepreneurial musicians got the bright idea to start bundling their culture and taking it on the road via traveling outdoor festivals. In 1991, Jane's Addiction frontman Perry Farrell launched Lollapalooza, a roadshow that brought acts like Nine Inch Nails, Siouxsie and the Banshees, and Butthole Surfers to fields and fairgrounds throughout North America. The following summer, Blues Traveler singer John Popper strung together a tie-dye-friendly lineup that included Phish and Spin Doctors for H.O.R.D.E., an East Coast summer tour the *Los Angeles Times* called "the alternative to the alternative." Sarah McLachlan also began planning Lilith Fair, which aimed to give female artists like Sheryl Crow and Fiona Apple more prominent main-stage placement. It was only a matter of time before someone found a way to pack the nineties punk boom into a neat package that could be delivered to cities and suburbs across the United States. And in 1995, that person was Kevin Lyman.

Lyman was not a musician. He'd roadied for bands like Fishbone and the Untouchables before booking and running shows for Los Angeles–based production company Goldenvoice. In 1995, he used his industry connections to launch Warped Tour, a twenty-five-date expedition that delivered punk rock and extreme sports to the masses with ticket prices about twenty bucks cheaper than its festival competitors. Dubbed "punk rock summer camp," Warped Tour and its crew trucked stages and halfpipes from city to city to bring kids the complete skate/punk experience. Each of the nineteen bands got thirty minutes onstage, with a schedule that rotated daily. Unlike other festivals, it had no clear headliner. This unconventional scheduling method was done not only as a way of keeping the tour an egalitarian operation, but also because there was no clear main act to speak of. Instead of investing in high-price artists, as Lollapalooza was doing with Pearl Jam, Beastie Boys, and the Smashing Pumpkins, Lyman built a whole tour out of undercard acts like Guttermouth, Quicksand, and Face to Face.

Warped's inaugural year was a victim of bad timing. Many acts on its lineup, like Deftones and CIV, were performing material that was just on the precipice of breakout success. Were the same lineup taken on the road the following summer, attendance could have reasonably doubled or tripled. "The first year was tough," admits Lyman. "We had Sublime and No Doubt that year, but no one knew 'em yet."

The next year, Lyman took a more expansive approach and landed a sponsor in skate shoe company Vans, who ponied up $300,000 in support. The larger budget allowed him to add a second stage and more acts. He booked a number of reliable draws from the booming punk and ska worlds, like NOFX, Pennywise, Fishbone, Lagwagon, and the Mighty Mighty Bosstones. Among the stacked lineup of more seasoned bands, the young Blink-182 got offered a slot on the smaller stage and a few bunks on Lyman's production bus, largely as a favor.

"I'd started to see Blink playing shows around town in L.A., so I became aware of them early on," says Lyman. "I became friends with Rick DeVoe, who was managing them at the time. Blink was a cool band, but I mainly took them to help out my friend who was trying to establish himself as a manager. They weren't worth anything that first year—very small. But I said, 'You know what, Rick? They can ride on my tour bus with me.'"

Lyman's decision to bring Blink along was also based on some light bullying from their friends in Pennywise. "I remember telling Kevin, 'You've got to take these guys on next year's tour,'" says Dragge. "And he was like, 'I don't know, we're gonna have a full lineup . . .' And I was like, 'No, no. You put them on next year and pay them a thousand bucks a night.' We wrote the contract out on a napkin and I forced him to sign it."

The tour kicked off on the Fourth of July in Phoenix, and Blink-182 immediately made themselves at home. Their sets didn't attract the biggest crowds most days, but they won over small smatterings of overheated onlookers, if not with their music, then with their relatability. With their baggy shorts, bleached blond heads, and sweaty, hairless torsos, they resembled most of the sunburned teenagers shuffling around Warped Tour. When Hoppus and DeLonge giggled and cracked their diarrhea jokes into the microphone, they came off like two punk kids who'd sneaked their way onto the stage to cause as much trouble as possible before security booted them, which wasn't far from the truth. They played their instruments like they were learning them as they went along, and spent a good chunk of their set riffing with the audience. When they rocked hard enough to get the crowd circle-pitting, the guys soundtracked their mosh movements with porno-style moans and grunts. Sometimes, to let the chain-smoking Hoppus catch his breath between songs, De-Longe broke out a thirty-second tune he'd made up, the lyrics of which were, in full: "Shit, piss, fuck, cunt, cocksucker, motherfucker, tits, fart, turd, and twat."

Warped Tour and Blink-182 proved to be the perfect pairing. The band's carefree, fun-loving attitude provided the ideal entertainment for the Warped Tour crowd, most of whom were skateboarders and surfers kicking back on summer vacation. "A band like us, we were a little faster and more aggressive," says Dragge. "But them, they fit more into the NOFX category. They had a friendlier feel. It was a have-fun, bounce-around pit, whereas we had a giant circle pit with a bunch of knuckleheads beating the shit out of each other. There were enough teenage girls there and people who were into the happier side of punk to make their shows great."

"The reason why Pennywise was always cool with Blink was because they never really took away from their audience," says DeVoe. "[Pennywise] sometimes got labeled jock-punk rock. It was for the bros. But Blink, they appealed to the girlfriends of those guys in the pit."

The tour hopped all around that summer, from Quebec to Massachusetts to Florida, and with each stop, Blink-182 spread their West Coast juvenilia. "You could see that underground word of mouth spreading," says Lyman. "People were going to Warped Tour in New Jersey and calling their friends in New York and saying, 'Dude, you gotta check out this band!'"

Like everyone else on the fledgling tour, Blink-182 was expected to earn their keep, and Lyman put Hoppus and DeLonge to work with a specific duty: press. "I was a little leery about talking to the press about Warped," Lyman says. "I was the background guy. I was pretty much the first non-band guy to start their own festival. You had Perry Farrell, you had John Popper, you had Sarah McLachlan—you had all these people who were artists [starting festivals]. Me, I was the guy who threw people off stages in L.A. and loaded trucks. So I told Blink, 'If any press wants to talk about Warped Tour, they're gonna have to talk to you. That's how you'll pay me for being on the bus.'"

As for why he designated, of all people, two wiseass miscreants like Hoppus and DeLonge to be the face of his costly operation, Lyman admits there wasn't really anyone else to do it. "NOFX was a big band, but they wouldn't do press," he says. "Pennywise was a big band, and Fletcher is one of my dear friends, but he was a little volatile at times. These kids—Mark and Tom—were *charming*. Back then, if you had a library card and a story in the school newspaper, you'd get a press pass. Anyone who wanted to come to cover it could. So, every day, Blink had to go be there for any kid that wanted to talk to 'em. It got them comfortable talking to the press."

Hoppus and DeLonge stood in blacktop parking lots across America in the oppressive summer heat and fielded questions from anyone with a fanzine or college radio show who was thrown their way. Mostly, they deflected any serious conversation topics with gag answers about their balls and their buttholes. But buried below the ball-and-butthole talk were two guys who could wax thoughtfully about punk when they wanted to. They also had a great deal of confidence in their band, and unlike many of their punk peers, they were unapologetic about their career aspirations. They wanted their songs to be played on the radio and they didn't care what the rest of the scene thought of that.

In one interview that summer, after recommending everyone try punching themselves in the nuts because, they swore, "when you *stop* punching yourself in the nuts, it feels so great," Hoppus and De-Longe discussed their views on the stigma surrounding major labels. It wasn't much of a concern to them, they claimed.

"I don't think, the way a lot of people do, that if you go to a major label you're a sellout or whatever," Hoppus said. "As long as you stay true to your style of music and don't get a big head about it and stay true to your fans."

"Basically, what we want is for our albums to be everywhere and for our label to have the capacity to go as big as we have the potential to," DeLonge added. "We don't want to be held back by any obstacles. If one of those is being on a small label and we have to go to a major, then we'll do it."

Hoppus laid out the criteria that would need to be met if Blink-182 were ever to consider signing with a major label, namely that the band would never want to lose control over their art, their singles, or their videos. "Things like that, you don't want to give up when you go to a major label," he said.

"One of the main things you don't want to lose as well," De-Longe said, with an upper lip that quivered as it struggled to suppress a smirk, "is your virginity."

$ $ $

In the last week of 1995, the *Washington Post* ran an article about *Insomniac*, Green Day's much-anticipated follow-up to their major-label debut, *Dookie*. Ten weeks after the album's release, it had yet to go gold. With a few hundred thousand copies sold in its first two months, *Insomniac* was doing respectable numbers by punk standards, but for Green Day, a phenomenon that had sold more than ten million copies worldwide the previous year, its performance was a tad underwhelming. It didn't have as many natural radio hits or MTV videos. Most singles were marred by censoring of the word "fuck" or "shit." It was a bit darker, a bit angrier, and a bit meaner than *Dookie*, which critic Mark Jenkins surmised was perhaps its intent—Green Day's way of "alienating some of its massive, unwieldy following." The headline captured the current state of pop-punk's golden boys: "It's Not Easy Being Green Day, the Sellout Band That Isn't Really Selling."

A few months later, around the time Blink-182 was preparing to embark on their first Warped Tour, major labels started taking interest in the San Diego band and sending A&R scouts to their shows. Whether these labels were on the hunt for Green Day's pop-punk successors or it was just a fluke, Blink-182 had no clue. They didn't know much of anything, in fact. "We were just idiots," says Hoppus. "We didn't really know what we were talking about. We had no idea how the music industry worked. We had these people coming out who had signed R.E.M. or who'd worked with the Go-Go's or whoever. Everybody had a story of someone amazing they'd signed, everybody had a huge track record. And we were just like, 'Uh . . . we just want to play fast punk music. We want to sound like Screeching Weasel.'"

DeVoe believes it was not only Blink-182's impressive indie-label sales that made them enticing, but their proximity to the profitable SoCal extreme sports industry. While Los Angeles had its celebrity hobnobbing and San Francisco had its respected DIY punk institutions like Gilman and *Maximum Rocknroll,* San Diego had its boards. In its backyard was Transworld, the media hub that published widely distributed magazines and videos about skateboarding, snowboarding, and surfing. The city had also birthed skate shoe company Airwalk, pro skate legend Tony Hawk, and Carlsbad Skatepark, the first one built in California.

"Everyone else was trying to be like Green Day, but they had no story, no identity. They were just copycats," DeVoe says. "So I tried to take Blink, who looked like any other punk band in the mid-nineties, and give them some sort of an identity, and tied them in with surf film producers and the company Billabong. I marketed them towards the action sports industry. It worked, because all the pro surfers and skaters picked them up. We were boiling up in this scene that no one in Hollywood and New York had any idea how to crack into, but they knew it was popular. Quiksilver, Billabong, Volcom—all of those brands were huge. The Southern California lifestyle was on fire, fashion-wise. We were *the band* for it."

Blink-182 found themselves taking lunches with employees from Atlantic, Epic, Interscope, and Columbia, and soon learned that their prank skills had done little to prepare them for business meetings. "I remember we had a show in Las Vegas and I think it was [Interscope president] Tom Whalley who took us on a helicopter tour of the city," says Hoppus. "There were important people coming to shows. There was a lot of pressure of 'Oh, this A&R guy is at this show' or 'This A&R guy is at that show.' Before we played, we had to go to dinner with this person or that person. We were getting caught up in this strange whirlwind, being taken out to dinners at restaurants that we could never be able to afford eating at."

"They were going from Taco Bell to Ruth's Chris," says DeVoe. "We'd be in New York and be in the elevator with these execs in button-up shirts and [Hoppus or DeLonge] would fake a fart. They'd try to punch them in the nuts, messing with their food, starting food fights. I always felt more uncomfortable for the executives, because they were trying to fit in, trying to talk like us, and it was just so obvious. A couple of these execs would try to make a fart joke and it was so awkward. That's when Mark and Tom would lose their shit."

Aside from the major-label offers coming in, there was also the option to move to a larger independent label by joining Epitaph Records, the thriving home to many of their friends and heroes, like NOFX, the Offspring, and Pennywise. "They really wanted to get on Epitaph Records," remembers Dragge. "If you were in a punk band on the West Coast at the time, you wanted to get on Epitaph. So I started campaigning to Brett Gurewitz about getting them on the label. He wasn't a huge fan of Blink, musically. He was like, 'Hey, they're great, just not my cup of tea, so I'm not gonna sign 'em.' I was like, 'Look, Brett, they've sold X amount of records on their label down there. If you sign them and you lose money, you can take it out of my paycheck.' He said it wasn't about the money; he just didn't think they fit the label at this point in time."

A few months later, Gurewitz had a change of heart and took an interest in signing Blink-182. He gave them a tour of the label's Silver Lake office, and the sight of framed gold Rancid records and stacks of Descendents CDs made them feel like they'd be in good company. "I remember walking through there and Tom got so excited," says DeVoe. "They were like kids in a candy store. But the problem [with Epitaph] was that we would be in the shadow of Pennywise, Bad Religion, NOFX, Rancid, and the Offspring. We'd be number six. Plus, the advance was not very good. It was small. All of the major-label offers were better than Epitaph."

There was another hurdle in acquiring Blink-182. Since the band was locked into a multi-album deal with Cargo, signing them would require paying the label for the remainder of their contract. Major label MCA had also grown interested in the band and was not only willing to buy out their contract with Cargo but was looking to essentially buy out the entire label.

"I remember specifically we had at one point decided we were going to sign to Epitaph Records," says Hoppus. "Brett had always supported us. He thought we were cool, and we visited Epitaph and it felt like a family. It felt like home. But at the same time, Cargo was being courted by major labels and was eventually bought or acquired or signed a distribution deal, whatever it was, with MCA. The deal with MCA made it so that it was pretty much impossible to go with Epitaph without Epitaph having to pay a big override. So we ended up going with MCA."

Billboard soon reported that Cargo had "entered into a multi-tiered pact with MCA Records" that would allow the two companies to launch a joint venture, Way Cool Records, and expand the San Diego label's distribution reach and increase promotional efforts. Although Blink-182 was not bound to MCA as a result of the merger, they still liked what the label had to offer, specifically that the band was assured they could maintain creative control of their next album. Additionally, they relished the notion of being the label's lone punk act among a roster that included Meat Loaf and Brian Wilson. "You wanted to go to Epitaph because that's where the cool kids were," says DeVoe. "But at MCA, there was no one like us. Anyone that was in a punk rock band all went to Epitaph or Fat. But Green Day stood alone on Warner, so we wanted to do the same."

"I talked to Rick and he said [MCA] offered more money than Epitaph wanted to pay," remembers Dragge, who'd been so loyal to Epitaph that Pennywise had become synonymous with the label. "I was like, 'What the fuck! You begged to be on Epitaph. I went to bat to the point where I offered my own paycheck. Then a major label waves around the big carrot and now you're gone?' I was pretty bummed on that."

Dragge was upset not just because he felt Epitaph had been slighted, but because he feared that Pennywise's punk protégés were about to put themselves at odds with their fans. "In those days the word 'sellout' was getting thrown out a lot more," he explains. "You had to worry about something like that becoming a reality if you went to a major label. Bands got a really hard time for that. That's what I was concerned about for them. Major labels were never about supporting artists. They saw dollars, and if you didn't have money coming in, you were done, your project was shelved. I figured a lot of their fans would turn their backs on them because they were on a major label and they'd get a lot of backlash."

"It was a touchy subject for a lot of people," says Hoppus. "The whole time, our stance was: 'If we are making the music we want to make and playing the shows we want to play, and we're not being told by anybody what to do or how to act, then how can we possibly be selling out?' It's exactly what we've always done, but with a bigger distribution channel to get our records into stores. You have no idea how distressing it is to be gone from home, living in a van, getting paid after a show, and looking at how far we had to drive to the next show, saying, 'If we each get one burrito at Taco Bell, we can have enough to buy gas to get to the next city.' When you're touring in that manner, and you get to these cities and people are asking, 'Hey, where can I buy your CD?' you're like, 'Well, why am I busting my ass on tour if people can't even get our CDs?' It's really upsetting."

Raynor, who'd been gung-ho on the idea of joining Epitaph, was also disappointed about being outvoted in the decision and began feeling disconnected afterwards. "Looking back, I marked the decision to go to a major over Epitaph as the point where I was only half-invested in Blink," the drummer later recounted to author Joe Shooman. "It's like that song says, 'I left my heart in San Francisco'; I left my heart in the office at Epitaph. After that compromise, I found it difficult to make further ones, and I felt like I was asked to make a lot. Eventually, there was not much of my heart in the band to justify my sticking around. I backed away. I was dead weight."

$ $ $

Blink-182 knew exactly who they wanted to hire to produce their first record for MCA: whoever had helped make their new favorite album, Jimmy Eat World's *Static Prevails*. After sharing a stage with the Arizonans in Denver, the band got their hands on an early cassette copy and played it until the tape wore out. "It just blew my mind," Hoppus remembers. "The guitars sounded *insane*. Everything just sounded so good. We listened to that cassette over and over and over in our tour van. We found out who recorded the album and we said: 'Him. *That's* the dude we want to do our record with.'"

As they'd soon learn, the studio mastermind behind the album was Mark Trombino, a fellow product of the San Diego rock scene. Trombino was a soft-spoken producer who now suddenly found himself wrangling three loudmouth pranksters at Big Fish, a studio in San Diego's North County. Blink-182's infantile demeanor aside, though, Trombino was surprised by the band's ambition and drive. "I was really impressed with their ethic. They knew what they wanted and they worked for it," he says. "They were the first band I worked with that wanted to be a big band. I was used to working with bands, like my own, that were just in it for the art of it or whatever. Maybe secretly they cared, but wouldn't outwardly project that they wanted to sell a lot of records, whereas Blink wanted to be big. They wanted to sell records."

Trombino, who was living in Los Angeles, saved commuting time by sleeping on a couch in the studio and woke up every day to the sound of the three Blink-182 members barging in and making fart sounds. "They were super funny and really nice to me. They really took care of me and brought me burritos for breakfast," he remembers.

Not only was Blink-182 afforded the luxury of extended studio time for their MCA debut, but with five weeks booked at Big Fish, they also for the first time had a leader challenging them to perform to the best of their abilities. "I'd listened to *Cheshire Cat*. I liked Tom's voice. He had a whiny, nasally punk-rock-sounding voice. And Mark sounded like he was talk-singing. So I wanted to hear Mark push his vocals a bit. I let Tom be Tom and pushed Mark to be a bit more aggressive," remembers Trombino.

"I needed that," says Hoppus. "Mark would say, 'No, that needs to be better.' Whereas my natural tendency is to go, 'Oh, that's fine.' I needed somebody in there saying, 'No, it's not fine. You need to do it again.'"

The member who struggled the most in the studio was Raynor, who'd broken both of his feet and was wheelchair-bound. "I think what happened was, they were celebrating signing to MCA and he was partying a little too hard and jumped off the second story, trying to go into a pool, and missed or something," says Trombino. "Fortunately, by the time we recorded, his bass-drum foot was fine, but his hi-hat foot, he couldn't really use it. But the dude played. As a drummer, I was impressed. He would wheel up in his wheelchair, lift himself onto his seat, and bust it out."

Although the Big Fish resources helped capture a tidier-sounding Blink-182, it would be hard to argue that the band did any maturing on their second record, from a thematic standpoint. Their sophomore album was rather sophomoric. They were still singing about their ineptitude with women, deeming their romantic skills "pathetic" and "retarded." They remained committed to giving their songs titles like "Dick Lips." And they were still more closely tinkering with their throwaway gags than with their actual songwriting. "We found a sound effects CD and we spent more time putting together these joke skits with that than we did trying to get perfect vocal takes," says Hoppus. "Mark was used to working with more professional musicians than us. I think he probably struggled with us."

But Trombino helped tighten up Blink-182's loose ends. Whereas the band had previously sounded like three musicians kind of playing the same thing at sort of the same time, they now sounded like a cohesive unit. A few tracks in particular, like "Josie" and "Apple Shampoo," felt like potential singles, but one song, "Dammit," was far and away the standout. "There were three that we really thought were the ones, but 'Dammit' was the number one. It was obvious that was the big one," Trombino says. "When you're making a record, you're hearing the same songs over and over again. I'd heard that song so many times and I still wasn't tired of it."

If a template needed to be drawn of a structurally perfect poppunk song, it would unquestionably look like "Dammit." It led with an earworm hook that sounded like DeLonge rushing through a guitar lesson before passing the ball to Hoppus, who delivered his best vocal performance to date. Instead of his usual ho-hum half singing, the bassist put oomph into each and every word. His verses had heart and his choruses had bite. But "Dammit" was more than the sum of the members' strongest efforts. After four years together, the guys had finally figured out how to write an actual song. Whereas most of their previous tracks were punky little fragments stitched together with stray vulgarities for two and a half minutes, "Dammit" had an arrangement that flowed soundly, from verse to chorus to a bridge that built up and up and up until it reached Hoppus's brilliantly simple, reluctant embrace of adulthood: "Well, I guess this is growing up."

"I thought that something cool was happening with 'Dammit.' It had an immediacy to it," remembers Hoppus. "We spent a lot of time in the studio on that song. That song almost didn't make the record. We had run out of time. It was nearing the holidays and everyone was breaking to go do different things. It was the last day in the studio and I shredded my voice singing 'Dammit.' I was smoking Marlboro Reds, I was drinking nothing but soda. Never a sip of water, never not smoking—the worst stuff you can do for your voice."

Blink-182 titled their major-label debut *Dude Ranch*. Given the album's themes of jacking off and bestiality, as well as the band's predilection for pornographic puns, many fans would interpret the album's title as a euphemism for cum, which Hoppus swears was not by design. "No, we never intended that!" he insists. "It makes total sense to me in the pantheon of punny Blink-182 album titles. That would be a genius one, but I never meant it as that. I just thought it was a funny combination of words."

For all the concern about major labels cleaning up Blink-182's rough edges, *Dude Ranch* was exactly the album the band wanted to make. There were no concessions, aside from their management talking them out of adding a parody of the "Macarena" called "Hey, Wipe Your Anus"—not because it was too stupid (though it was) but because they feared it might have been prohibitively expensive to license.

"When we recorded *Dude Ranch*, nobody from the label came to check in on us at all," says Hoppus. "We didn't have any direction from the label. We did what we wanted to do and put out the record we wanted to put out. That being said, I remember the day we finished *Dude Ranch*, we drove up from San Diego to Los Angeles to present the album to MCA. We brought the DAT there and we sat down in this lounge area at the label. Somebody walked around and said, 'Hey, Blink is here to present their new record!' Out of the entire office, five or six people came to listen. We played the first song, then the second song, then by the third song people started checking their BlackBerrys, saying, 'Uh, I have to go make a phone call.' By the fifth song, it was one person, who was on their BlackBerry the whole time. By song six or seven, it was just me, Scott, and Tom sitting there by ourselves. That was our reception from MCA when we presented our first major-label record, recorded in a real studio, with a real producer. We couldn't even get the people at the label to listen to the whole album."

$ $ $

Plenty of people stuck their necks out for Blink-182 in their first five years. The band had been taken to Australia as a favor, added to Warped Tour as a favor, and signed to Cargo as a favor. But by June 1997, they didn't need anyone doing them favors, because they had *Dude Ranch*.

The album captured Blink-182 at the peak of their talents—such as they were—and its production sounded worlds better than most of the releases by their pop-punk peers. Two weeks after its release, the band took it on the road on their second Warped Tour trek, where the positive reception to the new material was immediately apparent. The band graduated to the main stage, and were the least established band on there. Lyman had promised them the opportunity, which put him at odds with another act, Sugar Ray, who had a radio hit that summer with "Fly." "I had Sugar Ray's management and label yelling at me, saying, 'You need to move them to the main stage!' And I said no. I was willing to lose Sugar Ray, who was selling seventy thousand records a week, because I wanted to keep my word with Blink-182," he says.

The bigger stage meant bigger crowds, and it wasn't just attendees watching. Friends from other bands on the lineup, like the Vandals and Less Than Jake, started gathering around the stage to catch a band that was quickly becoming one of the festival's most talked-about acts. Even the older, humorless punks who didn't like the band could at least hum a few bars of "Dammit." "It was really the perfect tour at the perfect time," Hoppus says. "It was this perfect brew of everything that was popping off in the youth culture at that moment. To be part of that tour and have Blink taking off at the same time, it was like getting double-bounced on a trampoline. It just rocketed Blink up."

After letting "Dammit" simmer on Warped Tour, MCA serviced the single to radio, where it got gradual pickup through the fall, first catching on with California rock stations like KROQ, in L.A., then with others across the country. "Once KROQ jumped on it, it was like, *Ho-ly shit*. It crushed," remembers Dragge. "The guitar hook is insane, the lyrical content was perfect for your typical teenager, whether it's a girl or boy. It's just such a soundtrack to your life. You can't hear it without singing it in your head. It's just a well-written song. That's one thing those little fuckers can do, they can write some goddamn songs."

MTV's *120 Minutes* premiered the video for "Dammit." In it, Hoppus gets beaten up by his ex-girlfriend's beefy new man in a Hollywood movie theater, before she ditches both of them for the awkward concession stand employee, played by DeVoe. It might be a stretch to say the "Dammit" video (and the subsequent one for "Josie," starring Alyssa Milano) proved the guys had acting chops, but there was something magnetic about their performance. They were no thespians, but they could fall down like Chris Farley and ham it up like Jim Carrey. The channel started adding the video to its rotation after that, sending the song storming up the Billboard Modern Rock chart.

"The song blew up that September when we were on a tour with Blink and Frenzal Rhomb called the 'Race Around Uranus Tour,' which was coined by Mark Hoppus," says Less Than Jake frontman Chris DeMakes. "I remember sitting in a van somewhere and Hoppus came running up and he was like, 'Dude, MTV just added "Dammit!"'" It wasn't getting played every hour or anything, but it was getting played four, five, six times a day. It was in rotation at MTV, and that's when the gears started moving."

Once "Dammit" was on televisions and radios, the members of Blink started getting recognized not just at venues but at stores and restaurants. In punk vernacular, this is called getting rockegnized. Hoppus realized his life was changing when he was rockegnized at Disneyland, where he and his sister had season passes.

"The one I remember the most was that I was getting in line for the Casey Jr. railroad, which is a ride for little kids," he says. "Here we were, a bunch of punk rockers who all had dyed hair and tattoos, getting on this ride, and somebody was like, 'Are you the guy from Blink-182? Holy shit!' The reaction was more than just being in a local band where people say, 'Oh hey, what's up.' It was, 'Wow, this is really cool that I'm getting to meet somebody that I heard on the radio!' It was a different kind of fan interaction."

But with new fans came detractors. "I remember playing shows of decent sizes at venues like the Roxy, and having arguments with people that were saying, 'What are you doing? You're ruining the scene.' But I'd say, 'I want my music on the radio. I love our band and I want everybody to hear us. I want everybody to come to the party,'" says Hoppus. "I was once arguing with people in Lake Havasu, Arizona, in a parking lot—people who had been supporting our band for a long time—having a discussion about major labels. They were like, 'You're selling out our scene. People put their lives into this scene, and big companies come in and think they can just buy it all up.' I lost people I'd considered friends who stopped coming to the shows."

Their mentors in Pennywise were happy for their success, but they'd warned them what would happen once they crossed the major-label line. "I remember seeing Tom once and asking him how it was going," Dragge says. "And he said, 'Oh, you know, I'm either coming out of 7-Eleven to a bunch of teenage girls screaming and yelling and asking for autographs or I'm getting a Slurpee thrown at me by some dudes in a truck saying 'Fuck you, you fucking sellout!'"

$ $ $

The first time Blink-182 performed on *Late Night with Conan O'Brien*, in March 1998, they looked like extras from a PacSun commercial. Hoppus bounced around in a Billabong shirt and what were either awkwardly short pants or comically long shorts. De-Longe also repped Billabong with the company's sticker on his guitar. The band gave shout-outs to their friends watching at home, with Hoppus writing UL on his forearm (for Unwritten Law) and DeLonge wearing a homemade shirt that had both Pennywise's and the Vandals' logos drawn on it. As a special nudge to Vandals bassist Joe Escalante, he'd also written JOE LIKES BOYS.

The day after the guys appeared on *Conan*, they made their debut in *Rolling Stone*, in which writer Jon Wiederhorn led with the most fitting introduction: "At a time when even notorious punk rock brats like Green Day are singing acoustic ballads and ruminating about their fading youth, it's getting harder to find a band that just wants to get drunk and act stupid. Meet Blink-182. 'Our favorite things in the world are pee pee and doo doo,' says bassist Mark Hoppus."

The band had just returned from Australia, where they could now headline two-thousand-cap theaters. Upon landing in the United States, they hit another milestone: *Dude Ranch* went gold, thanks to the slow-burning radio success of "Dammit." Much to the grievance of parents' ears, the song's riff was screeching out of basements and bedrooms everywhere as aspiring musicians struggled to learn it on guitar. Blink-182 had tripped and fallen into the mainstream.

But as 1998 sent the band sailing upward, Raynor started holding them back. He grew disengaged with the other members, and his drinking and personal issues became problematic. Eventually he was asked to leave the band. "The best way for me to put it is that everything got kinda haywire in my personal life, and in the band, and with Mark and Tom," he explained to writer Jason Tate. "They wanted different things than me and at the same time our friendship was put to the test . . . and it kinda failed."

As a replacement, DeLonge and Hoppus poached the Aquabats' drummer, Travis Barker. A fellow product of the West Coast punk scene, Barker was a drum savant who had an athlete's discipline behind the kit. He'd filled in on a couple of gigs that Raynor had missed because of personal obligations, and allegedly learned the band's entire set in thirty-five minutes before their first performance together. The partnership was mutually beneficial—Barker was taking a lucrative touring opportunity and Blink was picking up arguably the scene's most skilled drummer. A man of few words, Barker later reflected in his memoir about joining one of punk's fastest-rising bands, describing himself as having felt "totally pumped."

The newly christened three-piece immediately locked into a groove. Not only did Barker add a firecracker pop to their pace; he proved to be the missing piece of the highly marketable identity of Blink-182. With his blue eyes, high cheekbones, and arms full of tattoos, he looked cool enough to fit in between Hoppus and DeLonge but knew enough to keep his mouth shut so as not to taint their perfectly balanced banter.

In the summer of 1998, the new and improved Blink-182 left for a huge North American tour, which included stops as far as Anchorage and Montreal. They brought along a rotating list of opening bands, many of which Blink had been opening for just a year earlier, including Unwritten Law, MxPx, and their favorite band, Jimmy Eat World.

These shows were intended to prove that the new lineup meant business. Blink-182 were no longer the scrappy San Diego underdogs who played empty weeknight shows for free Snapple. They were now a successful group of professional musicians who demanded to be taken seriously. And they called this venture the Poo-Poo PeePee Tour.

$ $ $

It was a beautiful night in New York City and everyone was out celebrating, even though the world was about to end. The nineties were coming to a close at midnight, and a few alarmists had predicted that the dawn of Y2K might trigger a computer glitch that would cause planes to malfunction midflight, banks to have their accounts wiped, and the end of civilization as everyone knew it. None of it would end up coming true, but it was scary enough to sprinkle a sense of exuberant doom throughout the city.

Downtown, at the intimate venue the Knitting Factory, Elliott Smith was onstage with his acoustic guitar and a bottle of champagne, toasting a few minutes early. "Have a good new year, y'all. It's gonna be a good year," the shaky-voiced singer assured the small crowd. Uptown, a tuxedoed Billy Joel was leading a packed Madison Square Garden in singing "Auld Lang Syne." "Happy New Year!" the piano man screamed. "Happy *millennium*!" But the real party was in Times Square, where a horde of onlookers on Broadway gazed up at the massive flatscreen outside MTV Studios and saw the twenty-five-foot-tall members of Blink-182. "You guys didn't even know, but you're on the Jumbotron out there in Times Square," host Carson Daly told the band in the studio. "There's two million people checking you out!"

It was fitting that Blink-182 ushered in the new millennium on MTV. Over the previous six months, off the success of their second MCA album, *Enema of the State,* the band had become fixtures on the channel, their faces as recognizable as pop stars like Justin Timberlake or Jessica Simpson. They appeared on the video countdown show *Total Request Live* so frequently that it might as well have been renamed *The Mark, Tom, and Travis Show.* "We were all over *TRL,*" remembers DeVoe. "It got to the point where I'd walk down the halls in their office and people knew my name. I was just some manager dude, and Carson Daly would say, 'Yo, DeVoe!'"

The band christened the year 2000 by performing "What's My Age Again?" and "All the Small Things," a pair of songs that were even catchier than "Dammit" and had brought them even greater fame. The frequently played video for "What's My Age Again?" saw the guys streaking naked through the streets of Los Angeles with porn star Janine Lindemulder, who also graced *Enema*'s cover. The "All the Small Things" video was a bit of self-aware parody in which they poked fun at the celebrity culture of which they'd become a part. They relentlessly mocked boy bands, even though they had in essence become the Billabong Backstreet Boys. Blink-182 was now a well-packaged group of cute man-boys with anti-sexual sex appeal —an 'N Sync with lip rings or a 98 Degrees with Dag Nasty tattoos.

Although *Dude Ranch* had taken Blink-182 to heights of which they'd only dreamed, it had proven to be merely the kindling for the blaze of its follow-up, *Enema of the State.* The album, released on June 1, 1999, sold 110,000 copies in its first week, enough to debut at number nine on the Billboard 200 chart, among A-listers like Ricky Martin, Backstreet Boys, and Jennifer Lopez. By the time the band performed the New Year's Eve bash, the album was days away from going triple platinum, with an astounding three million copies sold. And that number wasn't the result of any Y2K glitch. "We've already sold 100,000 in the first week," DeLonge bragged to *MTV News,* "but we're all shooting for higher. I want to sell fifty million. I'm thinking fifty or three hundred million—somewhere between there."

Hoppus, DeLonge, and Barker weren't just punk rock stars after the success of *Enema;* they were legitimate celebrities who rode limousines to red-carpet appearances where they flung their arms around the shoulders of Beyoncé. The three cemented their place in turn-of-the-millennium pop culture among other oft-naked men who behaved badly and dominated MTV, like Tom Green, Eminem, and the crew from the newly launched *Jackass.* Mark, Tom, and Travis were now household names.

After *Enema's* release, Blink-182 got bumped from the back pages of *Rolling Stone* up to the cover. "The biggest compliment of all is a kid saying we opened up his eyes to a new style of music," Hoppus told the magazine. "We're kind of like Fisher-Price: My First Punk Band." They even landed in heartthrob rags like *Teen* and *J-14,* causing countless copy editors to comb through their stylebooks to figure out whether words like "pee-pee" and "blow job" needed hyphens. Mainstream radio made hit singles out of three *Enema* tracks: "All the Small Things," a song whose rhymes of "Say it ain't so" and "I will not go" are so rudimentary an infant could enjoy them; "Adam's Song," a tonal departure in which Hoppus reflects more seriously on suicide; and "What's My Age Again?," the first hit song in radio history, Hoppus maintains, to use the word "sodomy."

The band continued their partnership with Lyman and jumped on Warped '99, their fourth consecutive year on the tour. "They kind of set the standard for a band that could break on Warped Tour," says Lyman. "They were the first band that really saw it as a multi-year plan." But the band's crowds had outgrown the tour in size and fervor. The guys suddenly found themselves being flashed by women in the crowd, a new phenomenon they handled with as much grace as might be imagined, usually by pointing and shouting, "Boobies!"

"They were the stars of the tour," says DeMakes. "They now had bodyguards, they had people following them to interviews. And it wasn't for show; they needed it. Everybody wanted to talk to them. It was that insanity and that hysteria that comes with having a hit."

As *Enema of the State* continued to go platinum multiple times over through 2000 and 2001, Blink-182 did arena tours around the world, headlining over some bands they'd grown up idolizing, like Bad Religion, and some of their favorite up-and-comers, like Alkaline Trio. They kicked off 2002 by announcing the Pop Disaster Tour, on which they were set to co-headline with Green Day, whose breakthrough success in 1994 had been instrumental in Blink's rise.

"They blazed the trail for Blink-182. Them, Rancid, the Offspring—all those bands opened doors that we walked through after them," says Hoppus. "But when we toured with Green Day on the Pop Disaster Tour, there was a mood in that camp that they were on the downslide. They were looking at artwork for their B-sides and rarities collection. While they were on the downslide and Blink was on the upswing, they were playing for some audiences who might not have listened to Green Day. It's funny to say, but they were kind of an older band. Older by five years, but at that point our fans thought of Green Day as an older band. And they performed so well at that tour that I think they started coming back up. I'd never take credit for that in any way—they resurged on their own merits—but we put them in front of a lot of people who saw how great they are."

The competitive sales numbers between Blink-182 and Green Day would lead punk fans to occasionally paint them as rivals, but in actuality the two bands owed a lot to one another. Without the foundation Green Day had built, a band like Blink-182 likely never would have been afforded the opportunity to release their music through a major label. And without Blink-182, the national interest in punk rock that Green Day had sparked might have been a fad that fizzled out and stayed behind in the nineties, along with Pogs and Beanie Babies. Major labels had taken dozens of gambles on bands from the genre in an attempt to duplicate Green Day's mega-success, but the San Diego trio proved to be the first one that truly paid off and shoved pop-punk into a new decade.

"I don't regret signing with MCA one bit. I don't think we could've done what we did without the help of a major label," says Hoppus. "Blink made our own success, and once we did that, the label was there to get the records out and do the things we needed them to do. That's what the problem is—I think a lot of bands think they're gonna sign with a major label and things are just going to happen, because the label will make it happen for them because they have all the connections. For us, it was building our own fan base, touring, recording, touring, touring, touring, touring, getting in as many people's faces as we could. And then, once we'd set the table, MCA came in and kicked the field goal . . . Fuck, I really mixed analogies there."

CHAPTER 5

AT THE DRIVE-IN

Relationship of Command

Grand Royal (2000)

ON THANKSGIVING EVE in 1994, Bill Lowery, a fifty-one-year-old traveling preacher and founder of the evangelical ministry Christ Is the Answer, stared into the TV camera in front of him, nervously adjusted the lapels of his gray suit, and realized he'd made a terrible mistake. He'd invited a young local musical group to perform on his KJLF-TV public access show, *Let's Get Real,* and during his monologue it was becoming evident that they were not the nice Christian boys they'd billed themselves as.

"The Drive-In Movie guys are here with us tonight," he told whatever viewers in the El Paso, Texas, area happened to be tuned in to Channel 65. "They're gonna do a little grunge-polka Thanksgiving music for you."

The five-piece band shifted around, wearing stifled smirks and white dress shirts with neckties that made them look like Mormon missionaries. Lowery asked them how long they'd been playing music together. Without missing a beat, frontman Cedric Bixler-Zavala, a wiry twenty-year-old with short, bleached blond hair, dark muttonchop sideburns, and intense blue eyes, deadpanned, "Since 1976."

With that introduction, the band, which was actually named At the Drive-In, got to work, tearing through their frantic punk jam. The volume of their amps was far too loud to be captured by the public access studio's low-grade equipment, leading all the sound to become muddled together in an obnoxious cacophony. For the duration of their three-minute song, Bixler-Zavala's feet hardly touched the ground. He was a bouncing ball of hyperactive energy that Lowery would later joke was akin to a Jane Fonda workout.

After their performance, Lowery invited the boys to take a seat on the couch of his talk show set for an interview. Bixler-Zavala and guitarist Jim Ward, a scrawny, baby-faced eighteen-year-old fresh out of high school, fielded questions about their stances on drugs, religion, and punk rock, a genre Lowery insisted had died ten years earlier. The band members took every opportunity to make a mockery of the experience and sneak juvenile gags into each reply. They subtly picked their noses, feigned narcolepsy when questions got boring, and at one point tried to convince Lowery that they were, in fact, Green Day. It was a televised showdown between an old square and a bunch of Gen X pranksters. And when asked what they thought about Generation X, Bixler-Zavala quipped, "They were a good band until Billy Idol went solo."

Then the conversation turned darker when Lowery brought up the recently deceased Kurt Cobain: "What about that one guy that shot himself in the head with a shotgun?"

"He went out like a king," defended Bixler-Zavala.

"Oh, he went out like a fool!" Lowery scoffed. "He died like a fool dies."

Bixler-Zavala momentarily dropped his mischievous facade to give Lowery a sincere explanation about the late Cobain's suicide and the price of unexpected fame: "He was the kind of kid that grew up and was picked on at school. He was the geek, the outsider. Then all of a sudden, his music made him big, and the dorks that would pick on him in high school were singing the words to his songs. How would you feel? Of course he's gonna hate the world."

$ $ $

El Paso sits tucked away in the westernmost corner of Texas and shares a border with Juárez, Mexico. The close proximity produces a cultural fluidity between them, like two halves of a single town separated by the Rio Grande. As a result of the area's binational makeup, the small, DIY rock gigs around town in the 1990s drew an ethnically diverse mix of local misfits. There weren't a lot of punks or metalheads in El Paso, but the few who lived there found one another and made noise together.

Jim Ward, a white student at El Paso High School, had grown up on the music of Billy Joel and Led Zeppelin and discovered punk rock at the age of twelve, when a friend gave him a copy of Subhumans' *From the Cradle to the Grave*. Ward's older sister had an interest in college radio that trickled down to him as he discovered the Cure and Siouxsie and the Banshees. The summer he turned thirteen, he wore out a cassette copy of Jawbreaker's *Unfun,* and its catchy song "Want" made him realize that writing and playing music was something he'd like to try. Once he learned the basics on guitar, he started joining bands to immerse himself in the local scene and quickly developed an insatiable taste for life as a musician.

Ward was a good student and had been saving money to attend college, but when asked by a guidance counselor in his senior year what university he wanted to attend, he told her that he'd gotten hooked on punk bands around town and no longer wanted to apply to colleges. The concerned counselor made a phone call to Ward's parents, and, around the dinner table that night, Ward repeated his intentions to them. "Well, if you want to be in a band, that's fine," his father said. "Just be in the best fucking band you can be in."

Ward met a number of young musicians in the El Paso scene, including Cedric Bixler-Zavala, a Mexican American classmate two years his senior. The son of a Chicano studies professor at the University of Texas, Bixler-Zavala describes himself as "the Latin Danzig" of his high school. In 1989, Bixler-Zavala watched the documentary *Another State of Mind,* which depicted the punk bands Social Distortion and Youth Brigade escaping the confines of their hometowns and embarking on international tours. From then on, he had his life mapped out. "That was always my blueprint," he says. "You just gotta get out and pave roads that aren't there."

Bixler-Zavala eventually dropped out to play in a handful of local bands, most notably drumming for Foss, a grunge rock group fronted by another former El Paso High School student named Beto O'Rourke. Bixler-Zavala had a simple goal with his music: "I was always aiming to just get out of El Paso. At the time, it was a pretty desolate place. Bands didn't really support each other and audiences didn't really support bands, so you'd play to nobody a lot of times."

When Ward heard Bixler-Zavala's stories of playing shows outside of El Paso, he saw a path out of his hometown as well. The two started playing music together, with Ward on guitar and Bixler-Zavala singing, and roped in a few other local musicians to practice in the living room of Ward's parents' house. The members were all approaching the project from different perspectives, but they found a common influence in Dischord Records bands, adding their own poppy spin on the D.C. label's legendarily angular approach to punk. The delegation of duties between Bixler-Zavala and Ward mimicked the one Ian MacKaye and Guy Picciotto shared in Fugazi. Bixler-Zavala took a loud, unrestrained approach that hit all ranges, from unsteady singing to desperate wailing, while Ward evened him out with grounded backing vocals. They called their group At the Drive-In (sometimes stylized as at.the.drive.in), a name borrowed from, of all places, a lyric by the eighties hair metal band Poison.

At the Drive-In played their small handful of songs at makeshift venues throughout El Paso and then expanded their horizons with a two-thousand-mile loop around Texas. Ward used his college savings to run a label, Western Breed Records, and pressed five hundred copies of At the Drive-In's first seven-inch, *Hell Paso,* a nod to their love-hate relationship with their hometown. The scrappy three-song EP was available by the end of 1994, and a second EP, *¡Alfaro Vive, Carajo!,* followed a few months later. They also bought a 1981 Ford Econoline van for $800 and booked their first journey through the United States—twenty-five shows in forty-two days.

Bixler-Zavala soon recruited a friend named Omar Rodríguez-

López to play bass. A year younger than Bixler-Zavala, the diminutive Rodríguez-López wore Elvis Costello–style glasses and was the runt of the El Paso punk scene. "I kept an eye out for Omar," says Bixler-Zavala. "He was really little and people picked on him, so I was like his older brother. We've been joined at the hip ever since."

The Puerto Rican–born Rodríguez-López was raised in a musical family and grew up on everything from hip-hop to dub music. The son of a former salsa dancer, he had started playing in bands at the age of thirteen, including a few alongside Bixler-Zavala. "I was in a band called Three Blind Bats and he was in a band called Startled Calf," remembers Bixler-Zavala. "We were the most notoriously rowdy of the punk bands in El Paso. Everyone in El Paso was so into Jane's Addiction and the Chili Peppers as the mainstream alternative, but we were always keeping it way back in the eighties with hardcore punk." The addition of Rodríguez-López injected even more frenetic energy into a sound that was already unwieldy on account of its many diverse influences.

At the Drive-In lugged their records to out-of-town gigs but could barely sell enough to pay for gas. "On our first tours, no one bought our merch," says Bixler-Zavala. "What we did was, we went to Juárez and bought like a hundred dollars' worth of wrestling masks and really shitty cigarettes called Faros that have no filter and are really awful. That's what kept us fed, just selling those."

At one early show, at Bob's Frolic III, in Los Angeles, the band played for nine people, one of whom was Blaze James, a writer for the long-running punk zine *Flipside*. James had come out to see the Long Beach locals Paper Tulips, but he stuck around to watch the El Paso band because they looked so pathetic. Being under twenty-one, the members weren't even allowed into the bar and had to wait out front until it was their turn to play. But once they were thirty seconds into their first song, James pitied those who had left early. The band was rough around the edges, but he was blown away by their boundless teenage energy.

James started talking At the Drive-In up to friends and making converts out of his *Flipside* colleagues, who began joining him at shows whenever the band came through town. "I saw them in a tiny clothing store in Silver Lake. The whole place was maybe seven hundred square feet, if that," remembers *Flipside* writer Todd Taylor. "They were pulling from so many different pools. Emo wasn't really defined yet, and it wasn't straight-up hardcore, but they had tons of energy. They were super aggressive but not tough; super emotional but not pandering. It was fantastic."

Eventually they captured their developing sound on their first LP, *Acrobatic Tenement,* which James arranged to have released via *Flipside*'s label, one of its last records before shutting down because of financial and legal troubles. *Acrobatic Tenement* sounded the way a record made in three days on a $600 budget might reasonably be expected to sound. Rodríguez-López's basslines were muddled and lumpy. The guitars sounded largely out of tune and lacked the bite of distortion, because Ward, under the impression he was laying down rough scratch tracks, didn't realize he wouldn't be getting a second crack at recording them. "Making records isn't something you're born knowing how to do," he says. "It takes work to learn how to do it."

At the Drive-In's first three years were marked by a good deal of upheaval and transitions. Ward left for a few months and then rejoined, Rodríguez-López switched over to lead guitar, they recorded another patchy EP, members cycled out, and James quit his *Flipside* gig to act as their manager.

It wasn't until the end of 1997 that the band started in earnest. They brought two new players into the fold: Lebanese American drummer Tony Hajjar and Mexican American bassist Paul Hinojos. Despite being avowed metalheads, the two were gentle and soft-spoken additions to the band. From then on, At the Drive-In was a unit built upon five personalities from five different backgrounds, which made them diverse in every way—culturally, ethnically, and musically. It was both a source of contention and their greatest asset. While their contrasting viewpoints often led to dysfunctional internal relationships, their combined power packed a dynamic punch that assured they'd never be mistaken for another band.

Their discord was evidenced onstage as the band was visibly divided into two sides—the structure and the spectacle. On stage left, the workhorse rhythm section of Ward, Hajjar, and Hinojos dutifully anchored their songs with reliable timing and technical efficiency. And on stage right, Bixler-Zavala and Rodríguez-López unleashed an onslaught that was impossible to look away from. Rodríguez-López's left-handed guitar was more weapon than instrument; throughout their performances, he'd swing it around viciously, sporadically holding it long enough to actually play it. Bixler-Zavala was an indefatigable blur of limbs and microphone cables—*un hombre salvaje*. The frontman possessed a beaming confidence and a reckless disregard for his own body. Any objects in his orbit risked being climbed on, leapt from, crawled across, or all of the above.

Most impressive was that these outbursts were not occasional flare-ups in an At the Drive-In performance; they were the entirety of it. The full force of this energy was packed into every single second of their set. Every night. Night after night. It was chaos for forty-five minutes, and then it was over.

$ $ $

In 1992, a twenty-eight-year-old investment broker named Bob Becker got the idea to start a label called Fearless Records as his way of helping local bands in Orange County, California. "The reason I called it Fearless was because I put out a record before I knew what I was doing," he says. "I felt I was being fearless for even venturing into releasing records."

While Becker didn't make enough money from Fearless's mail orders to quit his job, the wrinkled dollar bills he received in envelopes from around the world were more rewarding than his weekly paycheck. He'd grown up on SoCal punk bands of the seventies and eighties like the Adolescents, T.S.O.L., and Social Distortion, and proudly carried on the O.C. punk tradition with releases from a new crop of upstarts that included White Kaps, Glue Gun, and the Grabbers.

The label got a small boost from the punk boom of the mid-nineties, though Fearless wasn't a household name like Epitaph or Fat Wreck Chords. "I wasn't Brett Gurewitz, I wasn't Fat Mike. I was just Bob," he says. "It didn't have a defined sound like those labels, or a brand. I liked so much different music. It was a little hard for me, but I kept chugging along."

In 1998, Becker got a phone call asking if he might be interested in checking out a band from El Paso called At the Drive-In. "I knew a guy named Blaze James through shows. He was a writer for *Flipside*," remembers Becker. "He was working with the band and he'd shopped them to every label—Fat, Epitaph, Sub Pop. They got turned down by everybody."

"[Fearless] was, in my memory, the last label left. Everybody else said no," says Ward. "I remember hoping Jade Tree would sign us. I really wanted to be on Jade Tree. All the bands I loved were on these labels that didn't want anything to do with us."

"Secretly, I'd hoped Kill Rock Stars wanted us. The other dream was Dischord, but you kind of had to be local [to D.C.] to be on Dischord," says Bixler-Zavala.

James talked Becker into attending the band's show at Club Mesa, a small dive bar in Costa Mesa. The band performed with their typical intensity, which caught Becker off guard. "They were rolling all over the stage and throwing guitars around. I'm a guy who had been to GG Allin shows, but I was actually kind of intimidated. I was blown away and in awe," says Becker. He'd been invited to meet the band afterwards but instead slipped out of the club without saying a word to anyone, processing what he'd just witnessed the whole way home.

"Blaze called me the next day and said, 'What, you didn't like it?'" remembers Becker. "And I said, 'Are you kidding? Those guys were insane!' And he said, 'Well, why didn't you stick around and talk to them?' I said, 'About what? I was afraid! Those guys are nuts!'"

Eventually, Becker did get to meet the band and was surprised to find them warm and down-to-earth, nothing like the erratic madmen they presented as onstage. His wife, Michelle, who helped operate Fearless, bonded with Bixler-Zavala over their shared Mexican American heritage.

"Bob and his wife are great," says Bixler-Zavala. "They took a chance on us even though we were not that O.C. style. That was really cool of them. We didn't fit in there, but no one else would take a chance on us."

The way Becker saw it, At the Drive-In was taking a chance on the label, too. "I was pretty clear with them that our distribution was just okay," he says. "We'd do the best job we could, but we were just a small DIY label." They worked out a two-record deal and the band soon got to work on their first release for Fearless, *In/Casino/Out*.

With its newly solidified lineup, At the Drive-In crafted their first collection of songs that reflected the band's fractured identity. *In/Casino/Out* pulled from each of the members' disparate musical influences to create a mutated form of punk rock. On "Chanbara," high-intensity outbursts were smashed up against Hajjar's punked-up calypso beats, which featured bongos. On "Napoleon Solo," Bixler-Zavala shifted between emotive singing and ferocious screams as he invoked the memory of two friends who had recently perished in a fatal car crash. On "Hourglass," Ward took a cue from one of his first musical inspirations, Billy Joel, and led a piano-heavy ballad.

Since At the Drive-In's primary weapon in attracting new fans was the strength of their live show, the band's goal for *In/Casino/Out* was a recording that captured the raw energy of their performances. That meant largely doing away with overdubs, using first or second takes, and keeping the stray mistakes. "I thought they were nuts because they wanted to do the record live," says Becker. "They were known as a live band, so I get it. They were so afraid of making an overproduced, sterile record. I don't blame them. We've seen that happen plenty of times."

But producer Alex Newport says the scrappiness of the recording wasn't so much a deliberate choice as a product of necessity. "There was a very small budget for recording, and studio time is expensive, so we really only had a few days to record an album. We couldn't afford to be indulgent," he says. With limited time booked at Doug Messenger's Studio, in Hollywood, he did the best he could to stretch their dollars.

Newport kept the lights in the studio low to simulate the live show experience and gave Bixler-Zavala a handheld mic, encouraging him to move around the room as if an audience was watching. Sometimes the band came too close to replicating their wild live energy. "Omar would be leaping around so crazily in the studio that he kept missing his part, or the guitar was going so badly out of tune for that part that I had to ask him to try to keep still and focus on it," Newport recalls.

They recorded the entire eleven-track album, plus three bonus tracks, in three days. With only enough money to afford a single day in the mixing room, Newport mixed the album in one straight twenty-four-hour block without a break. Bixler-Zavala would later admit in a fanzine interview that while he liked the record, the band didn't get to execute "maybe 30 percent" of the ideas they had planned.

"I knew that getting a highly produced record was going to be impossible in that short amount of time," says Newport. "But I felt like the most important thing was to try to capture the spirit and energy of the live show on a record, get that out to people, and hopefully get them on the way to getting a bigger and better budget next time."

$ $ $

It was around the time *In/Casino/Out* was released, in the summer of 1998, that Bixler-Zavala and Rodríguez-López stopped cutting their hair. The fairly innocuous cosmetic decision would be mentioned in just about every write-up of the band from then on. Much attention, and sometimes mockery, was paid to the duo's curly Afros, because they were so distinguishing. Press and fans alike seemed incapable of describing the band without noting the hairdos of the guitarist and the singer.

What was less often noted, though, was that their high hair was a subtle defiance of the racial homogeneity of the predominantly white punk scene they inhabited. Chicago's Los Crudos, the most notable Latino hardcore band in the United States, played their final show that October. Bixler-Zavala and Rodríguez-López proudly picked up their torch, even if it meant being the butts of a few cheap

Afro jokes, as when the *Chicago Tribune* referred to the two as "human Q-tips."

"At one point I noticed Omar letting his shit go natural," says Bixler-Zavala. "You know this if you're Puerto Rican, if you're Mexican, if you're Black. That's just you going, 'You know what? I'm tired of putting this shit in my hair. I'm tired of waking up on a pillow slobbered with Murray's.' I didn't even use Murray's. I used Nu Nile. That's next-level straightening shit. For me, my homie's out here going natural. Why don't I just go natural? That's all it really was."

As At the Drive-In's hair grew, so too did their draw. *In/Casino/Out* finally armed them with a collection of songs befitting of their live talents, and their performances became more intense than ever. Sonically, the band didn't fit in with most of their peers, which sometimes made for odd tour pairings, but they could win over dubious fans across the genre spectrum, from pop-punk to hardcore.

"I'd put them on shows with some of the more punk artists on my roster," says Becker. "What we learned was that if you got those guys in front of people, regardless of the genre of the band they're playing with, a certain amount of people will come out of there blown away." A packed year ensued, during which the band jumped from tour to tour with anyone who would have them.

Right after the release of *In/Casino/Out*, they hopped on a tour of the Midwest and the East Coast, opening for the emo band Knapsack, a connection made through their mutual producer, Newport. "You could feel the upswing happening for them on that tour. You could feel that people were starting to know who they were and that people were talking about them," says Knapsack frontman Blair Shehan. "When they played, it was like watching popcorn pop. They had so much energy and charisma and style that it made me feel really antiquated. You'd feel sort of square or old-fashioned in comparison to this fresh thing that just blew into town." That tour, incidentally, would be Knapsack's last.

At the Drive-In then ripped through the South with the rising Jimmy Eat World, who were touring in support of their second album with Capitol Records, *Clarity*. "When we first saw [At the

Drive-In] play, they were so good and we loved watching them, but on the other hand, we were bummed. We were like, 'Fuck, we have to follow *that* every night?'" says drummer Zach Lind. "That tour helped them a lot, but it helped us, too. That was the first time we really thought about having to match someone's energy."

Knapsack and Jimmy Eat World's shared roadie, Paul Drake, was so impressed with At the Drive-In's performances that he started working for the Texans after that. The pay wasn't great, but he got to watch the scene's most exciting live band every night. "They put everything they had into their show," says Drake. "They got their sound exactly right at soundcheck. It wasn't pretentious or planned out, but they knew that they were gonna explode onstage every night. You wouldn't want to stand next to Omar's guitar amp. He really wasn't playing guitar most of the time, because he was throwing it around."

At the Drive-In also opened for the punk band AFI on a few West Coast dates, during which Becker remembers them facing a particularly hostile Los Angeles crowd. "It was ugly in Hollywood then. There was no bullshit," he says. "There were AFI fans who had their backs to their stage and were flipping [At the Drive-In] off because of how they looked or whatever, I don't know, but it was pretty brutal. The band then went into three straight songs and they didn't stop. The kids were just staring off like they didn't know what they were seeing. Then, after the third song, you just heard the audience erupt in applause and cheers. Those kids were all buying merch on the way out."

At the Drive-In even got to share a stage with their heroes Fugazi that year, in front of five hundred people in Des Moines, Iowa. They also took off for their first jaunt in Europe, hitting eleven countries in six weeks and winning over international crowds through the universal language of destructive punk performances.

Bigger audiences brought bigger problems, though. The more people At the Drive-In played to, the less control they had over them. The band viewed their shows as inclusive spaces for all misfits like them, so when they witnessed unruly slam dancers or large men ruining the experience for women, younger kids, and more vulnerable members of the audience, they put a stop to it immediately. Much like Fugazi was infamous for doing, At the Drive-In would shame people mid-song for stage diving, or stop playing until the aggressors left.

"I knew I was coming off like an uncool teacher, as Ian [Mac-Kaye] did when he had to call it out," says Bixler-Zavala. "But a lot of times, we had the aerial view. I'd see guys feeling up on girls, or assholes elbowing people, and that's what I wanted to stop." Sometimes he would ask politely, and other times he put his foot down when needed. His antiviolence stance sometimes came off as preachy or, for some scene newcomers, confusing. After all, here was a frontman so untamed that he would literally hang from the ceiling while simultaneously scolding the audience to "cut that shit out!" whenever their energy matched his. But it was the band's mission to rid their shows of the misogyny, homophobia, and macho bullshit that plagued the scene, and if that meant losing a few fans along the way, they were fine with that.

A handful of awkward incidents aside, tall tales of At the Drive-In's performances were drawing more and more people curious to see the southwestern quintet. The band wasn't getting much press outside of praise from the internet's notorious tastemakers *Buddyhead,* so they had to stay on the road to draw fans in. "Our records were not pushing people to our shows," says Ward. "Our shows were pushing people to the records."

Thousands of miles and many buckets of sweat went into selling the first thousand copies of *In/Casino/Out,* but gradually Fearless went through multiple pressings. "The record didn't come out and start off like gangbusters. It was a grind, a slow burn," Becker notes. But after a full year of touring, plus the release of a subsequent EP, *Vaya,* At the Drive-In became Fearless's most popular band, selling more than ten thousand records.

"Going from selling a few hundred records to ten thousand records in a year is great," says Ward. "When you hit that magic ten-thousand-record mark, all of a sudden people started calling. That means your shows in L.A. are now selling enough tickets that people at major labels were coming."

"The calls started coming in," says Becker. "I don't think they really even wanted to leave, but it was just getting bigger than Fearless. We couldn't fully compete with bigger labels. We were still a very small company."

Having grown up in an insular music scene that didn't concern itself much with punk politics, At the Drive-In didn't have many hangups about taking meetings with major labels. The way Bixler-Zavala saw it, the wider their reach was, the more their messages would resonate. "I always wondered what the hesitation was with major labels," he says. "Why not be able to walk into a Kmart and have your record there? Be a choice in that. Be the thorn in the side of society and let the weirdos take over."

Hajjar and Hinojos had been reared on thrash metal and weren't even familiar with punk's heated debates about selling out. "To them it was like, 'Yeah, give us that money so we can make a living,'" says Bixler-Zavala. But while the band had the attention of the majors, the majors didn't always have theirs.

"Omar used to have so much fun with that shit," Drake says. "He'd have a fake phone and he'd be fake-talking on the phone and then he'd dump it in a water glass. Everyone would be like, 'Whoa, what was *that* all about?'"

"You go on these orbits," says Ward. "You go to Reprise and then you go to Capitol and then you go to Warner, and someone gives you fifteen CDs and a free pair of Pumas, and then I felt like I had to wear the Pumas because they gave me them. You get into this shitty mentality where you take everything they give you, whether you want it or not. There was a point where [my girlfriend] said I couldn't take any more free shoes. I had so many pairs of shoes."

"The band didn't want to go to a major label," says Becker. "Those A&R guys can be stuffy sometimes, and didn't understand the band. The band was savvy enough to know that they could end up in a big, dark hole."

$ $ $

Like many tech startups of the nineties dot-com bubble, Digital Entertainment Network made a lot of cash and a lot of empty promises. Founded in 1998, the Santa Monica company had raked in a reported $58 million through investors that included music mogul David Geffen, movie director Bryan Singer, and former congressman Michael Huffington. "Executives from Disney and other major companies flocked to join the company. Digital Entertainment Network hired Hollywood directors and actors to create original programs for its Web site," the *Los Angeles Times* reported. "Advertisers including Ford and Pepsi eagerly plastered their logos on the DEN.net home page, and industry giants such as Microsoft invested millions of dollars."

DEN's objective was to lure young viewers away from television and onto the internet with original, youth-oriented digital video content. "It's a fusion of the marketing power of Madison Avenue with the technology of Silicon Valley and the entertainment of Hollywood," DEN's thirty-nine-year-old co-founder Marc Collins-Rector boasted in a promo video. How the company would actually turn a profit was anyone's guess.

The hot media company soon employed a staff of three hundred and produced a series of shows for the web, even though most American homes were using dial-up modems that lacked the bandwidth to stream long videos. The prospective audience, according to the *New York Times,* included "gay teen-agers, fraternity brothers, punk rockers and skateboarding 16-year-olds." *Fear of a Punk Planet,* a series produced by the Vandals bassist Joe Escalante, was a punk rock soap opera that featured cameos from NOFX, Sick of It All, and the Bouncing Souls. Another series, *Redemption High,* was a Christian high school drama that starred Judge Reinhold. The network's flagship series, *Chad's World,* centered around a teenage boy who moves to California to live in a mansion with his rich older brother and his boyfriend, played by Seann William Scott.

And, since young people listen to music, DEN also ventured into the record-label business with DEN Music Group. The imprint made high-profile hires with former Capitol Records president Gary Gersh and his business partner John Silva, who together owned G.A.S. Entertainment, an artist management company that represented Foo Fighters, Rancid, and Beastie Boys. The two reportedly received $600,000 annual salaries and million-dollar advances to come aboard at DEN. "The DEN Music Group will have promotion people and marketing people and A&R people and publicity people," Gersh told *Billboard*, assuring that the company would do everything traditional record labels did but with an increased focus on reaching online fans.

DEN Music Group had employees and funds and an abundance of slick tech-speak about things like "digital expansion" and "online footprints." They wielded everything traditional record labels did. Everything except for artists. In the hunt for their first signing, Gersh and Silva allegedly took the advice of Sonic Youth guitarist Thurston Moore, who tipped them off to At the Drive-In. "We got that Thurston Moore vote of approval, which I think was just a fucking lie," laughs Bixler-Zavala. But whether the connection was authentic or just label schmoozing, the band was still impressed with their résumés. "Gary and John had represented Nirvana. They managed the Beastie Boys. It was good company."

DEN was an unconventional home, and At the Drive-In was an unconventional band. They agreed to take a chance on the tech company, and in the fall of 1999, At the Drive-In became DEN Music Group's first signing. As a welcoming gift, the band was given digital cameras to document their lives on the road.

Shortly after signing the deal, the band agreed to tour with another act with an unpredictable live show, Les Savy Fav. At the Drive-In soon canceled, though, when an unexpected opportunity suddenly arose to do an arena tour supporting Rage Against the Machine—they had been personally handpicked by guitarist Tom Morello and vocalist Zack de la Rocha. "I didn't know Zack's hardcore history," says Bixler-Zavala. "I just knew that we showed up and he had a Los Crudos shirt on, so he knew what the fuck was up."

At the Drive-In would earn frequent musical comparisons to Rage, though they failed to see the similarities. Ideologically, though, the Texans seemed like a natural fit with the politically charged activists, who used their music as a weapon against American imperialism and capitalist greed. But the Rage shows would prove to be, by all accounts, brutal.

"Playing with Rage was one of the worst experiences of my life," says Ward. "Everyone in the front is there, one, for Rage and, two, to fucking murder each other. So when we came out and played, it was just shit being thrown at us and people flipping us off."

"That was the hardest audience to open up for. You gotta fight that audience," says Bixler-Zavala. "Moronically, DEN thought it would be a good idea to hand out our promotional CDs right before we played. So we got pelted with our own CDs, nonstop, and heard people yelling 'Faggot!' It got so bad that Tom Morello took it upon himself to announce us every night, in a tone that was like, 'Be cool, man!'"

During one performance, the band members felt the repeated sting of something hitting their backs and legs while they played. When they looked down, they saw nickels and pennies on the floor and realized the audience was pelting them with loose change. They tossed some of the coins back into the crowd, and a penny hit a girl in the eye, which would eventually lead her to threaten legal action against the band.

For Bixler-Zavala, the experience was a rude awakening about career growing pains: "It was like, 'Oh, so this is what happens when you get more popular?'"

$ $ $

Ross Robinson likens his process of recording studio albums to capturing ghosts. "There's a life-form that gets created through the members of a band—a pulse that happens and it creates this vibe," the producer explains. "It's a deeply spiritual process for me. We're chasing the only thing that's real."

Throughout the nineties, the ghosts Robinson had been capturing primarily belonged to a new breed of hard rock acts. His work behind the boards made mega-sellers out of debut albums from newcomers like Korn, Slipknot, Soulfly, and Limp Bizkit. Their downtuned, chugging guitars, combined with their coarse lyrics, birthed a new genre to which Robinson's name was inextricably bound, leading him to be known within the industry as the Godfather of Nu-Metal.

The nu-metal craze swept the country during the late nineties, providing the youth of the nation with an outlet for their suburban rage. And for his work igniting this international phenomenon, Robinson was rewarded with a number of gold and platinum records, which helped him land a lucrative deal with the hard rock label Roadrunner Records. When his contract with Roadrunner expired at the end of the nineties, Robinson shopped himself around to new labels. Although he'd found success within nu-metal, he was eager to move on to the next chapter. "I just wanted to rip into a new world and leave my past behind," he says.

In October 1999, Robinson visited the Santa Monica office of Digital Entertainment Network to meet with A&R rep Craig Aaronson about the possibility of working with some of his clients. Aaronson had recently come from Capitol Records, where he'd signed the teenaged Jimmy Eat World for the release of their 1996 album *Static Prevails*.

"I was in this meeting with Craig Aaronson and he asked, 'So what are you looking to do next?'" Robinson remembers. "I heard an echo of something from around two corners, from an office in the distance. I couldn't even hear a song, it was just an echo. And I said, 'That! *That's* what I want to do.'" What Robinson was hearing was DEN's first signing, At the Drive-In. Even from this faint whisper, Robinson could hear the future.

"Craig had just signed them. He was so excited," remembers Robinson. "He said, 'We'll fly you to their next show! They're in San Francisco. We'll get you on a flight and you'll be there the day after tomorrow!'"

Two days later, Robinson was at the Bottom of the Hill, where the band was opening for the Get Up Kids. Robinson, like many in the audience, wasn't sure what to make of At the Drive-In when they took the stage. Their frontman looked like he'd stepped out of a seventies after-school special, with his tight pants and shirt featuring the face of fitness expert Richard Simmons. "Bixler spent much of the show airborne, and even more time on his knees," *MTV News* wrote of the show. "He also hung from a ceiling beam, kicked at the wall and gesticulated at every chance, working up more of a sweat than the workout guru on his T-shirt probably ever did."

The band's energy radiated from the stage and made the entire room feel like a sauna. There was moisture on Robinson's face, but it wasn't entirely perspiration; it was from tears. "I started crying as I watched them," he recalls. "It was this amazing feeling of seeing something brand-new. They didn't play anything correctly, which I loved. I love violent music, and yet it was so emotional and sweet and sensitive. It was 'Fuck you' and 'I love you' at the same time."

After being blown away for forty-five chaotic minutes, Robinson went backstage to meet the band, worried that his nu-metal pedigree would put him at odds with their punk sensibilities. "That whole scene was so gnarly about outsiders. I was like, 'I need you guys to destroy everything I've ever done in my past,'" he laughs. And indeed, the members of At the Drive-In cringed at just about every band Robinson had worked with. But what the producer lacked in punk cred he made up for in shameless fanboy appreciation of their performance.

Robinson says, "I remember telling Omar, 'Whatever you do, never, ever let anybody tell you how to play your guitar. Just do exactly what you do, and that's all you ever have to know.' That was the first thing I ever said to him."

At the Drive-In was already set to return to work with Alex Newport and didn't have much use for Robinson. "I didn't want to work with Ross, but he kept hammering it and hammering it. He'd show up at shows and help us break down," says Bixler-Zavala. Robinson went so far as to book complimentary studio time, just so they could try him on for size. They recorded a song together, "Catacombs," a challenging audition that smashed together meandering spoken-word sections with extended full-volume screams.

"We did one song in Steely Dan's studio in New York," says Robinson. "I had this amazing analog keyboard I brought in from L.A. They fell in love with it. I told them, 'If you let me do your record, I will give you this keyboard!'"

The bribe would prove unnecessary, though. Much to their surprise, the band loved Robinson's rendition of their sound. "Catacombs" was the closest a producer had ever come to capturing At the Drive-In's live energy, and it earned him the gig. "We made a big change that day, and tasked Tony with the awful job of informing Alex that we were gonna go with Ross," says Bixler-Zavala. They soon made plans to record their first album for DEN, *Relationship of Command,* at Indigo Ranch Studios, in Malibu, where Robinson had done much of his previous work.

Over seven weeks at the start of 2001, Robinson chased the same evocative power of At the Drive-In that had brought him to tears in San Francisco. The producer had a reputation for taking extreme and unorthodox measures to provoke players into giving their most emotional performances—kicking trash cans or shoving musicians until he got the energy he sought.

"I would throw people into the 4Runner and turn 'Meowy Christmas' on full blast and do donuts in the lot," Robinson laughs. "Anything to turn the brain off, just to make it crazy and radical and unpredictable."

Robinson was especially tough on drummers, and once threw a flowerpot at Slipknot drummer Joey Jordison. When he noticed Hajjar kept a photo of his deceased mother by his drum kit, he encouraged him to think of the rhythm of the bass drum as the beat of her heart. The inspirational tactic crossed a personal line, though, and only irritated the drummer. Robinson pushed a frustrated Hajjar to his breaking point over the long weeks and then insisted that the drum tracks all be re-recorded. Robinson also admits to letting the dissolution of a romantic relationship at the time taint his attitude at work.

"Tony's fire and his red-hot Middle Eastern blood are just fucking gold. His value is priceless. I just wasn't mature enough to guide him," the producer concedes. "He was frustrated. I was frustrated. I wasn't the best with him."

Hajjar later told *MOJO* magazine about running into Robinson at their first show after recording, where Robinson apologized. "I broke down in tears," said Hajjar. "I told him that day, 'I better never fucking see you again.'"

"It kind of drove some people to not want to be in the studio anymore," says Bixler-Zavala, who was surprised to find that he actually enjoyed Robinson's wrestling-coach motivation. "He was up in my face and throwing shit at me and wanted to re-create what we were like live. Though there were times where I was like, 'All right, let's just record the fucking song, Ross. I'm tired of this Method acting shit.'"

Robinson also landed an impressive cameo for the album, rock legend Iggy Pop, who spent a day at Indigo with the band, laying down backup vocals for "Rolodex Propaganda." The Stooges frontman and Bixler-Zavala were situated to face each other as they sang. "I wanted them to see each other and go head to head," Robinson says. "To me it was like the ultimate with the ultimate." As the two famously unhinged frontmen went back and forth on their microphones, it was like a punk torch was being passed down through generations.

Despite all of the strife that went into *Relationship of Command,* or perhaps because of it, Robinson accomplished the impossible. He was able to hone At the Drive-In's complex identity into eleven tracks, striking a perfect balance between the band as a fiery unit and the sum of five contrasting personalities.

As with most subjects, opinions about the final result were divided among the band members. They were especially torn on the album's mix by engineer Andy Wallace, who'd mixed Nirvana's *Nevermind,* Bad Religion's *Stranger Than Fiction,* and Rage Against the Machine's debut album. Rodríguez-López would later gripe that Wallace's mix was his least favorite aspect of the record, calling the finished product "passive" and "plastic." A decade after *Relationship of Command'*s release, he would still be hung up on it, telling *Alternative Press,* "One of my only regrets out of anything I've ever done is the way that record was mixed. That record was ruined by the mix."

Conversely, Ward loved Wallace's take on their sonic identity. "When we mixed with Andy, he asked how we wanted the record to sound," he says. "I remember somebody saying, 'I want it to sound like a teddy bear getting hit by a freight train.' We had no other way to express how we just wanted to sonically assault the listener. And he was just like, 'Yeah, okay, no problem.'"

$ $ $

While At the Drive-In was busy capturing the ghost of *Relationship of Command* at Indigo Ranch, the company that was set to release it was haunted by scandal. Digital Entertainment Network had been set to launch an initial public stock offering expected to be worth $75 million, but plans were abandoned when its co-founder made headlines.

"Digital Entertainment Network—known as DEN—filed to sell shares to the public in September but chairman and founder Marc Collins-Rector hastily resigned a month later after settling a civil suit alleging he sexually abused a 13-year-old boy," the *New York Post* reported on February 11.

A front-page story in the *Los Angeles Times* would soon expose DEN's seedy underbelly. Collins-Rector's Encino mansion had served as something of a harem for him and his associates, who hosted late-night parties there with underage male employees. The scandal would unfold over the next few years and grow more disturbing as details surfaced. Collins-Rector was hit with a number of lawsuits from minors who claimed they were bullied, drugged, and coerced at gunpoint into performing sex acts. *Radar* reported that amidst the influx of lawsuits, he suddenly disappeared with what remained of his fortune, turning up two years later in a villa in Spain, where he was "arrested by local authorities, who uncovered 'an enormous collection of child porn,' according to Spanish police reports."

In an effort to salvage the tailspinning company, Gersh took over as chairman and gutted the place. "Gersh fired more than 100 workers, closed one of DEN's offices in Santa Monica, and halted production of new shows," the *Los Angeles Times* reported. DEN Music Group was also on the chopping block, but Gersh found a way to save its artists. He quickly brokered a partnership between his management company and Grand Royal, the record label run by his client Mike Diamond, of the Beastie Boys, wherein the label would absorb his DEN signings, which included At the Drive-In,

Scapegoat Wax, Bran Van 3000, and rapcore band Gangsta Bitch Barbie.

"We were in the middle of recording *Relationship of Command* and they told us, 'Good news, bad news: DEN folded, but now you're on Grand Royal,'" remembers Bixler-Zavala. For a Beastie Boys fan who had grown up on the hip-hop trio's 1989 album *Paul's Boutique*, the move was a blessing in disguise.

Diamond had launched Grand Royal in 1992 and amassed an impressive roster that included Luscious Jackson, Ben Lee, and Sean Lennon. While still carrying the hip vibe of a boutique indie label, the Beastie Boys association helped Grand Royal land a distribution deal with a major label, first with Capitol Records and later, thanks to Gersh and Silva, with EMI's Virgin Records. With their corporate backing, Grand Royal was able to get their releases into chain stores and provide international marketing. "It was a punk-rooted indie label with the power of a major behind it," says Kenny "Tick" Salcido, who served as Diamond's right-hand man.

Salcido recalls the first time he and Diamond saw At the Drive-In perform, at the Troubadour, in West Hollywood. While waiting in line, they ran into Rage's Tom Morello, who sang their praises. "Tom Morello said, 'Have you seen the band? They're fucking amazing!'" remembers Salcido. "We go inside, and I'm not a snob or an elitist, but I did work for the coolest band in the world, the Beastie Boys, so my bar was inexcusably high. The five of them got onstage and put on one of the best shows I'd ever seen in my life. I was in shock. Both of us were. We were just floored." Diamond was especially enamored with Rodríguez-López, whom he bonded with later that night over their vegetarian diets.

"That show was important for Mike. He needed to see it to get behind it," says Salcido. "That night, Mike bought in, and he bought in big. He got involved in all aspects of the band after that. He felt so invested. He was obsessed with them." Diamond even filmed a promo video in which he played a bigwig record executive who leaned against the marble desk in his high-rise office lined with gold records and pitched viewers on his label's "fine, upstanding, and dynamic young combo" At the Drive-In.

Diamond's passion trickled down until every employee at Grand Royal was under the spell of At the Drive-In. "In all my years in the industry, I've never seen a band where everyone was all in. Everyone in the building was a fan of them. We were geeks for these guys," says Salcido. "Mike D. was telling everyone he knew about them. Gary Gersh and John Silva were calling radio stations—personally calling all their contacts—saying, 'This is the greatest band in the world.'"

"They had this PR guy Steve Martin, who was in the band Agnostic Front," says Drake. "If he was your PR guy, you were gonna be on *Saturday Night Live.*"

Grand Royal's president, Mark Kates, who had brought Jawbreaker to DGC for the release of *Dear You,* was also fully invested, throwing money and resources at the record because, he says, "there was no question that At the Drive-In was poised for global success."

An advance copy of *Relationship of Command* was on constant rotation in the Grand Royal offices, and staff members were so confident in it that they were gloating to the press. "The emotion is so honest, so open, that you can't help be sucked into it," director of marketing Kristen Welsh bragged to *Billboard* a week before its release. "This band can save rock."

$ $ $

Relationship of Command's yellow cover featured a drawing of a Trojan horse, and the metaphor for At the Drive-In infiltrating the mainstream with their punk ethos would not be lost on reviewers. *Guitar World* called it "an apt image to adorn their own tool of subversion."

Upon its release, on September 12, 2000, *Relationship* was immediately flooded with more press than the band had received in the entirety of their first six years together, and it was overwhelmingly glowing. Almost overnight, At the Drive-In became music journalists' favorite act to heap praise upon. The band's stage swagger earned them frequent comparisons to venerated punk pioneers like Fugazi and Nation of Ulysses, and their battering-ram career momentum occasionally got them hailed as the next Nirvana. Afro jokes continued to pepper the praise as well, with *SPIN* likening their style to a mix of MC5 and *Welcome Back, Kotter.*

CMJ declared *Relationship* its number one album of 2000, beating out releases from veteran hip-hop trio De La Soul and Icelandic icon Björk. "I think *Relationship of Command* was so universally lauded by music critics because it was simultaneously like everything and nothing you'd heard before," says *CMJ*'s former Loud Rock editor Amy Sciarretto. "They proved heavy music could have a heart and didn't have to be meatheaded."

Rock snobs suffering from nu-metal fatigue were particularly fond of the band. "Frankly, it's a relief and a joy, in this rap-metal year, to hear a young rock & roll frontman actually sing," wrote *Rolling Stone*'s David Fricke. Similarly, *Village Voice* critic Robert Christgau gave *Relationship* an A-minus, noting that "in a bad time for young guitar bands, including many barely forgettable ones lumped under the trade name 'emo,' these ambitious yowlers are reason for hope."

British press had gotten a taste of the Texans and were especially laudatory, with positive coverage in the pages of *Melody Maker, Q,* and *Uncut,* who predicted that At the Drive-In "might well prove to be one of the most important discoveries of the last five years." *Kerrang!* deemed *Relationship* its number two album of the year, behind only Queens of the Stone Age's *Rated R. NME* put the band on the cover of the magazine, above the words "Brothers and sisters, are you ready for At the Drive-In, the best new rock band on Earth?"

The album's breakneck single, "One Armed Scissor," lit up college radio and hit number 26 on the Billboard Alternative Songs chart, with its concert-footage-heavy music video earning regular MTV rotation. The band also cut through the late-night talk show circuit, literally bouncing off the walls in instantly legendary performances on *Conan* and *Letterman.* They brought the same intensity overseas for a performance on *Later . . . with Jools Holland.* During their performance, Bixler-Zavala flung a chair across the room, to the bemusement of the British studio audience, which included pop bad boy Robbie Williams, who watched in dumbfounded amusement. When their song ended, the camera panned to Williams, who asked, "Can me mate have his chair back, please?"

Everything was happening so fast for At the Drive-in, and after a while they became powerless to slow things down as pressure took its toll on them. "They tried to be Fugazi on a major label. They were saying no to everything. There was always this clash," says Drake. Promotional radio station gigs, photo shoots, and interviews became a source of contention as the obligations began overloading their travel schedule. "I remember Mike D. had to come in to convince them to do some things they didn't want to do. They never wanted to do press, because the press would always only want to talk to Omar and Cedric."

"The year 2000 was easily the craziest year of my professional life," Ward says. "It started in January in Malibu, making that record, and I think I was only home for three weeks that year. So forty-nine weeks of touring or recording, and in the process, the record came out, it was blowing up, we were on the cover of every weekly in every city we went to, plus *NME* and all this stuff. That fucks with a twenty-four-year-old. And then pour a gallon of vodka in them a day and give them all the drugs they want? How are you supposed to hold it together?"

Drugs had long been a recreational element of At the Drive-In, but as stress mounted, they became a reliable way for some members to numb the pains of consecutive shows that were both physically and emotionally draining. Rumors of the members using crack and heroin circulated, and although Bixler-Zavala maintains that rumors of their drug use were largely exaggerated or complete fabrications, he does acknowledge that substances like weed, pills, and alcohol provided an escape. "At the time, we knew this kid in El Paso," he says, "and this is a shitty thing to admit, but he had cancer and knew he didn't have much time, so he had saved a gigantic stash of stuff. He traded it to us for merch or money. We had this stuff we didn't know what to do with, stuff you shouldn't be toying around with. I didn't remember any of the shows. I just wanted a break. There were no days off, and that's why I'd indulge in that kind of stuff."

The band spent October and November on the road, headlining over a cycling lineup of openers that included the Murder City Devils, the (International) Noise Conspiracy, and Cursive. Considering how fatigued and medicated they were, At the Drive-In still set an unrealistically high bar for every band they shared a stage with.

"The consensus among my group of music friends is that they are probably the best live band that ever played," says Cursive frontman Tim Kasher. "It was so much more visceral than anything else out there. There was an explosive nature to the way they would all erupt together. The way they would play, it was almost like they were rushing the crowd."

"After the first night it was obvious that we needed to step up our game, and I have to say that our game was pretty good to begin with," says Noise Conspiracy frontman Dennis Lyxzén. "At the Drive-In had this really primal energy about them, wild and savage but at the same time suave and cool."

But as had happened with Nirvana—to whom At the Drive-In's meteoric rise earned them comparisons—the more fresh fans their MTV exposure brought them, the more uncomfortable they became with their rising stature. Their relationship with their audience became more tense and combative as moshing and crowd surfing grew more prevalent.

Bixler-Zavala opened the tour's Detroit show by addressing the men in the audience. "If you guys wanna do that karate-kicking shit, if you wanna beat the shit out of each other, please don't do it at our show," he said. "I think it's about twenty years into this so-called punk movement where we need to reinvent shit. Slam dancing and the bastardized term 'mosh,' it doesn't exist with us." A week later, at a show in Cursive's hometown of Omaha, he took additional preventive measures by instructing the venue to keep the house lights on as a deterrent, insisting, "Keep the lights up so I can see the assholes beating each other up."

The next night, while driving through Sterling, Colorado, the band's van skidded on black ice, flipped over, and landed on its roof. "I don't know how my toenails came off, because I used to wear two pairs of socks back then, but they did," says Bixler-Zavala. "I landed on my butt and, magically, my shoes were right next to me. I crawled out and it was like Narnia—just white everywhere. Ryder trucks were all over and the contents of people's homes were spilled on the highway. Cars were totaled. We cheated death."

He and Hajjar were taken to the emergency room and treated for injuries. "The next day, we drove past the van and it was all smashed in like Godzilla had stepped on it," Bixler-Zavala says. They rented a new van, canceled their show that evening in Salt Lake City, and were in desperate need of an extended break. But, not wanting to let down the opening bands who were depending on them, they immediately bounced back to rejoin the tour for its next date, in Seattle.

The frontman opened the show by dedicating the set to their dear departed van. "We shouldn't even be here right now," he told the crowd. "I'd like to thank whoever our guardian angels are for watching over us, because we should be dead."

$ $ $

On January 25, 2001, George W. Bush was settling into his first week in the White House while the members of At the Drive-In, a product of the state in which he'd served as governor, were sitting in a television studio on the other side of the world, lighting a picture of him on fire. As a fourth-generation Texan with a tattoo of the Lone Star State on his right bicep, Ward got to do the honor of flicking a lighter until the forty-third president was engulfed in flames.

The band was in Australia, the farthest they'd ever ventured from El Paso, appearing on the show *The Joint*. They were promoting their upcoming dates on the traveling festival Big Day Out, on which they were slotted into a diverse lineup of international acts that included everyone from Rammstein to the Black Eyed Peas. Before signing off, the show's host urged viewers to check out *Relationship of Command* and left them with a sage piece of advice: "If you go to Big Day Out tomorrow, drink lots of water. It's gonna be a hot one."

By the time the band was preparing to take the stage in Sydney the following afternoon, the temperature had risen to a steamy eighty-six degrees. The At the Drive-In faithful waited patiently in the heat for the band's set to begin, and a few recognizable faces lined the sides of the stage. Legend of the must-see band had drawn members of other acts, who stood shoulder to shoulder to claim a prime viewing spot for the much-rumored wild men. "Queens of the Stone Age, PJ Harvey, Coldplay, all these other bands were on the side of the stage, watching," remembers Drake. "They were *the band* to watch."

Meanwhile, on the conjoining stage, nu-metal rockers Mudvayne were whipping their crowd into a frenzy. Adorned in gigantic overalls, clown makeup, and a braided, blue goatee that hung down to his navel, singer Chad Gray and his monstrous growls soundtracked a violent sea of circle pitting. "Put your fucking hands up in the goddamn air!" he snarled. "We are Mudvayne. Welcome to our fucked-up worrrrrld!"

As soon as Mudvayne's musical assault ended, a horde of their fans came stampeding to At the Drive-In's stage, looking for the next outlet to unleash their adrenaline. "I remember watching all the kids you'd expect to see at an indie rock show up front—all our little people with fucked-up hair and skinny bodies—then there was just this wave, this infestation of bros. I don't know any other way to put it," says Ward.

"Our audience was nerdy riot grrrls and the meek," says Bixler-Zavala. "The Mudvayne audience was nu-metal facepainters. That was the landslide of people who rushed over to our set. I saw them ruining everything. I started seeing people getting crushed and hurt. I literally saw people boogie-boarding on top of each other."

Bixler-Zavala began the set with a warning: "Just be nice to each other. Let's dance rather than beat the shit out of each other." He shook a pair of maracas to begin "Arcarsenal" while Rodríguez-López channeled the energy of his salsa-dancing father, hula-hooping his guitar around his torso while his Converse sneakers hopscotched across the sprawling stage. The song exploded and Bixler-Zavala threw his microphone stand ten feet up in the air, caught it, and spun around like James Brown. The row of famous musicians that lined the side of the stage looked on with their mouths agape.

If there was any question as to whether or not At the Drive-In had what it took to make the jump from small clubs to expansive festival stages, they answered it within the first sixty seconds. The members used every square inch of their new playground, as though the massive platform was where they'd always belonged. Bixler-Zavala somersaulted from end to end, performed handstands on the drum riser, leaped off Hajjar's bass drum, and was dancing before his feet even hit the floor. Even the cool-tempered axman Ward swung his guitar above his head like a tomahawk.

Midway through their second song, though, Ward looked into the audience and noticed the wincing faces of fans who were not having a good time. Aggressive moshers and crowd surfers had overtaken the space and were crushing the people up front. During the song's bass solo, while Bixler-Zavala was doing a flying push-up, Ward pleaded into the mic, "Could you guys stop crowd surfing, *please*? You're fucking hurting 'em!"

Then, after they played "Cosmonaut," the audience vibe turned even more malicious. "By the third song it was like watching people get pummeled," says Ward. "Nobody gave a shit. The people didn't stop. That was their mentality: 'We go to a show to pummel each other and this is fun.'"

When the song ended, Bixler-Zavala went on a tirade: "I think it's a very, very sad day when the only way you can express yourself is through slam dancing. Are you all typically white people? Y'all look like it to me. Look at that," he said, pointing to a crowd surfer who was saluting him with devil horns. "You learned that from the TV. You didn't learn that from your best friend. You're a robot, you're a sheep." He started bleating at them. *Baahhh, baahhh, baahhh*.

Finally, the band had seen enough. They unplugged after only three songs, stormed offstage, and left a bewildered crowd booing and flipping them off. "The amount of shit that was thrown onstage was really bad," says Drake.

The guys sulked back to their trailer, where they were chewed out by the festival's promoter for acting unprofessionally. "They said, 'This is your fault for not letting us do lights!'" Bixler-Zavala recalls. "I was like, 'A fucking light show is not gonna make people less violent!'"

"Everybody got in the little golf carts to go to the dressing room, but I walked," remembers Ward. "Between the stage and the dressing room, I decided what I was gonna major in in college. I thought: 'I'm fucking done. We're over. This is totally out of control. This is impossible to do. There's no way we can survive in this setting.'"

Later that night, Limp Bizkit walked onto Big Day Out's main stage in front of an endless ocean of people. An estimated fifty-five thousand attendees had gathered for their set, many circle-pitting and charging at each other before a note was even played. Immediately after the first song, the festival's security team was frantically rescuing people who were being crushed up front. "I told you before we came," frontman Fred Durst boasted, "I said, 'Put Limp Bizkit and sixty thousand Aussies in one place and this motherfucker is gonna go crazy.'"

Durst kept urging the crowd to take a step back and pick up anyone who had fallen, but he was losing to the pandemonium. Security guards apparently tried motioning to the frontman to stop altogether, but something was lost in translation. "What did you say, you punk motherfucker?" Durst told them. "What did that big faggot beside you say—that big punk right there?"

Dozens of security guards and medics waded into the front of the crowd, pulling limp bodies out and carrying them to safety. "Minutes later, the St. John Ambulance treatment area would look like a war zone," *The Advertiser* reported. Six hundred people received medical attention, mostly for dehydration, and six were hospitalized. One of the trampled bodies belonged to sixteen-year-old Jessica Michalik, who suffered a heart attack and asphyxiation. She was loaded into an ambulance, rushed to Concord Hospital, and put on life support.

The next morning, tabloids picked up the story of Big Day Out's fiasco and pitted Limp Bizkit and the festival against each other. The band claimed that their booking agent had insisted that a T-barricade be used as a safety precaution to break up the massive crowd and was ignored, while festival promoters accused the band of not cooperating with security personnel.

Limp Bizkit canceled their remaining Australian dates, boarded a plane, and returned to the United States, but At the Drive-In soldiered on to Melbourne, where they took the stage on a somber note. Ward opened their set by telling the crowd, "Some pretty bad shit happened in Sydney, not just for us but for a young woman who will probably never be the same." He asked for a minute of silence for Michalik, who was 450 miles away, hanging on for her life. Four days later, she was taken off life support and died in her hospital bed.

The black cloud hanging over At the Drive-In turned even darker after that. Following their stretch in Australia (which itself had followed a stretch in Japan), they headed to Europe for a grueling three-week run that included five German shows. "We did a tour in Germany and they used this really punk rock booking agent, Dolph," remembers Drake. "Dolph booked them on this tour where there were twice as many people outside than inside the venues. Every night was like this. It was really horrible. It was problems all the time—problems with the crowd coming to the shows with Afro wigs on, problems with people slam dancing, which pissed Cedric off. It was really tense."

The band had splurged on a bus instead of a van so they could slot more rest into their taxing schedules, but the luxury put them at odds with their staunchly punk European fans. "Somebody put two-by-fours with nails on them under our bus in Germany," remembers Ward. "To me, that was the most obvious way of saying, 'Who the fuck do you think you are, showing up in a tour bus?'"

"There were notes on our bus that said, WHERE'S THE ANARCHY NOW?" remembers Bixler-Zavala.

On their final German date, where they played to fourteen hundred rabid fans in Bremen, the crowd surfing started early. By the second song, the band was already fed up. Rodríguez-López took his guitar off and threw it to the floor in frustration while Bixler-Zavala reached into the audience and tried to yank a crowd surfer onstage by the arms. "Look, we will play no more fucking songs if you guys aren't gonna cooperate with us! This is why we turned into fucking assholes," he told the uncomfortable room. "Two years of this kind of bullshit, man. And people wonder why we act like jerks. Is it any wonder?"

The following night, February 21, At the Drive-In played at Vera, a venue in Groningen, Netherlands, and the band was running on the last drop of gas in their tank. "I remember looking over and seeing Omar just hitting the strings. Not fretting, just hitting the strings and standing there," says Ward. "It was heartbreaking."

Shikari, the Dutch screamo band that opened the show, later described it on their website as "a big circus. Professional photographers, reporters, camera/television/radio teams everywhere." Their recap read, "At the Drive-In plays pretty bad and, due to frustration, their guitarist smashes his guitar into the back wall. They leave the stage ranting and cursing and quickly disappear in the backstage, literally slamming the door shut in the media's face!"

"We used to have a rule—a six-month emergency button. When you hit that button, it meant—no questions asked—we're done for six months," says Ward. "We had built this into our ideology. That night, I remember everyone saying we had to push the button." Realizing At the Drive-In was hanging on by a thread, the guys canceled their remaining five shows in Europe. Drake hugged them as they parted and pleaded, "Go home and save your band."

"We took a picture of us all together," remembers Bixler-Zavala, "and we were like, 'This is the last one.'"

A week later, Ward attended the Brit Awards in London. Backstage, he spotted members of U2, who were scheduled to be presented with the Outstanding Contribution to Music Award by Oasis's Noel Gallagher. Ward tracked frontman Bono, waiting for his moment to approach. When Bono's handlers were distracted, Ward swooped in and tapped him on the shoulder.

"I pulled Bono aside at the rehearsal and I was like, 'I know you know who my band is, because I saw you talk about us on MTV.' I was crying. I was like, 'Everything is so fucked up. I don't know what to do,'" remembers Ward. Through tears, he looked behind Bono's blue sunglasses and into his eyes and told him about Big Day Out and all the stress that fame had brought them. He told him about the crowd surfing and the internal tension and pushing the emergency button. "He talked to me for twenty minutes while all these people were telling him he had to go. He told me, 'Look, I remember being there when the crowd was going crazy and not knowing how to handle it. You'll get through it. You'll find a way. Don't quit. Just give it time. All of us go through this.' This was the biggest guy in the world to me, telling me I'd be all right."

Everything wouldn't be all right, though. When Ward returned to the States, he started coughing up blood. He told a doctor that he was drinking a bottle of vodka a day on top of smoking a pack and a half of cigarettes, and often went days without much food or sleep. "The doctor was like, 'Well, yeah, that's what's wrong with you. You're dying inside. If you don't stop that, something bad will happen,'" he says.

Ward and his girlfriend were set to be wed a week later, and by that point At the Drive-In was caving in too fast for it to be saved. "It was a wildfire. It was already gone," he says. "I got married and the next day Cedric left the band. And that was that. I remember being relieved, honestly."

On March 27, just six months after the release of *Relationship of Command,* the band posted an update on their website, announcing that they were "going on an indefinite hiatus." Rodríguez-López said in a statement, "We need time to rest up and re-evaluate . . . just to be human beings again and to decide when we feel like playing music again."

The decision was met with resistance from the band's management and label, who begged them not to derail their red-hot momentum. Album sales were finally beginning to catch up to all of the hype and glowing praise the band had racked up. *Relationship* was selling ten thousand copies a week, the influential L.A. radio station KROQ was on board to give their next single, "Invalid Litter Dept.," a heavy push, and dates were already booked at two-thousand-cap venues for their next European tour.

But for the members of At the Drive-In, it came down to a simple choice: Kill the band or it would kill them first. "I could easily have seen someone dying. I don't think that's an exaggeration," says Ward. "It was a pressure cooker."

$ $ $

In the months following At the Drive-In's implosion, a clear rift between the members developed publicly. The structure and the spectacle had parted ways. By the end of 2001, Bixler-Zavala and Rodríguez-López had splintered off to form a new group together, the Mars Volta, which indulged the duo's penchant for spacey, psychedelic jamming. Meanwhile, Ward, Hinojos, and Hajjar launched the more straightforward rock outfit Sparta. Ward says their At the Drive-In connection made it "stupid easy" to get big-money offers from record labels. They signed with DreamWorks Records for the release of their 2002 debut, *Wiretap Scars.*

While both bands were well received and enjoyed their own respective successes, separating the members was like splitting apart a rainbow for its individual colors. The two groups had their own distinct charms but lacked the volatile chemistry that had made At the Drive-In a uniquely explosive powerhouse.

As their six-month rule approached its expiration, the chances of At the Drive-In ending their hiatus seemed less likely as it became evident that the two factions were not on good terms, and were perhaps even competitive against each other. In an interview with *Harp,* Bixler-Zavala recalled a night when Ward showed up intoxicated to a Mars Volta show at the Bottom of the Hill and laid into Rodríguez-López and his penchant for destructive offstage habits: "He was like, 'Yeah, that's cool, you guys go ahead and make your own band. That'll go really far. Yeah, you and Cedric, the responsible guys.'"

Ward's harsh words were like a bucket of cold water on his former bandmate, who realized he needed to drop the heavy drug use and take his music seriously. "I got sober that day," Rodríguez-López told *MOJO.* "I couldn't run the Mars Volta while I was still partying. It was like a challenge."

Not only did At the Drive-In leave behind a wake of disappointed fans, but their collapse created a sinkhole that dragged its surroundings down with it. At the end of August, Grand Royal announced that the label would be ceasing operations, citing "mounting debts, decreasing assets and exceedingly harsh industry conditions." The company would soon file for bankruptcy and auction off its assets online. The *New York Times* noted, "Initially, it looked like At the Drive-In might buoy the label. When Grand Royal released 'Relationship of Command' in 2000, the album sold well and landed on many critics' lists as one of the year's best. But the band unexpectedly broke up in March 2001."

It was a loss for the scene that had birthed them as well. The critical-darling band was on the verge of ushering their post-hardcore peers into the mainstream. But after their demise, tastemakers who had heralded them as rock's saviors promptly moved on to a new breed of tamer indie rock acts that included the Strokes and the White Stripes. While this era of rock's "rebirth" would reach greater heights of commercial success, not even its most celebrated bands could hold a candle to the sheer unbridled mayhem of their southwestern predecessors.

At the Drive-In was a force that shot out of a small corner of Texas like a rocket. For six years, they grinded their way around the globe to play for anyone who would watch them. It was only in their last six months together that the rest of the world caught up long enough to get a fleeting glimpse. But in the end, the velocity, the attention, and the intense pressure of it all rendered them too unstable to last. They hit a brick wall at a thousand miles per hour and left behind a spectacular explosion.

"Maybe it was always supposed to be that way," says Ward. "It was just like the live show: it was chaos for forty-five minutes, and then it was over."

CHAPTER 6

THE DONNAS

Spend the Night

Atlantic Records (2002)

THE DAY AFTER a talent show at David Starr Jordan Middle School in May of 1993, Brett Anderson's classmates started pulling her aside in the hall. "Don't tell anyone," they'd whisper, "but your band was actually my favorite." Her rock band, Screen, had performed in the battle-of-the-bands-style show and, although the thirteen-year-old was proud of their short set, in which she and three other girls ripped through covers of songs by L7, Shonen Knife, and the Muffs, the student body seemed more interested in Verbal Constipation, a singerless band of boys who played a fine, albeit predictable, instrumental cover of Nirvana's "Smells Like Teen Spirit." It was only in furtive murmurs that Screen received any compliments. "Like, what the hell?" Anderson recalls. "Don't tell me you *secretly* liked us! But that was just the climate in 1993."

Anderson had started Screen with three friends and fellow eighth graders—guitarist Allison Robertson, bassist Maya Ford, and drummer Torry Castellano. The four had learned to play music together by covering the songs of their favorite bands, like R.E.M., Faith No

More, and Sonic Youth. They gave themselves the name Screen because, she says, "it was a name no one could make fun of. If people said it was dumb for one reason, we could just say it meant something else."

By the time they entered their freshman year at Palo Alto High School that September, Screen had changed their name to Ragady Anne and were practicing regularly in Castellano's garage, where neighborhood boys would occasionally pass by to tease them about their cheap guitars and handed-down drum kit. Ragady Anne wrote a bunch of fierce songs in which they railed against these annoying boys as well as the evils of vapid Valley girls and fake feminists. Their demo recordings sounded as if they'd been captured in a pet shop, with Anderson barking, screeching, and squealing her way through them with an adolescent ferocity. Meanwhile, the rest of the band used speed to gloss over the weak spots in their still-developing musical chops. "It was just a mishmash of everything we were listening to," Castellano says of their style, "and we liked making everything faster, because then it sounded tighter."

Ragady Anne began playing shows around town at community centers, where they got a taste of how unwelcoming the music scene would be to an all-girl band. "From the moment we started, there was a lot of shit that was thrown our way about being girls in a band. It happened right off the bat and it never stopped," Castellano says. "Even when we were playing our very first shows in ninth grade at a community center, you had to go to a meeting beforehand to show that you were gonna show up to play the show. We were the only girls, and the boys wouldn't even sit at the same table as us. They literally said they didn't want to play the same night as us. It was that explicit."

Occasionally the girls would open their lockers at the end of the school day to find insulting notes from male classmates stuffed into them. The misogyny in the messages was so on the nose that it was hard to tell if their authors were being sincere or satirizing the stereotype that girls couldn't play rock music. Either way, the girls found them comical enough to stick a particularly mean one in the liner notes of Ragady Anne's first seven-inch: "Hey Allison—Stupid little bitches like you shouldn't write or play guitar 'cause you suk at both!"

But while their male peers continued to mock them, Ragady Anne amassed a small fan base of local girls their age. "They played a show I put on and all these kids showed up, all these little high school freshmen and eighth graders," says Mark Weiss, who booked shows around Palo Alto, California. "Most of the other shows were people in their twenties and thirties, but a hundred kids from Palo Alto High School or the junior high would show up for them. They were sort of a word-of-mouth phenomenon."

It wasn't just the size of the band's fan base that was impressive, but its dedication. Weiss says he later booked a young Blink-182 in the same community center, but Ragady Anne's audience was noticeably more passionate. "Blink's crowd was probably the same size —about 150 people—but the energy these ladies had, and the bond they had with their audience, was incredible," he remembers.

Sometime after freshman year, Ragady Anne changed their name again, this time to the Electrocutes. "We got made fun of a lot," says Castellano. "We were called the Ragadies by guys in bands, so we were trying to get away from that. Plus, our sound was changing. We just felt like we needed a change." With the Electrocutes, the four maintained their primitive, tantrum-pitch approach to thrashy rock music but also started leaning into their other musical love: heavy metal, a genre that had inspired the members' musical awakenings in the eighties. Castellano even paid homage to Metallica in her yearbook entry, writing, "METAL UP YOUR ASS MO'FO'!"

The Electrocutes eventually began venturing out of the comfort of Palo Alto, taking gig opportunities thirty minutes north in the Bay Area, at clubs like the Chameleon, Gilman Street, and Bottom of the Hill. Being too young to drive, they relied on rides from their parents, who would drop them off and wait outside the venues until the show was over. "We didn't want them to come in," Anderson says. "Sometimes they'd come in wearing hoodies and hang out in the back. That's not really a disguise! People know it's you! We were a little bit embarrassed, but we also liked our parents for the most part."

But even in the Bay Area, which prided itself on its diverse and communal music scene, the Electrocutes didn't feel embraced, whether because of their age, their gender, or their zip code. "I think, because we were from Palo Alto, we were seen as bridge-and-tunneling it in," Anderson says, "and there's a truth to that."

The more indifference or hostility the girls faced from the scenes they inhabited, though, the more it pushed them closer together and strengthened them as a unit. "We got made fun of a lot, so we became insular and moved as a group at all times," says Castellano. "We always thought of ourselves as a gang, like it was us against the world."

$ $ $

In their sophomore year, the Electrocutes shared the stage with a surfy garage rock band called Car Thieves at Harry's Hofbrau, a German beer hall and restaurant in Oakland. Car Thieves had just released a seven-inch entitled *Everybody's Going Ape!* and, in full commitment to the bit, the members performed while wearing gorilla costumes.

Car Thieves belonged to a collective of bands that were part of Radio X and Super*Teem!, two small indie labels both run by a prolific twenty-nine-year-old musician named Darin Raffaelli. The labels' acts were all cut from the same cloth, united by their dedication to a retro, lo-fi sound. The bands all had distinct, kitschy personalities, which Raffaelli often helped craft and direct—not necessarily joke bands, but not fully sincere, either. As Anderson puts it, "All of the bands could have had action figures." In addition to Raffaelli's own act, Supercharger, there was also the Vulcaneers, five men seemingly playing both the bully and geek roles in *Revenge of the Nerds,* with songs that were about *Star Trek* but named after frat houses. There were also the Bobbyteens, whose members often dressed like a 1950s motorcycle gang, custom matching jackets and all.

Raffaelli had been kicking around an idea for a new project in which he envisioned young women playing in the bubblegum punk style of the late seventies, like the Undertones or the Buzzcocks. When he saw the youthful stamina that fueled the Electrocutes' performance as they opened for Car Thieves that night, he knew he'd found the perfect candidates.

After introducing himself to the band, he told them about his idea and asked if they might be interested. The Electrocutes were green, but were still knowledgeable enough about music history to be wary of the proposition. They feared that working with a male ghostwriter would only increase the sexism leveled at them and draw comparisons to producer Kim Fowley's managerial work with Joan Jett and the Runaways, or Phil Spector's often exploitative relationship with girl groups of the 1960s. "Even then, we knew that if we recorded songs that someone else wrote, people were gonna say, 'You girls can't write your own songs and need your own Svengali.' We were always really worried about that," says Castellano.

"When Darin said he wrote some songs we'd be perfect for, we were like, 'That's so lame. What are you, Kim fuckin' Fowley?'" Anderson laughs. "But we figured, 'Let's try it'—almost as a joke. So we wrote some songs with him. I think he wrote the first four songs, but it was more integrated after that."

Although some found it odd that Raffaelli was spending time with a group of high school sophomores nearly half his age, the girls found him remarkably normal, and were won over by his goofy humor, boundless creativity, and supportive encouragement. Over the next year, the girls would release ten tinny songs across three EPs with Raffaelli, including a cover of the Crystals' 1963 single "Da Doo Ron Ron," a cheeky mocking of the notion that he had a Phil Spector–like role within the band. Unlike Spector, Raffaelli didn't have the means to work at famous studios and instead held recording sessions after shifts at his day job. "He worked at a Mail Boxes Etc. in Half Moon Bay, so we'd record there at night after-hours, just standing behind the counter," remembers Anderson. "People would come in to get mail out of their P.O. box and we had to stop playing." Raffaelli used the Xerox machine to photocopy the EPs' inserts, which featured black-and-white photos of the girls leaned up against a schoolyard jungle gym, looking very nonthreatening.

Buzzsaw guitars carried the foursome's fast and fuzzy tunes about being in high school, crushing on boys, and going to the big dance alone. What they lacked in production value they made up for in peppy energy, as if the cheerleading team rejects had started a punk band. Their style would earn them frequent comparisons to the Ramones, and with good reason beyond their simplistic sonic similarities. For the project, the four took on a new band name they'd all decided on: the Donnas. Just as each of the four members of the Ramones had adopted Ramone as his last name, all four members of the Donnas claimed Donna as their first name, distinguishing themselves by the initials of their real last names. And much like the Ramones had primarily sung about what they did and didn't wanna do ("I Wanna Be Sedated," "I Don't Wanna Walk Around with You," etc.), so too did the Donnas, in songs like "I Don't Wanna Go to School" and "I Wanna Be a Unabomber." Where the Ramones had coined phrases like "gabba gabba" in their lyrics, the Donnas created their own slang with "rab," "glitch," and "mano," words that could seemingly be used as verbs, nouns, or adjectives.

As Raffaelli's friends in the garage rock scene took notice of the project, the girls started getting opportunities to play more shows as the Donnas than the Electrocutes, which came as a surprise to them. "We looked at it as this silly, funny band that we did—a side project almost," says Castellano. "The Electrocutes was our real band. We were doing the Donnas because it was fun, and musically it seemed really simple and easy. But then people started really liking it, and who's gonna say no to playing shows? We wanted to play and have fun."

They got pastel T-shirts printed with their stage names—Donna A., Donna F., Donna C., and Donna R.—and those became the band uniform. The outfits were advantageous not only in driving home their Ramones-tribute persona, but in helping audiences differentiate the Donnas from the Electrocutes. The girls played into the roles of their alter egos, even creating a bit of a faux rivalry between the two acts.

On October 4, 1995, the Donnas, accompanied by Raffaelli as their mock wrangler, played a set on *Wednesday Night Live,* a show on Stanford University's radio station, KZSU. They exuded a good-girl-gone-bad attitude, going so far as to trash-talk their counterparts in the Electrocutes. When the host mentioned that they had a pair of EPs available on Radio X, they retorted, between snaps of gum, "Yeah, what of it?"

As the Donnas ingratiated themselves with the garage rock scene and received more attention, the teenage girls who made up their fan base got some company. Suddenly, more men in their thirties, forties, and fifties were showing up to see the band. "It was a lot of older dudes and younger girls at venues together, which was a real combustible situation," says Anderson.

By the time the young musicians reached their senior year, in 1996, their joke band had overshadowed their real one. The Electrocutes had recorded an album but were having difficulty finding the funding or interest to release it. Conversely, Raffaelli was already working on releasing the Donnas' first full-length LP, with a record release party booked that January at Slim's, in San Francisco, alongside the Mr. T Experience. The Donnas were getting booked on more shows, usually fetching between 100 and 150 bucks, and were drawing bigger crowds.

"We loved the Electrocutes, but people tended to like the Donnas better," says Anderson. "When we played live, the Donnas was a bit easier to dance to, because the songs were more predictable. To dance, you kind of have to know what's coming."

Raffaelli had also been mailing the Donnas' records to a friend in Japan, Pinky Aoki, a connected scenester and member of the psychrock band the Phantom Gift. The Donnas' style of classic American punk rock was connecting with locals, and Aoki offered to fly them over. The girls talked their parents into letting them take a week off from school for the international trip, and the experience made them realize there was an entire world outside Palo Alto High. "Pinky had a little record store in Japan," says Anderson. "He booked a four-show tour for us there when we were sixteen. Darin came with us. We wouldn't have been allowed to do that on our own. He was sort of the chaperone." When the band arrived at the airport in Japan, they were surprised to find that there were fans there waiting to greet them.

The Japan trip saw the Donnas skipping several steps in the traditional career trajectory of a band, as they had yet to even play outside of their home state. "We'd played around the Bay Area, we'd played L.A. maybe once, and up north in California one time. And then we went to Japan. It was crazy," says Castellano.

While the Donnas were making their debut in Asia, they were getting their first taste of press back home. That week, the *Palo Alto Weekly* ran the paper's first prominent feature on the up-and-coming local band, capturing the members at the crossroads of pending adulthood. "Their upcoming graduation from high school signals a fork in the road," it read. "To the left is the rock 'n' roll lifestyle—gigging, touring and trying to make it in the music industry. To the right is college."

The members were still undecided about their futures, they admitted to the reporter, but there was one thing they knew for sure: Their funny little side project, the Donnas, had run its course and was soon to be laid to rest. "The Donnas aren't going to be together for that much longer," guitarist Allison Robertson said. "But the Electrocutes have bigger and better plans and we all know it."

$ $ $

Larry Livermore was working alone in the Lookout Records office late one night in 1997, thinking about how much his tiny label had changed in the four years since his prized act Green Day left to become one of the biggest bands in the world. What was once a three-person operation scraping by on a shoestring budget had ballooned into a multi-million-dollar business that provided salaries and benefits to eighteen full-time employees. He still proudly adhered to the label's founding principles—providing artists with 60 percent of profits and paying their royalties like clockwork—but with a larger profile came greater concessions.

Knowing the label was flush with cash, many Lookout bands were coming to Livermore with their hands out, seeking heftier recording budgets, broader advertising for their releases, or money for van repairs and new equipment. What became most frustrating for him was the mounting expectations. Other bands wanted to know why they hadn't enjoyed the same skyrocketing success as Green

Day, as if he could simply snap his fingers and magically produce another media firestorm. "I'm not a very diplomatic person," he admits. "I'd simply say, 'Well, you're not as good as they are. Maybe practice more. Write better songs and maybe you'll have their success.'"

Even the building Livermore was sitting in had changed. No longer was he working in the cramped one-room office that also served as his bedroom, having recently been talked into relocating to a more suitable six-room suite on University Avenue in Berkeley, which also housed the label's own record shop on the ground floor. As president, he had his own office, furnished with a blue denim couch, an ergonomic chair, and a real desk, an improvement over the loose door he had previously used as a workspace.

As he burned the midnight oil, signing off on invoice payments and balancing the books, a thought that had been on his mind a lot creeped up on him: this was no longer the life he wanted. Lookout had started as a way to avoid working a normal job, but over the past decade, running the label had become one.

Around 4 a.m., the forty-nine-year-old Livermore hunched over his computer and began drafting an email to his employees, explaining that he had made a decision. He was stepping down as the head of Lookout, he wrote, and would be leaving the label in the capable hands of his twenty-four-year-old protégé, Chris Appelgren, who'd been a Lookout employee since the age of fourteen. Sunlight from a new day was starting to fill his office when he finally finished the message. Satisfied with his words, he pressed "send," sat in silence for a few minutes, and took a final look around the punk rock institution he'd built by accident. Then he cleaned out his desk and left the building.

After his departure from Lookout, Livermore took an extended trip to London to decompress from the profitable but stressful few years that Green Day had brought him. Appelgren and his wife, Lookout's general manager, Molly Neuman, took the reins of the business. "It was both exciting and a little scary," Appelgren says. "Scary because Green Day's success had plateaued a little, and the ancillary success of everyone on Lookout also plateaued and maybe even started to come down from its peak."

In their new roles, the young couple quickly incurred more stress and increased demands from bands on the label. Suddenly the entire punk scene was vying for their time and attention, asking for things Livermore had previously shot down. Of course, there were also perks to being in charge of an influential punk label with a virtually limitless checkbook. With their elder leader out of the picture, the two were free to lead Lookout into a new era and sign bands that would usher the label into the future. No longer did Lookout need to be relegated to the same circle of sloppy Bay Area pop-punk bands with interchangeable members. The label could branch out to keep up with punk's ever-evolving sound.

One new act the couple had kept their eyes on was the Donnas, whom they'd found through Raffaelli. Neuman and Appelgren had shared the stage with the Donnas in their own band, the PeeChees, and a kinship had developed between the two groups. Having grown up in Palo Alto himself, Appelgren felt an affinity for the Donnas, and Neuman, who'd played drums in the seminal riot grrrl band Bratmobile, was an idol to them.

Livermore continued to pop his head into the label in his semi-retirement and didn't fully understand his successors' interest in the Donnas. "I told Chris and Molly, 'They'll do all right, but they're not gonna do what you think they're gonna do. Fifty thousand, sixty thousand records maybe, but they're not gonna be the next Green Day,'" says Livermore. "They dismissed my concerns. Maybe it was that I was older and not really active in the business anymore and they were younger."

"I don't believe Larry was very enthusiastic," Appelgren remembers. "I think he thought they were kind of limited. That was his criticism of a few bands that we worked with at the end of his tenure."

"I remember going to see them at a Lookout showcase," Livermore says. "I knew all of the other bands that were playing. They were all the kinds of bands you'd associate with Lookout, and the audience was a Lookout audience—fairly young people bouncing around being goofy. Then the Donnas came on and it was almost like you pulled the plug and all the water went out. All the bouncy kids disappeared and all these older men with raincoats stood on the edge of the stage and started leering at them. I'm exaggerating, of course, but that was the vibe to me. It didn't feel like Lookout. It felt like they were a little bit of a novelty act aimed at someone different."

Despite Livermore's objections, it seemed like an opportune time to invite the Donnas aboard at Lookout, since the four were nearing graduation and mapping out their futures. When asked to sign with the label, the girls convened a meeting with their parents. After some deliberation, the plan they all decided upon was that they would attend their first semester of college and then defer a year of classes to record an album and tour. Spending a year as a touring band would offer rare life experiences that they wouldn't learn in any classroom, they all agreed. "We wanted to go to college, we were all about it, but it was all happening. There was no way to do it in the other order. We had to know if it could be something or not. If we didn't do it, we would never forgive ourselves. We would have wound up beating our children, saying, 'I could've *been something*!'" Anderson laughs.

Anderson attended UC Berkeley in the fall, while Ford and Robertson roomed together at UC Santa Cruz. Castellano was admitted to NYU but, due to school policy, couldn't enroll for a single semester, so she instead stayed home and got a job at a video rental store. On weekends, they met at Trainwreck Studios, in Oakland, to write and record their Lookout debut, *American Teenage Rock 'n' Roll Machine*.

When they all reconvened in Palo Alto on winter break, the Donnas floored the gas, knowing they had only a few months in which to fulfill their rock aspirations. *American Teenage Rock 'n' Roll Machine* didn't mark the death of the Electrocutes so much as the birth of a new identity. The way the members saw it, it was a merger of the two bands.

It was around this time that Raffaelli faded from the picture, in an effort to combat the annoying rumors that had been circulating that he was the mastermind controlling his Donna puppets. "I probably encourage them more than anything. It wasn't like I was telling them what to do. They had their own ideas. I think [encouragement] is what they needed, because there was a lot of talent there," he told *BAM* magazine that year. And when asked to define his role within the band, he said simply, "I just consider myself probably their number one fan."

Free to indulge their own musical passions, the Donnas pulled more influences from their unabashed love of hair metal. Robertson, in particular, was developing into a monster shredder and could inject more ripping riffs and solos into their songs, giving them a Punk Goes Sunset Strip sound. "With *American Teenage,* it was much more hair-metal-influenced," says Anderson. "We were much more into KISS and Mötley Crüe and Ratt and Poison and W.A.S.P. And when you put that through the filter of what we were, that's the sound you get. That's what happens when you play Def Leppard through a tiny speaker."

Armed with their first Lookout album, some cash from their parents, and a new fifteen-passenger van, the Donnas took *American Teenage Rock 'n' Roll Machine* on the road while their schoolmates began their second semester. Their first national tour kicked off in February '98—six weeks in support of labelmates Groovie Ghoulies. From there they headed to Europe, a tour that saw them returning home early because of poor planning by the booking agent. They spent the summer opening a stretch of West Coast shows for Rocket from the Crypt, where they took not only the crowds by surprise, but the headlining band itself. "I remember the first day of tour, they were setting up for soundcheck, and as each one of them tried their instrument out, there wasn't much of anything going on," says Rocket drummer Atom Willard. "But then they started playing a song and I was like, 'Holy shit! That's not what I expected at all!' They sounded so full when playing together. It was rad."

As summer wound down, the Donnas once again found their academic responsibilities in direct conflict with their American teenage rock 'n' roll dreams. With their fall semester quickly approaching, tour offers came in to support fellow Lookout acts the Crumbs and the Hi-Fives. Plus, the band was getting favorable press for their album, which had already sold around twenty thousand copies. *SPIN* gave it a B rating, claiming the band "squeezed ten pep-rally pom-

pom stomps into 24 shiny minutes of party-metal hairspray." The *Los Angeles Times* said it "vividly recalls the classic punk-pop of the Ramones and the boisterous sexuality of '70s girl rockers the Runaways." *Rolling Stone* declared that "the collective musical chemistry between the four Donnas and their instruments is a force to be reckoned with."

The Donnas even cracked into Hollywood. Their cover of KISS's "Strutter" was used in the film *Detroit Rock City*. The band was flown to Los Angeles to film a scene in the Rose McGowan movie *Jawbreaker,* in which they performed their song "Rock 'n' Roll Machine" as the high school prom band. They also appeared in the teen rom-com *Drive Me Crazy,* in which they again portrayed the prom band and, in a nod to their own high school experience, performed in front of a giant neon flag that read ELECTROCUTES.

The more opportunities arose, the less likely their return to school seemed. Turning the Donnas into their full-time gig had never been the plan, Castellano swears. "We just thought of it as a year off." But they'd accomplished more in just a few months than most bands do in their entire careers, and there were more and more fans packing into their shows wherever they went. Why pull the plug now?

$ $ $

The Donnas didn't return to college. Instead they recorded a follow-up album for Lookout in 1999, *Get Skintight,* and sped off on a thirty-day headlining U.S. tour in early 2000, supported by labelmates the Smugglers, a group of five men from Vancouver who prided themselves on their sense of humor and their sense of style, donning dapper suits and rubber boots onstage.

"It was quite difficult for most bands to break through the Donnas' exterior shell. They were a tight group, insulating themselves as a protective measure from what was out there," says head Smuggler Grant Lawrence. "Only a few people were able to break through that shell. We were just nice Canadian guys and they let us in."

Lawrence remembers being awestruck by the buzz building around the Donnas and the white-hot spotlight they were under for the entire month. "There aren't too many tours like that, where almost every single night is sold out. It was a fever pitch," he says. "Everybody wanted to see the Donnas. Their guest list was a who's who; our guest list was a guy named Steve." Over the course of the tour, which looped through Los Angeles and New York, he recalls encountering members of the Go-Go's, the Runaways, Green Day, Motörhead, and even *Star Trek* actor William Shatner, who was dating Anderson's aunt. "Kim Fowley was at the show in New Orleans," Lawrence recalls. "He was totally creepy but also completely fascinating. He's like six foot seven or something, and he showed up in a crimson-red suit with a white shirt, white tie, and red alligator skin shoes. There was a real second-coming-of-the-Runaways vibe around the Donnas."

The Donnas would even make their television debut, on *The Late Late Show with Craig Kilborn,* at the end of the tour, with Kilborn introducing them by saying, "My next guests are giving new life to one of our favorite concepts, the girl group." They performed "Skintight," a song that relied on a looping, string-bending guitar lick, and the studio audience erupted every time Robertson tore through it.

But while the Donnas boasted a number of notable members in their growing fan club, dubbed the Donnaholics, they were also attracting more admirers waiting for them outside with Sharpies and records. Livermore called them the Raincoat Brigade. The Smugglers had another name for them. "We called them GBGs—Girl Band Geeks, these middle-aged creepy men who'd hang out after the shows and wait for the Donnas to get them to sign stuff and give them gifts," says Lawrence. "Sometimes the Donnas would be exhausted and there would be ten guys who looked like extras from *The Lord of the Rings* hanging out in the back alley with various crystals and goblets to present to them."

At one of the tour's smaller shows, at Bernie's Bagels & Deli, a two-story venue in Columbus, Ohio, that housed a delicatessen upstairs and a tiny dive club and distillery downstairs, a combination of heat from the ovens, intoxication, and cramped space led to, as Lawrence puts it, "one of the most insane events I've ever been a part of." The stage was only a few inches off the ground, and the ceiling wasn't much more than eight feet high, with protruding pipes and wires hanging everywhere. A sweaty, overzealous audience was squashed so close to the front that the Donnas kept getting pinned to their amps or knocked over as they struggled to play. Songs had to be restarted as the band's instruments kept getting unplugged. Anderson pleaded with the crowd, "We'll play for you, but we really don't wanna die!"

A gaggle of male hecklers grew so loud that they were nearly drowning out the volume of the amps. "Hey, suck my dick!" yelled a voice from the crowd. Anderson, who'd become an expert in defusing loud, drunken men, snapped back, "Suck *my* dick, baby."

When the situation became near-riotous, the venue employees, still dressed in their deli aprons, linked together to form a human chain to protect the band. "These big bouncer kind of guys had to lock arms and create a barrier between the stage and the audience," remembers Castellano.

"One audience member tried to climb onto the stage by monkeying along the exposed wires in the ceiling. That was until he grabbed onto a live wire and was thrown to the floor in a shower of sparks and vodka. Others climbed up the PA speakers, toppling them like children's blocks," Lawrence later recalled in his memoir, *Dirty Windshields*.

With a few songs still left in their set, the human chain broke and the Donnas gave up. Lawrence remembers, "They unplugged their guitars and ran out of the venue and the audience chased them. They ran upstairs, went outside, and jumped into their van. The audience was so out of control that they surrounded the van and were rocking it, just out of drunken hysteria. It was absolutely apeshit insane."

While hiding in their locked van as it was encircled by a frenzied mob, the Donnas came to a conclusion, Castellano says. "That was a moment where we realized: 'Maybe we need to start playing bigger places.'"

$ $ $

To commemorate turning twenty-one, the Donnas chose a bluntly autobiographical title for their third album with Lookout: *The Donnas Turn 21*. It was their first album to crack into the Billboard Heatseekers chart, selling four thousand copies in its first week. Not only was the band continuing to transition into an arena-metal sound; they were also adopting the personalities behind it. Inspired by the hypersexual machismo that oozed from lyrics by male-led bands like KISS, AC/DC, and Guns N' Roses, the Donnas sang their own songs about drinking, hooking up with guys, and hard partying. Songs like "You've Got a Crush on Me" and "Midnite Snack" objectified the male objects of their desire, taking the clichéd rock 'n' roll gender tropes and flipping them on their heads.

One song, "40 Boys in 40 Nights," was a two-and-a-half-minute brag about collecting "boys all over the road." It wasn't out of the ordinary for male artists to gloat about this kind of promiscuous tour behavior in song, of course. In fact, just a few months later, rapper Ludacris would have a hit single with "Area Codes," his raunchy chronicling of having "hoes in different area codes." But when a group of freshly minted drinking-age women did it, it became noteworthy. Ironically, the members of the Donnas felt little to no identification with their bawdy stage personas.

"In a way, it was like a character and a persona, but in another way it was aspirational. Like, *if only* we could have forty boys in forty nights. *If only* it was like it was for the dudes we were emulating," says Anderson. "It's funny. The best thing you can do for your sex life as a guy is to just pick up a guitar. The worst thing you can do for your sex life as a girl is to start a band. People will say, 'Oh, you're lesbians, you're witches.' We definitely were repellent to what you would think of as a groupie."

It was a no-win situation. In abstaining from tour debauchery, the Donnas earned a reputation for being too uptight. When the band played Warped Tour in the summer of '99, an experience Anderson says "sucked balls," they felt criticized just for dodging male attention. "It was the first time we'd ever had a bus, so we'd be watching *Twin Peaks* in the back lounge and playing video games. Then we heard that people thought we were too stuck up to come off the bus," she says. "People threw shit at us onstage. They changed the lineup every day on Warped Tour, so one day we played between NOFX and MxPx, which is the worst thing that could've happened.

They were throwing CDs at us, flip-flops, cigarettes, spit, all kinds of shit."

Questions about groupies came up routinely in interviews, particularly among radio DJs, who Castellano says almost never grasped the band's tongue-in-cheek shtick. "It was all of these sad versions of Howard Stern. They would always ask if we got our periods at the same time or they would ask if we showered together." Journalists at magazines and newspapers tended to be in on the joke, and the Donnas racked up more thoughtful press in outlets like *CMJ*, the *Washington Post, Alternative Press,* and *Entertainment Weekly*. Journalist Rob Harvilla wrote, "Horny teenagers and horny old rock critics immediately adored them—it's entirely possible the band received more column inches of press than every other post-Green Day Lookout band combined, a media obsession that only escalated as their photos got more glamorous and their sound veered farther from the Ramones and closer to Mötley Crüe."

The band was getting so much attention, in fact, that it became a source of friction within Lookout's roster. Other Lookout acts started to gripe that Appelgren and Neuman were putting more resources into the Donnas than anyone else. Not helping dispel their perception of bias was the fact that Neuman had taken on the role of the band's co-manager. The Queers felt so neglected by the label that had released four of their albums that they wrote a snotty song, "Molly Neuman," airing their grievances: "Molly Neuman won't return my calls / Molly Neuman manages the Donnas."

"The bands that were wondering why we were spending so much time on them had to kind of begrudgingly acknowledge that they were a great band, though. They quickly became one of our top-selling bands," says Appelgren. (True to Livermore's premonition, sales of *Turn 21* landed between fifty thousand and sixty thousand copies.) "They were new and different, and I think that was compelling. I remember talking with the guys in the band AVAIL about why we were doing so much for them. But really, we were just responding to the inbound interest."

"Even before the label started heavily promoting them, the mainstream rock media showed more interest in the Donnas than they did in any Lookout band, including pre-*Dookie* Green Day," Livermore later recalled in his memoir, *How to Ru(i)n a Record Label*. "It was the novelty factor, I warned, and wouldn't have staying power, but nobody was interested in my naysaying. Chris also didn't think it was funny when I snarkily suggested that sending every kid in America a $15 check to spend on a Donnas CD might be cheaper than the marketing campaign he was running."

It wasn't just their label peers who were taking notice of the Donnas' rising star. With 110,000 total records sold on Lookout, A&R reps at bigger labels had also gotten wind of the band and began requesting meetings with them. "We would get A&R people coming to our shows since we'd started at Lookout," says Castellano. "We never thought it was the right time, because we'd heard a lot of horror stories from bands who had left the indie label, gone to the major label, and totally got fucked over. We were really worried about that."

"I think we were pretty hard on the label guys," she continues. "We were like, 'What are *you* gonna do for *us*?' We wanted a presentation. We were probably ridiculous, but it was good to not be afraid of them. We met with this one A&R guy in L.A. and he was like, 'I really want to sign you guys. I think it's gonna be really great. The one thing I think you should change is: drop the instruments and then you can sing and dance.'"

"First of all, we can't dance. Secondly, we don't want to. Thirdly, playing instruments is what got us here," adds Anderson.

"And then he went off and signed Christina Aguilera and everyone was happy," Castellano laughs.

The most important selling point to the Donnas was the assurance that they would be able to maintain creative freedom. This is the top priority for most bands from the punk world considering a jump to a major label, but it was particularly pressing for a group of young women who feared they'd be talked into changing their sound into something cutesy or dressing up in revealing outfits.

The label that was most supportive of their identity was Atlantic Records and its A&R consultant Mary Gormley. "My sister was a huge Donnas fan. They were on Lookout at the time, so I just kind of followed what they were doing," she says. Gormley first saw the band at Irving Plaza, in New York, on October 8, 2001, just a few weeks after the terrorist attacks of 9/11. The mood in the venue was somber, but she was still impressed with the band's ability to liven up a grieving crowd. "It was the first time I'd been out after 9/11 and we were all pretty traumatized. Just even being in a big place with people felt strange. But the show was great and I really enjoyed meeting the girls."

"We had a real bidding war between the labels," says Joey Minkes, who co-managed the band with Neuman. "Another label came in at the end with a bigger offer, but the Donnas turned it down to go with Atlantic. They thought the bigger label would want to change them too much. They felt more comfortable with Mary."

"They were already established and accomplished musicians," says Gormley. "They knew who they were. I thought they were so good that if they had the support and tools of a major label, they could make bigger videos, get on the radio, and get more exposure. They seemed ready for it. In their hearts, they're just independent girls."

As negotiations grew more serious, the band felt guilt over the thought of leaving Lookout, the label that had worked so hard for them since they were teenagers. But Appelgren and Neuman were supportive, recognizing that the Donnas were hitting their heads on the ceiling of the indie world and were primed to be breakout stars. "I don't know that we could've done a lot more with them at that point," says Appelgren. "I think trying to restrict them would've been doing them a disservice."

The Donnas signed with Atlantic Records in December 2001, the first Lookout band to make the major-label jump since Green Day. But unlike their Bay Area predecessors, the Donnas weren't too concerned with the blowback they might receive from the scene. Green Day, conversely, was still publicly at odds with their old stomping grounds. In fact, the year the Donnas had signed to Lookout, Green Day released their fifth album, *Nimrod,* which took aim at *Maximum Rocknroll* founder Tim Yohannan. The raging "Platypus (I Hate You)" was a two-and-a-half-minute score-settler with Yohannan, a smoker who was ill with lymphatic cancer. "Shit out of luck, and now your time is up / It brings me pleasure just to know you're going to die," frontman Billie Joe Armstrong snarled. Six months later, Yohannan was dead and Armstrong expressed no remorse.

"We weren't as afraid as some other bands," says Castellano. "Yeah, we played Gilman and punk clubs, and yeah, we were on Lookout, but we never claimed to be this punk band. We never went out and said, 'We're never selling out! Fuck corporations!'"

"Towards the end of the nineties and into the 2000s, selling out wasn't the worst thing you could do anymore, and I do feel like there were some people who felt things were handed to us on a silver platter," says Anderson. "Our attitude was: 'You can't reject us if you never accepted us.' We were immune to that shit. We were never really welcomed into a scene. We were our own scene."

$ $ $

As was the case with all of the Donnas' previous albums, the four members graced the cover of their major-label debut, *Spend the Night*. The front cover showed the band engaged in a slumber party, looking prim and proper in bathrobes and pajamas. On the back was a photo of a trashed bedroom with a passed-out guy lying on the floor, a red lipstick kiss on his cheek, among a mess of half-eaten pizza slices and Cheetos.

When *Spend the Night* hit stores, in October 2002, it joined a long list of other albums released by female artists that year. A staggering number of women from a wide variety of genres had releases that dominated the charts, including Avril Lavigne, Celine Dion, Norah Jones, Sheryl Crow, Faith Hill, Brandy, Alanis Morissette, Vanessa Carlton, Kylie Minogue, Jennifer Lopez, and Christina Aguilera. But, along with Dixie Chicks, the Donnas were unique in that they worked as a group, and were determined to keep it that way. "We made that choice together," says Anderson. "We split everything four ways, which we'd learned from R.E.M. We were a democracy. We were egalitarian."

In an effort to avoid any member being singled out and positioned as the band's star, the Donnas insisted on being interviewed and photographed as a foursome. It was also a way to offer one another support through the particularly demoralizing interviews that focused on the band's lip gloss rather than their gear. "We'll talk about music, and then the only thing they print is what's in our makeup bags," Ford griped to the *Boston Globe*. "We get mad and totally despise the people that wrote it. We would like to have a web site called getyourownbandandshutup.com."

The Donnas were a welcome addition to Atlantic's roster, and were supported by an enthusiastic team. "Everyone [at the label] was really excited to have them," remembers Gormley. "The young people working there were so happy to have a cool band. It was a turning point for Atlantic in some ways. They didn't have cool girl rock bands. There were very few, and [the Donnas] kicked ass."

With the backing of Atlantic's publicity team, the Donnas were showered with more coverage than ever. They landed spreads in the usual music outlets, but also broke into young women's magazines like *Teen Vogue* and *Seventeen*. *Rolling Stone* called them "punk rock girls playing with the big boys," and *SPIN* deemed them "the most atypically ass-kicking band in America." The *Village Voice* noted, "It's all been said before, but few penis carriers put it so consistently or succinctly."

"The Donnas were a press dream," publicist Nick Stern told *Billboard*. "They wouldn't say no to anything unless it was something raunchy like a *Playboy* spread or taking their clothes off for *Maxim*."

The band liberally licensed their songs to movies, TV shows, and video games. "Who Invited You" was used in PlayStation 2 games like *True Crime: Streets of LA*, *MVP Baseball 2003*, and *Splashdown*. Their straight-ahead style of cocky, no-nonsense rock was especially popular in teen comedy flicks, getting added to the soundtracks for Lindsay Lohan's *Mean Girls* and Amanda Bynes's *What a Girl Wants*.

While hesitant at first, the Donnas also became more comfortable with the idea of using their music to hawk brands and products after some encouragement from the label. "We sat with the band and talked about our ability to co-opt all the relationships we have at every level of the business, from AOL to the Budweiser deal to an Urban Outfitters tie-in to securing them a consistent run of major tours," Atlantic co-president Craig Kallman told the *Los Angeles Times*.

The band appeared together in a Budweiser ad, and Castellano participated in a drum-off with Cheap Trick's Bun E. Carlos for a holiday Target commercial. Traditionally, lending songs to commercials was a kiss of death for an indie band's credibility, perhaps even more sacrilegious than signing to a major label. But to the Donnas, indie cred was less important than exposure. If sticking one of their songs in a commercial helped them reach a wider audience, they were open to it.

"We were on board for pretty much whatever," says Anderson. "We didn't care if we 'sold out,' because our only measure of integrity was if we liked the music we were doing." The only line they wouldn't cross was when they received offers to promote brands aimed specifically at women, which felt like being typecast. "The worst, lamest one I can think of was that they wanted us to cover 'We're Not Gonna Take It' for a Yaz commercial, which is a birth control pill. Conceptually, it's fucked up, because it's a pill—you *have* to take it! We just didn't want to be associated with feminine products. We did have a lot of offers from Stayfree and Kotex and shit. I love women and want to support women, and I love birth control, but I just didn't like how we were positioned. Like, 'Why can't we just do Budweiser?' . . . And then we did!"

They returned to the late-night circuit, this time hitting *The Tonight Show with Jay Leno* and *Late Night with Conan O'Brien*, gifting each host a pair of pajamas and toothbrushes to match *Spend the Night*'s sleepover party theme. They also landed the prestigious booking as the musical guest on *Saturday Night Live,* alongside host Ray Liotta.

Spend the Night's release was perfectly timed to catch a shift at MTV's popular after-school show *Total Request Live*. In an effort to steer the show away from the boy groups and teenage pop stars who'd dominated its programming for years, MTV executives pushed for a new direction. "There were times when 'TRL' seemed like an hourlong commercial for [Justin] Timberlake's boy band, 'N

Sync," the *New York Times* wrote. "These days, though, teen-pop is in remission, and MTV executives think they may have identified its successor: punk rock. On 'TRL' this is 'Spankin' New Bands Week,' which means performances from five punk-inflected bands in five days: the Donnas, the Used, Simple Plan, New Found Glory and Good Charlotte."

Having already put in a decade of work, the Donnas weren't exactly "spankin' new," but they still welcomed the opportunity to perform for a new audience. Castellano was a frenetic ball of hair and drumsticks in MTV's Times Square studio, while Robertson ripped solos on a Les Paul that matched her orange dress. Thunderous riffs boomed out of her Marshall amp, which had a sign taped to it: HI MOMS! MTV2 also picked up the video for "Take It Off." It depicted the Donnas beating a male band (played by themselves, donning the most heinous fashion item of the early aughts: trucker hats) in a school's battle of the bands, their overdue revenge for Verbal Constipation upstaging Screen at Jordan Middle School.

Every television performance by the Donnas was airtight, almost formulaic, a level of perfectionism that was very deliberate and hard-earned. They took their responsibility as female rock ambassadors incredibly seriously, and weren't about to screw up on live TV. The week of their *SNL* debut, the band locked themselves in a rehearsal space in New York and practiced their two songs for several hours each day, until every second was perfect, right down to Castellano's stick twirls. "We put a lot of pressure on ourselves our whole career, but especially for moments like that," she says. "If I messed up on a fill-in or something, people would seriously say, 'Ah, well, girls can't really play drums.' So it felt like 'Well, fuck, we've got to be beyond perfect on these things.' It was a lot of pressure to represent that we could do this. We felt like we had pressure to prove girls can play."

And for all their hard work striving for perfection and exposure, the Donnas did see their sales spike and their audience expand, with a growing number of female Donnaholics up front at their shows when they opened for bands like the Strokes, Jimmy Eat World, and OK Go, or played festivals like Lollapalooza, where they were one of only two woman-led bands on the main stage, along with the rowdy L.A. punk band the Distillers. In its first year, *Spend the Night* sold an impressive 360,000 copies (with Lookout handling the vinyl edition) and spent twenty-six weeks on the Billboard 100 chart, peaking at number 62.

Although the Donnas were happy to provide female music fans with an alternative to the proliferation of professionally styled, immaculately groomed teenage starlets who had dominated Y2K-era pop culture—*The Hollywood Reporter* described them as the "anti-Britneys"—it was a position that, Anderson admits, didn't always feel flattering.

"Sometimes it really sucks to be the role model of imperfection. It sucks to be like, 'You don't have to be skinny, you can be like Brett!'" Anderson laughs. "Maybe you can't sing like Christina Aguilera, but you can sing like me, for sure. The talent realm was attainable. It was for girls who said: 'Fuck that. I don't want to be backstage, I want to be *on* stage.'"

$ $ $

The cracks were starting to show in the operations of Lookout Records. It happened shortly after the Donnas had set sail for Atlantic. Since its inception in 1987, Lookout had been so committed to treating its bands with transparency and goodwill that they had a rule in place that stipulated that a band would receive royalty checks every three months, and if they fell behind by more than two payments, they were free to pull their albums from the label and take them elsewhere. In more than a decade in business, it had never been an issue, even in the label's leanest times. But in the years after Livermore relinquished control to Appelgren and Neuman, he started getting panicked phone calls from bands asking if he knew where their payments were. Some complained that they hadn't received money in months; others claimed it had been more than a year. Rumors started to circulate that Lookout, a label that had raked in $10 million in a single year at its peak in 1995, was in financial trouble.

"There is stuff I'm not so good at in running a business, but one of the things I was undeniably good at was picking bands that would do well," says Livermore. "So when I started stepping away from that and letting other people pick bands, the results were often not good, and it diluted the whole image of Lookout."

In addition to the Donnas, Appelgren and Neuman had invested heavily in a new cluster of signings at the start of the 2000s that diverged from the pop-punk sound the label had built its name on. Among them were Ted Leo and the Pharmacists, the Phantom Surfers, Communiqué, the Oranges Band, Black Cat Music, and Pretty Girls Make Graves. Some, Livermore thought, were a good fit; others he found too hip for Lookout's vibe. But none of them, in his opinion, were going to pay off enough to recoup the exorbitant amounts Neuman and Appelgren were spending to promote them. Lookout had traditionally never spent much more than a couple hundred bucks to promote an album, placing a monthly ad in *Maximum Rocknroll* and mailing a hundred promo CDs to fanzine writers and college radio stations. Now the label was paying for costly music videos, taking out ads in mainstream magazines like *SPIN*, flying bands to tastemaking music industry conventions like CMJ, in New York, and SXSW, in Austin, and mailing press copies to more than a thousand contacts.

It wasn't just overblown promotional spending that was cutting into Lookout's profits. A lopsided negotiation to purchase a sub-label from Screeching Weasel frontman Ben Weasel resulted in a devastating financial hit. The label also switched distributors at the end of the nineties, from the punk-friendly Mordam to the more corporate RED, causing album prices to rise and retail distribution to drop. "We moved to a Sony-controlled RED Distribution, where there was a higher cost of operating. At that point our margins evaporated," says Appelgren. "There was also a shift away from physical products. We noticed a severe polarization with the way our total catalog performed. That could've been market conditions, it could've been all the competition with other labels and bands."

As Lookout continued to be short on the income necessary to cover royalty payments, even the label's most loyal stalwarts started to pull their catalogs or depart for other labels. AVAIL, Pansy Division, Blatz, Filth, Enemy You, Neurosis, and others jumped ship. "Nobody really wants to fuck Lookout over, but they don't want to sit there and let Lookout fuck them over, either," Lookout accountant Bill Michalski told the *East Bay Express*. "So a lot of bands have waited a really long time before they took any action. People gave [Lookout] a lot of slack."

The two bands owed the most money were Operation Ivy and Green Day, whose three combined releases were the label's top sellers. Green Day was cautiously patient with Lookout, in hopes that sales and licensing of their two records would help keep their former home afloat. But as the amount the band was owed neared half a million dollars, they had no choice but to pull their catalog. "I feel we've more than honored our handshake agreement with Lookout. I think that's really fair," bassist Mike Dirnt said to the *Express*. "There comes a time where you're like, 'Okay, how long do you want to support your record label?'"

Lookout not only had failed to uphold their end of their financial deal with Green Day but had broken the promise Livermore had written into their arrangement—that "the truest contract is one based out of trust and friendship."

Soon after Green Day pulled their records, Operation Ivy followed suit. The label began downsizing after that, laying off employees and halting the release of new albums. Many hoped Appelgren would be able to salvage the beloved institution by running it at a reduced capacity, but the task was too insurmountable, and Lookout Records was effectively dead. "I'm not necessarily happy with the way it ended, but I don't know that I would've wanted it to continue on indefinitely the way it was," he says. "Everything comes to an end."

$ $ $

Lookout Records wasn't the only label grappling with the shifting trends of a new millennium. The entire music industry was faced with a new enemy. As internet speeds increased on users' home modems in the early 2000s, peer-to-peer file-sharing applications became a more popular means of downloading music, and soon this began cutting into label profits. Even as hefty lawsuits shut these sites down, online piracy was a leaking dam that couldn't be plugged.

As one shuttered, two more popped up in its place—Napster, Kazaa, BearShare, Grokster, Morpheus, LimeWire, the Pirate Bay, etc. While the legal teams at record labels played whack-a-mole with these emerging networks, the creative teams put their heads together and came up with a solution to fend off the pending obsolescence of the physical CD: they were quite literally planning to double down.

DualDisc was a new technology unveiled at the National Association of Recording Merchandisers convention in August 2004. It was a double-sided compact disc with standard audio tracks on one side and DVD capabilities on the other, which allowed for 5.1 surround sound and digital space for various visual goodies like music videos, photos, and interviews.

"The world is going toward more visuals in the entertainment sector," BMG Distribution vice president and general manager Jordan Katz told *Billboard*. "People [are spending] more screen time, whether it's a computer, television or videogames. It's a natural progression for music to have a visual attached to it."

Believing DualDisc was something consumers would be willing to pay an additional two dollars for in the face of free music sharing, major labels all designated select titles as their guinea pigs for the fall launch of this industry-wide experiment. Sony Music Label Group offered up releases from Good Charlotte and Incubus; Universal Music Group elected Keane and Snow Patrol; and Warner Music Group, which included Atlantic, put their stock into Simple Plan's *Still Not Getting Any . . .* and the Donnas' second release with the label, *Gold Medal*.

"We were really sold on it, but it wasn't something we were particularly excited about," says Castellano. "But if the label was excited about it in terms of promoting our record, then we wanted them to do it."

Gold Medal was highly prioritized at Atlantic, and thousands of DualDisc copies shipped to stores across the country for its October 26 release. The CD's special edition jewel case came wrapped in a black felt slipcase. Inside were an explainer on DualDisc technology and a download card for official Donnas ringtones. Its DVD side featured the music video for "Fall Behind Me" plus fifteen minutes of behind-the-scenes footage. The video, made to look like "a black-light poster come to life," as Anderson described it, was filmed entirely in front of a green screen, which didn't make for particularly engaging bonus content.

But when fans who purchased the album played it on their stereos, they were left scratching their heads. Just fifty-three seconds into the album's final track, "Have You No Pride," the music abruptly cut off with two minutes still remaining in the song. It went silent right as Anderson was singing, "All eyes on you and they're burning holes," an ironic place for a technical glitch, given how closely monitored the DualDisc experiment was within the music industry. "It was really stressful," says Gormley. "Whatever happened between the mastering lab and the production facility, something went wrong. And we printed a lot of those CDs—*a lot.*"

Atlantic ate the cost and issued a statement to the Donnaholics via the band's website: "If you would like to return the DualDisc, please go back to your local retailer with your original receipt and they will replace it with the regular 'Gold Medal' CD. Feel free to keep the special black velvet limited edition cover."

"Radio play is based on how many records you ship on release date. All the records shipped in huge numbers and we were so excited," says Anderson. "And then the day our album dropped, we started getting calls that the CDs were defective. The last half of the last song was cut off, and people were returning them. So they just shipped them all back. Our first-day numbers got fucked because of this glitch, and then there's no coming back from that. So our radio play was fucked."

"It was always a fight to get on mainstream rock radio," says Castellano. "They'd literally say to us, 'We don't play girls on our station.' Or they'd tell us that they had two slots and they were full with No Doubt and Evanescence."

Gold Medal's only single, "Fall Behind Me," didn't catch much airplay, whether that was a result of the DualDisc calamity or the fact that *Gold Medal* saw the Donnas taking a more mature approach to songwriting. They'd dropped their Donna monikers for this album cycle and were less focused on rocking out and more concerned with expressing their emotions. They were experimenting with slower tempos and new soundscapes. "The Gold Medal," a song about never being accepted in the Bay Area music scene, did away with their reliable distorted riffs and instead employed an acoustic country twang. "The recycled riffs and too-easy lyrical cheese are occasionally still in play," *Pitchfork* said in a middling review. "But on *Gold Medal,* even when they fail, it seems as if that failure is a result of the Donnas trying to carve their own identity rather than just being a cute cover band that ran out of ideas."

Gold Medal enjoyed a small fraction of *Spend the Night*'s sales numbers, moving about 79,000 units in its first twelve months. Like many artists, the band was trying to adapt to an industry that was rapidly changing in the face of emerging digital platforms and illegal downloading. Overall physical album sales were starting to plummet. The selling power of major labels became less reliable, not just to the Donnas but to many indie acts that had made, or were considering, the jump.

"The Great Label Debate," a cover story in the March 19, 2005, issue of *Billboard,* analyzed the current state of the indie-vs.-major dispute and the modern industry challenges developing artists were facing. The article examined a number of acts from the new crop of indie rock—Bright Eyes, Arcade Fire, the Shins—and how they viewed the choice in labels. Against Me!, a red-hot "acoustic-flavored pop-punk act" from Florida, had recently "shunned mega-advances from major labels" to stay proudly independent. Conversely, Death Cab for Cutie, whom Gormley had also recently ushered to Atlantic from indie label Barsuk Records, was touted as a promising new addition to the major-label system. But the Donnas were cited as an example of a major-label signing whose results were "mixed."

The article noted that, while the Donnas had been taking many high-profile opportunities—signing on to open a tour with Maroon 5 and licensing songs to video games like *Gran Turismo 4* and movies like *The Sisterhood of the Traveling Pants*—sales of *Gold Medal* were at a standstill. Atlantic had relied on many of the same promotional tricks that had now sold more than 400,000 copies of *Spend the Night,* but to diminishing results. The Donnas again dominated the talk show circuit, performing on the *Late Show with David Letterman*, *The Late Late Show with Craig Ferguson*, *Jimmy Kimmel Live!*, and *Last Call with Carson Daly*. Songs appeared in more TV shows (*Charmed*, *Veronica Mars*), more movies (*Herbie: Fully Loaded*), and more video games (*Guitar Hero*), but the media blitz wasn't translating into album sales. It seemed as though the shine on the band was wearing off.

Failure to move the sales dial was creating a strain between the band and their label. "I feel like the Donnas are an important group, culturally, and I hope [Atlantic] understands that," a trepidatious Neuman told *Billboard*. "Yes, this record has been challenging, but a lot of careers have that story in them. Most of the bands who have hit it have taken a little bit of a turn south."

But the Atlantic team that had enthusiastically signed the Donnas two years earlier had changed as well. A year after the release of *Spend the Night*, Time Warner had sold Warner Music Group to a new group of investors for $2.6 billion, in an effort to shave down debt it had amassed after a disappointing merger with America Online in 2001. Personnel shake-ups had displaced much of the Donnas' original team by the time *Gold Medal* was released. New management came in, and what staffers remained were fearful of losing their jobs in the transition.

Atlantic's contract with the Donnas provided for two albums, with an option for a third. The band wrote a handful of songs in hopes of proving they could produce a crossover hit on their next record, but Atlantic didn't bite. The label and the band parted ways in early 2006, on terms that were "mutual and completely amicable," according to a post on their message board. "We were really happy with the way they let us go," Anderson says. "They could've kept the masters for the second record, but they let us go with the masters. They were really generous. They could've fucked us over, but they didn't."

Following their release from Atlantic, the band couldn't return to Lookout, because there wasn't much of a Lookout left to return to. They entertained offers from other majors for their next record. With more than half a million records sold and a proven record of commercial utility, the band was still an attractive signing. Ultimately, though, they passed and formed their own label in a joint venture with Redeye Distribution that gave them a fifty-fifty split in profits, a more generous share than they'd seen from Atlantic. "To the girls' credit, they saw the writing on the wall," says Minkes. "Technology was going to change everything, and these girls are smart and they knew they had to try something else. Why push a rock uphill?"

As the Donnas returned to their independent roots in the years following their major-label stint, the band members exhaled and realized how tense they'd been throughout their four years on Atlantic. From the day they signed on the dotted line, they were always on the defensive, constantly ready to fight any label exec who dared ask them to dress sexier, make their music poppier, or drop their instruments to sing and dance. They were so concerned about everything that could go wrong that they hardly had a chance to stop, take stock of it all, and savor their success.

"I think I'd do it again," Castellano says of her major-label experience. "We were so nervous about being fucked over the whole time that I don't think we had fun with it. I mean, we had a lot of fun, don't get me wrong, but I'd try not to be so worried all the time. It's hard—it's your band, which is your entire life. For us, it was our job, our creative outlet, and our best friends. It was everything to us. We didn't have many friends outside the band. It's hard not to be protective over that. But I still wish I'd just enjoyed it."

CHAPTER 7

THURSDAY

War All the Time

Island Records (2003)

THERE WAS A spray-painted sign hanging in the corner of Geoff Rickly's basement that read WATCH YOUR HEAD, and it was there because, well, people kept hitting their heads. The ceiling wasn't much more than seven feet from the ground, and anyone over six feet tall was bound to bump their skull against the protruding pipes and low-hanging light bulbs sooner or later. From an architectural standpoint, the cramped subterranean space was not the ideal place to host a gathering of several dozen people, but for punk shows it was perfect.

The concrete-walled basement sat below a three-bedroom house at 331 Somerset Street in New Brunswick, New Jersey, a college town between New York City and Philadelphia. The area was home to Rutgers University, whose sprawling campus spread across town and packed in more than thirty thousand students during the school year. Rickly, a bookworm and aspiring teacher, had moved into the house with friends in his freshman year, in 1998, and started hosting punk and hardcore shows there as his way of connecting with the community.

Rickly wasn't alone—there was an underground network of students putting on word-of-mouth gigs in their homes. Shows that outgrew the basements were moved to the nearby Melody Bar, the Court Tavern, or local VFW halls. The vibrant scene became such fertile ground that after a while, some touring bands found just as great a payoff in a New Brunswick stop as they would at New York's prominent DIY space, ABC No Rio.

Rickly's house hosted between one and three shows a week. Most cost five bucks at the door and crammed in about fifty to a hundred people. At the particularly packed shows, crowds pinned the bands right up against their amps, and enough dust would get kicked up to leave attendees sneezing black globs for days. To avoid drawing noise complaints, Rickly had the bands park their vans as close to the house as possible to block the sound from escaping.

Each show's bill paired touring acts like Florida's Hot Water Music and D.C.'s Q and Not U with local mainstays like thrashy punks the Degenerics and screamo favorites You and I, whose guitarist lived in the bedroom across from Rickly's. The biggest name in the area was Lifetime, whose swift and bratty punk songs made them New Brunswick's most revered band and, if the title of their 1997 album was to be believed, Jersey's best dancers. The record even featured the scene's unofficial anthem, "Theme Song for a New Brunswick Basement Show."

On New Year's Eve in 1998, Rickly went from being a spectator at these shows to a participant. Itching to take a more active role in the scene and looking for an outlet for the lyrics and poetry he scrawled in notebooks, he'd been practicing with a band he was able to scrape together called Thursday. The incipient band didn't have many songs to their name and were still finding their identity. They sounded like an amalgamation of elements from the dozens of bands who'd passed through the basement over the years, with some parts that were gentle and melancholic and other parts whose unfiltered noise felt loud enough to put cracks in the cement floor. Whether or not they were ready to try out their stuff, Rickly added Thursday to the flyer for that day's show with Miami's Poison the Well and two Jersey upstarts, Midtown and Saves the Day.

Rickly paced back and forth in his kitchen until it was time to perform for the few dozen people downstairs. When he finally held a microphone in his hands, it only made the young singer appear more exposed and vulnerable. Rickly was underweight and lanky, with a bad haircut and ill-fitting clothes. Whenever he opened his mouth to sing, it showed off the prominent gap between his two front teeth. He had a pair of piercing blue eyes, but he was so nervous that he kept them tightly shut through the majority of the band's set.

Thursday raced through their short repertoire in a matter of minutes. When Rickly finally unclenched his eyelids after the last song, he was relieved to see that it was all over. But it was actually just beginning.

$ $ $

Rickly had assembled Thursday from connections he made in the New Brunswick scene. He first hooked up with Tom Keeley and Tucker Rule, two Rutgers classmates who had been friends since high school. The three shared a common interest in hardcore and bonded over their love of everything loud, from the thinking man's approach of Fugazi to the blunt-force assault of Integrity. They were especially enamored with Philadelphia's Ink & Dagger and the sense of theatrical danger they injected into their live show via vampire makeup and fake blood. It was rumored that their antics had earned them a lifetime ban from playing Rutgers's student center.

The trio started jamming together, with Keeley on guitar, Rule on drums, and Rickly singing. Needing a bassist, they roped in an unwitting Tim Payne, whom Keeley knew through art classes. Payne was an indie rock kid who would rather listen to My Bloody Valentine than Integrity, and he wasn't much interested in joining their band. "Geoff said they were gonna sound like BoySetsFire and all this hardcore stuff and I was like, 'I don't know what the hell you're talking about,'" Payne remembers. But since he couldn't think of a worthwhile excuse to get himself out of the invitation, he started showing up to band practices. They rounded out their lineup with a second guitarist, Bill Henderson.

The group wrote and recorded a four-song demo and started passing around copies to friends. The songs laid the groundwork for the defining elements of Thursday's sound—soft melodies that built up to loud, intense sections, which sometimes collapsed into textured chaos. Rickly's voice swung between tender crooning and full-on screaming. A kind interpretation of his vocal approach would call it passionate and earnest, with a distinct charm. A more cynical description would be that he was off-key and tone-deaf. And indeed, Rickly's frequent mangling of pitch and frequency earned him the nickname Tone Geoff. But it was the imperfections that became Thursday's calling card, as if the band had accidentally stumbled into a style that sounded just wrong enough to be right.

"At first I thought, 'This kid's voice sounds fucking weird.' I wasn't sure how I felt on the first listen. Then by the second listen I was like, 'Okay, there's something special here,'" remembers Alex Saavedra. Saavedra ran a small, local record label called Eyeball Records, which had released EPs by street-punk bands like the Casualties and L.E.S. Stitches, as well as moshy hardcore acts like Breakdown and Terror Zone.

"I got a copy of their demo from this kid named Gabe Saporta, who was in a band called Midtown," he remembers. "Gabe was living in New Brunswick and was going to school with all those other nerds there. That kid connected everyone. He was always up in somebody's fucking business. He was like a seventy-five-year-old woman playing mah-jongg—just knew everything that was happening in town."

Saavedra and Rickly met in a Burger King parking lot one night and ended up talking for hours while sitting on the hood of Saavedra's white Chevy Blazer, which he was also living in at the time. The two became fast friends, and by the end of their conversation Saavedra had convinced Rickly that Thursday should record a full album and that Eyeball should release it.

But while Thursday's four recorded songs were enough to earn them the backing of a local record label, their live show needed work. "Geoff was awful in the beginning. He would do these stage antics in spots where he didn't have the confidence to pull off the vocals. He would intentionally crawl on the ground and get all emotional or drop the mic—stupid shit. The kid had zero confidence," Saavedra says. "He would pop and lock, and people didn't know how to react to it, but I thought it was awesome. He was a cross between Ian Curtis from Joy Division and a B-boy."

Through contacts Rickly had accumulated hosting touring bands at his house, he was able to book out-of-state gigs and weekend tours for Thursday, and the road quickly sharpened the band's skills. "They went on tour for the first time, and when they came back, you could see the confidence building," Saavedra says. "Geoff wasn't just screaming anymore, but trying to sing. He wasn't doing it well, but he was trying. You could see a definite change once they got a few miles under their belt."

True to his word, Saavedra paid for the pressing of a thousand copies of Thursday's debut record, *Waiting*, which the band recorded at Big Blue Meenie, a studio in Jersey City run by owner Tim Gilles and producer Sal Villanueva. Although the two constantly ribbed the young band with relentless barbs akin to a Jerky Boys routine, the session perfectly captured Thursday's developing sound.

The thousand copies of *Waiting* lasted Thursday nearly a year. A handful of them sold at each show around the tri-state area, where the band's name was becoming more familiar among dedicated fans of underground screamo and hardcore, ranking among other basement shriekers like Neil Perry, Orchid, and Yaphet Kotto. Saavedra's business partner at Eyeball also happened to be the buyer at the influential Manhattan music store Generation Records, a connection that helped distribute a slew of copies to indie shops.

Eager to get *Waiting* out into the world, Thursday booked themselves more dates in more cities. When Henderson realized he couldn't abandon the responsibilities of school and work to keep up with the pace of the band's growth, he was replaced by a friend named Steve Pedulla. The longer Thursday spent away from New Jersey, the more they realized there was more to learn on the road than in class.

$ $ $

The idea to start a record label came to Tony Brummel in a fever dream. The eighteen-year-old Chicago native was running a temperature of 103 degrees one night in 1989 when the premonition hit him that he should launch a company called Victory Records and that its logo should be a snarling bulldog. So when he woke up, that's what he did.

Brummel had never owned a business or a bulldog, but the label did well and the logo stuck. Over Victory Records' first decade of operation, the beefy canine stamped onto every release became an appropriate symbol not only for the heavy-hitting hardcore acts the label signed, but for the pugnacious reputation of its founder. Brummel, a straight-edge college dropout with a shaved head, ran a fiercely independent label that snubbed its nose at the majors. He viewed the music industry less like a competitive business than a war zone, and once told an interviewer that he wanted his tombstone to read, "That was a crazy motherfucker who gave a shit. He liked the music; and he wanted to win."

Tony Victory, as he came to be known, cast an imposing shadow over the hardcore scene. He became a divisive figure and the frequent target of irate fanzine writers who portrayed him as a villainous kingpin for putting dollar signs on independent artists and for injecting tough-guy machismo into a genre that was meant to be a sanctuary from the jocks of the world. A number of bands mocked him in their music. Reversal of Man, Charles Bronson, and Good Clean Fun all penned anti-Victory anthems in the late nineties, although Chicago's MK Ultra may have written the most scathing one with their forty-second ripper "Bring Me the Head of Tony Victory."

But while Brummel's tactics may have drawn detractors, his methods were effective from a business standpoint. His aggressive marketing campaigns helped bands like Hatebreed, Snapcase, and Earth Crisis reach levels of commercial success previously unheard of in hardcore. He also got Victory releases into chain stores and worked with overseas distributors to broaden the label's reach, making it one of the most internationally recognized brands in hard rock.

By the year 2000, Victory Records had more than a hundred releases under its belt and employed a staff of fifteen people in its Chicago office. Heavy music was always emanating from the speakers, and when one of his employees started playing a copy of *Waiting* she'd gotten through Saavedra, Brummel was immediately intrigued.

"Their music was being passed around the office, and after thirty seconds I said, 'How fast can we see these guys?'" Brummel remembers. An employee soon flew to New Jersey to see Thursday open for At the Drive-In at the Wayne Firehouse. The label also arranged for the band to play an afternoon set at the Cubby Bear, in Chicago, a sports bar across the street from Wrigley Field, to a crowd that was mostly Victory employees and a few confused Cubs fans.

"That was one of the first soulless shows I'd ever experienced," remembers Keeley. "Up until that point we were just playing because it was fun and we had zero agenda, and we were surrounded by weirdos and punk kids. Now suddenly we're on this stage, no one's there, and it felt like a showcase where we were being observed, and I didn't like it."

Not long after Thursday's test run for Victory, Keeley was finishing up a work shift at the Rutgers student center when he looked up to find a contract with a bulldog logo on it lying before him. "I'm working at the convenience store there, and next thing I know Geoff walks in and throws a pile of paper in front of me and says, 'We're getting signed to Victory!'" he remembers.

Thursday had no management or lawyers helping them look over the contract, and they signed it without much consideration. "The negotiation was painless," Brummel recalls. "Basically, I made an offer and they took it." What the band didn't realize, though, was that a deal with Victory often meant being locked into a multi-album contract that gave the label publishing and merchandising rights.

"The one thing that sticks with me was that he was like, 'You guys need a van, right? Here's this little contract and we'll throw you five or ten thousand dollars; it's just a formality,'" remembers Payne. "So we signed it and got some money, but it was the publishing for [the album]. It's like, 'Well, that was not aboveboard.' That was on us."

There were early warning signs that gave Thursday pause, like the reaction Rickly got from fellow Victory bands like Snapcase and All Out War. "I remember after we signed, I ended up at CBGB and All Out War was playing," he says. "I was like, 'Hey, man, I'm Geoff from Thursday. We just signed to Victory, too.' And they all just started laughing. They were like, 'Oh, you guys are so fucked!' I thought they were joking around, but after the third Victory band said the same thing, I was like, 'Oh man, that can't be good.'"

"At the time, newer bands on Victory were having a lot of turmoil with the label and quickly falling out with them after having some success with record sales," says Snapcase frontman Daryl Taberski. "I remember telling [Thursday] not to get into debt with Victory and to keep their touring budgets independent of recording budgets so that the label wouldn't have more leverage on them. I also told them to go through royalty statements with a fine-tooth comb."

Red flags aside, Thursday gladly accepted Victory's modest budget to begin work on their sophomore album, *Full Collapse,* which brought them back to Big Blue Meenie. *Full Collapse* captured the band at an ideal moment in their evolution. They'd been around the block enough times to work out their kinks but were still green enough to radiate with youthful poise. The addition of Pedulla proved to be the final missing piece of the band's sonic identity. The occasional guitar lick he tossed onto breakdown sections threw a stadium rock element onto their anthemic post-hardcore style.

Whereas *Waiting* was often personal and introspective, *Full Collapse* turned the energy outward with its choruses built for audience participation and scream-alongs. Thursday gifted themselves a treasure trove of stage-scorchers with songs like "Understanding in a Car Crash," "Paris in Flames," and "Cross Out the Eyes."

The emotional resonance of *Full Collapse* would get the band tagged with the increasingly common and often unflattering "emo" tag, which would lose them respect among more snobbish listeners. Keeley laughs that "the tastemakers never liked our band." Buddyhead, the internet's most influential shit-talking music website at the time, described Thursday's style on *Full Collapse* as "real whimpy boys-fun rock and then super tough guy hardcore 'let's point at each other' stuff." And that was a positive review. *Pitchfork* characterized it more succinctly, calling it, in a word, "shit," before wrapping up their review by advising readers to check out At the Drive-In's *Relationship of Command* instead.

But Thursday's peers who witnessed the album's immediate and undeniable impact firsthand knew better. Adam Turla, frontman of fellow Eyeball Records band Murder by Death, remembers getting a burned CD-R directly from Rickly after the two bands played a show together at an anarchist bookstore in Turla's hometown of Bloomington, Indiana. "Somehow Geoff had gotten my address and he showed up at my door at midnight after the show," he says. "He was like, 'Hey, we've got this new record. I really want you to hear it!' He handed off a copy of *Full Collapse* that they'd recorded but wasn't out yet. He was just so proud of it. I had never heard anything like it. Most of the hardcore and emo that I'd heard had a really different sense of dynamics. The first thing I noticed, as a huge fan of the Cure, was that there were more new-wavy guitar elements, not just the heavy, chugging stuff. It just stunned me. We listened to the hell out of that record."

Thursday spent the last month of 2001 on the road, opening for their Garden State brethren Saves the Day and Hey Mercedes, a new band made up of ex-members of Braid. The venues on this tour were not the basements and small clubs to which they'd grown accustomed; they were now playing for a few hundred people at places like the Trocadero, in Philadelphia, and the House of Blues, in Las Vegas. Chalk it up to a combination of pure adrenaline and blind ambition, but the bigger stages didn't seem to faze Thursday. In fact, the added space and new faces only further empowered them.

"They were the openers, but every night they became certified rock stars," remembers Saves the Day frontman Chris Conley. "I'd never seen a band like that. Their energy was unmatched, and the audience went nuts every night. Their music was just electrifying."

Rickly in particular stepped up his game, transforming from a gawky teenager with goofy pop-and-lock moves to a full-blown showman. No longer concerned with hitting his head on the basement ceiling, he bounded off every corner of the stage, swinging the microphone above him in huge concentric circles. He roped the front rows into the performances, making every audience member within reach feel like an honorary member of the band. The more people screamed his lyrics back at him, the more fearless he became. Rickly made Thursday a band that was impossible to simply witness; Thursday had to be experienced.

"I don't think too many people knew who we were, but we played for a half hour, and by the end the entire room felt like everyone was on the same page," says Payne. "It was one of those moments where it felt like there was something tangible happening. That was when we started to develop an overwhelming amount of confidence."

Thursday was selling more merch than they could keep up with. Shirts and stickers emblazoned with their logo, an outline of a dove, were quite literally flying off the table. Some nights it felt like they'd sold a *Full Collapse* CD to every kid who walked in the door. The strength of their live show even started garnering them new fans off the road when a music video they'd made for "Understanding in a Car Crash," which featured tour footage of the band, started getting played on cable television.

"When we did that Saves the Day tour, we didn't have cellphones, so I'd call my friends back home from a pay phone and they'd be like, 'Dude, I saw your video on MTV2 like eight times today. You guys are famous!'" Payne remembers.

To keep each other humble, the bands pulled nightly pranks on one another, culminating at the tour's final stop, at El Corazón, in Seattle. As Thursday finished their set, Saves the Day and Hey Mercedes ambushed them onstage with an arsenal of Silly String cans and toilet paper rolls. Payne received the worst of it, getting duct-taped to a pole while still trying to pluck his bass.

Thursday left the stage a colorful wreck that night, and as they surveyed one another's Silly String–covered faces backstage afterwards, everyone agreed that something had happened out there. They weren't sure what, exactly, but they could feel that their little band's world was about to change.

"On that tour, we all realized how special it was. It was palpable," says Conley. "We all knew we were riding a wave that was just gonna get bigger."

Thursday stopping for a photo in the Southwest on their tour with Saves the Day and Hey Mercedes, December 2001. *Mike "Hoss" George, courtesy of Thursday*

The members of Thursday watching intently as frontman Geoff Rickly fields interview questions at Big Day Out, 2004. *David "Rev" Ciancio*

The Distillers making their CBGB debut in 2003. Brody Dalle plays guitar with RED HEADS DO IT BETTER inked on her forearm.

Theo Wargo / WireImage / Getty Images

A pre-Frank Iero My Chemical Romance getting their first promo photos taken, at Factory Studios in New Jersey. *Eyeball Records*

Rise Against taking a break from recording *Siren Song of the Counter Culture* in Vancouver to play a few holes of Frisbee golf. *GGGarth*

Rise Against begrudgingly posing for a photoshoot on the streets of Chicago, 2004. *Lisa Johnson*

Against Me!'s Laura Jane Grace in her Chicago home with her collection of decades' worth of ticket stubs. *Dan Ozzi*

$ $ $

Thursday felt invincible. After their tour with Saves the Day, they could now headline shows in medium-size clubs for several hundred people. They were an especially attractive booking in their home base of New Jersey, where they could reliably draw more than a thousand locals. Very often, fans would hang around before doors opened, hoping to pour their hearts out to Rickly, whom they treated like a mixture of lyrical genius and therapist. A few diehards even flashed him their fresh dove tattoos.

"They were the snowflake rolling down the mountain," says the band's manager, David Ciancio. "They were gaining speed and went from a snowflake to a snowball to a full avalanche. When I started working with them, we were fighting for scraps—four dates with Skycamefalling here or three dates with From Autumn to Ashes there. We would take whatever we could get. I was calling people, begging them to book the band. Then, suddenly, people were calling me."

The twenty-seven-year-old Ciancio had first seen the band play at the Hard Rock Cafe in New York City before the release of *Full Collapse* and felt in his bones that he was destined to work with them. "They played in the room where people dine, and it was totally awkward. People were wrapping up their nine-dollar chicken entrees before going to some Broadway show or whatever," Ciancio remembers. "Thursday came out and it was like a clap of lightning came rolling off that stage. Everybody that was there already knew all the lyrics, and I have no idea how. The energy was consuming."

Before the last note of the band's set rang out, Ciancio stuck business cards in their faces. "I didn't even give them a chance to take their guitars off. I ran up to them onstage and said, 'I love your band, I'm gonna manage you, and you're gonna be huge. We're gonna meet this week and talk about how to get this out there.' That definitely threw them for a loop," he laughs.

Things were going so well for Thursday by their senior year of college that they dropped out in the last semester to focus on touring. Their van became their classroom, and when they looked at the path ahead of them, they saw nothing but open road. The only speed bump that occasionally threw them off course was the rocky start to their relationship with Victory Records, whose response to *Full Collapse* felt disheartening.

"I think they were underwhelmed by the album at first. I remember there was a band called Student Rick that was on the label at the time. I think they thought it was the Student Rick record that was gonna do things for the label," says Rule. "Even when our record was doing well, I felt like they were always on to the next thing, looking for something that could do better." Keeley adds that it was "the first and only blockage in our momentum. It was the first brick wall we'd ever experienced."

Communication between Thursday and Victory deteriorated as Brummel realized he had little patience to deal with Ciancio. "I'd always talked to the band [directly], and then they got a manager, Dave. Dave is an internet reverend, so he started calling himself the Reverend. Anyone can go online and become a reverend for like thirty bucks. And he wore a cowboy hat and tight jeans, and he didn't have a full mastery of the King's English," says Brummel. "I know it's gonna sound pompous, but I wasn't gonna talk to someone who calls himself the Reverend when I'm a Roman Catholic who went to Catholic school. I want to talk to the band; I don't want to talk to this goofball."

"They had no interest in talking to Tony," Ciancio says of Thursday. "Any relations we had to have with the label went through me. Then it got weird with Tony, where he didn't want to talk to me, so I had to talk to somebody else at the label. We still got everything we needed. I think it was just part of the Tony thing."

"I was spending so much money on the band that this guy should've been shining my shoes. Instead he was getting in the way and he wasn't bringing any value," says Brummel. "[Managers] think they're helping, but it's actually anti-help. It's like, 'Dude, if you did nothing, you'd be helping. Every time you open your mouth, you're fucking something up.' He would've added more value if he drove their tour vehicle and did their laundry."

Thursday's frustrations with their label piled up and intensified until things hit a tipping point—one that came in the form of a whoopee cushion. The members had caught wind, very literally, that Victory had printed whoopee cushions with the band's name and logo on them as novelty promotional items. Without telling the band, Victory Records had sent a few hundred of them to radio stations in an effort to get songs from *Full Collapse* added to rotation.

"It seemed like at a certain point they started treating us like a gimmick," Payne says of Victory. "We were all putting our entire selves into what we were doing, and then that got distilled down to this thing that you sit on and it farts. At the time, it was like, 'Fuck you!'"

"That was something that was done as a goofy promotional item to get people who hated this kind of music to actually pay attention," says Brummel. "It wasn't something we sold, it wasn't something for fans. It was something for radio people. People in radio, they like goofy stuff. I don't know, what if we'd sent them a bunch of dildos? It'd get their attention. We had to do something to make it stand out."

Brummel didn't think much of it, and once the band voiced their displeasure, the remaining whoopee cushions were thrown away, he says. "Every label would send tchotchkes," he notes. "This wasn't something Victory invented. People have been sending things to get their product attention forever." But to the members of Thursday, the whoopee cushions just served to emphasize that they were stuck on a record label that didn't appreciate them or share their artistic vision.

"We were just not on the same page, the band and the label," says Rule. "You're young and you care so much about your art, and it's bad enough you're dubbed this fucking 'emo band,' and then it's like, 'Well, now we're a fart-emo band.'"

"If I could go back, yeah, maybe we should've run that by the band and maybe they would've had a better idea," Brummel says. "But it was moving so fast, nobody thought about it. All we cared about was getting them results." And, to his credit, Brummel was getting Thursday results. *Full Collapse* had strong placement in major retailers like Best Buy, "Understanding in a Car Crash" was popular on college radio stations across the country while the video continued to get play on MTV2, and the album even sneaked onto the Billboard 200 chart for a week in April 2002, at number 178. "It grinded—five or six hundred units a week," Brummel says. "It wasn't like it was twenty thousand units a week, but it kept building. When you see something building over time, you can justify continuing to invest in it. So I just kept spending and didn't think about it. I didn't even run profit/loss statements on it, because I didn't care."

"That guy's all bark. He's a real bastard," Rickly says of Brummel. "But he'll put out your record and do a good job with it."

$ $ $

Ben Lazar first saw Thursday on a Friday. The band was on the bill for a show at the Wetlands, in Manhattan, on May 4, 2001, three weeks after the release of *Full Collapse*. "They were playing some benefit show and there were, like, ten people in the room. That's when I saw them play for the first time," he says. "Within ten seconds, I knew I had to sign them. I fell in love immediately."

A former employee of Elektra and EMI, the thirty-year-old Lazar had recently been hired as director of A&R research at Island Def Jam and was on the hunt for his first signing for the label. One of his scouting tactics was to call around to record stores and ask employees which indie artists were selling well. He had called a few stores in Central Jersey, like Vintage Vinyl and Curmudgeon Music, and the name Thursday kept coming up.

"There was one guy who kept mentioning them, and the tone of his voice when he spoke about them made me really curious," he remembers. The clerk touted their live show and alluded to their upcoming Wetlands gig, which Lazar put in his calendar.

Thursday didn't necessarily play Lazar's favorite type of music. In fact, he hated every other band from their scene. "I thought all that shit sucked, and still do," he says. A self-professed Deadhead with eclectic tastes that ranged from Springsteen to hip-hop, he found himself drawn to bands less for their sonic features and more for their artistic DNA. "I was interested in the frequency of artists. Certain bands have the right frequency, regardless of genre, and I was interested in finding them."

Something about Thursday's Wetlands performance resonated with Lazar. The band wielded a mix of art school acumen and street grittiness, he thought. They were a band with pretensions but not pretentious—a refreshing antidote to the indie rock snobbishness he felt emanated from stodgy labels like Matador Records. He was especially taken with Rickly's heart-on-sleeve approach on the microphone. "They played with love, they played with heart," he says. He was further impressed after the show when he talked to Rickly, whom he found intelligent and thoughtful. Lazar left the show that night sweaty and fully sold on Thursday. He had received his New Brunswick baptism and become an overnight convert. When he reported back to the office on Monday, he sent an email to his colleagues:

"Thursday was extremely impressive at Wetlands on Friday night. They're the real deal. Within 20 seconds of the first song, it was obvious that they're a band to be reckoned with. The lead singer is very charismatic and very physical and passionate on stage, and the band's playing is tight and pretty thunderous."

Lazar was the first A&R rep to make contact with Thursday, but he wouldn't be the last. As legend of their cathartic live show grew, more and more reps reached out to the band, until they'd been approached by someone at almost every major label. At the end of their tour with Saves the Day, Ciancio rounded up the interested parties and started scheduling meetings and dinners with the band.

"It felt awkward. I was out of my depth. I didn't know how to relate to these people. I didn't know what they wanted from me and I didn't know what I wanted from them," Keeley remembers of the meetings. "They're showering you with praise and talking to you about all this money and the careers they can make for you. They make a lot of promises, but they may as well be speaking Greek to me. What they're talking about was so far out of the perceived realm of possibility, they might as well have been aliens coming down from the moon."

"There was a show we did with Taking Back Sunday at the Sahara, which was a weird club on Long Island, and there were probably five different labels there to talk to us," says Pedulla. "It was so overwhelming. You just want to hang out with your friends and then it's like, 'Okay, I have to go to three dinners now.'"

"We had one dinner in Little Italy and they rented out a private room at some super old-school Italian restaurant," remembers Payne. "They kept bringing us more food and more food and at one point I had to get up and leave because I almost threw up on the table."

"We played one club in Albany. It must've been a five-hundred-capacity club, but I think they put eight hundred people in it. It was insane," says Rickly. "They were like, 'You can't go on yet,' and when I asked why not, they were like, 'Tom Whalley from Warner Bros. flew in on a personal jet and he's coming to the show.' And I was like, 'I'm not waiting for fucking Tom Whalley. We didn't even invite him!'"

The more meetings Thursday took, the more in demand they became. Labels grew competitive with one another as talk of the band's potential circulated. Some of the A&R pitches were flattering. "We met Gary Gersh, the guy who signed Nirvana, and he got us," says Rickly. "When the guy who signed Nirvana tells you you're gonna be the next Nirvana, that's a pretty big deal."

But some meetings were greased with enough music industry slime to make the band's skin crawl. "I remember one guy coming in and saying, 'Listen, we're not gonna swing our big dicks around,' and then proceeded to do just that. Immediately we were like, 'Nope,'" Pedulla says. "The guy opened the conversation like that, and then talked about all these bands we could give two fucks about, whether it was Third Eye Blind or bands in that genre. It's like, 'This has nothing to do with us. I don't think you have any sense of who we are or who we want to be.'"

"One of the heads of the label offered for us to fuck his personal assistant. We were gone—never talking to that person again," Rickly says. "He would tell us we'd have 'the biggest market share in the business.' We just started calling him Market Share Guy."

As the weeks went on, Thursday met with more and more A&R guys who threw out large sums of money and promised more market share. But the band always knew that the standout suitor in their minds was Island, a label that was home to mega-sellers like U2 and Bon Jovi. Beyond Island's impressive roster, Thursday felt most comfortable with the label's staff. Not only had Lazar been the first rep to take notice of Thursday, but the band was drawn to Island's top brass, Lyor Cohen and Julie Greenwald, whose backgrounds were worlds away from New Jersey basements. Cohen had played a significant role in the crossover success of hip-hop acts like the Beastie Boys and Public Enemy in the 1980s, and along with his protégée Greenwald, he was now leading a new era of artists at Island Def Jam that included DMX, Ludacris, and Jay-Z.

"Lyor and Julie came from Def Jam. The ethos was completely different. They articulated a vision that was incredibly compelling," says Lazar. "Who was cooler than Jay-Z in 2001? Lyor was involved in the birth of the most fundamentally important musical genre at the end of the twentieth century. No one else had that."

Pedulla recalls an intense meeting with the two immediately after news broke that a video had surfaced depicting Def Jam artist R. Kelly allegedly urinating on an underage girl. "It was weird to be a fly on the wall for that, but also, seeing their reaction made us realize that these people actually gave a shit and took something like that seriously," he says. "That meant more to us than someone saying he was gonna swing his big dick around."

Rickly remembers the band's first encounter with Cohen and Greenwald over dinner: "When we first met Lyor Cohen, who is this legendary character from every rap song of the last two decades, he took us to Mr. Chow's, a very upscale Chinese restaurant. Sean Penn was at the next table. The dumplings come out and we're just really hungry. So we're eating the dumplings and dipping them in this sauce. The Island people are looking at us across the table, and then they just slowly dipped their hands into what we thought was dipping sauce and they started washing their hands. They were finger bowls! We were dipping our dumplings in hand water—so uncultured. The president, Julie, was watching me do it and wouldn't break eye contact. I think maybe that sealed it for them. They must've thought: 'These kids don't know anything. We can show them the ropes.'"

Once word made its way to the Victory office that major labels were keen on poaching one of its rising acts, Brummel's bulldog instincts were triggered and he grew protective. "I think it was when [*Full Collapse*] had sold over 100,000 copies, that's when I started getting intel on the street that all these major-label A&R guys were trying to cozy up to the band," says Brummel. "I'm pretty sure that I threatened some of those people. I mean, what would you do if someone broke into your house and tried to steal something from you? There's no difference."

A proud indie-label torchbearer, Brummel harbored no respect for delegates of the corporate music machine and was obstinate in his interactions with them. "If you sit in a room with ten major-label A&R guys and you're not running to take a hot shower in the next fifteen minutes, there's something wrong with you," he says.

And, for their part, the A&R guys didn't much care for Brummel. "I fucking loathed Tony Victory. I thought he was the biggest fucking asshole hypocrite. I respected him—he's smart and he worked his ass off—but he was a toxic piece of shit," says Lazar. "He'd always talk that indie propaganda bullshit and then he'd sign these bands to slavery deals. It still makes me fucking nauseous."

$ $ $

On May 28, 2002, Geoff Rickly hovered his mouse cursor over the "post" button on his computer screen, clicked it, and "the Magna Carta," as Thursday had been calling it, was up on their website for all to read.

"Hello Everyone," the fifteen-hundred-word statement began. "We've noticed that there have been a lot of rumors floating around on the internet and especially on our message board and we'd like to set the record straight. We hope that this clears some things up."

The statement went on to air Thursday's grievances with Victory Records and Tony Brummel. It claimed that Brummel had tried to push the band in unwelcome creative directions, like including a scant one-page insert with *Full Collapse,* instead of the full booklet the band had designed, because "it would be cheaper" and because the band's lyrics "were unimportant and should be left out of the packaging." It chronicled their communication difficulties with

Brummel and accused him of only showing interest in Thursday after their successful tour with Saves the Day. It mentioned that they'd heard rumors that Brummel was looking to sell part of Victory to the major label MCA. (Brummel claims he did this "to cockblock Island.") It also told their side of the whoopee cushion fiasco, which was so inherently comical that it would become the focal point among many Thursday fans.

"Victory Records helped us very much," the statement continued. "They helped us to make a record and to get it out to people. However, we have realized that we are not and never will be creatively aligned with Tony and his vision for our band and his company. The idea of family is very important to us, members of a family should treat each other in a forthright, honest, respectful and supportive manner. This is not the case with Victory because of the way Tony has acted towards us. We have been deceived, bullied and compromised to an unsatisfactory end. This is not to say that we don't care about members of the Victory staff. We wish them all the luck in the world. We simply want to continue autonomous from Victory."

The Thursday-vs.-Victory feud made for juicy punk drama on internet message boards, but the real takeaway of the statement was tucked into its latter half: Thursday was leaving Victory to sign with Island Def Jam. It read, "While our deal with Island is subject to our getting released from Victory Records (which Victory is obligated to do according to the contract), we are confident that we will soon be a part of the Island family."

This public declaration was designed to put pressure on Victory to release the band from their contract. Since Thursday was on the hook for more releases with Victory, they were legally bound to deliver more material before moving on to another label. At one point, Island had even considered purchasing a stake in Victory Records, just to obtain Thursday, according to Lazar. "Lyor explored doing a deal with Victory. I remember we brought in all the Victory CDs to the office and listened to them, and they were fucking unlistenable. I mean, just shit; awful fucking music," he says. "Lyor and I flew out to Chicago to meet with Tony in August of 2001. He didn't really know how hot we were for Thursday at that point. He was talking about this band Student Rick, as if they were gonna be the thing. I kept my mouth shut. You could tell he didn't know what he had with Thursday, because he had no fucking ears."

Thursday combed through their contract with Victory and eventually discovered a back door out. "The only loophole we found was that we could have our contract bought out by a major label," says Rickly. "That was how we got out of our contract with Victory. It was either be on a major or be on Victory; that was the choice."

While Thursday's online manifesto provided Victory-hating punks with more ammunition, Brummel maintains that it helped his label in the long run. "It's funny, because when that happened, we had more bands calling and showing up to the office and sending demos," he says. "It was actually counterintuitive. People were like, 'Ah, that must have really sucked. You must have been really distraught.' No, it was great! All it did was give us more attention. Other bands were like, 'These guys are bitches, man. You need to sign us. We'll be loyal.'"

Thursday's deal with Island benefited Brummel financially as well. Victory pocketed around $1.2 million, Rickly says, assuring Thursday would have a hefty bill to recoup with Island Def Jam before seeing much of a profit themselves. Victory also squeezed one more release out of Thursday, a five-song EP entitled *Five Stories Falling,* whose contract-fulfilling nature Thursday was upfront about at their shows as they encouraged crowds to illegally download its sole original track, "Jet Black New Year." The deal even stipulated that Victory's bulldog logo would appear on the back of Thursday's next two albums with Island.

"I didn't buy a house or a fucking Bentley. I just cranked that money into other bands," Brummel says. "I pumped the money into Taking Back Sunday, and Atreyu, and Hawthorne Heights."

Signing to a major label had never been on the road map for Thursday, but this was the corner into which they were backed. Unless they ended the band completely—a solution they considered in their bleakest moments—they had no choice but to sign to a major. "We didn't want to sell out, but we had no option to go to another independent label. We had to go to a major. That was the only way to get out of our contract: to get bought out," says Rule. "So, as a band, we wanted to release something that aired our grievances and let people know: 'We're not fucking sellouts. You want to hear more music and we want to make more music, so this is how it has to be.'"

"This is the tragedy of all this DIY punk shit, that everyone has to pretend like they don't want it," says Lazar. "For a scene that prides itself on authenticity, it's such a bunch of fucking bullshit."

"We'd always said we were never gonna do the major-label thing," says Rickly. "We saw how it went for Jawbox and Jawbreaker and Shudder to Think, all our favorite bands who did one more record and that was it. We thought we'd learned enough and knew better. And as soon as you think that, you're totally fucked."

$ $ $

After laying down his ninth take of the same song at Big Blue Meenie Studios, Tucker Rule stomped down to the basement, threw his drumsticks at the wall, and let out a primal scream. The studio engineer had hired a "drum doctor" to help Rule get his beats to sound just right, and the good doctor was losing his patient on the operating table.

"There were three drum kits, and I had to do three perfect takes on each kit. So I did nine takes of each song," says Rule. "I was enamored with the fact that I got to use all these fancy drum kits, but at a certain point I was fucking exhausted. My arms were like the Hulk's."

The drum tracking alone on Thursday's major-label debut, *War All the Time*, ate up two and a half weeks—as long as it had taken to record *Full Collapse* in its entirety. All told, *War All the Time* would take more than six months to record.

The band found themselves in a difficult position—torn between wanting to stay true to their New Jersey punk roots while also needing to prove that they were the visionaries that all the industry sweet talk and high price tags had made them out to be. "We also had this chip on our shoulder about going to a major when we didn't really want to," says Rickly, "and we thought we had to make a way more difficult record, more angular and weird."

Before even setting foot in the studio, the band had undergone an arduous writing process in Northern New Jersey, following a year and a half of relentless touring in support of *Full Collapse*. "We got some weird rehearsal space in Weehawken. We'd show up at noon and write until midnight," says Payne. "I think we wrote the bulk of the record in two months or less. It was exhausting, but we were so focused."

Thursday returned to Big Blue Meenie to work with Tim Gilles and Sal Villaneuva, but the band's new resources made for a totally different experience than they had on *Waiting* or *Full Collapse*. No expense was spared in regard to money or time. If they wanted to experiment and needed new equipment to do so, they bought it without much hesitation, even if the final result never made it to the record. Unlike with *Full Collapse,* whose speedy and raw recording process held little room for second-guessing, every minute detail of *War All the Time* was nitpicked and overanalyzed.

"It was the same producer, same studio," says Rickly. "But *Full Collapse* took two and a half weeks and cost about $20,000 to make. For *War All the Time,* they charged $550,000 to Island. Put that together with the 1.2 million, plus gear and everything, and we're two million dollars, unrecouped, right out of the gate."

A portion of the budget was used to hire one of Rickly's friends, Andrew Everding, as a studio intern. Rickly had invited Everding to join Thursday as an unofficial band member after his house in Syracuse, New York, burned down. Everding, who had been playing keyboards and doing some guitar-teching for the band on tour, now found himself running personal errands for them.

"Those dudes made a big mistake," Everding says of Thursday. "They told Sal and Tim what the budget was, and they spent everything. Tim bought himself a rack of gear that was like a hundred grand."

"Some of the budget for *War All the Time* was us doing those guys a solid," Pedulla admits. "When we'd made *Full Collapse,* I think we spent $20,000 on it, but that's not what it would have actually cost. Those guys went above and beyond on it. It probably would have cost more like $50,000. So a lot of the reason we turned a blind eye during *War All the Time* was that they'd done so much stuff for us over the years, from *Waiting* to *Full Collapse,* that they deserved to make some money."

War All the Time didn't allow for the fun, breezy times they'd shared while recording their first two records. There was suddenly a lot more pressure to make something their new label could sell. "I walked into the live room and there were fifteen rigs set up—fifteen different amps with fifteen different cabinets," remembers Keeley. "I'm ready to rip some guitars, and before I can do that I have to spend two days playing twenty seconds of a riff through every amp, over and over and over, trying to decide which one is the smallest of degrees better-sounding. And this is our major-label debut record, so I'd better pick right."

As the face of the band, Rickly was put through the wringer the hardest. "I was in the studio for months after the band had stopped going," he says. "I had been taking vocal lessons, but how far along can you come that quickly? You can only grow so fast. I wasn't going to go from being half tone-deaf to suddenly being this amazing singer overnight. So I did feel this impossible pressure."

After months of meticulous work, Thursday was content with the batch of songs they'd laid down and sent the fruits of their labor to Island. But Lazar didn't think they were finished. "I get the record and I'm like, 'Well, it's good; it ain't great, and it ain't gonna do great. We don't have singles,'" he remembers. "We didn't have that song that was going to galvanize an audience. To me, the record was not artistically complete until we had that song."

Thursday was burned out from endless days at Big Blue, but Lazar kept dropping by to pump them harder and harder for a single. "I visited them in the studio and told them, 'You guys need to record more.' They kind of erupted. Geoff started crying. Steve called me a major-label pig," he says.

Inspired by the lore of Bruce Springsteen composing "Dancing in the Dark" in a hotel room overnight after being pushed to his breaking point by his producer for a last-minute single, Lazar ordered half of Thursday to go on a writing retreat. "He had this grandiose rock 'n' roll dream of sending Tom, Steve, and Geoff to a hotel room in

Manhattan to write for three days," says Everding. "Granted, everybody lives, like, five minutes from this fucking place."

From there, Lazar booked another session for the band at Long View Farm, a studio in an isolated, rustic barn in North Brookfield, Massachusetts. The supplementary time generated three more songs: the moody "Division St.," a somber piano ballad from Everding called "This Song Brought to You by a Falling Bomb," and their most accessible output to date, "Signals Over the Air," a straightforward, mid-tempo rock song with a jangly hook. "Signals" saw Rickly waxing about sexuality and the reductive ways in which it's marketed, with lines like "They stole the love from our lives to put sex on the radio." At long last, Lazar believed Thursday had written their single, and *War All the Time* was officially complete and scheduled for release in the fall of 2003.

The recording process was so drawn out, draining, and at times absolutely miserable that the members of Thursday were unsure how they felt about the finished product. They sometimes heard moments of genuine magic when listening back, and other times heard nothing at all.

"I remember thinking, 'This is great, this sucks, I love it, I hate it, the drums sound amazing, the drums sound like shit.' It was all over the place," says Rule. "When you're listening to your own band in the studio on these pristine speakers, it sounds like, as they used to say at Big Blue, 'Christ on a flaming jet ski.' But then you listen to it in your car and you're like, 'Hmm, where's the kick drum?'"

$ $ $

Thursday kept hearing from their contacts at Island that, thanks to an intense marketing push, *War All the Time* was on track to sell 100,000 copies in its first week. The number sounded so astronomical to the band that they joked that they'd probably shit their pants if they actually sold that many records. So the members of Thursday made a wager among themselves on the album's sales: if *War All the Time* sold more than 100,000 copies in its first week, they decided, they were all going to get in the van together and shit their pants. When the SoundScan numbers finally came in, the album ended up landing shy of the six-figure mark, and they lost the bet. Or won, depending on how they looked at it.

War All the Time's first-week showing was strong, though. The album sold 74,000 copies and debuted at number seven on the Billboard 200 chart on October 4, 2003—one slot below Beyoncé's *Dangerously in Love*. For Thursday, these were milestones beyond anything they'd ever imagined. Their little hardcore band had crawled their way out of the basements of a college town in New Jersey to make a top ten record. "It's sort of surreal. It doesn't even make sense to me," Rickly told *Billboard* that week.

"I felt like I was master of the universe," remembers Keeley. "It felt like the world turned and suddenly we were these people who did something no one had ever done."

Thursday felt more supported by their new label through the release of *War All the Time* than they'd felt at Victory. On Victory, the band was one screamy rock band on a roster of many, but at Island, Thursday was treated like rock's saviors. And, in contrast to their publicly tumultuous relationship with Brummel, the band was getting along famously with Cohen and Greenwald. A four-page feature on the band in the November 2003 issue of *SPIN* mentioned that Cohen had gifted Rickly a $90,000 Yoshitomo Nara painting and that "Island Records president Greenwald claims to have wept the first time she heard *War*." She boasted to the interviewer that Thursday was "a top priority" for the label and said of Rickly, "Geoff would kill me for saying it, but he is so sexy! The only thing I ask is give me some more butt shots [in the video]!" Two issues later, the magazine would award *War* the number seven spot on its 40 Best Albums of 2003 list, one slot behind Jay-Z's *The Black Album*.

Lazar's demand for a Springsteen-esque single in "Signals Over the Air" was validated by a review in *CMJ*, which likened the band to the patron saint of the Garden State: "Much like The Boss, Thursday uses vivid detail and gruff emotion to paint pictures that aren't beautiful, but they're magnetic celebrations of human imperfections."

On the streets of New York, Thursday's dove logo was spray-painted all over sidewalks by hired street teams. In Los Angeles, a huge dove appeared on a billboard above the Whiskey a Go Go, on Sunset Boulevard. "I'd go to the store and someone would recognize me. For me, as a bass player, to get recognized, it was crazy," says Payne.

"Things that were supposed to happen were happening," says Ciancio. "We were getting budgets to make videos that were just insane. We were living this life that we'd asked for and wanted, but it was weird once you were in it."

"The big change was that we now had international help," says Rickly. "Victory had distribution in other countries, but they didn't have PR teams over there. So all of a sudden, *NME* was calling us the future of punk rock. *Kerrang!* was saying that when we played the side stage at Reading, we were in a whole other league from anything else on the bill."

On Halloween night in 2003, Thursday made their network television debut, playing "Signals Over the Air" on *The Late Late Show with Craig Kilborn*. The host gave them a hell of an introduction: "*New York Times Magazine* compared our next guest to both Metallica and U2," he said, holding a *War All the Time* CD. A month later, Thursday played the album's titular track on *Late Night with Conan O'Brien*. Neither performance successfully captured what made the band special, though. Thursday was at their best when they were feeding off the energy of a room packed with sweaty kids, not trying to impress a seated studio audience hoping to see a young U2.

"It was horrible. I didn't think we played well. It felt like one of those showcases. We just don't translate that way," says Payne, whose idea it was to play the meandering, four-and-a-half minute "War All the Time" on *Conan*. "It's one of those songs that you feel naked when you're playing it. It's like, 'Holy shit, is this song a half hour long? Is it ever gonna stop?'"

"In those moments, when we were on the fringes of our reach, it did not feel inviting. It felt like a hard sell," adds Keeley. "All the stuff we could control felt bulletproof. We could steer our own ship pretty handily. But when we would have these 'career-making moments' that bands dream of—being on TV for the first time, playing Coachella's main stage in front of eighty thousand people—anything like that, we bombed."

"Signals Over the Air" didn't fully land with radio listeners, either. A shortened version of it got some pickup on rock radio stations, but it didn't produce the momentum needed to roll out subsequent singles, as was Island's original plan. Plus, like most labels at the time, Island was still trying to navigate the industry's rapidly changing landscape. Music fans were migrating en masse to the internet, and the label was struggling to convert Thursday's online popularity to physical album sales.

"True 'emo kids' didn't want to listen to the radio," says Ciancio. "That was the time when media consumption really shifted. It was just after Napster and streaming and social media and Myspace. Young people didn't want to listen to Bob Olson on the radio telling them about this cool new emo band."

Lazar remembers accompanying Lyor Cohen to a Thursday show at Roseland Ballroom, in New York, with Island labelmates Thrice. The two watched three thousand people screaming along to "Signals Over the Air" and other songs from an underperforming *War All the Time*. That was when it dawned on them that their business was on the precipice of a seismic shift. "I remember Lyor going, 'Every fucking kid downloaded this record, I know it! Everyone knows every single fucking word.' That audience was ground zero for downloading," he says.

"There was this great white hype," Ciancio says of Thursday. "All this money, all this drama, all this investment. Big-budget videos, big-budget this, and big-budget that. I think the band did everything the way they wanted with integrity, but I think Island had expectations that they'd signed the next Nirvana. I think they thought they were gonna put out a single and it'd roll out three more singles. After we took that first single to radio, it had a small pop. They were expecting a fireworks show and just got some sparklers."

"I thought it'd be a hit. I still do," says Lazar. "If there is a God, and when I die he says I can ask him any question, I will ask why 'Signals' wasn't a hit."

$ $ $

Four months after *War All the Time*'s release, Thursday was in Australia when they received news they didn't expect or want: Lyor Cohen and Julie Greenwald were jumping ship at Island Def Jam to take positions at Warner Music Group. The company was about to be restructured, and the band knew that without their two biggest advocates in their corner, they were about to find themselves stranded on a deserted Island.

Thursday soon learned that their label would now be headed by Antonio "L.A." Reid, the former Arista Records hotshot CEO who had overseen the runaway success of rising pop stars like Avril Lavigne, P!nk, and Ciara. "It's like having a new dad. He comes in with his own kids and inherits you. He doesn't have the same emotional investment in you," says Ciancio. "He was a pop/R&B guy—really smart and super friendly, but we couldn't expect him to walk in the door and think Thursday was amazing."

Much to their surprise, though, Reid was initially intrigued by Thursday. "L.A. Reid came out to a Warped Tour, and I remember because he was wearing this really expensive sweater and it was like ninety degrees. He looked sharp, just swagger," says Rule. "He watched our set and was blown away. Coming from his background, I just don't think he'd seen stuff like that."

"L.A. Reid loved the band at first," says Lazar, who stood beside Reid during Thursday's Warped Tour performance. "He turned and said to me, 'These guys are great! They're much better than Thrice.' When they played 'Signals,' he goes, 'This is a hit, right?' And I said, 'Nope.' He said, 'How is this not a hit?' I said, 'I have no fucking idea, man.'"

"He came backstage and he was freaking out. He was so psyched," remembers Rickly. "He was like, 'You guys are fucking stars. You're *stars*! You're gonna be the biggest band in the world. You're amazing live. You have magnetism. All we gotta do is get you the right person to write singles for you.' And we were like, 'We don't do that.' He just said, 'Okay.' And that was it. He totally checked out."

The pressure Thursday put on themselves to impress Reid and live up to their label's impossible expectations was starting to break them. One lyric on *War All the Time*'s "Tomorrow I'll Be You" proved especially prescient after a year of constant international touring, press interviews, and live radio performances: "How long can the wheels maintain a spin at this velocity?"

The members were growing sick of one another and sick in general. "I kept losing my voice because we were playing like three hundred shows a year," says Rickly. "The EMT said it was probably acid reflux. So he gave me whatever the purple pill is for acid reflux, but I was allergic to it. I was constantly shitting blood and feeling really sick. I got anemic and started bruising everywhere. It was one of those things where I was like, 'I deserve this. I sold my soul to the devil' or whatever. I really put that on myself. If you grow up punk and a Catholic, that's how you think."

The band took a brief hiatus before regrouping at the end of 2005 to record their follow-up for Island, *A City by the Light Divided*. For the first time, they left the familiar comfort of Big Blue Meenie to record in Cassadaga, New York, with producer Dave Fridmann, who was best known for his work with bands like Weezer, the Flaming Lips, and Mogwai.

City marked a shift for Thursday, but it wasn't clear in what direction. After desperately trying to make a commercial record with *War All the Time*, the band was now unconcerned with producing singles. They instead wanted to make something weirder, something more experimental, something that challenged listeners. Rickly's ailing vocal cords had been given a rest on the album, so it largely lacked the band's trademark gnarling bite. The departure from form left Thursday without a clear identity. *Rolling Stone* didn't appreciate the band's new direction and closed a dismissive review of the album by quipping, "This Thursday may make you long for Friday."

"[It] was a hollow echo of their best shit," says Lazar. "It had the sonics of Thursday, but it didn't have the heart. Working with Fridmann was not the right move. He served their intellectual art school thing. When it went too intellectual, it stopped working."

By the time the band completed the album, they felt they'd completely lost the attention of Reid. The label had releases scheduled that year from reliable sellers to concern themselves with. Rickly remembers walking into a meeting where Reid made it clear that Thursday was no longer a priority. "He had me come into the office to play him the singles, and made me wait a really long time, which is fine. I figured he was busy. I didn't think he was making me wait as a power play," Rickly says. "I come in and sit down and he asks me about the record, and as soon as I start talking, he opens up a newspaper and starts reading it in my face. And I was like, 'Oh, this meeting is to show that we're not important because we didn't play ball.' Once I got that, I had to laugh. Because the thing about L.A. Reid is, his desk was on a raised pedestal so he's always above you. This is his whole thing—to play games to assert his dominance."

In June 2006, a month after *City*'s release, Ben Lazar was among several employees laid off from Island in a company downsizing. "Sales were going down. They had to cut people," he says. "I didn't belong there anymore. The world was moving to pop and hip-hop. L.A. didn't want to deal with failure. How was that team gonna support that record? At that time it was still all about radio, and there were no radio songs on that record." The label was, as he puts it, "in full internet collapse."

Eventually, Thursday was informed that their budget had been cut and they wouldn't be seeing another dollar in support, which didn't bode well for their tour schedule, already booked for the next five months through North America, Europe, and Australia. "I remember sitting on the bus with everybody when they broke the news to us," says Everding. "They'd sent out two shitheads from Island who could give two fucks and they tried to explain it. It was all bullshit. We were pissed off."

Thursday found themselves stuck between a rock and a hard place. Their contract gave them the option to make another album, which they wanted to take, but they knew Reid would never give them the budget to do so. They were deeply indebted to a label whose investment they'd never be able to pay back, left to eternally wander the dreaded record-label purgatory. "It felt like a movie where the astronaut floats out to space forever," says Keeley.

Once the writing was on the wall, Thursday wanted out. Ciancio sent the band an email urging that their priority should be getting dropped from the label and that they needed to approach this move "with an iron grip and with venom on our teeth." Without an A&R rep at the ready, Ciancio no longer had a label contact to handle Thursday's affairs. He called the Island office every day for weeks but couldn't get anyone to return his calls. Ciancio claims to have threatened to stand outside the Island offices with a baseball bat if that was what it took. Once he finally heard back from Reid, he set up a meeting between the CEO and Rickly just before Christmas in 2006.

"When I went in this time, he was highlighting something in a booklet from a CD," Rickly says of Reid. "I was like, 'Whatcha doing?' And he said, 'I'm highlighting the number one songs that I wrote.' I just thought he was doing it because it was something he had to do. I realized later he was a hitmaker. That record wasn't new. He was just showing me he'd made all these hits."

Rickly cut to the chase: "I said, 'We were thinking maybe it'd be good for us to go back to being what we are, which is an indie band.' He was like, 'That makes some sense.' I said, 'But we know we owe you. Nobody here is trying to get in a fight with the label. We figured we'd like to leave and thought it'd be no skin off your back.'"

It seemed like Reid appreciated the candid approach. He told Rickly that he would take the holiday break to consider the proposal and crunch the numbers. The two shook hands on it and Rickly left. As promised, Reid reached out to the band at the start of 2007 with an answer. Rickly remembers, "The new year came and he said, 'You guys are free to go.'"

Island Records and Thursday cut their respective losses and went their separate ways on a handshake, and both parties were happy enough. The label moved on to their next big thing, and the band considered themselves lucky to part on good terms and in one piece. "It tried to break us, and we bent; we nearly snapped, but we kept it together somehow," Rule says of the experience. "But you've got to take those chances. No matter what anyone says, sometimes you've just got to take that leap of faith."

Thursday spent nearly five years on a major label, and for a group of college kids from New Jersey, their success vastly exceeded their

CHAPTER 8

THE DISTILLERS

Coral Fang

Sire Records (2003)

GEOFF RICKLY HAD a big, bloody gash on his forehead. The Thursday frontman had picked up the injury the previous night, after opening for Deftones in Chicago. Although the chaos of his band's live shows had inflicted a number of bumps and bruises on his body over the years, this one came courtesy of the Windy City itself. A stiff gust had blown open the door of a production truck behind the Aragon Ballroom. Rickly ducked, but it was too late—the metal clipped his skull, and the next thing he knew, his face was covered in blood.

It couldn't have come at a worse time, since Rickly was now in New York, getting prepped to be photographed for the cover of *SPIN*'s Next Big Things issue. The magazine, due to hit newsstands in February 2004, spotlighted Thursday as one of the four "cool new bands you need to hear now!"

As stylists worked to hide the wound with makeup and strands of his hair, Rickly sized up the other three Next Big Things on the set. Drinking a Heineken and doing the *New York Times* crossword puzzle was Paul Banks, frontman of the rising New York indie rock band Interpol, looking unassuming and dapper in his usual dark European-cut suit. The other Next Big Thing, Justin Hawkins of British stadium rock revivalists the Darkness, was more flamboyant, in a long white overcoat and pink candy-stripe bell bottoms. But even in a room full of hot young singers poised for rock stardom, the fourth Next Big Thing stood out. She was, as Rickly recalls, "clearly the magnet in the room."

Brody Dalle, the twenty-four-year-old frontwoman of the Los Angeles punk band the Distillers, stood five foot eight but seemed to tower over everyone. She had a pale complexion and a dark aura. A mop of jet-black hair shrouded her eyes, which sometimes looked green and sometimes blue, depending on the light. Her bright red lips were pierced with a lip ring, and her left shoulder was covered with a tattoo of a skull and crossbones adorned with a dainty pink bow and the words FUCK OFF. She wore a black corset top, and as for the rest of the outfit, that was a source of contention.

"I'm not wearing this," she told her label handlers, rolling her eyes as she pointed to a puffy white tulle skirt by designer Betsey Johnson. "None of these guys are being asked to wear this ridiculous shit. So why should I?" She wasn't wrong. The photographer had given Rickly little more sartorial instruction than to hike up his pants a bit to accentuate his sneakers and white tube socks.

The conversation grew tense as the team from Dalle's record label pleaded with her to try it on. The *SPIN* people wanted her to wear it, they told her, and if she didn't, it might irrevocably damage her relationship with the magazine. Finally, after much debate, Dalle relented. "Fine," she said. "Give me the fucking tutu."

$ $ $

Brody Dalle was born Bree Joanna Alice Robinson on the first day of 1979, and grew up in Fitzroy, a suburb of Melbourne, Australia. She was the daughter of a single mother, and her early childhood was marred by familial turmoil and the seedy undercurrent of her hometown.

"Australia, it's built on fuckin' convicts, man," she says. "Melbourne, particularly, was very violent and dark, whether it was romper-stomper-style beatings, which were quite regular, or seeing men expose themselves pretty much on a daily basis as a schoolgirl. They're called flashers and, seriously, I saw them all the time. But I was not afraid. I would go for it: I'd be like, 'Motherfucker, I'm gonna kill you!' I'd chase them and throw shit at them and scream at them—all the things that they did not want to experience. It made me so fucking angry. It was such weakness to me."

Dalle had developed her tough exterior early on, after being molested at a young age. "I was sexually abused by two different men who actually lived next door to each other," she says, "one of whom was my childhood best friend's father. He sexually abused both of us—his own daughter. She ended up moving into our house and we went to court against her dad. They came from money and had high-powered lawyers. Because we couldn't provide dates—because we were like four and five—he got away with it. But the court believed us, so they compensated us."

The young Dalle attended Catholic school, where she had a hard time making friends. "I was hardcore bullied at school by girls," she says, "whether it was getting physically dragged up and down the playground or picked on or left out or talked badly about." She began fighting back and got kicked out of school at fifteen. She fell into the habit of running away from home and squatting on the streets, where she experimented with alcohol, pills, and heroin.

The only constant in her life was music. She'd latched on to American exports like Cyndi Lauper and Bruce Springsteen at a young age. At twelve she discovered Nirvana, and absorbed every band in their orbit. Later, in her teen years, she was clued in to English punk rock by an older boyfriend. "I was dating this guy called Andy the Anarchist, this dirty crust-punk guy," she says. "Between him and my friend's cousin, I was exposed to Discharge and Disorder and everything from Oi Polloi to the Exploited and the Clash. And then through that I found the Dead Kennedys."

Dalle began playing music through Rock 'n' Roll High School, a Melbourne collective for aspiring female musicians run by Stephanie Bourke, a music instructor and drummer for the bands Hecate and Litany. It was there that Dalle assembled her first band, Sourpuss, with three other girls. Sourpuss's downtrodden delivery of angsty lyrics sounded very much in line with the mid-nineties alternative rock scene, earning them comparisons to bands like L7 and Hole, whose raspy-voiced frontwoman, Courtney Love, Dalle would frequently be likened to. But after a while, Dalle began to feel limited by the confines of an all-girl collective, an attitude that put her at odds with the other members. "I didn't like playing under the banner of a girl school," she says. "I thought it was more damaging than anything, to be defined in that way. It was uncool and we were made fun of for it. Eventually, [Bourke] ended up managing us and we just rehearsed there instead of falling under [the Rock 'n' Roll High School] moniker."

Under the guidance of Bourke, Sourpuss released a pair of EPs through Fellaheen, the Australian label that was home to artists like Pavement, Ben Lee, and Superchunk. The band also landed some opening slots on high-profile shows and tours throughout Australia, sharing stages with Hole, Dinosaur Jr., and another up-and-coming local alternative rock act, Silverchair.

On the last day of 1995, Dalle's final day as a sixteen-year-old, Sourpuss played a daytime slot at Summersault, an outdoor festival in Sydney, which also hosted Bikini Kill, Beck, and Foo Fighters, as well as Jawbreaker, on what would be the band's final international tour before imploding. Although Sourpuss was assigned a less-than-desirable midday slot, they earned some important new fans when members of Sonic Youth and Beastie Boys lined the stage and nodded along.

Backstage, Dalle met another headlining act that was playing the festival, Rancid. The spiky-haired Bay Area band had been one of the biggest successes of the post-*Dookie* punk boom of the mid-nineties. Their new album, . . . *And Out Come the Wolves,* had infiltrated the mainstream through exposure on MTV and rock magazines, and was three weeks away from going gold. Most impressively, Rancid had achieved their success while maintaining their punk cred, having proudly stuck with Epitaph Records, the indie punk label founded by Bad Religion guitarist Brett Gurewitz, for all their releases. Dalle immediately clicked with the band's mohawked thirty-year-old frontman, Tim Armstrong, a lean and handsome punk poet with whom she shared a chemistry that felt instant and natural.

A few months later, Rancid was scheduled to play the traveling North American festival Lollapalooza, and Armstrong reached out to Dalle with an invitation. "He wanted me to come out to Lollapalooza, so he flew me out and I was on tour with him for a week and a half, just hanging out on tour," she says. The pair grew closer as Rancid's bus rolled through the Northeast and Canada that summer with bands like Metallica, Soundgarden, and the Ramones, who were playing the final shows of their career. Although they spent only a handful of days together, the two bonded immediately and deeply over late-night talks, sharing intimate details about their troubled upbringings.

When the Lollapalooza run was over, Dalle and Armstrong made plans to meet up again, but things went inexplicably awry. "I flew home and Tim was going to come visit me," she remembers. "He called and my mom answered the phone. He said, 'I'm coming out tomorrow,' and then he never showed up. I couldn't get ahold of him for six months. I was fucking devastated. I didn't have a contact, there was no way to get in touch, I had no idea what happened. I was this seventeen-year-old girl who'd just moved back home. In the six months, I slashed my wrists and then went into some hardcore therapy."

Dalle suffered more heartbreak that October when Sourpuss dissolved, for tragic reasons. "Sourpuss had been through twelve drummers," she says. "Our main drummer we ended up settling with was named Ineka Hinkley. She told us she was going to hitchhike to Coffs Harbour, which is up on the New South Wales coast. We begged her not to, but she was older than me by four years and she had her mind made up and off she went. Three days later, we found out that she had been raped and murdered and thrown in a ditch on the side of the freeway."

The Australian newspaper *The Age* reported that Hinkley's body had been found lying faceup in the bushes at a truck stop, "naked from the waist down and police said the body was in an advanced state of decomposition. Strewn about the area was a backpack containing personal items and clothing." An autopsy confirmed that she had been strangled to death but did not determine whether she had been sexually assaulted. The twenty-year-old was one of six young women, all hitchhikers, who were murdered in the area that year by what investigators believed to be a series of killers.

The loss only made Dalle's depression grow worse. When she finally did hear from Armstrong in early 1997, he made up for the radio silence with a grand gesture, inviting her to move to Los Angeles to live with him. Without a second thought, the lovestruck Dalle packed a couple of bags and, using the money she'd received from her childhood abuse case, bought a plane ticket to America. "I had no plans, no idea. I kind of just flew by the seat of my pants," she says. Upon landing at LAX that April, the Australian teenager felt an immediate culture shock.

"I hated it," she remembers of L.A. "I thought it was really ugly and strange and confusing. Everything was so different—the architecture, even the road is a different color. Everything was so fucking far away. I think I spent twelve grand on cabs in three months."

The eighteen-year-old Dalle and the thirty-one-year-old Armstrong were married that summer in Nevada, easing the constraints of her visa restrictions, with Dalle taking Armstrong's last name thereafter. His name wasn't the only trait she'd adopt. Knowing no one in her new city but her husband, she glommed on to his lifestyle to get assimilated. His friends became her friends; his hangouts became her hangouts. She spent her nights tagging along at shows in Hollywood and her days hanging around the Epitaph Records office in Silver Lake.

As she would quickly discover, the Rancid/Epitaph crew was tight-knit, insular, and sober. Bad habits had nearly derailed both the band and the label early on, with Armstrong's alcoholism having gotten in the way of his early music career and Gurewitz's heroin addiction leading him to briefly walk away from the label and check into a rehab facility. As a result, anyone who stepped into their orbit was expected to follow suit and check the substances at the door. Any lingering interest Dalle had in drugs or alcohol would have to be left in Australia.

Even Dalle's music didn't fully belong to her anymore. She didn't have a guitar of her own in America, and taught herself to play Armstrong's left-handed guitar upside down. The first song she wrote in her new city, "L.A. Girl," was inspired by the not-so-warm welcome she'd received from Armstrong's female friends upon her arrival. ("*Do ya wanna go home soon?*")

"I had no direction," she remembers. "I was like, 'I need to start a band.'" She recruited Kim "Chi" Fuelleman, an employee of Epitaph, to play bass, and Matt Young, a connection she'd made through her new friends in the Adolescents, on drums. The three found a rehearsal studio on Cahuenga Boulevard in Hollywood and began jamming together.

They called themselves the Distillers, and their earliest songs were fast and trashy cuts of unruly punk rock. Musically, the band didn't break new ground, but their standout feature was Dalle's voice, which had grown feral since her Sourpuss days. Her volume and pitch flared wildly and unpredictably, from scratchy howls to hoarse harmonies. Her mumble-mouth enunciation stretched and twisted syllables around like taffy. Even simple words, like the "women" in "L.A. Girl," became *wom-oy-wenn* after Dalle got ahold of them. It's a technique, she admits, that took a good deal of inspiration from her husband. "I was definitely emulating Tim's singing style, for sure," she says. "I really loved Rancid. They were rad. We spent a lot of time around them, and I was still finding my legs."

Armstrong offered to release the Distillers' first four songs as a seven-inch through Hellcat Records, a subsidiary of Epitaph he'd launched two years earlier that aimed to be a hub for modern punk and third-wave ska acts. *Give 'Em the Boot*, a widely distributed $4.99 compilation CD, introduced the world to its roster, which included the Slackers, Hepcat, and U.S. Bombs.

"Tim wanted us to be on his label," says Dalle. "At the time, I didn't really even think twice about it. It wasn't until later that I thought about looking at options. But he was very adamant that I couldn't do that—that I 'keep it in the family.'"

Dalle's introduction to playing American punk gigs came when the Distillers opened for a band that was performing a Ramones cover set at an East Hollywood bar called the Garage. "They had the wigs on and everything," she remembers. "Then these jocks came into the bar and got into a fight. There weren't that many people there, so everyone in the bar jumped into the fight, too. I was standing up on a table, just watching it. The band got off and beat the shit out of these guys and then got right back onstage. It was wild."

The Distillers played more shows around Los Angeles, Orange County, and San Francisco. With the help of their label connections, they got booked on their first tour in May 2000—six weeks opening for Dropkick Murphys, the Bouncing Souls, and the Dwarves on Epitaph's Punk-O-Rama tour. In need of a roadie to handle merch sales and guitar repair, Dalle approached Tony Bevilacqua, an intern she'd befriended at the Epitaph office. "I'd just gotten hired there," Bevilacqua says, "and then four months later she was like, 'We're going on our first tour. You wanna come with us?' And I was like, 'Yeah!' I'd just started working at a record label and then I quit. I didn't really even like punk rock like that back then. It wasn't my thing. But her voice, man. I'd never heard anything like it." It was a guttural roar that Gurewitz once described to the *SF Weekly* as sounding "like a gravel truck with a broken axle, but she never misses a note."

After going over well with Punk-O-Rama crowds, the Distillers hopped on a few more tours and made their first trip to Europe, sharing a bus with the New York hardcore band Agnostic Front for six weeks. "We did, like, thirty days in a row in Germany," remembers Dalle, who welcomed the grueling introduction to touring abroad. "We played squats. It was awesome—a dream come true." They'd also added a second guitarist, Rose "Casper" Mazzola, to round out the lineup.

A small cult quickly grew around Dalle. It wasn't just her talent that drew curious punks in, but her style and attitude. She was a sneering, cursing, spitting machine in tattered tank tops, studded belts, and hair that was often glued up into a mohawk or liberty spikes. "All the early shows, you could tell right away there was something special about Brody," Bevilacqua says. "She's just a rock star, man. She's got *that thing*. There's just something about her that kids looked up to. Even when there were just a couple of kids, I remember seeing them crying and telling her life stories and showing their tattoos. That shit started right at the beginning. People would lose their shit in front of Brody."

In the spring of 2000, the Distillers released their first album, via Hellcat, a fourteen-song, self-titled LP that featured a black-and-white photo of a snarling dog on its cover. It's a debut that Dalle describes as "terrible" and looks back at with regret. "It's like having someone read your first diary," she winces. "It's so immature and ridiculous. There are aspects of it that I love, like the melodies and stuff. Melody was always really important to me. I think it's my strong suit." But the main source of the album's weakness, in her mind, stemmed from her lyrical delivery, which was still largely imitative of Armstrong's. "In discovering yourself, you do emulate people, but it's just so apparent on that record."

That the Distillers had effortlessly earned a slot on a reputable label, coupled with the fact that Dalle's musical style bore noticeable similarities to her husband's, earned the band a good deal of petty criticism. Much like rumors had circulated that Kurt Cobain had ghostwritten songs for his wife, Courtney Love, Dalle had to stomach a few hurtful accusations of getting writing assists from Armstrong or being a shameless, social-climbing gold digger.

Despite the naysayers, the Armstrongs remained happily in love as punk rock's power couple. Dalle even commemorated their union with a tattoo on her right hip bearing the name TIM inked in the middle of a red heart, above the word EVERLASTING. The Distillers were seeing success as well, with their album selling around twenty thousand copies and expanding their fan base. "It was the gamut," Dalle says of Distillers fans. "Skater kids, punk rock kids, punk girls, and a few skinheads sprinkled in there."

The record was fairly well received, garnering a few positive press write-ups. One review in the *Village Voice*, though, would stick with Dalle forever. The review was generally favorable—"I like this record a lot," wrote critic Frank Kogan, who compared Dalle to punk greats like Patti Smith and Joe Strummer. But its main critique of the album boiled down to: *What the fuck is this woman saying?* "The Distillers' actual lyrics seem not to coalesce into anything colossal, or even understandable," Kogan wrote, pointing to slurred, seemingly nonsensical words and phrases like "night irreverential" and "carneleby." The review stung, not because it was mean but because it was accurate.

"He was like, 'What the fuck is this word? What does this even mean?'" Dalle recalls. "I was like, 'Oh my God, he's right.' I'd never focused much on my lyrics, and I was kind of cramming the last part of that record without really even thinking about it. I was making sounds, but there weren't really even lyrics behind them, which makes singing those songs really difficult now, because it's like, 'What the fuck am I even saying?'" Reading the review served as a challenge for Dalle to up her songwriting game and to discover her own musical identity outside of her husband or anyone else. "From then on, I was so determined to find my own style. Writing and lyrics became super important to me. It changed my fucking life."

$ $ $

Not long after the release of their debut album, Brody Dalle broke the band up. The Distillers was her brainchild and she needed bandmates willing to fall in line behind her, which she felt was not the case. The band was being pulled in too many different directions and she was losing control of the project. "After the first record, I fired Matt and Kim because I felt like there was collusion going on," she says. "It was this dynamic where people didn't like that I was running the show. It hurt and it was problematic for me."

Needing a few trustworthy players to support her vision, she filled the drum seat with a gentle brick wall of a man named Andy "Outbreak" Granelli. "Brody actually broke the band up, but she had this tour booked and I filled in, and then stayed forever," Granelli laughs. "I just wouldn't leave."

Dalle had met Granelli through the Bay Area scene at Gilman Street, where his band, the Nerve Agents, were regulars. "Everything happened because of Gilman Street, at least in my life as a musician," Granelli says. "That's where I met Brody and Tim. Brody and I became fast friends and I really loved her and her band. She's got a knack for the hook, and I love a good hook. Plus, in Nerve Agents,

I was kind of tired of the boys' club shit. So to have the opportunity to back up a woman like Brody was a dream come true."

Dalle replaced Fuelleman on bass with Granelli's friend Ryan Sinn, a metalhead guitarist and record store employee. "Andy called me one day and asked if I played bass. I said no," remembers Sinn. "My boss said I was an idiot and that I should call him back. I had four days until my audition. I borrowed some gear, learned to play the first album, and I was in. My first show with them was in Phoenix, Arizona, on the first day of Warped Tour. I was told that if I fucked up, [Rancid bassist] Matt Freeman was gonna finish the set. He was kneeling onstage about ten feet away, staring at me. My knees had never knocked so hard. I was absolutely petrified."

With the two new members locked in, Dalle decided to soldier on with the Distillers, embarking on a stretch of U.S. shows in November 2000 on which they opened for Rancid and AFI. The new members would soon learn about Rancid's stringent rules against tour debauchery, and keeping the backstage dry.

"Coming into the band, I was told that if I was caught drinking, the tour was done, the band was done, and Brody would be in rehab," says Sinn. "The first drink I had after joining the band was in Amsterdam after five weeks of touring with three bands on one bus. We had one day off in the middle. We got our meal tickets and I went down to the restaurant and I got a vodka cranberry for some reason. I sat at the back table, a spot where I could see both doors, and I just inhaled it. Even if I wanted to have a beer off tour, too. Like, I remember the new Satyricon album came out. I picked that up and got a bottle of Thunderbird and was hiding in my bedroom with it. It was just that feeling of being watched."

With this revamped lineup, the Distillers wrote and recorded their sophomore album, *Sing Sing Death House,* released on Hellcat in January 2002. Mazzola left the band shortly after, reducing them to a trio. With the sting of the *Village Voice* review still fresh in her mind, Dalle took a more thoughtful approach to her songwriting this time around. What came out was twelve tracks that blended her natural gift for catchy punk hooks with more mature lyrics that often leaned autobiographical. On "The Young Crazed Peeling," she sang about growing up in Fitzroy with a "working single mother in an urban struggle" and about falling in love with Armstrong: "I love a man from California / He's the prettiest thing, we got the same disorder." She still maintained a bit of distinctive drunk-punk slur and sneered accentuation on her words, but had dropped the incoherent drawl.

Sing Sing Death House was striking, even before a note of it was played. When the jewel case was opened, it revealed a neon-green compact disc with a black outline of Dalle's profile, a foot-tall mohawk fanning around nearly half of it. The world would soon get a glimpse of Dalle's spikes when MTV featured the Distillers on *You Hear It First,* a three-minute video segment that spotlighted up-and-coming acts. Host Sway Calloway touted the Distillers as "a band that gives a spark to the world of punk rock, and it doesn't take the resident expert to know how much it's needed. The female lead is definitely genuine, and the Distillers pick up where legends like the Runaways left off."

The segment showed clips from their music video for "The Young Crazed Peeling," in which Dalle and her pointy liberty spikes turn heads as she saunters through the streets of downtown Los Angeles. An accompanying interview with the band showcased a demure but effortlessly cool Dalle, begrudgingly fielding questions in an oversize olive-green hoodie. When asked if the intimacy of her songwriting made her feel vulnerable, Dalle shrugged and said, "I don't really give a fuck what people think." For a new generation of budding rock fans, especially female ones, Dalle provided the same first eye-opening glimpse at punk culture that her husband had done years prior when Rancid's "Salvation" video was played on MTV.

A coinciding feature on the MTV News website, which included a free download of "The Young Crazed Peeling," sang further praises: "Not since Courtney Love wanted to be the girl with the most cake has a woman so embraced her role as a sleazy punk *femme fatale* on par with the first woman to push the role to the extreme, the Plasmatics' Wendy O. Williams. With so many immediate comparisons and that ever-present 'women who rock' tag hinged upon her every move, Armstrong might have buckled under such extraneous pressures, but she'll leave that to a chick without *cojones.*"

"After we did that segment, that's when it started to blow up for us," remembers Granelli. Over the next year, the video got added to rotation on MTV2, the album's catchy single "City of Angels" became one of KROQ's most requested songs, and the band even got mentioned on an episode of *Gilmore Girls*. *Sing Sing* never broke into the Billboard 200 chart, but it did well for Hellcat, selling more than 100,000 copies, making it one of the label's most popular releases.

By this time, a few of the bigger press outlets had also taken notice of the hot young band. In a positive review, *Rolling Stone* praised *Sing Sing*'s sound as "pure garbage-truck scuzz." *CMJ* said that *Sing Sing* was "not only one of the best punk albums of the new year, it's also a step in the right direction for raging women to bring their lethal charms to the mic." And Dalle's underrated shredding skills were recognized with a write-up in *Guitar Player*.

The band even got a glowing feature in the *Village Voice*, in which writer Jeanne Fury praised the improvement Dalle had made as a songwriter since leaving the paper's critic scratching his head with their debut. "*Sing Sing*'s songs are haughtier and groovier; melodies bubble up and rock side-to-side," it read, going on to praise Dalle as an important female rock figure whose songs "would leave stretch marks on the mouths" of Yeah Yeah Yeahs' Karen O and Bikini Kill's Kathleen Hanna: "Her power lies in a don't-even-think-about-fuck-ing-with-me attitude. It's immediate, forceful, and unwavering—and too many girls still need to be convinced this is a beneficial way to be. Ignorance is not tolerated, and there is no discussion."

On the heels of this momentum, the Distillers spent most of their time on the road and took bigger tour opportunities, some of which broke out of the confines of their narrow punk world. At the end of 2002, the Distillers played their biggest shows to date—seven weeks on an arena tour supporting two major acts, No Doubt and Garbage. It was there that Dalle found a mentor in Garbage front-woman Shirley Manson.

"I just walked into her dressing room on the first day and I was like, 'Here I am,'" Dalle remembers. "And on the spot, we fell in love. I didn't leave her side that whole tour. I was really looking for that. I'd always liked having strong female mentors."

"The fact that she just walked into my room like that—that tells you a lot about somebody's balls," says Manson. "She was so young —she was a baby! And she had a full-on mohawk, wore unflattering eye makeup, and was making herself look 'ugly' at a time when we were dealing with the Jessica Simpsons and the Britney Spears of the world. I've always been repulsed by the idea that women need to play up to the male gaze, so I was right behind her, 100 percent, from the second I met her."

As the Distillers reached larger audiences on the tour, playing to thousands each night, they landed on the radar of a few major labels whose curiosities were piqued by the exciting young punk band and its fiery frontwoman. A cover story in the February 2003 issue of *Alternative Press* would capture the high demand surrounding the band: "Sony. Def Jam. DreamWorks. They've all come knocking at the Distillers' door over the past year, on the heels of the group's cult-level sophomore success, *Sing Sing Death House*."

"Of course record companies were interested. They thrive on ambitious people like her," Manson says of Dalle. "Brody is a star. There's just no other way of putting it, really. She's an incredible singer, she's an incredible guitar player, she's really charismatic, and she's ridiculously beautiful. I kept calling her the Ava Gardner of punk rock. But she also had this band of incredible characters. It wasn't like some background musicians that merged into one. They all had specific personalities."

Having come from the Gilman scene, Granelli was initially wary of the major-label interest. "We always had our guard up a little bit. You never knew if labels had ulterior motives," he says. "Tim would tell us stories about the guy who signed Green Day taking a meeting with Rancid and dying his hair green to seem punk. Everyone from that era has a story about some A&R guy cheesing it up for cred."

"We heard some ridiculous shit," Dalle remembers of their conversations with labels. "'If you guys don't sell a million records, I'm gonna quit my job.' That came out of the mouth of an A&R guy."

"We played in New York and [Island Def Jam co-president] Lyor Cohen was supposed to come and check us out," Granelli says. "He ended up not even talking to us. I heard he watched the band and thought we played a hardcore set to piss him off and didn't spend time to talk to us afterwards. To us, that was like: 'Yeah, see—these know-nothings don't even listen to our records!'"

Ultimately, it was Warner Bros. who appealed to the band the most. The label's Sire Records imprint had an impressive history of punk rock bona fides, touting the Ramones and the Dead Boys. The band was also won over by the personal investment of Sire co-founder Seymour Stein and Warner CEO Tom Whalley, who took them out to late-night dinners at restaurants they never would've been able to afford. "Seymour Stein and I got lobster and wore the bibs and everyone made fun of us," remembers Sinn. "They were just people we could hang out with and have fun talking about music. It felt like our people."

Sire's other big draw was the A&R guy the band was dealing with, Craig Aaronson, who had worked with Jimmy Eat World and At the Drive-In. Aside from his A&R duties, Aaronson had a lot of pull within the company. "Our A&R guy was Craig Aaronson, who was also the VP," says Granelli. "That was a big thing for us . . . If you deal with some junior guy, you might get buried or lost in the machine. But if the VP was gonna be our A&R, that sweetened the deal."

After some consideration, the band decided to take Aaronson, Whalley, and Stein up on their offer, inking a deal with Sire Records for their third record. The agreement would even allow for the release of the record to be a joint venture with Hellcat, with immediate advance payouts. "They gave us all checks," remembers Granelli. "I got like thirty grand as a signing bonus, so that was cool. It felt real."

But while the Distillers' lucrative new opportunities and nonstop touring schedule were exciting, they were also starting to put a strain on Dalle's marriage. "I was gone most of the time," she says. "I remember coming home from tour and Tim was like, 'I'm lonely. I miss you. You're never around.' And I was just like, ' . . . Tough shit? You're a fucking grown-ass man.' I was twenty, twenty-one. And he was in his mid-thirties. 'I'm not here to fix you.' I was a kid. I was a fucking kid!" Leaving Hellcat to sign to a bigger label only made the situation more personal. The word that most frequently came up, she remembers, was "loyalty."

"Right before that, I'd said I wanted to explore my options—maybe I'll talk to Fat Mike or maybe I'll talk to whoever, see what else there is. He was so furious about it," Dalle says. "The concept was so alien to me. 'Loyalty?' Fuckin' . . . *what*? To not be able to make my own autonomous decisions outside of someone, it was a shock. It was one of the reasons it started to dawn on me that I needed to get the fuck out of there."

$ $ $

Loyalty, honor, allegiance. These were all qualities firmly embedded in the fabric of Rancid. "It's like the Mafia," guitarist Lars Frederiksen once told the *Washington Post*. "We keep it in the family."

Loyalty was a major theme in a cover story about the largely press-averse band in *Alternative Press* that year—loyalty to one another, loyalty to their crew, loyalty to Epitaph Records and its founder, Brett Gurewitz. "If there were one adjective to describe Rancid, it's loyal," Gurewitz told the magazine. "I'll always be grateful for how loyal they've been to me. But that's just how they are as people. They're that way with one another, and with anyone they choose to work with. And that's something very rare in this business."

The article, billed as Rancid's first interview in five years, caught the band as they readied their forthcoming album, *Indestructible,* their sixth consecutive full-length with Epitaph. "We're with Gurewitz for life," Frederickson said of the label head, who also had a hand in producing most of the band's work. Originally, the article said, the new record had been largely about death, taking inspiration from the recent passing of Joe Strummer, Joey Ramone, and Frederiksen's brother.

But while Rancid and Gurewitz were holed up in the studio in January 2003, finishing the recording of *Indestructible,* Armstrong was blindsided by a phone call from Australia. It was his wife, telling him that after nearly six years of marriage, she wanted a divorce. The stunned frontman later described the split to MTV as "the most devastating thing that's ever happened to me."

Armstrong sought consolation from his bandmates and Gurewitz, who immediately ceased production on *Indestructible* to give him time to recover. "[Tim] told us on a Sunday morning, and we went in and talked to Gurewitz and said, 'That's it, we're stopping.' We stopped the record cold," Freeman told the *Cleveland Scene*. "By Sunday afternoon, me and Tim were driving up Highway 5 back to the Bay Area. He just had to get out and process this shit."

"We shut down and we didn't know if we were gonna make the record," Armstrong recalled to MTV. "And then I went back home to the Bay Area and I listened to what we had done and started writing some new songs. And I [found the process so therapeutic] I said, 'Fuck it, man, let's get back in the studio.'"

When the band regrouped weeks later, the scorned Armstrong brought with him a new heap of breakup tunes he'd written. On "Tropical London," he lamented that his heart had "been ripped wide open" by a girl from Melbourne. On "Fall Back Down," he sang of betrayal and finding light through darkness with the help of his friends. "I'm very lucky to have my crew," he boasted, with the gang-vocal backing of his bandmates: "She's not the one coming back for you!"

On one song, "Ghost Band," Armstrong seemed to take aim at not just his ex but her entire band, playing into the notion that the Distillers were a cheap Rancid knockoff: "There's a ghost band, girl, playing our songs now." But the song wasn't just a bit of bitter lyricism; real-world repercussions followed the couple's split. Armstrong, a powerful and influential figure in the world of punk rock, made life difficult for the Distillers, they say. It felt like there was an industry stink on them as fewer and fewer people and bands were willing to work with them. Their world had shrunk, and they suddenly found themselves very alone, the scene's punk band non grata.

"Everything I knew was through Gilman Street, so when Brody and Tim split up, all the friends I had and everyone I knew from playing music shunned us," Granelli says. "They were really fucked up to us. 'We'll kick your ass if we see you around town'—that kind of vibe. It's like, 'Man, we're just trying to play music.'"

"We couldn't do certain festivals because Rancid was gonna be there," Bevilacqua says. "There were certain things that couldn't happen anymore."

"Other bands that I'd go and see and hang out with, they wouldn't talk to me anymore," says Sinn. "That time was weird for me. I had RANCID tattooed on my hand. *Let's Go* was a big influence on me. All of a sudden it felt like we were public enemy number one as far as Hellcat was concerned. We became very protective of each other. We were fists-up towards anybody coming at us."

"I had friends be like, 'Hey, look, I love you, dude, but I can't go to the movies with you. If Lars sees us at Japantown, it's curtains for me and my band. Sorry, bro,'" says Granelli. "It sucked. It made us feel like shit. It also made us turn inward. We were our own crew. We had each other's backs."

As tensions between the two camps boiled over that spring, the June 12, 2003, issue of *Rolling Stone* threw ten gallons of gasoline on the fire. Inside was a giant photo of Dalle gleefully and sloppily kissing her new boyfriend, Queens of the Stone Age's tall, redheaded frontman, Josh Homme. "I remember seeing that in *Rolling Stone* and being like, 'Ho-ly shit . . .'" Bevilacqua laughs. "It was shocking."

"The *Rolling Stone* thing came out real fast," Granelli remembers. "It was like a week after Brody and Josh hooked up. It was fucked. People were calling me—lots of hurt feelings."

The divorce forced the Distillers to change their summer touring plans, as *Rolling Stone* reported: "The Distillers were originally slated to play the Warped Tour but dropped off the bill after singer Brody Armstrong split with her hubby, Tim Armstrong, of Rancid, who are headlining the festival. Brody's band was quickly snatched up as a second-stage headliner for Lollapalooza, whose lineup includes Queens of the Stone Age main man Josh Homme. 'I've never been more blown away by a band than I am by Queens,' she says."

On a night off from Lollapalooza in July, the Distillers played an intimate show at the iconic New York club CBGB. Rubbing a bit of salt in Armstrong's fresh wound, Dalle performed with the words RED HEADS DO IT BETTER written in huge letters across her left forearm. (Rancid, who had never played the long-standing punk mecca in more than a decade together, were suddenly moved to book their first show there at the end of the year as well.)

"We played CBGB's, which was a huge deal for us," remembers Bevilacqua, "and some kid held a sign that said TAKE TIM BACK." Dalle saw the sign and responded the way her instincts guided her. "I kicked him in the head," she told *SPIN*. "All the kids around him cheered when I did it. I didn't realize how hard I kicked him until I saw his head wobble. I was like, 'Oh, shit. Not a good sign.'"

The CBGB incident was not unique. Dalle routinely had run-ins with irate Rancid fans. The *Los Angeles Times* reported that outside a sold-out show at the Glass House, in Pomona, a few weeks later, "a kid was handing out flyers with Armstrong's picture and the words 'Money Whore.'"

"Shit like that would happen at least once a show. This one girl wrote RANCID on our bus. Brody saw it and she, uh . . ." Bevilacqua says, before cutting himself off. "Well, it was *a whole thing*. Those people turned their backs on us—really high school shit. That stuff just pushed us to be like, 'Fuck you! We never needed any of you.'" The Distillers even embraced the venom, naming one stretch of shows that year "The Most Hated Woman on Earth Tour."

But while life on the road was increasingly combative, life at home was dreamy for the frontwoman, who was falling fast in love with Homme. She soon dropped the Armstrong name and adopted Dalle, after the provocative and controversial French actress Béatrice Dalle. "You know that gut-sick feeling, that lovesick feeling? I have that all the time. He's the most beautiful man I've ever seen in my life. He's 6ft 5in and looks like a red-headed Elvis," she told the *Guardian*. The two were deemed "a striking couple" in the article, and Dalle's growing reputation as a troublemaker was captured in its headline: "Move Over, Courtney Love. The Rock World Has a New Woman It Loves to Hate."

$ $ $

Budding romances weren't the only source of scandalous punk drama in the summer of 2003. The same week that rumors of Dalle's relationship with Homme went public in the pages of *Rolling Stone*, another rumor that had been circulating about Rancid was leaked in the press as well. It turned out that the band had also worked out a deal with Warner Bros. Records for the release of *Indestructible*. An unnamed Epitaph representative confirmed the arrangement to *Billboard,* saying simply, "This is true."

A spokesperson later added that it was a "unique deal" that didn't "play by the traditional record biz rules," implying that it was perhaps a distribution deal and Rancid would not officially be on the Warner roster. Frederiksen provided a statement, but his contradictions and lack of details only made the nature of the venture more murky: "We have absolutely no complaints with Hellcat. Yes, we are considering additional support that Warner Bros. might be able to provide, but whatever happens, we're sticking with Brett Gurewitz. All I care about and all I have is my music, my bandmates and my band. We are going to do whatever we need to do to survive."

Comments piled up by the hundreds on Punknews, the website where the story had broken. Many were in all caps, many used exclamation points liberally, and all contained very strong opinions. Some were furious and derided the band as hypocrites and sellouts. ("Honestly, there is no way to reconcile this with what they've said and stood for in the past.") Others defended their punk heroes and pledged to stick with them. ("Who are we to say whether or not Rancid has sold out? Who cares. Rancid is still perhaps the greatest living band right now. They are the Clash, reincarnated. Period.") But the most common reaction was one of shock. Shock that Rancid, of all bands, had finally crossed the line.

Rancid had famously brushed off the opportunity to jump to a major label at the height of their breakout success during the mid-nineties punk explosion, a time when they could have joined their Bay Area brethren Green Day in superstardom. The offers were there, but Armstrong and company snubbed their noses at them. A 1996 feature in the *New York Times Magazine* documented the music industry's intense courting of the band: "Madonna started coming to Rancid shows, and sent a naked photograph of herself, pleading with the band to sign with her label instead of Epic, which offered a deal worth $1.5 million. At the peak of the bidding war, Rancid turned them both down."

The band had even reiterated their allegiance to Epitaph as recently as their June *Alternative Press* story, which made no mention of Warner Bros. whatsoever. So why now? And why Warner Bros.? And why so quietly?

These were questions the Rancid camp was too tight-lipped to answer. A reporter for the *East Bay Express* went digging for explanations and was met with a wall of silence. No comment from Rancid, no comment from Gurewitz, no comment from anybody. "Don't ask me about Rancid," Epitaph publicist Hilary Okun told the paper. "It's kind of something we just don't talk about. It's a big, sad gulp in our throats."

The band's new label was equally unhelpful. "Rancid are on Warner Bros.," label PR head Luke Burland commented. "You wanted to know our relationship—our relationship is great."

Even Canada's most relentless interviewer, Nardwuar, couldn't get clear answers out of Frederiksen. "We haven't signed anything," the guitarist told him. "We'll stay with Brett forever. Brett's our guy. He's the one who produced this new record, *Indestructible,* that's coming out on Hellcat."

It was only an anonymous source at Epitaph who talked to the *Express,* insinuating that Rancid's label news came as a surprise to everyone in the office, even Gurewitz: "I mean, Brett Gurewitz produced the record—put his blood and soul into producing it—and we thought it was going to be an Epitaph release. But then everything kind of changed once Brody and Tim went their separate ways and a whole bunch of new songs were written and the record was put on hold. That's when the changes came about."

$ $ $

Rancid and the Distillers had their Warner Bros. releases scheduled two months apart in 2003. *Indestructible* hit stores first, on August 19. Its cover was conspicuously absent of any major-label logos; in fact, the back of it instead bore Hellcat's logo of a puffed-up black cat.

The music video for "Fall Back Down," the album's first single, matched the song's lyrical themes of camaraderie and loyalty —plenty of arms around shoulders and stiff upper lips, with lots of who-needs-you-anyway posturing for the camera as Armstrong played dominoes with friends. Among the frontman's supportive pals featured in the video were Armstrong's protégé and Good Charlotte guitarist Benji Madden, as well as reality TV star Kelly Osbourne.

The airing of dirty laundry among high-profile rock stars and famous socialites pushed the situation from punk circles to tabloids, especially in the sensationalist UK media, who ate up the drama like candy. Dalle found herself dragged into a strange time in early-aughts pop culture, during which the media was highly invested in the personal lives of punkified pop stars like MTV power couple Avril Lavigne and Sum 41 frontman Deryck Whibley.

Homme, Armstrong, Dalle, and Osbourne traded verbal darts about one another in the press. Osbourne bashed Dalle in interviews, calling her a "talentless fake," a "poser," and a "Courtney Love wannabe." "I don't remember seeing the video, but I know that she attacked me in the press, so I clapped back," Dalle says. "It's funny, years later I saw her at an event and she ran and hid. To this day, that girl is afraid of me."

Indestructible drew a line in the sand for Distillers fans, many of whom had found the band through their devotion to Rancid. Suddenly they were like the children of divorced parents, being forced to choose a side. "I think our fan base was torn in two," Dalle says. As divisive as *Indestructible* was in the punk community, though, the members of the Distillers say they didn't bother with it. "I had no desire to listen to his record," Dalle shrugs. "Someone said there was a song called 'Tropic London,' which was maybe about me and Melbourne. I still haven't heard it."

"I stopped caring about their art because they tried to step in my way," Granelli says of Rancid. "The way they treated us made us pissed. So I didn't want to listen to the record—'Fuck it, I don't give a shit.'"

Two months after the release of *Indestructible,* on October 14, Dalle and the Distillers fired their own shot with *Coral Fang.* If the band's previous work had gotten them labeled as Rancid copycats, *Coral Fang* saw them putting miles between them. It was a bold statement, their own flag in the sand. It was Dalle bursting into the room and saying, "Here I am."

The album had been recorded over the spring at the Site, the same remote studio in the redwood forests of San Rafael, California, where Queens of the Stone Age had captured their widely praised 2002 album *Songs for the Deaf*. Its eleven songs got a sheen from producer Gil Norton, who had previously worked with Pixies, Patti Smith, Foo Fighters, and Blink, the Irish pop act that had forced a pop-punk trio from San Diego to add "-182" to their name.

Norton's production added a new dimension to the Distillers' sound by amplifying Dalle's strengths, namely her gift for sharp hook writing and her inimitable voice. Bevilacqua, who had been made an official member of the band just prior to *Coral Fang*'s recording, provided depth to her guitar playing as well, throwing his own stray licks on top of Dalle's driving rhythm work.

The band still charged through a few straight-ahead punk rippers in which Dalle's voice unfurled wildly with piercing shrieks and rusty growls, but they also slowed their pace at times, giving themselves room to spread out. It turned out that, when freed from the confines of hundred-mile-per-hour rhythms, Dalle could croon with the best of them, easily sliding into sultry murmurs and seductive hums.

Coral Fang possessed a duality that captured Dalle's shifting life at the time—a mean and ugly record that was also harmonious and graceful. It was an album about life and death, love and hate, killing and fucking. Its cover was just as gruesome—a crucified naked woman, bleeding a stream of red razor blades from her ribcage. The interior artwork was even more extreme, with women hanging from umbilical-cord nooses and blood gushing from between their legs.

Sire, which had been hands-off during the production of *Coral Fang*, started growing more intrusive about how the album and Dalle should be marketed, an overstep that had never been an issue at Hellcat. Knowing that national chain stores like Walmart and Target were unlikely to carry copies of a record with such obscene artwork, the label suggested the band provide a second cover for these retailers. "They told us that something like 80 percent of CD sales were through Walmart, but CD sales are less than 2 percent of Walmart's sales," remembers Sinn. "So Walmart's not gonna give a shit [about not carrying the record] from a business standpoint. But for us, we might be denying our fans who live someplace where Walmart may be the only spot they can get a CD."

"They were like, 'You need to make a *safe cover*,'" says Bevilacqua. "We were smart-asses, so we made a cover with animals on it and it said SAFE COVER. In retrospect, we could've done something else."

"We were so offended at the time. It was unbelievable," says Dalle. "We went from running our own ship to having someone else control it. All of a sudden, there were rules and regulations. We lost the freedom to do whatever the fuck we wanted. It wasn't just that. I'd go to a photo shoot or something and they'd say you have to wear this stupid fucking tutu like I wore on the cover of *SPIN* magazine. It was kind of like manipulation. I felt forced to do some things that I really didn't want to fucking do."

The press, in particular, became a regular source of contention, as interviewers were largely uninterested in talking to her bandmates and only wanted divorce dirt. In the quest for juicy ex-husband bashing, critics picked through Dalle's lyrics, which were rife with imagery of blood, fangs, and murder. "In light of Armstrong's separation from her husband, Tim Armstrong of Rancid, it's hard not to hear *Coral Fang* as a breakup album. Behind the cryptic goriness and the veneer of rage . . . there is a bruised and bandaged heart," read a *Rolling Stone* review.

For her part, though, Dalle claims that "most of *Coral Fang* was not about him. 'Die on a Rope,' maybe, or 'For Tonight [You're Only Here to Know].' But I think a lot of it was about my childhood, being sexually abused. 'Coral fang' symbolizes the male anatomy. I don't think a lot of people got that." She described the writing process to the *Los Angeles Times* as "total liberation . . . Just feeling like a caged animal for most of my life and someone breaking the cage open. Actually, it was I who broke the cage open. I bit through the chain-link fence and let myself out."

The Distillers released their own subtly confrontational music video for album opener "Drain the Blood." The opening shot saw the band descending into a sewer, an apt metaphor for their place in the music scene after their blacklisting from the Rancid crew. Then Dalle strutted onto the screen wearing a cropped leather jacket and low-rise pants. The camera followed from below with a tight shot of her swaggering hips as she strummed the opening chords. What was most noticeable, to anyone looking closely, was the tattoo on her right hip. The heart was still there, but something was different. The name TIM had been blacked out.

Dalle and her covered-up tattoo soon hit the covers of a number of magazines like *NME, Kerrang!,* and *SPIN.* But even though she had penned her strongest collection of songs to date with *Coral Fang,* her musicianship was overshadowed by the drama surrounding her messy divorce and public feuds. "Everyone wanted to talk about my personal life and less about music," she says. "I spent more time defending myself and things I didn't want to talk about."

Nearly every piece of coverage alluded to her estranged husband or her current boyfriend. Some made dutiful, passing mentions, but in too many instances, the love triangle became the focal point. Tabloid rags and radio DJs in particular were shameless in their muckraking. Dalle endured daily intrusions on her privacy and crass interview questions about her love life. "It was so fucking overwhelming and I don't know if she was fully ready for it at that time," says the band's publicist, Brian Bumbery. "It was difficult to navigate it."

"It was really painful," Dalle says of the press. "I didn't realize until years later that it's so fucking sexist. I literally read the worst shit—the meanest, most awful, brutal shit that someone could say about me, without even knowing me. It doesn't bother me anymore, but at the time, the boys would see me cry. There was a *Q* article that was so awful and had nothing to do with the Distillers or our record. It was talking about how ugly I am and about my pockmarked skin. I don't even have pockmarked skin! I was like, '. . . *Why?* Why have I been painted as this villain? Why am I someone's punching bag?' There was no recourse. There was no accountability and people could say whatever the fuck they wanted."

Dalle started dragging Granelli along to interviews for support.

The drummer frequently relied on his quick wit and humor to break up awkward conversations and change topics. It also didn't hurt that the six-foot-six Granelli was an imposing figure, in case any journalists really stepped out of bounds. "Andy would do interviews with her because he was the Chewbacca to her Han Solo," says Bevilacqua. "If some interviewer was being an asshole or getting out of line, making her talk about shit she didn't want to talk about, Andy would step in and be like, 'What the fuck, dude?' They had a good dynamic. Andy had her back in those situations. Still, she had to deal with that every day. There was an interview or photo shoot every day at the shows. It was always something."

"She ended up bringing me to deflect," Granelli says. "There were a lot of shitheads who would ask stupid questions. Everybody loves drama, and Brody had drama. On one hand, you know the press is gonna ask that shit. You kinda can't blame 'em, but sometimes people get nasty. So it's nice to have your friend with you."

The most frustrating part about sitting through invasive radio interviews was the fact that the Distillers' singles weren't actually getting much radio play. "I remember being in a meeting with Craig Aaronson," says Granelli. "'Drain the Blood' had come out and we were talking about the different radio stations that were picking it up and the ones that weren't. And Craig said, 'Well, you know, with commercial radio, there's really only room for one or two women in rock. Courtney Love is gonna be the first one, and they just chose Evanescence instead of the Distillers.' I remember looking around and thinking, 'But that band sucks!'"

Dalle took one demoralizing radio interview on the chin after another. It wasn't until February 2004, when she was photographed licking a novelty guitar carved in the shape of a red dragon for the cover of the British style magazine *The Face,* that she opened up. "I really waited until *The Face* to let my side of the story out," she says. Dalle dished about the unpleasant final three years of her marriage, during which she and Armstrong were in counseling and had stopped making love, she claimed. She spoke of feeling "dead" and "drained." "He wasn't physically abusive," she clarified, but he was "a very, very controlling man." She felt "like a child being reprimanded, constantly, for being in trouble. He'd threaten me with divorce. I was constantly humiliated in public."

She talked about how restrictive it was living in the world of her husband and his band. "The way he runs his business is very mafioso," she said. "And I didn't like being married to the mob. And I was. I didn't just marry Tim, I married all of them."

Her bandmates chimed in with stories about being "blanket-ostracized by the scene that had created them," and about how Rancid and their crew spread malicious rumors about them after the divorce. Homme had also received death threats, Dalle told the magazine, and her friends had been confronted by Armstrong in public —one was allegedly cornered by Armstrong and given the instruction "Tell that fucking bitch she's a fucking cunt and I fucking hate her." She had to get a restraining order against her ex, she claimed to the magazine. "He can come a certain distance, but he can't say anything nasty or he'll literally get thrown in jail."

It was a new world for the Distillers, and there was no going back. There was no longer a scene for them to call home. All they had now was each other. "When I got the divorce, people drew the largest line in the sand that I have ever witnessed," Dalle said. "I lost everybody. Everybody. The only people who were there for me were my boys. My band."

$ $ $

In the two years after Dalle's divorce, the Distillers toured relentlessly in support of *Coral Fang*. They tore through Europe, Australia, Japan, and Canada and hit festivals like Reading and Leeds, Download, Lowlands, and Pukkelpop. Along the way, they shared stages with Red Hot Chili Peppers, Pixies, and, whenever possible, Queens of the Stone Age. It all started to blur together as days blended into weeks, and weeks into months. "I feel like I'm on this train that doesn't have any stops," Dalle told *SPIN*. "You just stay on and watch the scenery go by."

No longer bound to the strict sobriety rules of the Rancid/Epitaph scene, the band made up for lost time with hard partying as drinking and drug use grew more prominent within the band. "It was sort of like being a tiger in a cage," says Sinn. "You're watching prey go by all the time and you can't touch it. Then one day some-one opens the cage, and as soon as the lock was off, it was playtime."

Meth became Dalle's drug of choice, because, as she says, "I had done so much cocaine that I actually couldn't snort it anymore. The people I was hanging out with, [meth] was what they were doing. As a girl with ADHD, who takes legal speed now, I was like, 'Oh my God, I found my fucking thing!'"

"We were on tour for two years and we went *hard,*" says Bevi-lacqua. "All these managers and new people were working for us, but playing shows was all I concerned myself with. Tour was all I thought about. We were really wild at that time, and we were with bands who were also wild, like the Bronx."

"We toured the world together and everybody was *going for it,*" says Bronx guitarist Joby Ford. "I blame it all on the record labels. They would show up with bags of this or handfuls of that. They al-most encouraged it. It was crazy."

But after a while, the long, drunken nights and drug-fueled weeks on the road started to take their toll on the relationships between the band members, as well as their personal health. "We were two years deep into a tour cycle. We had fractured apart," Dalle says. "I was doing meth and gallivanting around the world with either my boyfriend at the time or on tour. We had all become drug addicts."

"When you're partying all the time, you're not sleeping good and you're making bad decisions," says Granelli. "Everyone was wasted all the time. You party on tour, then go home and it turns into party-ing at home. There's this cycle. You're fucked up all night and hung-over all day. No one is communicating. People go to their own cor-ners. We were all doing the same things, but kind of doing it behind each other's backs."

"At the Kerrang! Awards one year, I drank three or four bottles of Jägermeister, fell down a flight of stairs, and was carried into a cab," says Sinn. "My bass tech put me in a luggage cart and brought me up to a hotel room and called the paramedics. I woke up with an IV in me. It got really bad for me at times. If it was going to continue like that, one of us was gonna die."

There was something else that wasn't adding up. When the band members came out of their hazes to check their bank accounts, there wasn't as much money in there as there should have been—not for musicians who'd spent most of the year playing lucrative gigs, had an album crack into the *Billboard* charts, and had sold more than 100,000 records. "It was tax time and my taxes were due," remembers Granelli. "I kept bugging the accountant for numbers—'Can you bring the reconciliation papers for the last three tours?' She brought them and it was like a stack of nonsense. None of the numbers made sense. It was all this money on a bus company that ended up being a tour manager double-dipping on the bus, all this fucked-up shit."

"We were so young and so green. We were getting fucked left, right, and center," says Dalle. "We toured and toured and toured—where's the money? We didn't see budgets; we didn't even know to ask for budgets. It was a huge learning curve."

"I feel like we made more money before we were on a major label," says Granelli. "You get to this echelon—you're on Warner, you're flying on a private jet, and suddenly you have to carry management. At the time, it felt like if you were playing with the big dogs, you had to hire the big dogs. But I think the big dogs were kind of ripping us off. So that thirty grand was great, but it ended up being the only money I got for two or three years."

On November 14, the Distillers played their last show of 2004, a slog of a daytime set at Holiday Havoc, an outdoor festival in the parking lot of Angel Stadium, in Anaheim, California, with the Buzzcocks, the Offspring, Pennywise, and Finch. By this point, music had become nothing more than an excuse to do drugs. "I remember playing that show and being more interested in getting back to L.A. to party," Bevilacqua says.

After that, Dalle flew back home to spend the holidays sleeping off the past two years. "I went to Australia for three months to get away from meth and get away from everyone," she says. "It was killing me. I was completely out of my fucking mind. I became completely psychotic and paranoid. I'd be up for three days at a time. I once sat in a car and wrote down every address that I could find in the navigation, for seven hours. I heard Mickey Mouse in the drain, I heard people having sex all the time. I cut down a tree with an electric chainsaw after being awake for three days and almost cut my fucking legs off. I was just a fucking maniac and I would not sleep. That was a dark period for me. It was probably the closest to the devil that I've ever come."

While detoxing in Australia, on the first day of 2005, Dalle's twenty-sixth birthday, Homme proposed and she accepted. But while Dalle was off getting engaged, Granelli started feeling restless in California as his wallet grew thin and his drum kit collected dust. The Distillers had another record in their contract with Sire, but they only had a handful of half-finished songs for it and no map for what came next. "I felt like there was no plan," he says. "I was getting antsy and broke. I felt like the level we were at required constant maintenance. Either we had to keep touring or keep releasing records, and if we didn't do that, then it would go away."

To keep himself occupied and pick up a few bucks, Granelli joined a band called Darker My Love, made up of some friends in San Francisco. When word reached Dalle through mutual acquaintances, she took it as a personal affront. "When I found out that he had joined Darker My Love, I was devastated and hurt," she says. "I was like, 'All you had to do was tell me. Why did I have to find out like that?' It felt like a betrayal."

Tensions ran high as the two bickered about it over the phone. Looking back now, they both agree that the smart move would've been to communicate that they should take a break and regroup a few months later. But through a fog of drugs and heated arrogance, all that came out was yelling and arguing. "I remember thinking, 'I'm about to quit the band, and I really wish I was sober enough to figure out if what I'm doing is the right thing,'" says Granelli. "I quit the band and we just fought and fought. It was unnecessary and it sucked. And it was because of drugs, 100 percent."

As the call wound down, it was clear that the Distillers had reached the end of the road. Dalle started crying and hung up the phone, but the crying didn't stop then. She wept through the night and woke the next morning to find that she was still crying. "I cried for forty-eight hours straight," she says. "I've never cried so much about anything."

$ $ $

Dalle tried to keep up appearances through 2005, but it was hard to argue with the reality that the Distillers were falling apart. "The band is not breaking up but there's been a little movement of the members (both loss and gain)," their management assured in a statement. But as bandmates began announcing their departures—first Granelli, then Sinn—it became obvious that it was over.

"I'm no longer part of the life I knew so recently," Sinn posted on his Myspace. "Distillers are no more and it feels like a weight has been lifted. However, I'll never get rid of the disgust inside from it all."

"I had my own demons then, so it felt like one less thing I had to deal with," Sinn recalls of his reaction to the abrupt way the band ended. "It kind of felt like a pressure had been released." Following his departure from the Distillers, the bassist joined Angels & Airwaves, the new project from Blink-182 guitarist Tom DeLonge, after Blink announced their own hiatus.

But Granelli didn't get to spend much time touring with Darker My Love, having been involved in a serious accident that left him unable to play drums. "I ended up getting hit by a car within a year after I quit Distillers," he says. "I broke both my arms, I couldn't tour. Then the band I'd joined ended up being the backing band for the Fall with Mark E. Smith, so I missed out on all that. I sat around at home doing nothing. I was so mad at music that I quit and got a day job. I had my head shoved up my ass and wasn't thinking clearly."

With another record still remaining in her Sire contract, Dalle enlisted her loyal friend Bevilacqua and a few other musicians to help her work on a collection of new songs. The result was Spinnerette, a project that tilted away from the scathing punk bite of the Distillers, and leaned more toward dancier electroclash. It dulled the razor-sharp attitude Dalle had been known for, and Sire was not pleased. "They paid for it, and I walked away with my record because they didn't like it," she says. "I basically got a free record out of it."

The self-titled Spinnerette album eventually ended up finding a home with Canadian indie label Anthem Records, whose biggest claim to fame was a few early releases from Rush. "I didn't want to do a fucking monkey dance for people who don't care about art," Dalle told the *Guardian* of the Sire split. "I want to be more art-focused and call the shots." The record was not particularly well received, even among outlets that had previously championed Dalle. *NME*, which had once labeled her "the most important new rock star in the world," now claimed that she had "mellowed from the fiercely gobby, punk vixen whose blood-red lips we all instantly fell for." *Pitchfork*, which had called *Coral Fang* "a proud achievement" in an 8.0 rating, trashed *Spinnerette* with a 2.7, claiming that Dalle had gone "genre dumpster-diving."

Spinnerette didn't gain much traction with fans, either, not solely because of Dalle's drastic sonic departure but also because she was busy with a new chapter of her life that prevented her from doing much touring or promotion. In January 2006, she gave birth to her first child, Camille Harley Joan Homme.

In the end, the Distillers released only one album on a major label, the most ambitious one in their catalog, and Brody Dalle fought the world to get it heard until the band ultimately self-destructed. "When I look back, I'm amazed that that was my life," she says. "I'd never let anyone treat me like that now. A label, an ex-husband, people, press—I would never allow it. And I could give a shit what people say about me at this juncture. In the grand scheme of life, there is so much stuff that does actually matter. What someone thinks of me is none of my business. So selling out ... yeah, maybe we did, but ultimately we were like: 'Whose fucking career is it, yours or ours? Fuck off.'"

CHAPTER 9

MY CHEMICAL ROMANCE

Three Cheers for Sweet Revenge

Reprise Records (2004)

GEOFF RICKLY WAS cornered at a house party in New Jersey. This had been happening to the Thursday frontman more frequently, he noticed. Ever since his band's new album, *Full Collapse*, had started getting a little buzz, people back home wanted his time and attention. Not that he was an international superstar or anything, but he could stand on the stage of any local club from South Amboy to Cherry Hill, point his microphone at the crowd, and they'd sing his words back at him. By Garden State standards, he was a scene celebrity. And as such, people often pitched him about projects they were working on or dropped invitations for Thursday to play their shows, leading Rickly to learn the subtle art of feigning interest. So when Mikey Way, a twenty-one-year-old intern at Eyeball Records, trapped him into a conversation about the new band he was starting with his older brother, Rickly fought to keep his eyes from glazing over.

A music geek with an encyclopedic knowledge of rock history, Way was like the kid brother of Rickly and everyone at Eyeball.

He'd played in a few bands here and there, but his excitement about this project was noticeably more intense. It wasn't much more than a name and a few rough songs, Way told Rickly. They were going to be named My Chemical Romance, and they had a song he swore Rickly would love called "Vampires Will Never Hurt You."

"Hang on, I'll show you," Way said. He grabbed a guitar off the nearby wall—it was out of tune and missing strings, a decorative thing, really—and made attempts at plucking the song's odd chord patterns. He raced through the jangly intro but kept missing notes and starting over.

"He started trying to play me this song," Rickly recalls. "And I was like, 'Uhhh, sorry, I don't know what you're doing, man.' Finally, he was like, 'Wait, I'll give it to my brother. He'll know how to play it!'"

Gerard Way soon awkwardly shuffled into the room, visibly uncomfortable about the idea of performing in front of people. The older Way gave the guitar a tuning while Rickly and other partygoers waited impatiently. He finally got the instrument going and took a crack at the song, but it still didn't sound like anything Rickly could make heads or tails of. Not picking up on Rickly's disinterest, the two brothers went on to tell him that they were going to write more songs and record an album for Eyeball. "They were like, 'You should produce it!'" Rickly remembers. "And I was like, 'Uh-huh, *suuure.*'"

Not long after, Thursday was packing up their van for a tour one morning when Mikey Way came running up to them with something in his hand. Rickly rolled down the window and Way handed him a burned CD-R. "Hey, here's our song!" Way told him. "Let me know what you think."

"I remember thinking, 'Ugh, now we gotta listen to this fucking song,'" Rickly says. He took the CD and slid it into the van's stereo as Thursday sped down the New Jersey Turnpike. To his surprise, the recorded version of My Chemical Romance far exceeded what he'd heard at the party. "It wasn't what I expected at all. I'd given them an Ink & Dagger record at some point, and it had a little of that same angularity to them and the chorus was really interesting." The lyrics—the ones he could make out, anyway—were telling some sort of noir tale about hanging out with corpses, putting stakes through hearts, and pumping venom into necks.

"I played it again, and then again, and after the third time, a few guys in the van were like, 'What *is* this?'" Rickly remembers. "And I said, 'It's those fucking kids that asked me to produce their record.' And they were like, 'So are you gonna do it?' I said, 'Well, I didn't think so . . . but now I feel like I should.'"

$ $ $

By 2001, Eyeball Records was stable enough that founder Alex Saavedra no longer had to live out of his Chevy Blazer. He set up shop on a floor he rented above an office space in Kearny, a New Jersey suburb thirty minutes outside Manhattan. The Eyeball House, as it was known, was not only the label's base of operations; it was a place where all touring friends were welcome. It had enough bedrooms for bands to crash for the night and enough safe parking where they could leave their vans without fear of break-ins. Impromptu parties and gatherings often broke out at the Eyeball House that went well into the night. Fortunately, the architect who rented the office below was a friendly ex-metalhead who never complained about the noise.

"I grew up struggling, a lot more than the people around me," Saavedra says. "So when I got that place, it ended up being the house where anyone could live, anyone could stay there, any bands that were coming through could go there. My door was always open. A lot of people who have never been there might think it's a shitty punk house. It wasn't. It was actually clean and organized and a safe place to go."

The Eyeball House had its regulars. Members of local bands like Thursday, Midtown, and Saves the Day could usually be found hanging around among Rutgers students and other Jersey scenesters. One regular who practically lived there was Mikey Way, a rail-thin, bespectacled twenty-year-old from Belleville, a town two miles north whose claim to fame was being the setting for a few episodes of the popular new Mafia drama *The Sopranos*. Way was at the house so often that Saavedra put him to work as an intern, tasking him with the hundreds of small jobs it takes to run an independent label—"packing mail order, doing press shit, picking people up and driving them around. Whatever we needed, Mikey was always helpful," he says.

"I really liked Mikey. Just a really funny, really smart kid," says Rickly. "He liked stuff that the other punk kids didn't like. He liked bands like Suede and Portishead. He loved British bands especially, even the glammy stuff."

Way was introverted but came to life once he got a few vodka cranberries in him, often bending the ears of those around him about the merits of Radiohead and Blur. He'd occasionally allude to his brother three years his senior, Gerard, but no one ever saw much of him. "Everybody joked about [Gerard] being a hermit," says Rickly. "The first time Mikey mentioned him, he was like, 'He's probably at home in his underwear right now, drawing comic books.'"

Gerard did spend most of his time alone in his bedroom in his parents' basement, a cramped space with a tiny window that only let a sliver of sunlight peek through. Since he couldn't see much of the world from his room, he created his own. Way had an active imagination and a flair for illustration. Stacks of sketches and notebooks piled up around him as he designed universes full of fictional characters that existed in his mind.

"Gerard was this nerdy kid that we used to tease and call the Campbell Soup kid," says Saavedra. "We had common nerdy interests—horror movies, Houdini, secret societies, comic books, straight-up nerd shit. The dude was majorly agoraphobic, but when you could get him to come out, he was a funny guy. I know it sounds silly, but you get the vibe from him immediately that he's just a kind dude and a good person."

"Once I finally met him, I immediately loved Gerard," says Rickly. "He was soft-spoken, obviously super talented, and clearly had been the one who had fed Mikey the British glam stuff." Way himself was so enamored with Rickly and Thursday that he left his basement on occasion to head to the Loop Lounge, in Passaic, to stand up front and watch the singer command the room.

At twenty-two, Rickly was two years younger than Gerard, but he took him under his wing. The two bonded over their shared love of comic books and bands like the Smiths. Rickly was encouraging of Way's talents as an illustrator, and commissioned him to draw a design for a Thursday T-shirt. The band called it "the super dove," a take on their logo featuring a mechanical drawing of the inner workings of a bird.

Way had graduated from the School of Visual Arts, in Manhattan, a few years earlier and was putting his BFA to use at internships or low-level gigs at places like DC Comics and Cartoon Network, including a brief stint at a firm designing toys and action figures for Marvel. Way found these office jobs limiting, though, and he struggled to get his creations noticed. He came close to getting one of his pitches green-lit at Cartoon Network. It was a show called *The Breakfast Monkey* that centered around a magical chimp who worked at a diner, but ultimately the network deemed its oddball food-centric humor too close to another show they'd recently acquired, *Aqua Teen Hunger Force*.

One September morning in 2001, Gerard was commuting to his office job when he looked up from the Hoboken station to see thick clouds of smoke. Across the Hudson River, the Twin Towers were collapsing. Way watched in shock and disbelief as commuters around him cried and phoned their loved ones. He suddenly found himself reevaluating his life's priorities and was struck by a thought: "Fuck art." The years he'd spent years trying to get his illustrations noticed had amounted to nothing but a daily grind, and a commodified version of what he loved most. He would later explain to *Rolling Stone*: "I thought, 'Art's not doing anything for you. It's just something on a wall, it's completely disposable, and it's not helping anyone.' And I was like, 'Fuck *Breakfast Monkey*, because all it's gonna do is line somebody else's pockets.' I felt like I had given my life to art and that it had betrayed me."

Every comic book hero has an origin story, and this tragic day would kick off the mild-mannered Gerard Way's journey to form a band called My Chemical Romance. The protagonist put away his pencils and began bringing his intricate fantasy worlds to life with his Fender Strat. Although he wasn't as naturally gifted as a musician as he was an illustrator, he did his best to translate his talents between mediums. His first songwriting effort, the rudimentary "Skylines and Turnstiles," channeled the emotional gut punch of having a mundane Tuesday upended by the terrorist attacks of 9/11. The song also laid the groundwork for what he envisioned his band would represent: turning collective fear and anxiety into a message of positivity, hope, and empowerment that would inspire anyone who heard it. "And if the world needs something better," he sang, "let's give them one more reason now, now, now!"

To help fulfill his vision, he began recruiting musicians who could round out a band. His brother Mikey had no bass skills, but swore he could learn on the fly, which was good enough. Though he originally had aspirations to sing and play guitar, Gerard abandoned the idea when he realized he lacked the coordination to do both at the same time. He in turn invited the best shredder he knew, Ray Toro, a local virtuoso reared on Metallica and Megadeth. Way played "Skylines" for Toro, who immediately had ideas for technical improvements on Way's rough framework. The guitarist stuck sharp little melodies in here and there, and the next thing he knew, he was showing up to weekly practices.

"Ray was this really nerdy kid who was very ambiguous," Saavedra says. "We couldn't figure out if he was a punk kid or a metal kid. He had this goofy haircut and big Coke-bottle glasses, and his voice sounded like Mickey Mouse when he talked. But Ray was such an incredible guitar player and I had no idea, because he'd been in such terrible bands."

One of said terrible bands was called the Rodneys, whose drum seat had been filled by Matt Pelissier, a mechanic whom everyone called Otter. "He was sloppy and didn't seem to have any discipline," says Rickly. "To me, that's an important part of being a drummer is being super disciplined." But what Pelissier lacked in skill he made up for by having an attic in which the four could practice, so he was in.

Saavedra witnessed the nascent group turn their early ideas into songs at practices and immediately loved what he heard. It was a strangely compelling mashup of punk, metal, emo, and Britpop.

Whenever they were ready to record material, he told them, they'd be more than welcome to release it through the increasingly eclectic Eyeball.

My Chemical Romance evolved quickly, and the more Saavedra and Rickly heard, the more they felt foolish for doubting the two weird brothers who hung around the Eyeball House. Rickly agreed to produce their album in between Thursday tours. Although he'd never served as a producer, there was clearly something unique about the band that was worth attaching his name to. What he most appreciated was that, even though their music was moody, there was a self-awareness behind it. At a time when the entire scene was concerned with the right cut of jeans and the perfect color of New Balance sneakers, My Chemical Romance wasn't trying to be cool, tough, or stylish; they were indulging their own fantastical interests.

"They were tongue-in-cheek in a way that no one was doing in the punk scene, where everything was very sincere. They did dark music that was still kind of winky. So I told them to push that," Rickly says. "I told Gerard, 'You're a comic book writer. Write yourself. Imagine yourself as a superhero version of who you are.' I think that was a big moment for them, to have someone encourage that side of them. And they just ran with it."

$ $ $

Sarah Lewitinn was sitting in the passenger seat of her mother's Toyota Camry as it sped up the Palisades Parkway, frantically flipping through the pages of the book *All You Need to Know About the Music Business* as if she was cramming for a test. The twenty-one-year-old had talked herself into a gig managing My Chemical Romance, and as her mom gave her a lift to the band's recording session at Nada Recording Studio, in upstate New York, it was dawning on her that she was in way over her head.

Lewitinn's connection to the band had started three years earlier, on America Online, where she forged friendships with fellow music fans under the screen name Ultragrrrl. One day, she searched the member directory for Blur, Oasis, Radiohead, and Placebo, and up popped a profile for a user with the screen name MikeyRaygun. The account belonged to Mikey Way, a seventeen-year-old who told her that he worked at a supermarket corralling shopping carts during the day and slept on his parents' couch at night. The two began exchanging music recommendations and flirty IMs, and she found him clever and funny. After a few months of messaging, she suggested they finally meet.

"We didn't know how each other looked," remembers Lewitinn. "I think he said that people had told him he looked like Leonardo DiCaprio. He sent me this blurry photo of half his face, and that was all I had to go off. The first time I met him was at the Starbucks outside the West Fourth Street station, in the West Village. But the person that was chatty on text and IM was completely different than the person I experienced in person. He was so painfully shy."

Yet even through his timidity, Lewitinn could tell Way had ambition. "I remember going to Hot Topic and Virgin Megastore and all these places with Mikey, and he'd say, 'I'm gonna be in those magazines one day, I'm gonna be on the covers, I'm gonna be on lunch boxes.' He had a vision, from the moment I met him," she says.

The two shared a teenage romance that lasted a few months. Way would take the PATH train into Manhattan and Lewitinn would ride the bus from her parents' house in Tenafly, New Jersey. "We made out on every street corner in New York," she says. The long make-out sessions were Lewitinn's way of distracting herself from the fact that the boy she really wanted to be talking to was the outgoing MikeyRaygun. "Also," she adds, "he was a great kisser."

Once Lewitinn finally accepted that she was never going to get the charming online version of Way to come to life, she ended their fling, but was adamant that they stay friends. She didn't hear much from him over the next couple of years as she began working her way into the music industry, but one night in the fall of 2001, she was sitting in her bedroom in her parents' house when a message from MikeyRaygun popped up on her computer screen.

"He reached out to me and said, 'I'm starting a band with my brother. You're not gonna like it, it's not your thing, but I'm really excited,'" she remembers. Lewitinn braced herself for songs that emulated the music she knew Way loved—"quasi-sci-fi, futuristic Britpop bullshit," as she puts it. But when he sent her two mp3s, "Skylines and Turnstiles" and "Cubicles," neither sounded anything like what she was expecting. "He was right that it was not something I'd listen to, but it was fucking great. It was this visceral thing I couldn't even put my finger on. Just so much energy, so much excitement, so much thoughtfulness, and it grabbed me right away."

Way bragged that they were working on an album they'd convinced Geoff Rickly to produce. "I knew who Geoff was because anyone that worked in the music industry knew who Thursday was at that point. They were poised to be the next Nirvana," Lewitinn says. She begged Way to let her manage the band and, after talking it over with the rest of the guys, he agreed. She didn't have any real managerial experience, but, she says, "I just knew I could fucking kill it." It also didn't hurt that she was willing to work for free.

My Chemical Romance got themselves booked on their first show in October 2001, at an Elks lodge in Ewing, New Jersey, opening for Pencey Prep, a brash hardcore band fronted by their friend Frank Iero, and Iero's cousin's band, Mild 75. The members of My Chem were so nervous about their first public performance that they downed a case of beers beforehand to calm their nerves. Once they were full of liquid courage, they sized up the room of about forty people and jumped into "Skylines and Turnstiles." After rushing their way through it, they surveyed the crowd to find that, as far as they could tell, people actually liked them. They loved them, in fact.

"The room felt electric," recalls Iero. "I remember standing on a chair at the merch table in the back and watching them play. They were all drunk, but it was still incredible. It felt like it could fall off the rails at any moment, but somehow it stayed together. They might have played for twenty minutes. There was a Smiths cover in there —'Jack the Ripper.' If they played eight songs, that would be a lot. But I remember being like, 'Holy shit, there's something really special here.' And everyone knew it. *Everyone* knew it."

While most of the band stood with their feet firmly planted like cement blocks and dutifully ran through their songs, Gerard Way was already working the room like a veteran frontman, shedding his bashfulness the second he got the microphone in his hands. There was no stage, so he paced back and forth, claiming as much floor space as possible. His live persona took a little inspiration from his influences—the pained emotional delivery of Geoff Rickly, the operatic metal grandiosity of Iron Maiden's Bruce Dickinson, the pompous swagger of Morrissey, and, like any good product of New Jersey, the ghoulish brooding of the Misfits' Glenn Danzig.

Way wore a homemade shirt that read THANK YOU FOR THE VENOM, a phrase he'd coined that would eventually become the title of one of the band's songs. "We used to have this joke where you can't wear your own band's shirt unless you were Iron Maiden," says Saavedra. "And those kids were wearing their own shirts immediately. They were so confident that they were gonna be like Iron Maiden."

"Gerard, especially, exuded a confidence of being whoever the fuck he wanted to be and didn't give a shit," says Iero, "which is weird, because offstage he was very introverted and self-conscious. But when he got up there, that unlocked something." Iero made a point of seeing My Chem whenever they played from then on and considered himself their number one fan. He became part of the band's small cadre of supportive friends, family, and girlfriends who reliably turned up to every show at Legion halls, VFWs, and small clubs throughout the tri-state area.

"They handed out a demo, and it had Mikey's email address on the CD-Rs," Iero remembers. "There was something special about those songs. I'd play them over and over again and say, 'How is this so good? These kids came out of nowhere to put these three songs together and they're fucking incredible.' It was unlike anything else going on at the time. It was a bit alien in its voicings. There was almost a classical influence that Ray had. His chord progressions were off the wall. And of course Gerard's singing just set it apart."

After getting eleven local shows under their belt, My Chemical Romance decided that there was something lacking in their sound. Toro was a skilled guitarist, but there was a limit to how much he could pull off alone. Adding a second axman could help the band beef up their tone, they thought. Plus, having another member who wasn't so stage-shy might inject more energy into their live show.

At the suggestion of Rickly, they considered Iero. It was the perfect time to poach him, since Pencey Prep was winding down, clocking in their final show that year at CBGB. Iero already knew My Chem's songs and also had a chaotic and unpredictable stage presence that took inspiration from his favorite punk band, Black Flag.

At first, Iero felt uncomfortable with the idea of joining a new project that didn't include his Pencey Prep pals, with whom he'd played music since high school. But the allure of My Chemical Romance was too undeniable to pass up. "Somehow, in some way, we all knew that My Chem was gonna do something important," he says. "But I felt weird about leaving my friends behind; I felt bad about it. At the same time, My Chem was my favorite band in the entire world. It's like being a kid and having your favorite band ask you to be in it. It's a no-brainer."

"It was a four-piece and then Frankie came in," says Lewitinn. "He was a fucking star, and I was glad he was in the band, because all eyes were on Gerard, but someone needed to alleviate him at some point. It wasn't gonna be Mikey, because he was scared shitless to be onstage. Their drummer, Otter, was fine, but he was like a bro, not really commanding any presence. Ray was technically wonderful, but he wasn't commanding the audience in the same way that Frankie could."

Not only did Iero help thicken the band's rhythm section; his occasional shrieking backup vocals added a spazzy hardcore element to My Chemical Romance that borrowed from the screamo sounds commonly heard in New Brunswick basements. He became the band's wildcard, always leaping off the bass drum or writhing around on the floor.

As soon as Iero joined, the newly minted quintet trekked up to Nada Studios to get their debut album recorded. The band took to their first official studio experience like kids on Christmas. Nada was a small setup in the basement of engineer John Naclerio's mother's house. The ceilings were low, the rooms were cramped, and the recording booth was accessed through a laundry room. But the sight of real mixing boards and soundproofed walls made the band feel like professional rock stars.

"It was a home studio, but it might as well have been Electric Lady to them. Ray, especially, was like a little kid. He was so excited," remembers Saavedra. "There were a few times when his legs were shaking and it was picking up on the recording. We were like, 'Dude, you gotta stand still!' And he was like, 'All right, I'm sorry! I'm just so excited!'"

With only enough budget to cover two weeks of recording time, the band got to work rushing through their debut LP, *I Brought You My Bullets, You Brought Me Your Love*. The members' wide array of musical tastes produced eleven songs that were scattered and uneven, but that was part of their charm. "Early Sunsets Over Monroeville" was a five-minute homage to nineties emo in the style of the Promise Ring. "This Is the Best Day Ever," with its galloping punk beat, took a cue from revered Jersey veterans Lifetime. The most structurally disparate track, "Honey, This Mirror Isn't Big Enough for the Two of Us," shifted abruptly between styles like a car with a broken transmission. Pure metal-worship riffs dissolved into melodic verses randomly peppered with abrasive screaming, throwing the kitchen sink of influences at the listener.

The band's amateur energy produced plenty of serendipitous compositions, but when Lewitinn was dropped off by her mother, she was faced with her first managerial crisis: her band was having trouble getting decent vocal takes out of their singer. "Alex was like, 'We can't get Gerard to record. There's something wrong with his ears and he's not feeling well. We need every day we can get, because we don't have a lot of money,'" she remembers. "I'm fretting because I have zero dollars. I can't pay for more studio time."

"He had a terrible earache and this pain in his head," Saavedra says. "We couldn't figure out what was going on with him. The dude was really in major pain, but we needed to finish this fucking record. We kept bringing him to the ER and they were like, 'There's nothing wrong with you!'"

"So I go out to the car and ask my mom what to do," Lewitinn remembers. "She was like, 'Get Gerard in the car right now. We're going to the hospital!' We get to the hospital and she's telling [the staff], 'You're taking him right now! He's recording a record, he needs to have this done, you have to see him right this second!' He ended up needing a root canal or some dental work, but she insisted on waiting with him. She stayed with him the whole time. After that, my fifty-five-year-old Egyptian mother was in love with Gerard."

Way's swollen jaw did lead to one bit of studio magic. As the singer's pain grew stronger after the procedure, vocal takes started coming out flat and lacking in emotion. "I just wasn't happy with what he was doing. Neither was Alex," says Rickly. "Alex stole his pain meds and told him he couldn't have any more and needed to record."

After depriving Way of his Vicodin and giving him several unsuccessful pep talks, Saavedra tried one more motivational trick. "I punched him in the face," he says. "I thought I knocked him out at first. It shocked the shit out of him. In hindsight, it was very jock-ish, but at the time it made sense. I think the masochist in him really enjoyed it. It definitely hurt, but it amped him up. It was a different kind of pain. He slayed that vocal take right after that."

Saavedra's fist not only slugged better performances out of Way; it also pounded a notion into the singer's head that would become an integral part of how My Chemical Romance operated. Sometimes, Way learned, he'd need to embrace the pain.

$ $ $

Although Lewitinn was young and inexperienced, her hustle made her a good manager for a new band to have in its corner. She networked her way through three shows a night in Manhattan and spent her days spreading music gossip online. As soon as she got hired by the band, the hyperconnected manager sang My Chemical Romance's praises from her keyboard. She emailed their demo songs to her friend who did A&R at Atlantic Records and to her friends who were writers at *SPIN* and *NME;* she posted about the band on Thursday's message board and fired off IMs to tastemakers. The buzz she stirred up was enough to get the band written up in Hits Daily Double, a hot spot for A&R chatter. The band's songs bounced around the music industry after that, and before she knew it, she no longer had to tell anyone about My Chemical Romance. People were now coming to her.

"All these label people were calling me all of a sudden," she says. "I suddenly had people flying in to New York to see the band play at the Loop Lounge. Rob Stevenson, at Island Def Jam, was interested in signing them because his rival at Island had signed Thursday, so he wanted to have My Chem. It was moving superfast. It went from zero to 120 overnight."

It wasn't just industry insiders who were discovering the band through the internet. The band members, particularly the Sidekick-addicted Mikey Way, had a sixth sense for using the web to their advantage, and were corralling new fans wherever they gathered online. The band's name got around on local message boards like TheNJScene and on social networking sites like Friendster, Live-Journal, and the alt-culture favorite Makeoutclub. Hype around My Chemical Romance spread the old-fashioned way—by word of mouth—but thanks to the facility of the internet, it was happening at a rapid pace.

"Mikey lived online," says Lewitinn. "The internet was fucking huge for them. That was how people found out about them. They had their EP on their website, where people could download the songs or snippets. Any opportunity we had to spread their music digitally, we would do it. I was selling merch at their shows and giving people their website, making sure kids were signing up for mailing lists. I'd sit there and type in everyone's email and send out newsletter updates."

By the time Eyeball Records released *I Brought You My Bullets,* on July 23, 2002, it seemed as though My Chemical Romance was already on the lips of every record company. "All these labels were hitting me up, and I was taking the band out for meetings. It was all happening so fast and effortlessly," Lewitinn remembers.

"Finally one day the band asked me to meet up with them," she continues. "They were like, 'We love you, we think you're amazing, we're thankful for all the help you've given us, but we feel like you're pushing us too far. It's too much, too soon. You're trying to give us the big time and we're not ready for the big time yet. We want to be a punk band, we want to build up, we don't want to take the fast route.' That's the best way to be fired: being told you're doing too good of a job. I was so surprised, but I couldn't be bitter about it. I had to respect their vision and their goals. Similar to my breakup with Mikey, I wanted to continue helping this band any way I could. So when I got a job at *SPIN,* any opportunity I had to write them up, I was taking it."

"At the time, I remember thinking Sarah wasn't the best manager for them," says Rickly. "But in retrospect, she had a big influence on how they thought about what was going on. She pushed them to embrace the androgynous or feminine aspects of the band. So to minimize her contribution to their savviness is a huge mistake."

But even after Lewitinn was let go, opportunities continued to fall into the band's laps. In August, shortly after *Bullets* was released, they were contacted with a last-minute offer to fill in for Coheed and Cambria, who had to drop off a date in nearby Allentown, Pennsylvania, opening for the Juliana Theory and Jimmy Eat World. But it wasn't at a midsize club or hall; Jimmy Eat World could now fill a sprawling fairground, thanks to a wild breakout year. After two failed releases that had gotten them dropped from Capitol Records, the Arizonans self-funded the production of their follow-up, *Bleed American.* It was a record so undeniably accessible that labels started sniffing around again. "Word of mouth had gotten around that the material was strong," says drummer Zach Lind. "Hollywood Records was really interested, MCA wanted it, Sire wanted it, Atlantic wanted it. Even Capitol got interested again. It was total FOMO." They were pursued so intensely that eventually producer Mark Trombino had to start locking the door of their studio. The winner of the bidding war, DreamWorks, had its investment immediately pay off when the band's single "The Middle" found success and broke into Top 40 radio thanks to its sugary chorus. The song became a top-five *Billboard* hit and, in the month the band was set to play Allentown, *Bleed American* went platinum.

"That was [My Chem's] first break. Jimmy Eat World was huge at the time," says Saavedra. My Chemical Romance realized they were in over their heads as soon as they pulled into the parking lot and saw how ridiculous their cheap rental van looked alongside the other acts' massive buses. "I remember the stage manager was like, 'Do you have your stage plot?' And the guys were like, 'Yeah, hang on.' Then they went back and were like, 'Uh, sorry . . . what is that?' They were a baby band. They'd never played on a stage like that. They were playing little halls and Maxwell's, in Hoboken. They didn't know anything about stage plots."

If My Chemical Romance had been skittish about playing in front of a few dozen people at a New Jersey Elks lodge, they were scared out of their minds when they looked out onto the thousands of people gathered at the Allentown Fairgrounds. But even though he was petrified, Gerard Way became another person when he looked out onto the faces in front of him, like a man possessed. The massive stage didn't overwhelm him; it actually fueled him.

"Me and my girlfriends watched from side stage and we were freaking the fuck out," says Lewitinn. "We'd only seen them on tiny little stages—rec centers in Jersey. I'd seen them play CB's once. But I was finally seeing My Chem on a stage big enough for them."

Iero was so nervous that he clenched his eyes shut through the first few minutes of the set. The band played "Headfirst for Halos," whose mathy guitar intro, like something nicked from a Rush song, was built to rock arenas and stadiums. Midway through, Iero looked up to find that a sea of people were jumping up and down to the beat. "I remember we got the crowd to bounce," he says. "And we all looked at each other like, 'Holy shit, there are thousands of people here. This is crazy!' It was the biggest show we'd ever played, it was the best response we'd ever gotten, it was the best feeling we'd ever had."

My Chemical Romance had gotten their first taste of rock stardom that night, and they were hooked. From then on, Iero says, the band was committed to doing whatever was necessary to make that feeling happen every night, no matter how much time, work, and faith it took to get there.

"I signed my first autograph at that show," Iero says. "I felt really weird about it. I remember thinking, 'I shouldn't be signing this. I'm not even supposed to be here.' And my friend Eddie said, 'Think about it: if you were this kid, you'd want someone to sign this for you.' So I wrote my name and the kid was like, 'Can you please sign more than that?' So I wrote, 'Keep the faith.'"

$ $ $

I Brought You My Bullets, You Brought Me Your Love was released to little press reaction in America. Strangely enough, the UK newspaper the *Guardian* was one of the few outlets to devote ink to the debut album, though they weren't much impressed with the American band's displays of overt narcissism. "Nil points for urban credibility, then, but top marks for self-absorbed 'emo' angst," wrote reviewer Caroline Sullivan. "It would be surprising if they'd ever faced anything more dangerous than a runaway lawnmower."

At home, though, the members of My Chemical Romance earned some bragging rights around town when "Vampires" got played on WSOU, the venerated college radio station of Seton Hall University. Within two months of *Bullets'* release, Eyeball sold through the first printing of about two thousand copies, an impressive feat for a band that had barely left New Jersey.

Having gotten a taste for big crowds and big stages in Allentown, though, My Chemical Romance was eager to conquer the world outside the Garden State. The band added two new members to their team to help achieve this—Matt Galle, a Boston booking agent hired to land them as many tours and gigs as possible, and Stacy Fass, a lawyer brought on to handle everything else. "We had a lawyer and a booking agent," says Iero. "We were set. That's all we needed."

The Way brothers' grandparents cobbled together enough cash to buy them a run-down van, which the band used to hop from tour to tour throughout 2002 and early 2003. Armed with *Bullets,* they hit the road in the United States and Canada and played for anyone who would have them, from hardcore heavy hitters American Nightmare to perky punk favorites Piebald. That My Chem didn't sound like any other band was both a hindrance and a benefit as a touring band. They weren't a natural fit for most bills, but their eclectic pedigree allowed them to be slotted in alongside anyone, from screamo bands to indie rock acts.

Their first tour saw them opening for a poppy emo band out of Alabama called Northstar. After that, they supported Christian metalcore act Underoath. "That was huge for us, because they were really seasoned," says Iero. "They knew what they were doing and were super nice to us. Being Christian, they really looked out for us. We had no clothes and they'd give us T-shirts. One of the guys who managed them told us that if you call venues ahead of time, you can get chips and salsa. And we were like, 'Chips and salsa, are you fucking kidding me!' So we called everybody and asked for chips and salsa. We found out later that if you're a little bigger, you can ask for peanut butter and jelly."

Not every show was a knockout. Gerard Way's penchant for theatrics, in particular, elicited some eye rolls from older cynics who found the group too wimpy. The band wasn't for everyone, but the people who got into them *really* got into them. At every show, a dozen or so MCR faithfuls waited sheepishly in the corners for the band to take the stage, then pushed through the crowd to sing along up front. The band identified their handful of people every night and played directly to them, with an attitude that said "Fuck everyone else."

"Coming up, we'd play punk shows, we'd play hardcore shows, we'd play with Christian rock bands, but we didn't fit in anywhere," says Iero. "Very few people were nice to us. It wasn't cool to be our band. There was a bit of a flamboyance to it, a bit of theatrics to it. We didn't have breakdowns, we didn't sound like what was cool. But I think there were kids that were hearing our band who didn't fit in anywhere else and were like, 'That's me. I'm a fucking weirdo. I also don't belong anywhere else. Maybe I belong at these shows.'"

Geeks, nerds, outsiders, and misfits gradually gravitated to My Chemical Romance, and collectively dubbed themselves the MCRmy. Whether they were too scrawny, too overweight, not cool enough, or not cool at all, they were accepted by the band for who they were. No matter how excluded a person felt by the outside world, when they stepped into a My Chem show, they belonged to something bigger.

"From the very beginning, they'd say, 'If you're racist, if you're sexist, if you're homophobic, get the fuck out of the audience. We don't want you,'" says Cassie Whitt, a fan and MCRmy archivist. "They were creating this environment where we were all celebrating each other for being weird, or different, or women, or people of color, or trans, whatever we were. 'My Chemical Romance said it was okay, so if you don't agree, fuck you.' They never once encouraged the machismo that was prevalent then. They poked fun at that, even. A lot of the way Gerard presents himself is quite feminine. As a young girl, you could see some hypermasculine guy onstage and feel intimidated, whereas these guys were the opposite of that."

Women, especially, were made to feel welcome by My Chemical Romance. "They were a feminist band early on," says Lewitinn. "They had a female manager, they had a female lawyer. Their world was filled with strong women, which I think was representative of how they felt about women. That whole scene was such a boys' world, but My Chem did a really good job of making women feel included. If a girl was in the mosh pit, Gerard would shout her out for being unafraid. They made them feel welcome, and not as eye candy. As a female, we were seen as commodities. We were walking wallets. But he made them feel like they were part of something, and more than just tagging along with their boyfriends or buying T-shirts."

My Chemical Romance's new fans were particularly drawn to the band's increasingly dynamic frontman, who absorbed all the insecurity in the room and beamed it back out in the form of concentrated confidence. He had dropped some of the baby fat of his youth, revealing cute but peculiar good looks. His facial features were angular, almost elvish, like an anime rendering of a young Billy Corgan or a bad boy in a Tim Burton movie. He started embracing a darker image in his stage persona, letting his jet-black hair swoop across his face and wearing a tattered hobo blazer over ratty hoodies. He would also soon incorporate eyeliner into his look, which only further aggravated the rigid male hecklers in the room. "People at the very beginning would call us faggots and stuff like that," Gerard told the magazine *Big Cheese*. "We were being discriminated against from early on. The minute you open your mouth to stand up for yourself or to say something different from what everyone else is saying, people will start hating you. You pose a threat to them. People don't like it, and this band is a very threatening thing to a lot of people and that's the beauty of it."

"Gerard *thrived* on that shit," says Whitt. "If a dude was calling him a slur, he'd say, 'That's all right, I'm meeting up with your girlfriend in the parking lot later.' Or 'C'mon, dude, let's have a dance contest!' Or 'You want a kiss? C'mon up here and give me a kiss.' He would egg those dudes on."

Sometimes the singer would provoke a hostile crowd by strutting over to Iero and giving his guitarist a big, wet kiss. The band's androgyny and sexual ambiguity were embraced more immediately by British audiences on their first trip to Europe, in March 2003. The Brits, who'd been primed by decades of gender fluidity, from David Bowie to the Cure, were more open-minded and latched on quicker. The internet had helped spread word of the band internationally, and they were amazed to be greeted by kids at venues in England who wore homemade MCR shirts.

After returning home, Gerard got the chance to stand out among his male rock peers in his first major photo shoot. Lewitinn was now an assistant editor at *SPIN* and had been tasked with selecting a hot young singer for a fashion spread entitled "A New Breed of Cool from the Frontmen of Five Up-and-Coming Bands" which included the Apes, stellastarr*, A.R.E. Weapons, and Elefant. She suggested Gerard, who took to the modeling gig like a seasoned pro.

"Terry Richardson ended up shooting it, which was a pretty big fucking deal," she says. Richardson was notorious in the art world for his highly sexualized photos that appeared in edgy publications like *Vice*. He instructed the frontman to pick a CD in his studio and start rocking out while he snapped shots. Way threw on Black Flag's "Nervous Breakdown," clenched the microphone, and went berserk. An assistant spritzed water at Way's hair while Richardson's flash hit his face. A full-page photo of Gerard soon graced the July 2003 issue of the magazine. He resembled a young Danzig, with his black leather jacket, strands of greasy hair covering his steely gaze, and not-to-be-fucked-with Jersey sneer.

"I remember the fashion editor saying all those bands were great, but Gerard was something else," Lewitinn says. "The photo came out amazing, and Terry Richardson loved him. There was no situation I could put Gerard in where people didn't think he was amazing—everyone from my mom to Terry Richardson. How universal is this guy's appeal that everyone's so obsessed? He's just got the X factor—a person who looks you in the eye and all of a sudden you're the only person in the room."

$ $ $

Although they'd been on the road for barely a year, My Chemical Romance was ready for whatever came next. They all wanted to look out onto the crowds Jimmy Eat World saw every night, and they knew they needed more resources to get there. So when major labels came knocking on their door again in 2003, this time they let them in. "We'd done some touring and the band was getting big," says Iero. "This was something we wanted to do eventually, so why not do it now?"

"It became more work than Eyeball could handle," says Lewitinn. "There were distribution, marketing, and promotion elements that Eyeball just could not fulfill. The band built up the fan base and the credibility with the first record, but they didn't need to do that with the second record. They needed to go big, which is what they did."

Plus, in the wake of Thursday's recent high-profile signing to Island Def Jam, the prolific New Jersey scene and adjacent Long Island scene were being mined by record labels for promising stars in the burgeoning worlds of emo and post-hardcore. But for every respectable band like Thursday who'd earned their way into a record contract through sweat and sincerity, a dozen Diesel-jean clones were handed lucrative opportunities. A casual fan might not immediately spot the sonic or sartorial differences between these acts and My Chem, but a number of them represented the complete opposite of what Way stood for. Many of the prevalent ex-girlfriend-bashing lyrics traded at best in mopey misogyny and at worst in murder fantasy, frequently inflicting their macabre wrist-slitting or chainsaw imagery on the "whores" at the wrong end of the male singers' ire. A line from Thursday's "For the Workforce, Drowning" became prescient: "Just keep making copies of copies of copies of copies. When will it end?" My Chemical Romance didn't want a watered-down, misogynist copycat version of their band stealing all the glory. If anyone was going to make it, it was going to be them.

The band got taken out to restaurants and bars by A&R reps, most of whom knew better than to try to impress five comic book nerds with trips to strip clubs and bottles of Cristal. "The big three that came first were DreamWorks, Warner Bros., and Roadrunner," says Iero. "They wanted us bad and kept coming around. I remember Warner being like, 'Hey, we're gonna buy you guys pizzas.' But the pizza place wouldn't take cards, so we had to buy the pizzas. And then another time they just took us to Denny's. It was never extravagant. Someone told us later that they'd heard we weren't impressed by that kind of stuff, so they just took us to shit places."

Of all their potential suitors, the guys narrowed it down to DreamWorks and Warner Bros. The latter had an impressive history with Green Day, having made international superstars out of the Berkeley punk trio a decade before. DreamWorks boasted a more recent success story with Jimmy Eat World, who were still riding the wave of 2001's *Bleed American*.

"You have to fall in love with the label and not the A&R," says Iero. "We loved the A&R at DreamWorks, but the label itself we knew wasn't the right place for us. I remember meeting with Mo [Ostin], the head of DreamWorks Records at the time, and he had no idea who we were. At Warner, Craig Aaronson was our A&R, but I think it was [CEO] Tom Whalley who really sold us. Craig was incredibly passionate about the band. He was a wonderful person, but he was a bit much at times. He had really great qualities but really annoying qualities, too. But I will say this: as a champion of his bands, there was no one who fought more for his bands than him."

As the summer wound down, My Chemical Romance made their

decision. They would be signing with Warner Bros.' Reprise imprint for the release of their sophomore album. "We did not sign what you call a money deal," Gerard explained to *Alternative Press*. "A money deal is where right off the bat you go and buy houses and Ferraris and shit. Our deal is based on having a career, so we didn't ask for a fuckload of money. We just wanted to work and tour and so when you make your album the label says, 'We don't have to bank on any hits with this band to get our money back.'"

The label jump was a risky move, considering that the band owed much of their rising profile to the intimate relationship they'd formed with their community of devoted fans. Leaving their roots behind to get in bed with a big corporation like Warner Bros. might seem like an act of betrayal. To nip any conversations about selling out in the bud, the band posted a lengthy statement on their website that August, much like Thursday had done when they left Victory Records for Island. It wasn't a justification, the message clarified, but "a declaration and a threat."

"At that time, there was a sellout witch hunt going on," Iero says. "[The statement] was just explaining our point of view. We felt like this was our chance to take this shit and run with it and be who we wanted to become. It's not about who is super punk rock; it's about taking this opportunity and doing the best we can."

For several paragraphs, Gerard Way rambled cryptically about elitism and respect in music and alluded to forthcoming changes. Almost as an afterthought, the statement concluded with a call to arms and a bit of news sneaked in at the very end:

> I wanted to be the first to tell you before the gossip and the hearsay, I want to shout it from the street-lamps to the coils, in every fucked up slum, where every seedy club lives and breathes.
>
> > We are coming to your town.
> > *We are taking back what's ours.*
> > We're all in this together . . .
>
> And by the way . . . we've signed to Reprise and we are fucking ready for the world to hear us scream.

$ $ $

My Chemical Romance wanted to make a bold statement with their major-label debut, *Three Cheers for Sweet Revenge,* so they sought a producer who specialized in bold albums. One of their top choices was Jimmy Eat World's go-to guy, Mark Trombino. "We loved the *Bleed American* record, so we thought it'd be cool to work with Trombino," says Iero. Reprise booked a tryout session with the producer at which the band recorded a track, "It's Not a Fashion Statement, It's a Fucking Deathwish."

"I remember getting in the studio with Mark and recording all day," says Iero. "We finally finished it and I remember him being like, 'You guys aren't ready. You guys don't have it.' It was deflating. Then you start thinking, 'Well, shit did we make the wrong decision?'" (Trombino's account differs. The producer says he "would have died to make a record together" and suspects the label's preference in producers may have stood in the way of doing so.)

The label brought a handful of their preferred producers by the band's practices to see which ones they had the best chemistry with. The producer most of the guys agreed on was Howard Benson, who had an uneven background. He'd worked with some abysmal bro-rock bottom-feeders like Crazy Town, P.O.D., and Zebrahead, but had also collaborated with reputable heavy acts like Motörhead, T.S.O.L., and Ice-T's heavy metal project Body Count. "I didn't particularly like Howard Benson, but everyone else did," says Iero. "I remember butting heads with Howard a bunch, but ultimately I think he taught us a lot. He was very concerned with Gerard. He didn't care about anyone else. He never even was in the studio when Ray and I were recording."

While Benson's focus on Gerard's vocals might have left the rest of the band in the shadows, *Three Cheers for Sweet Revenge* did a commendable job of capturing what made Way a unique rock vocalist. The singer leaned further into his theatrical side, with a more sassy delivery than what he'd given on *I Brought You My Bullets.* He got a few vocal assists in the process, too, with "You Know What They Do to Guys Like Us in Prison" featuring a guest spot from Bert McCracken, of labelmates the Used. And it seemed fitting for an album centered around the idea of revenge that Keith Morris, who once sang punk's most famous revenge track, should appear on the record. The Black Flag singer—whom the band later claimed to interviewers they'd cornered at a gas station and begged to sing on the record—provided a hidden, enigmatic spoken-word section in the middle of the western-twanged "Hang 'Em High," whose meaning fans would endlessly dissect.

The record tackled heavy subjects—depression, suicide, and doomed love—but did so in a way that was either empowering or winking at their own melodrama. Opener "Helena" was a gut-wrenching personal exploration of the remorse and self-hatred Gerard felt after his pursuit of rock star dreams had caused him to miss the last year of his grandmother's life. Conversely, songs like "Give 'Em Hell, Kid" and "It's Not a Fashion Statement" are cuts of third-person storytelling that continue the saga of the Demolition Lovers, a fictional man and woman (depicted on the cover's artwork, created by Gerard) whose reckless love affair was cut short by a gunfight. The album's clear standout was "I'm Not Okay (I Promise)," a dejected youth anthem that Gerard would later describe to the press as a cry for help trapped in a pop song. The sum of all these ambitious parts was an album that would fit in just as well on the shelves of a comic shop as it would a record store.

Three Cheers for Sweet Revenge was released on June 8, 2004, and the band celebrated with their first in-store performance, at hometown mainstay Vintage Vinyl. The album sold about as many copies in its first week as their previous album had sold in its first year. "I remember the first week we sold over eleven thousand copies of *Revenge*," says Iero. "And we were like, 'How is that even fucking possible?'"

"Its first-week sales blew everybody away," says Jeff Watson, Warner Bros.' vice president of digital marketing. "Those aren't huge numbers, but we were all like, 'Shit, maybe there's something here.' What happens after that is the coffers open. Labels sit around and wait for some kindling to start, and once they see a spark, any good label will throw money at it. You get more money to go to radio, you get more in tour support, you get endcaps at stores."

The label's increased resources could be felt that summer as My Chemical Romance won over young audiences around the country on Warped Tour, along with fellow Jersey road dogs Senses Fail. "We'd done a proper tour together and no one came," says singer Buddy Nielsen. "We'd played Delaware, Detroit, all these places, and maybe a hundred people came every night. Then they released *Three Cheers* and we had *Let It Enfold You* come out, and we shared a bus on Warped Tour. That's when they were blowing up and we were blowing up. Then we did a tour home from Warped Tour and everything changed. It was fucking wild. Here we are playing two-hundred-cap venues and there are massive lines down the street, all to see My Chem. And we were headlining! That kind of growth within that short of a time, I'd never seen that. We were like, 'I don't know what this is, but something's going on here.'"

Sometimes, Nielsen says, the room would clear out immediately after My Chem's set. "They're like Slayer fans," he says of the MCRmy. "You could be the most metal band ever, but they don't care—they're just there to see Slayer."

As My Chemical Romance gained velocity, though, a crack was starting to show in their engine. After a brief trip to Japan following Warped, the Ways, Toro, and Iero decided that Pelissier had to go. They'd long felt that the drummer was unreliable onstage and wasn't up to snuff in the studio, especially as the band was headed for larger venues in the coming months. It was putting a damper on the band, so he was subsequently fired. Pelissier lashed out on the band's message board, claiming that he'd "been shafted." "I never got a band meeting to discuss this," he posted, "just the boot for messing up."

The rest of the band largely refrained from publicly responding, to avoid messy online drama. "This was a painful decision for all of us to make and was not taken lightly. We wish him the best of luck in his future endeavors, and expect you all to do the same," Iero wrote on his blog. Saavedra is less diplomatic in his recollection: "No one wanted that dude Otter around. He was a total asshole. He was the fuckin' pits." They filled the position with Bob Bryar, a sound tech they'd met while touring with the Used the previous year.

My Chemical Romance's new lineup was scheduled for a hefty tour in February 2005, again joining Senses Fail as well as the Used and Killswitch Engage on the inaugural year of Taste of Chaos, a heavily promoted winter tour package launched by Warped Tour founder Kevin Lyman. A month before the tour started, Nielsen was at home watching TV and heard a familiar sound. While flipping through channels, he landed on MTV's *Total Request Live*, the video countdown show whose studio segments were typically reserved for frosted-tipped boy bands and belly-ringed pop starlets du jour. An opening riff started and he recognized it right away. It was My Chemical Romance, live in the show's Times Square studio, performing "I'm Not Okay (I Promise)" for a screaming audience. Donning matching black shirts and red ties, the band held the predominantly female onlookers in their hands and played with such fury that a freshly mohawked Iero toppled their new drummer's kit.

"I was like, '*What . . . the . . . fuck,*'" remembers Nielsen. "I don't know if there was another band from our world who had been on there yet. They all had makeup on and these outfits. I was like, 'Holy shit, they're *going for it!*' Then a few weeks later we did Taste of Chaos . . . and they were the biggest band in the world."

$ $ $

The music industry was standing on the edge of a new dawn by 2005, one in which an artist's worth would be measured not in record sales or radio plays but in downloads and friend counts. Sales of physical albums were falling into a tailspin from which they'd never recover. Instead of spending cash at stores like Sam Goody, listeners were now prone to buying mp3s through online retailers like iTunes and streaming songs through subscription services like Rhapsody. Or they simply pirated them via the digital Wild West of file-sharing networks and BitTorrent sites. The most stubborn artists desperately clung to conventional models, and would soon learn that they were doing so at their own peril. But My Chemical Romance, a band that had been promoting themselves on the internet since the days of America Online, was ready to lead the charge in this new world.

The band became the darlings of Myspace, a rapidly growing new social networking site that had amassed five thousand bands and 1.2 million users in its first three months, most of them in the sixteen-to-twenty-four demographic. The site provided an inexpensive way for bands to distribute their music and connect directly with music fans and other artists. Emerging acts were sometimes able to get internet famous before having left their hometown or even playing a single show. Myspace's rising popularity among teens raised on webcams and dial-up modems blurred the line between the underground and the mainstream.

"Primarily, it was a discovery tool for culturally ravenous teenagers for whom weekly magazines and music video channels simply weren't enough," says journalist Emma Garland. "It mashed together social networking and A&R in a way that allowed anyone and everyone to discover and promote things for themselves. It was also the first site to completely obliterate the gap between band members and their fans. While previously you'd have to post shit to someone's P.O. box or hurl a message in a bottle into the ocean and cross your fingers, on Myspace you could just message Frank Iero asking for hairspray tips."

Believing Myspace to be a passing fad, some record labels were sluggish to embrace it, but Reprise saw the marketing potential early and used the data to their advantage. The label gave exclusive MCR tracks to Myspace and other sites where scene kids congregated, like PureVolume and AbsolutePunk. Once they had a sense of what was resonating with users, they were better able to plan going forward. Instead of telling kids what they should listen to, as labels had done for decades, Reprise let user feedback determine the singles. The label's approach was so successful that it was cited as a winning strategy in a marketing book, *The Long Tail: Why the Future of Business Is Selling Less of More*.

"Once the tracks were out there, Reprise could watch how they did," author Chris Anderson wrote. "Using BigChampagne file-trading data, the label could see growing interest in 'Not OK,' but also heavy trading and searching on the track 'Helena.' On the basis of that, it made 'Helena' the next single, and, helped by requests from the band's core fans, that song got airplay. By the end of the summer, 'Helena' had become the band's biggest radio single by far."

Online success soon translated to the real world. "Helena" was the band's first single to break out of the *Billboard* rock charts and into Top 40 radio, peaking at number 32. Additionally, gigs around the world were selling out well in advance. "They are the social media band," Saavedra says. "Prior to them, everybody had to struggle like normal human beings. Then, out of nowhere, these guys are worldwide. Even their first shows in Europe, kids already knew the words, and we didn't have distribution over there. I remember being like, 'How the hell do these kids know the words?'"

Traditional print media wasn't completely abandoned in the release strategy, however. My Chemical Romance became favorites among the readers of *Alternative Press*, making the cover of the magazine for the first time in December 2004. It was a bittersweet achievement, though, given that they'd clearly surpassed their Jersey mentors Thursday, who'd appeared on the cover just a year earlier but whose current major-label struggles now rendered them a blip in the corner that read, "The End of Thursday?"

"That was still in the day when people would write actual letters to the editor and we would have mail to open," says Leslie Simon, who wrote the magazine's earliest features on MCR. "Aside from the regular and consistent Juggalo mail we'd get asking when Twiztid was going to be on the cover, it shifted to being all about My Chem, Fall Out Boy, and AFI to an extent—all those Warped Tour bands. It wasn't even just the newsstand sales, but back issues. People were buying multiples of them."

Much like Mikey Way had prophesied on his teenage dates with Lewitinn, he and his bandmates were not only on the covers of magazines but were being immortalized as collectible items for sale at the mall. *Rolling Stone* reported that year that "My Chemical Romance's gear is second only to Green Day's among the top sellers at Hot Topic, the country's largest retailer of band merchandise." And it wasn't just T-shirts and magazines; a set of MCR action figures practically sold out before even hitting shelves in 2005. The former toy designer Gerard told the *New York Times,* "What we would really love is for people to see that even regular people can end up as toys. You just have to chase it."

There was also a changing of the guard in music television, and My Chemical Romance took full advantage of its timing. After MTV largely abandoned music videos in favor of reality and celebrity shows like *The Osbournes* and *Punk'd,* the recently relaunched channel Fuse aimed to take its place. Ads for the network featured slogans like "where the music went" and "the alternative to mainstream music television." Fuse featured video countdowns and interviews with emerging artists, and My Chem quickly landed among the channel's most requested acts. "My Chem were so well received by the Fuse audience because the band mirrored the fans, emotionally as well as aesthetically," says Steven Smith, host of *Steven's Untitled Rock Show.* "Kids really connected with them because they were sincere."

A no-budget video for "I'm Not Okay (I Promise)" made with slapped-together tour footage became popular among Fuse viewers, prompting Reprise to pay for a new, more professional version. The revamped edition was made to look like a trailer for a fake Wes Anderson–style movie in which the band portrayed prep school outcasts who got bullied. It became an instant teenage classic and a top-five track on the Billboard Modern Rock chart, pushing the album past gold. Budgets got heftier and video treatments got more elaborate from there. Their second video, "Helena," was a mock funeral shot in a church and featured choreographed dance numbers, while their third, "The Ghost of You," was an epic wartime saga shot on a half-million-dollar budget.

"With that video trilogy, the image of them and what they represented was so vivid," says Simon. "It was sort of gothy but not too depressing, sort of poppy but not too bubblegum, sort of edgy but not too rebellious. It was just rebellious enough for people who didn't like where they were but weren't sure where they were going."

Their message tapped into a cultural moment in a way that felt bigger than them. Much like Green Day had inadvertently captured the collective feeling of suburban teenage ennui in the nineties, My Chemical Romance spoke to the next era of young music fans who were even more burned out, more jaded, and more paranoid. For a generation that came of age watching the Twin Towers crumble and was about to have two forever wars dumped on their laps, the band offered an escape from, or at least a method of coping with, dark and uncertain times.

"I think one of the elements that connected them to people after 9/11 was that they added this element of abandon," says Rickly. "Like, 'We're all depressed, but let's laugh about it.' Laughing about depression has become such a cultural phenomenon. I don't know that you could say [My Chem] was the starting point for it, but in music it certainly was."

"We would be on the bus and there would be a line of kids outside, all makeup-ed out or in their My Chem shirts," says tour manager Jeff Pereira. "You'd walk off the bus and instantly, the first thing you'd hear was 'You saved my life!' I'd never heard that said more than when I was with Gerard."

"We were trying to come to grips with all these strange things that were happening in the world around us," says Whitt. "We were thinking more about tragedy, and everything felt more serious. Their forums back in the day were one of the first places where I saw people talking about mental health."

Entire corners of the internet were devoted to MCR fandom. The MCRmy endlessly dissected lyrics and videos on message boards and forums, cobbling together elaborate theories. Gerard Way fan art became a popular category on art-sharing sites like DeviantArt. Some fans penned fanfic about the band members in which they were vampire hunters or outlaws, while others dragged them into erotic territories.

"A tattoo in the MCR fandom is small fries," laughs Whitt. "I have friends in the UK who followed them all over Europe and then Australia and Japan and the U.S. It's not super common among their fans, but common enough that I know five to ten people who've done it, where they take out loans or open a bunch of credit cards to follow the band."

"My Chemical Romance wasn't just a band," she continues. "It was this all-encompassing experience. They built art and narrative around the music that you could get lost in and interpret. Fans created their own art around it and it became an eternal cycle. I think they really fostered that environment. It became people's lifestyle."

$ $ $

Three Cheers for Sweet Revenge's pop melancholia reached the computers of disenfranchised teenage music listeners in the year following its release, thanks to a combination of nonstop touring and a cunning marketing push from Reprise. Within fourteen months of its release, it sold more than a million copies and was certified platinum. It won a Kerrang! Award for Best Album, while "Helena" won Best Video and also racked up five nominations at the MTV Video Music Awards. My Chemical Romance landed on the cover of *SPIN* after practically sweeping the magazine's Readers Poll, winning Band of the Year, Song of the Year, and Cover of the Year. Gerard even won the vote for 2004's Sex God. "I am who I am. There is no façade," he told the magazine. "And being voted sexiest doesn't concern me. Maybe that's the sexy part."

Despite the newfound fame that allowed them to play for thousands of adoring fans every night, the band in many ways remained the same small-town geeks they'd always been. "When Mikey finally got a lot of money, he bought this gigantic fucking house in Jersey," Lewitinn says. "I remember teasing him and saying he was Tom Hanks in *Big*. There were times where I'd show up and there would be someone there and I'd be like, 'Who the fuck is this?' And they'd be like, 'Oh, that's Randall. Mikey met him on *World of Warcraft*.' Mikey was still meeting people off the internet and not telling them who he was and they were showing up to his house. There was always some random sketchy dude around."

But in other ways, the sudden success and the strenuous schedule required to maintain it were taking a toll, physically and psychologically. Gerard was in need of mentoring on how to adapt to the growing pains of reaching a new level of fame, one that brought sobbing fans who foisted emotional stories of depression and suicide attempts on him. He took advice from another frontman, Green Day's Billie Joe Armstrong, who had recently been put through the fame wringer himself. After three albums that saw diminishing returns in the decade after the *Dookie* boom, the band shocked the world with their triumphant return—2004's punk rock opera record *American Idiot*. It became their first number one album in the United States, went platinum in less than two months, and helped Green Day reclaim their seat on the punk rock throne. Gerard rightly described their wild revival to *SPIN* as "the story of the year and the comeback of the decade." Green Day took a victory lap around the world on a tour that lasted fifteen months, with My Chemical Romance opening five weeks' worth of dates, during which Armstrong took a liking to the MCR singer.

"I had conversations with Gerard," Armstrong recalled to *Kerrang!* "He was feeling a bit uncertain at the time and I just told him not to be afraid. I think he was shying away. He was at that point where a band reads too much of its own press, and they start to internalize everything. To the point where they become boring. So I told him that it's okay to be a rock star. It's okay to be that, because the world needs good rock stars. We've got enough boring people."

Still, the pressure to be good rock stars was mounting within My Chemical Romance, and old friends were starting to notice a change in them. "I think it fucked them up," Saavedra says. "For a few years, I felt they had quite an inflated ego, where they were completely different people. If everyone's kissing your ass all the time, you don't realize you're fucking up."

In the year on the road promoting *Three Cheers for Sweet Revenge*, substance use became more prominent among some of the members, particularly the Ways and most particularly Gerard. "Certainly, drugs were involved. It was mostly pot—*lots of pot*—and a ton of alcohol," says Lewitinn. "They were *Alternative Press* stars, but they really wanted to be the Gallagher brothers—the riffraff that was talked about in British press. That was our idea of stardom: being bonkers British artists. They saw themselves as future *NME* stars."

But the self-perpetuating cycle of drunken rock star antics was going too far. For Gerard, drinking turned from recreational to habitual to detrimental. He'd often relied on alcohol to invoke the spirit of the wild, tortured showman he portrayed onstage every night, but after a while it was hard to tell where Gerard the character ended and Gerard the person began. Not helping mark the distinction was the fact that he never cleaned or took off his stage outfit.

Entire months of shows blurred by in a haze of alcohol, sweat, and makeup. The 2004 Warped Tour was particularly grueling. Hot summer weeks on a diet of beer and cigarettes were starting to show on Gerard's face. His speech was stuck in a state of perpetual slur, and his step had a soused wobble to it. He became notorious for his excesses, which were evidenced onstage, where the frontman was prone to vomiting, falling over, or losing his pants. He'd always kept the lesson he learned from Saavedra's fist in the back of his mind, but he'd begun to embrace the pain too intensely.

"I'd been on Warped Tour with him when he was indulging a lot, and it was hard to watch," remembers Simon. "There were times when he was performing when he was puking off the side of the stage and then going back. And he did not wash that suit all summer. It smelled like a diaper filled with baby vomit; it was *dis-gust-ing*."

"It was a vicious circle," Gerard told *Blender,* which reported that he'd been dabbling in Xanax and cocaine. "I needed it to function, but it made me want to kill myself. It made me extremely unpredictable and dangerous to myself. I didn't want it to get to the point where it became like a VH1 *Behind the Music,* where they show this really bad picture of me thirty pounds overweight, throwing up on the floor in Berlin. I didn't want that to happen to this band."

He hit his lowest point on a trip to Japan, where he was wasted, suicidal, and hell-bent on annihilation. "I went to Japan not thinking I was coming back," he told *NME.* "I got on that plane and I packed real light. I was so addicted to self-destruction—I think more than the drugs. There was something very romantic about it. I didn't pack anything. I packed show clothes and they smelled awful. They smelled like I lived on the streets. I really thought I was gonna die."

After spending his last hours in Asia with his head hovering over a garbage can full of his own puke, Way made the decision to get sober. He kicked the substances cold turkey and sweated out three years' worth of alcohol on the painfully long flight back to the

United States, determined to stay clear-eyed for what awaited him on the other side.

$ $ $

As the 2000s wore on, the descriptor "emo" started to morph and mutate until no one was really sure what it meant anymore. It took on different connotations to different age groups. Once used to label bands of the punk scene's more thoughtful variety, like Texas Is the Reason, the Promise Ring, and Sunny Day Real Estate, emo became something else entirely after the internet took hold of it. As the scene migrated from VFW halls to social networks, a new breed of digitally active, fashion-conscious bands kicked their way into the genre until the e-word became an all-purpose title, at once signifying everything and nothing. "Emo" now encompassed the gamut of alternative music, from the folksy acoustic approach of Bright Eyes to the whiny metal stylings of Hawthorne Heights.

By 2005, Jawbreaker, widely acknowledged as one of the forebears of emo, had been defunct for nine years. Frontman Blake Schwarzenbach's follow-up project, Jets to Brazil, had also run out of gas. Jawbreaker's initially misunderstood *Dear You,* which had served as a cautionary tale of major-label disaster scenarios since its release by DGC in 1995, was starting to take on a second life, though. A new generation of bands—emo and pop-punk alike— were beginning to discover the complex album and cite it as a seminal influence on their own work. A 2003 compilation, *Bad Scene, Everyone's Fault,* featured eighteen bands paying homage to Jawbreaker, with acts like Fall Out Boy and Bayside tackling *Dear You* songs.

"When bands like Fall Out Boy and Panic! at the Disco came along, I looked at some of their songs and there were things that were direct lifts from, and absolutely inspired by, *Dear You,*" says the album's producer, Rob Cavallo. "It wasn't anything you could make a claim on, but you could hear it: This guy listened to 'Jet Black,' or this guy listened to 'Accident Prone.'"

For the most part, Schwarzenbach didn't recognize the remnants of his work in his predecessors, and when he did, he didn't much care for what he was hearing. "I don't like the boy-centric stuff that was really ubiquitous after us, and with which we were constantly associated," he says. "That wasn't what we were doing. We weren't from the suburbs. We were an urban band from New York and San Francisco and L.A., and we sang about urban alienation. It wasn't about 'Hey, my mom's out of town, come over,' like New Found Glory and these fucking bands. I totally don't like those people, personally. I dislike the personalities behind that music."

But in My Chemical Romance, Schwarzenbach finally saw a musical heir in which he could take pride. "I really like that band, and I like how self-possessed they are," he says. "It seems like a vision, and it's fearless in a way that I don't classify as 'emo' or commercial emo—Hot Topic emo or whatever."

For better or worse, My Chemical Romance cemented their place as the poster boys for the new internet era of emo, though it wasn't a title they relished. "I think emo's a pile of shit," Gerard told the college newspaper the *Maine Campus*. "I think emo is fucking garbage, it's bullshit. I think there's bands that unfortunately we get lumped in with that are considered emo and by default that starts to make us emo. All I can say is, anyone actually listening to the records, put the records next to each other and listen to them and there's actually no similarities."

Pile of shit or not, the marketable "emo" brand carried weight in the music industry throughout the early aughts. Independent labels like Drive-Thru, Victory, and Vagrant had rosters full of bands in this nebulous new wave of emo that had been flirting with crossover success. Some of them, like Dashboard Confessional and Taking Back Sunday, had even racked up gold records. But *Three Cheers for Sweet Revenge* was the rare case of an emo album that broke through and crossed the million-copy mark for Reprise, prompting other major labels to take notice. What Nirvana had done for grunge and Green Day had done for pop-punk, My Chemical Romance did for emo. "The scene became oversaturated and unfortunately every label then needed a My Chem," says Simon. "And then it became the same thing with Fall Out Boy and Paramore and All-American Rejects, those tentpole bands—all the labels wanted one."

The more My Chemical Romance was saddled with the dreaded emo tag, the harder they kicked against it. When they started planning their third record at the end of 2005, they aimed to scrap everything people had come to associate with the band and distance themselves from the emo craze in pursuit of something timeless and classic. They began thinking of it outside the confines of a traditional album. What had started out as a comic book idea evolved into something larger—a full-on rock-opera experience that would involve a cast of characters, elaborate costumes, and winding storylines. They weren't looking to make another record or redefine emo. They wanted to redefine My Chemical Romance.

Their idea was so wide in scope that it would require the expertise of a producer with a big imagination, one who specialized in expansive, blown-out records. Given how red-hot the band was, they could have had their pick of talent, but the one they had their eye on was Rob Cavallo. "Every big producer in the world was trying to get to them," Cavallo says. "And for some reason, I hit it off with them."

Cavallo's landmark album, Green Day's *Dookie,* was still a sales phenomenon a decade after its release. It had hit the elite-level diamond certification, selling well over ten million copies. His résumé had grown even more impressive since his *Dookie* days. Not only had he risen to the rank of chairman at Warner Bros., but his production work continued to elicit hits from Goo Goo Dolls and Phil Collins. Most impressively, his efforts on Green Day's *American Idiot* had just been rewarded with a Grammy for Best Rock Album, and it would eventually go on to spawn a Broadway musical.

But it wasn't Cavallo's success in the pop world that most appealed to My Chem, Iero says. It was, out of all the releases in an impressive discography, his masterful capturing of Jawbreaker. "*Dear You* is a direct reason we went with Rob Cavallo," says Iero. "Even with all his achievements, that motherfucker did *Dear You*!"

The band met with Cavallo over a cold winter to lay out their plans for their grandiose project. Over dinner, they told him about its three-act story arc centered around life and death, joy and sorrow, celebrations and funerals. They talked about pulling from a totally different palate of instruments like organs and xylophones and strings—an entire string section, in fact. And marching bands, too, while they were at it. They played him demo versions of songs they'd written—tunes that sounded better suited for a three-ring circus than a rock album.

"I went to New York and they played me a couple of songs," Cavallo remembers. "They played me 'Mama' and I actually leaped up out of my chair and started jumping around. I thought: 'Whatever that is, it's gonna lead to one of the greatest, darkest, most theatrical records ever.'"

Cavallo asked the guys what they were planning on calling this monument to their wild ambition that would surely go down as their magnum opus. Given the all-or-nothing stakes behind it, they joked that its working title was *The Rise and Fall of My Chemical Romance*. But by the time it was released, in October 2006, it would go by a different name: *The Black Parade*.

CHAPTER 10

RISE AGAINST

Siren Song of the Counter Culture

Geffen Records (2004)

LIKE COUNTLESS PUNK bands before them, 88 Fingers Louie found themselves idly flipping through the menu at a Denny's in the middle of nowhere. The Chicago four-piece was sitting at a booth at "America's diner" in Casper, Wyoming, halfway into a cross-country drive to Portland, Oregon, where they were scheduled to play the first show of a six-week tour with AFI in the summer of 1999. By the time their food arrived, though, the band had decided to break up instead.

The split had been a long time coming. The band had formed when the members were carefree teenagers, but after six years together their priorities had changed. Singer Denis Buckley now had a toddler back home, whom he missed on the long weeks on the road. The rest of the band sympathized, but at the same time, it felt disingenuous to keep going through the motions. So, after a long-overdue talk about the future of the band, they agreed to call it quits right there at the table. The group paid their bill, got back in the van, and, instead of continuing west, drove sixteen hours back to Chicago.

Not a single word was spoken on the long ride home, and the uncomfortable silence gave bassist Joe Principe plenty of time to reassess his life. He had been served well by 88 Fingers Louie, but he realized it was a project he'd outgrown. While he was proud of what they'd accomplished in their time together, there was a juvenile silliness to their persona that he connected with less and less as he'd grown older. The more he thought about it, the band that had released a record called *88 Fingers Up Your Ass* no longer seemed appealing.

By the time they arrived back to the Windy City, Principe had decided he was going to start a new band, one that would stand for something meaningful and galvanize the next generation of kids the way Black Flag, Bad Brains, and 7 Seconds had done for him in the eighties. He knew from studying bootleg videos of those bands that the key was finding an impassioned vocalist, and he was very specific about what he wanted in one. He needed someone who could scream, but with controlled pitch. Not a barker who growled with reckless abandon, but someone whose yelling had both an urgency and a melodic quality, like his hero Ian MacKaye had done in Minor Threat.

The other two members of 88 Fingers Louie, guitarist Dan "Mr. Precision" Wleklinski and drummer John Carroll, agreed with the new direction and were on board for whatever came next. Once word got around Chicago that members of one of the city's most popular bands were starting a new project, there was no shortage of people clamoring to try out for the open position. The trio auditioned more than a dozen vocalists over the next few months, but none of them were the right fit. Some grunted with too much toughguy aggression, while others lacked the in-your-face bite it took to front a punk band. After a while it felt like they'd tried out every aspiring punk in the state of Illinois.

On October 9, Principe drove to Indianapolis, where AFI was playing with Sick of It All, Hot Water Music, and Indecision at the Emerson Theater. He was catching up with frontman Davey Havok in the lobby after the show, still apologizing profusely for bailing on their last tour, when he spotted a face he recognized from the Chicago scene.

The face belonged to Tim McIlrath, a shy and scrawny twenty-year-old who was always slouching and stuffing his hands in his pockets. His sandy-brown hair shagged in his face, obscuring his striking case of heterochromia, which rendered his right eye hazel and his left eye crystal blue. Principe introduced himself and mentioned that he was friends with McIlrath's girlfriend, Erin. He told him he'd seen his band, Baxter, play a VFW hall in the area and was impressed with his guitar playing and singing style. Baxter had an artsy, off-kilter take on punk that reminded him of Ian MacKaye's post–Minor Threat project, Fugazi.

The two came from separate corners of the Chicago punk scene, but they found common ground when they realized they were both straight-edge, following MacKaye's famous credo that denounced drugs and alcohol. As they got to know each other, the conversation eventually turned to their own projects.

"So what's going on with 88 Fingers Louie?" McIlrath asked. "I heard a rumor that you guys broke up."

"Actually, we're starting this new band and we're looking for a singer," Principe said. "You wanna try out?" The proposition came as a surprise to McIlrath, who enjoyed singing but considered himself more useful with an instrument in his hands.

"Well, I play guitar, you know?" McIlrath said. "I'm not much of a singer."

"That's not a problem," Principe told him. "What we need is someone who can scream."

$ $ $

Principe called his new band Transistor Revolt, and they landed a record deal before even playing a single show. The bassist leaned on his connections at Fat Wreck Chords, the Bay Area punk label that, in its infancy, had released 88 Fingers Louie's early records. As soon as he had enough Transistor Revolt songs to fill a demo tape, he sent them to label co-founder and NOFX frontman Fat Mike Burkett.

"Mike didn't want to sign us at first," Principe says. "I sent him the demo, and a week later he called me and said, 'I'm not into it, sorry.'" Over the next month, Principe submitted it to other labels—Victory, Nitro, Epitaph—but didn't get any responses. Then Burkett called back one day to say he'd had a change of heart.

"That was because everyone at Fat was saying it wasn't good, but I kept listening to it and said, 'No, actually, this is great, and I'm going to sign them,'" says Burkett. Ever the office contrarian, he wasn't concerned that Transistor Revolt had yet to play a show or earn a single fan. "I very rarely sign bands as an investment. I sign bands if they're good punk bands that write good songs," he says.

Burkett remembers Transistor Revolt sounding "like 88 Fingers Louie but with a better singer." And indeed, half of their demo songs had originated as ideas Principe never got the chance to employ with his former band. McIlrath's voice was the clear selling point. The frontman possessed a bag of vocal tricks that allowed him to shift rapidly from harmonious singing to a more high-intensity shout to a blistering roar. In its most natural state, McIlrath's voice had an alterna-rock quality that gave the band a sound that might be more palatable to the average listener, Burkett thought. They sounded, as he puts it, "like a punk rock Bush."

Transistor Revolt's novel twist on punk came along at an ideal time in the history of Fat Wreck Chords. The label had benefited from the post-*Dookie* boom with a roster of bands that shared a similar pop-punk DNA. But as the nineties drew to a close, Burkett was trying to cater to punk fans' evolving tastes by signing more diverse acts. "I didn't want to go outside the punk genre, but I was going for bands that were melodic—bands that had singers that sounded different, more hardcore singers, bands with more of a Minor Threat aspect," he says.

"At that point, the label's sound was changing," says McIlrath. "When I was growing up in the nineties, it was No Use for a Name, Lagwagon, Strung Out; it had a Fat sound. But all of a sudden, Fat was signing AVAIL, Anti-Flag, and Sick of It All."

Burkett's sole condition for taking on Transistor Revolt was that they change their name. "I've done that quite a few times," he says.

"I did it with Lagwagon, who were called Section 8 at first. Mad Caddies were called the Ivy League. What can you like about the name Transistor Revolt?"

The group put together a list of potential names, each one worse than the last. There was the Chicago Tar, It's the Cops, and, most repulsive of all, Jimmy Crack Corn and the I Don't Cares. Finally, the name Rise Against was suggested, and it sounded too good to be true. "We thought there had to already be a band called Rise Against," says Principe. "But there wasn't, so we went with that."

Although Rise Against found a label and a name without much trouble, their early days were otherwise marred by stumbles. McIlrath wasn't a natural fit on the microphone, and it took several practices to jell with his bandmates, who already had a shared chemistry.

"It was a rough start, because we were trying to get a feel for one another. He was used to doing his thing and I was used to doing my thing, as far as musical styles go," says Principe. "But then it just clicked. I remember him bringing a vocal idea for a song we had and it was exactly what I wanted. I thought, 'Oh shit, this guy gets it, and this is gonna be rad.' He got where I was coming from and vice versa. It was a weight off my shoulders."

But as soon as McIlrath found his footing, the band's drummer quit. They scrambled to find a replacement before their first performance, a daytime gig at a skate park in Woodstock, Illinois, on August 4, 2000. "Our first show was at a Tony Hawk Boom Boom HuckJam event, and it was horrific," remembers Principe. "At that point, we had this guy Joe playing drums for us. He didn't have the stamina to play fast, so he'd just stop in the middle of songs. Plus, we played on top of the vert ramp, and we were so exposed up there. It was just a terrible setup. Most of the kids couldn't give a fuck about us. They just wanted to see Tony Hawk, and I didn't blame them."

Lineup changes would become a recurring problem for Rise Against as McIlrath and Principe struggled to hold a steady roster together. They were able to recruit guitarist Kevin White and drummer Toni Tintari early on, but both left shortly after the band signed to Fat. Through their friends in Fat Wreck labelmates Good Riddance, McIlrath and Principe heard there was a drummer named

Brandon Barnes who might be up to the task. The problem was, he lived in Colorado. Barnes flew in for a tryout and impressed the guys with his style, which was at once laid-back and aggressive. He had a wonky kit setup where his drums were tilted downward at an awkward angle, which caused him to hunch like a caveman as he played, yet rapid-fire beats flowed out of him as if he was barely breaking a sweat. Barnes was offered the gig and he promptly dropped out of college and moved to Chicago.

Rise Against's new lineup made the rounds at local venues like McGregor's, in Elmhurst, and Logan Square mainstay the Fireside Bowl, where their pedigree could reliably draw a few holdover 88 Fingers Louie fans. They soon set their sights outside the Midwest and bought a fifteen-passenger van, in the back of which they built bunks in the hopes of putting as many miles on it as possible. When Fat Wreck Chords' more established bands needed an act to fill opening slots for a few bucks, Rise Against always raised their hands and weren't precious about the opportunities they took. They were willing to play with any band, anywhere, for any amount of money.

"With Fat, you didn't just sign to a label, you signed to a family. And so the next two years were spent opening for Fat Wreck Chords bands," says McIlrath. "We'd tour with Sick of It All and then jump on tour with Mad Caddies, so we'd go from hardcore bands to ska bands." Rise Against became a chameleon act, able to fit on any show's bill and trying their hardest to win over every crowd. After a few trips through the Northeast, the West Coast, and the South, they'd amassed a small but diverse base of fans who knew Rise Against as that band they'd seen open for their favorite band.

Sometimes Rise Against sneaked onto tours on which they hadn't even been invited. "The first year they played Warped Tour, Volcom invited them to play their stage for, I believe, one date. They went out, played it, and then essentially followed the tour," says their booking agent, Corrie Christopher Martin. "They had all these friends on the tour who helped squeeze them into the lineup when they could, and it worked. They ended up playing a ton of dates. They didn't make any money, but they sniped their way in."

It was an exciting time in which anything felt possible, especially for McIlrath, who was still new to touring. "The first time we went to Europe, I treated it like the last time I'd ever be there, like I'd won a fucking contest," he remembers. "I was singing for a band, traveling across the world, and figured one day I'd tell my kids that. I thought I'd be able to tell my kids that I was cool for a minute, and now I sell car insurance or whatever."

$ $ $

Rise Against's debut album, *The Unraveling*, was released by Fat Wreck Chords in April of 2001, just before they embarked on a tour of Canada, opening for NOFX. The culture clash between the two bands was immediately apparent. NOFX was famously hedonistic when it came to drugs and alcohol. The band was touring in support of an album called *Pump Up the Valuum*, and Burkett's general rule with substances was that if he could chug it, smoke it, or snort it, he would. Rise Against's version of post-show debauchery, conversely, typically involved pizza, Diet Coke, and intense games of Scrabble. (Principe loved pizza so much, in fact, that he wound up getting a tattoo on his right bicep of a slice, drawn by the artist who designed *The Unraveling*'s cover.) Burkett was so frustrated by the younger band's unwillingness to imbibe that he tried bribing them.

"Fat Mike would offer us money," Principe says. "He'd say, 'I'll give you a thousand bucks if you take a drink.'"

"Not the whole band, just Joe," Burkett clarifies. "How can you go through life not trying things? It's no way to live! Joe is like that with everything. He likes pizza and soda; that's it. It wasn't that I wanted him to become an alcoholic, I just wanted him to *try* things."

The divide between the two groups was evidenced onstage, too. NOFX was an established act with a nearly twenty-year legacy and a predilection for off-color banter and poking fun at their audience. The scrappy Chicago punks in Rise Against, on the other hand, treated the opportunity to play music with gratitude and humility. They won crowds over by being younger and more relatable. With McIlrath's baggy shorts and Principe's dyed-blue hair, the band looked like four fans who'd been plucked from the crowd.

Not long after their Canadian tour, Rise Against had a messy split with their lead guitarist. Wleklinski's bitter departure served up punk drama as the two parties traded barbs in respective interviews. Word circulated on message boards that Wleklinski had been kicked out of the band because of his long hair, though Rise Against disputed this accusation. "I can only assume Dan spread this rumor maliciously to hurt us as a band and to deny the personality flaws that brought about his departure," McIlrath commented in an interview.

Burkett, however, claims that Wleklinski's hair, which went past his shoulders, his thigh-high shorts, and his general "*Dungeons & Dragons*–playing metal dork" appearance didn't match the band's aesthetic and prompted his dismissal. "It was his image," Burkett asserts. "Image matters! I'm sorry, but it does. If you want to be part of a band, you have to fit the image. If there was one Bosstone who decided he didn't want to wear plaid suits, the Mighty Mighty Bosstones wouldn't have worked."

Wleklinski was eventually replaced with Todd Mohney, who was McIlrath's roommate, co-worker, and former bandmate in the hardcore act the Killing Tree. Additionally, McIlrath had begun playing rhythm guitar to supplement his singing duties, a role in which he felt more comfortable.

In the rare times when Rise Against was home from tour, they holed up in their practice space, a dingy room above a run-down antique store in nearby Evanston, where the owner would bang on the ceiling with a broom if their amps got too loud. It was there that they crafted the songs that would constitute their sophomore album, *Revolutions Per Minute*. Determined to enter the studio with a sharp arsenal of tracks, the band spent long nights there after working shifts at their part-time day jobs, hammering out the kinks. "We went into that record fully prepared," says Principe. "We had every song written. It was a very well thought-out record."

The Unraveling had often been touted as "the album by the ex-members of 88 Fingers Louie," but with *Revolutions Per Minute* the band aimed to make the name Rise Against known. It was their first album since the terrorist attacks of September 11, and the volatile mood in America became the backdrop of the record. McIlrath's lyrics did away with metaphor and flowery language and spoke of political resistance in raw plainspeak, singing of "clenched fists" and "money-hungry governments." Even the title was a sarcastic dig at the glut of bands throwing the word "revolution" around until it had lost meaning. It was a message McIlrath was determined not to take lightly.

Rise Against was unable to book their first choice of producer, Brian McTernan, who had recently worked on albums by Snapcase, Hot Water Music, and Cave In. "The label manager of Fat called him and he turned us down. He said he didn't want to do a Fat band," says Principe. Their second choice, Ryan Greene, had no aversion to Fat bands, having worked with more than forty of them, but his calendar was all booked up. So the band turned to their third choice and booked time at the Blasting Room, the Fort Collins, Colorado–based studio owned by Bill Stevenson, drummer and songwriter of legendary punk bands Black Flag, Descendents, and ALL.

Stevenson's reputation as a cantankerous grump preceded him, and Rise Against found him to be an intimidating presence at first —a true product of the combative punk scene that had birthed him. But by the end of the first week of recording, they'd warmed up to each other, and the band formed a deep and personal kinship with Stevenson. There was a shared set of punk reference points between them; when Stevenson suggested to Principe that a bassline should sound "a little more Bad Brains than NOFX," he knew exactly what he meant. Members of Rise Against would go on to cite Stevenson in future interviews as a friend, a mentor, a musical soulmate, and an honorary member of the band.

"I like the way they put their songs together. There's no bullshit," says Stevenson. "They draw from a lot of the same influences I love, so we just have fun doing it."

The band spent the last two months of 2002 at the Blasting Room. Throughout the process, Stevenson challenged each of them to push themselves beyond the extent of their talents. He injected a bit of Black Flag's relentless work ethic into their operation, which valued playing a song with technical perfection second to playing it with blunt force. When they listened back to the recordings, the band heard a version of themselves that surprised them. They sounded like the kind of punk band they'd wanted to play in as kids. For four guys who had learned to play their instruments by studying Stevenson's bands as teenagers, the session was part work and part education.

"He showed me how Black Flag songs are *actually* played, because there's stuff you miss on the records," says Principe, who studiously absorbed Stevenson's lessons in strumming to help tweak his approach. "It was almost like passing the torch to the next generation so it wasn't forgotten."

After long days of recording, Stevenson regaled the band with tales of his days on the road with Black Flag in the seventies and eighties, and the antagonistic attitude the punk pioneers brought to their live shows. He told story after story about showing up to clubs full of kids who spit at them, cursed them out, and threw punches, and how the band spit and cursed and punched right back. The young band reveled in hearing anecdotes of cops shutting down Black Flag's shows and shoving the members against walls or dragging them to jail. Stevenson told stories of nightly violence, and how it felt like it was Black Flag against the world.

"When they'd play shows, they were challenging people to beat them up," says McIlrath. "If you could beat up Black Flag, you were cool. He said it was fucking gnarly." Stevenson instilled in McIlrath a lesson the young frontman would keep in the back of his mind every time Rise Against stepped onstage: Don't start a punk band unless you're willing to go to war every night.

$ $ $

A phrase the members of Rise Against often found themselves saying was: "Good for them." They shared a lot of stages with a lot of bands in their first three years, and it seemed as though all of them were suddenly getting swooped up by major-label A&R reps. They were on tour with BoySetsFire and Thursday in 2001 and watched as both bands were slipped business cards after shows. *And good for them,* they thought. When they heard about AFI cashing a hefty paycheck from DreamWorks Records in 2002, they felt like their brothers had struck it big. *Good for them,* they thought again. But even though they were happy for all their peers who were becoming hot commodities in the music industry, Rise Against never stopped to think that it might one day happen to them.

"We saw a lot of bands from our world getting attention. But as a spectator, that made sense to me," says McIlrath. "It made sense to me that Bert McCracken was gonna take over the world with the Used. I saw them and was like, 'Yeah, this dude's the second coming of Kurt Cobain.' With Thursday, Geoff Rickly had an incredible persona. I could see that on the cover of magazines. Thrice was amazing; they could be the next Deftones. Poison the Well was so fucking heavy; they could be the next Slipknot. But I didn't see us in that equation at all."

"So many of those bands had an image, whether they were trying for it or not," he continues. "I always looked at us as a band without the image that a major label would be interested in. We didn't have a shtick. We weren't made for TV."

The first time Rise Against learned that anyone at a major label had even heard of them was in the summer of 2003, a few months after the release of *Revolutions Per Minute*. The band returned home from a European tour with labelmates the Lawrence Arms, Mad Caddies, and the Flipsides, and there was a message waiting for Principe on his answering machine.

"I still lived with my mom, but I had a separate phone number," he remembers. "It was a message from this guy Ron Handler at DreamWorks. He was like, 'Hey, I want to talk to you guys about maybe coming over here to DreamWorks.' We never sought that out. We'd never even thought about it. I thought it was one of my friends fucking with me."

Principe called the number back, fully expecting that he was stepping into a practical joke, but to his surprise, there really was a DreamWorks A&R rep on the other end. Handler wasn't pushy, and simply told Principe that he'd been listening to *Revolutions Per Minute* and was a big fan of their sound.

"I used to listen to that album all the time. I just loved it," says Handler. "It was the power of the band and their playing, for sure, but the lyrics were more radically political than what anyone was doing at the time. In my mind, I knew Rise Against was going to be a big band. I had no doubt about it."

After that, the band started hearing through their Los Angeles–based booking agent, Corrie Christopher Martin, that it was more than just Handler who'd caught wind of them. "She was the first person who came to us and said, 'Hey, people in L.A. are talking about you,'" remembers McIlrath.

"I was working with Yellowcard, and when they went to Capitol Records, all the A&R guys said, 'What's next?' I said they had to check out this band Rise Against," remembers Christopher Martin. "They weren't much on people's radars. They were an underground band on a small punk label. I set up a show at the Troubadour to give these labels an opportunity to see the band. The Troubadour doesn't have a barricade; it has a low stage. It was the perfect place to see Rise Against. All the fans were singing every word, and it was clear that they were part of a community and had something to say. The energy was so intense. It was undeniable."

The Troubadour show was impressive enough to earn the band a few meetings. "We met with a handful of labels—DreamWorks, and then Island Def Jam, who was signing Thrice and Thursday. I think we met with Capitol, Hollywood Records, and probably a bunch more I don't remember," McIlrath says. "Bear in mind, we still didn't have a manager, and Joe was the only one who had a cellphone. Corrie was the closest thing to a manager we had. We were just fucking lost. I didn't even know the questions to ask a major label."

The members of Rise Against may have lacked the business acumen to talk dollars and cents with label reps, but as ardent punk fans, they sought one thing above all: creative control. "The fear of a major label is that you're gonna get some slick A&R guy who's Mr. Hollywood who wants to make you this cheesy rock band. We weren't gonna let anyone do that to us," says Barnes.

"As a music nerd myself, who'd read Steve Albini's diatribe against major labels and who grew up reading *MRR* and who was a Jawbreaker fan and who'd watched all these bands get signed in the nineties, I was skeptical, as any punk rock kid should be," says McIlrath.

The most surprising takeaway from these meetings was that A&R reps were not the slimy businessmen the punk scene had made them out to be. In fact, many of them came from the punk scene themselves. "We met with Pete Giberga, who was at Sony at the time," says Principe. "He came from the New York hardcore world and was friends with Sick of It All and Gorilla Biscuits. That was reassuring. I was like, 'Oh, holy shit, these people from our world are in this mainstream world as well?' I'd always thought it was just dudes in suits."

"It felt like we were in a post-major-labels-destroying-your-band era. I felt like we'd all learned the lessons," says McIlrath. "These A&R people, they were Jawbreaker fans. They got it. They were not much older than me and had grown up going to the same shows."

At first, Rise Against wasn't sure what a bigger label could offer that Fat Wreck Chords couldn't, but once they learned about the benefits of international distribution and the potential to reach a worldwide audience, they grew more intrigued. They weren't so naive as to think they'd become an overnight success, but larger labels clearly wielded more selling power than their indie label. Unless they wanted to work boring side jobs for the rest of their lives, this seemed like the more sustainable path.

Of the many label reps the band met with that summer, the one they felt the strongest connection with was Ron Handler, especially after meeting with him after their Cleveland stop on Warped Tour. "I went to see them and the band Coheed and Cambria," recalls Handler. "Coheed were on the stage next to Rise Against and had this following that went all the way back. Rise Against only had a couple hundred people there, but they played like they were at a stadium."

Not only had Handler been the first to contact them, but the label had recently signed other bands in Rise Against's wheelhouse. Jimmy Eat World's first post–Capitol Records release, *Bleed American,* had just gone platinum with DreamWorks. The label had also recently convinced a number of similar independent bands to make the jump, including AFI, Saves the Day, and Jim Ward's post–At the Drive-In project, Sparta.

The label, co-founded by director Steven Spielberg, seemed like a welcoming and stable home for young rock bands. "When Sparta signed to DreamWorks, they told us, 'We have more money than God,'" remembers Ward. "That was a real quote that they told us."

When Rise Against informed Handler that they were ready to give DreamWorks a try, a sharp sting of punk guilt immediately hit them in their guts at the thought of having to break the news to Fat Wreck Chords. But, much to their surprise, when they brought it up with Burkett, he encouraged them to go see what they were worth.

"Mike said, 'Go ahead and sign. I want what's best for you guys,'" remembers Principe. "He goes, 'It's a win-win for me, because if you blow up, your records that are on Fat will sell, or if you get dropped, you can come back to Fat.'"

"I don't begrudge anybody," Burkett says. "I'm still friends with all the bands that left Fat Wreck Chords. A lot of them have left and come back. That's why I do one-record deals. You want to go somewhere else? Go somewhere else. You're always welcome back."

And in their hearts, that's what Rise Against assumed would happen. They figured they were betting on a million-to-one shot and would eventually come crawling back to their punk roots. "The chances of it being successful were pretty slim," says McIlrath. "We thought we'd probably get dropped, and we hoped our world would take us back. We thought we'd go back to Fat Mike, licking our wounds, and hopefully keep a career after that."

$ $ $

Tim McIlrath was having a restless night in Los Angeles. He and Principe were sharing a hotel room near the DreamWorks Records office in Beverly Hills, where they and the rest of the band were due at 10 a.m. to put their signatures on a five-record deal. The twenty-five-year-old frontman was tossing in bed, thoughts racing. Maybe the band was making a big mistake. Maybe they were about to sign their death warrant. He envisioned his hard-won fans turning on him and Rise Against repeating the same major-label fate as Jawbreaker and Jawbox and so many of the punk bands that had come before them.

Just after 8 a.m., as he drifted in and out of sleep, the phone rang. It was his girlfriend, Erin, calling from the doctor's office in Chicago with some news: she was pregnant. The couple hadn't been planning this, and the news stunned him. When he was finally able to put words together, he told Erin that he loved her and that it would all work out, and then he hung up.

A groggy Principe rolled over in his bed to see what was up. "Joe was like, 'What was that about?'" McIlrath remembers. "I was like, 'What? Nothing. Uh, Erin had to go to the doctor. I don't know. Go back to sleep.'" McIlrath lay back in bed and stared at the ceiling. He wasn't just worried anymore; he was now, as he puts it, "scared shitless." A new set of anxieties about trying to raise a child on a musician's salary raced through his head as he got up, showered, and made his way to the DreamWorks office.

When the band arrived at DreamWorks, McIlrath's head was somewhere else. There was a thousand-yard stare in his two-toned eyes as employees toured the guys around the office and caught them up on the company drama of the day: one of their biggest artists, Nelly Furtado, had just informed the label that she was pregnant and would need to cancel a slew of upcoming bookings. McIlrath was suddenly snapped back to earth by an elbow in his side.

"I was only half listening, because I was in a daze," he remembers, "but someone turned to me and joked, 'So yeah, Tim, don't go get pregnant!' And I was like, 'What? What did you say? Who said that? Who told you?'"

The offer Rise Against accepted from DreamWorks wasn't at the level of Nelly Furtado. It wasn't even as much as some of their rock peers had received, like Jimmy Eat World for their heavily sought-after *Bleed American*. But for Rise Against, a band with an acute inferiority complex, it felt appropriate for their position in the scene at the time.

"In that era of the punk and emo explosion, there were some huge offers going around," says McIlrath. "There were huge bidding wars with some of those bands, and we were hearing about some of those prices, but I think that era was already over by the time Rise

Against signed. We were one of the last bands in our world to sign to a major label, and there were just sort of crumbs left. Labels had banked hard on some of these bands to get big and spent a lot of money. It was already starting to not pan out, and people were getting skeptical."

"Rise Against weren't trying to get a massive deal. That wasn't what the band was about," says Handler. "They just wanted to be safe enough at a label where they could make good records and have people support them. Some people have stars in their eyes and dream of limos and fancy houses. That's not the kind of guys they were."

"We actually took less money to sign to DreamWorks to have more creative control," says Principe. "I want to say we got $500,000. We got a little advance out of the recording budget to buy gear and stuff. As far as business goes, it's not free money. You still have to pay it back. They're basically a bank with a crazy-high interest rate."

Rise Against may not have struck it rich, but they saw this as a positive. They figured a lower paycheck meant lower expectations. "There were definitely a lot less zeroes at the end of our offer," says McIlrath. "But we knew that the money they were gonna give us was also how many claws they were gonna dig into us. So we figured if they had less investment in us, there would be less claws dug into our skin. We'd be able to create something that wouldn't put us in life-long debt with these people."

No matter how little money they pocketed, though, the band knew that the main takeaway for their fans would be that Rise Against had sold out. A political punk band working with a corporate label was bound to turn people off. So, like Thursday and My Chemical Romance before them, Rise Against took to the internet to get ahead of any blowback by posting a statement online.

"Hey, we just wanted to let everyone know what's been going on in the Rise Against camp as of late and keep you in the loop," the statement began. It went on to explain that the band had been approached by "over a dozen labels" during their summer on the Warped Tour, and after consulting their friends in other bands, particularly AFI, they'd made the decision to sign with DreamWorks.

The McIlrath-penned credo explained, "I understand that some of you will be angry about this, and that some of you couldn't care less because over half the bands you listen to are on majors anyway. To those who are angry, I assure you we are not abandoning you. There will be no compromising what we do and how we do [it]. There will only be a bigger push behind what we have to say and how we can say it."

The lengthy message ended with a line in the sand: "To those of you who have read this and written us off, so long and thanks for the memories! To those of you who feel Rise Against the way we feel it at every show, with every note and every word, we are still here for you . . . and we're not going anywhere."

"I think people like to feel more included in that kind of thing," McIlrath says of the statement. "I don't think there's ever been a time in history when a fan was excited when their favorite band signed to a major label. 'Good for them, they have families' — no one's ever said that. I figured all I could do was be transparent with our fans, because our fans had been so cool with us until that point. So I was asking them to take this leap of faith with us."

Some fans took that leap and appreciated the candor. To McIlrath's surprise, many of them were even happy to see their favorite underdogs finally getting their due. A few, predictably, decried the band's decision and wrote them off before a note of their major-label album was even recorded. But for McIlrath, none of the criticisms ever stung, because he had already grown accustomed to them.

"I grew up in a really PC hardcore scene in Chicago, with everything from Los Crudos to Earth Crisis," he says. "There were a lot of lines you had to toe. Like, if the van you pulled up in was too nice, it was like, 'Where'd you get that van?' If your guitar was too nice, it was like, 'Where'd you get that guitar?' If your seven-inches were too nice, it was like, 'You didn't screen them yourself? Fuck you.' So, in my world, just joining a band with the guys from 88 Fingers Louie, I was already a sellout. I'd been a sellout from the time we played our first song. Just signing to Fat Wreck Chords, all my friends called me Rockstar. We put *The Unraveling* out and they treated me like I was David Lee Roth. A lot of them were joking, but still, they didn't treat me the same. They saw me as an outsider. So when my closest friends walked away from me, there was very little that the mainstream world could do that would hurt my feelings. My ship had sailed a long time ago."

$ $ $

Barely a month after Rise Against signed to DreamWorks, Joe Principe was driving to an Alkaline Trio show at Chicago's Aragon Ballroom when he got a call that made him pull over. On the side of the road, he learned that the label had been sold to Universal Music Group. The $100 million acquisition left the future of the label, as well as the band's career, in serious jeopardy. "I thought for sure we were fucked. It was scary," says Principe. "I thought we were going to get dropped before even working on the record."

Universal ended up folding DreamWorks into its Interscope Geffen A&M label, and an internal restructuring soon eliminated a number of positions. Fortunately for Rise Against, Ron Handler was kept on board, but much of his team was displaced. "There were only six or seven people kept on, and about a hundred people got fired," he remembers.

DreamWorks' dire straits weren't unique. Just days prior, Sony and BMG had also reached an agreement to combine forces. Mergers and acquisitions were becoming commonplace survival methods throughout the industry as sales of physical music nosedived. The world of major labels was quickly shrinking with the ascendancy of digital music, and the Big Six, as they were once known, were crumbling. An article in *The Economist* that week painted a grim picture of the industry climate: "Music executives prefer to talk of synergy, rationalisation and strength through partnership. But the fact is that big music firms are in deep trouble because sales are falling fast; merging is one of the few things they can think of doing."

"It's like every other cookie-cutter story of a label: your label folds, your people there are gone, and you're an orphan. All those typical things all happened to us," sighs McIlrath. The band feared the phone would ring any day and someone would be informing them that their record was being scrapped. "We were just waiting for the other shoe to drop. We figured they'd pay for the record, because they were contractually obligated to do that, but we worried it'd get shelved. That'd be the worst-case scenario. We all knew it'd have a great chance of falling apart. We just didn't think it would fall apart so fast."

"I was worried that the band could fall through the cracks in that transition between DreamWorks and Interscope," Handler says. "Bands like Papa Roach, they were big already. But if anyone could fall, it would be Rise Against. My mission was to get this band off the ground."

Although the stability of DreamWorks hung in the balance, Handler encouraged Rise Against to begin work on their album and assured them he would handle the rest. Their first big decision was choosing a producer. "The label suggested a few pop producers," says McIlrath. "With Rise Against, there's a pop side to our band and then there's a heavy side of our band. And we figured, 'Let's do a record that brings out the heavy side of our band and get a producer that understands that.'"

They arranged to work with Canadian producer Garth Richardson, who went by the nickname GGGarth, a nod to his prominent stutter. Richardson had worked with a number of heavy bands that, while commercially successful, rubbed Rise Against's punk instincts the wrong way. His résumé included hard rock and nu-metal acts like Trapt, Mudvayne, and Chevelle, but he also had a few credible albums under his belt. He'd produced Rage Against the Machine's debut album in 1992, a record that not only was a bestseller, but leaned heavily on radical political messaging. He'd also worked with Rise Against's friends Sick of It All, on their 1997 major-label record *Built to Last*. For better or worse, Richardson knew how to make a band sound like a fist to the head.

Once the decision was made to book time with Richardson at a Vancouver studio, Rise Against's punk guilt flared up again. They felt bad for abandoning Bill Stevenson, whose guidance had shaped the band's identity. For a while, Rise Against tried keeping Stevenson on the payroll. "Because we were such fucking amateurs, in our heads we were like, 'We'll do the record with both of them!'" says McIlrath. He remembers flying Stevenson to Chicago to help the band with the album's pre-production work, which only caused confusion. "I think Bill thought he'd been hired to do the record. We told him we loved him and we just wanted him there. He was like, 'That's not how it works, guys. If you're doing a record with Garth, do a record with Garth.'"

"There wasn't anything secret or underhanded going on. I just think they weren't sure what they were doing," says Stevenson. "I got the feeling, when they signed to a bigger label, they felt pressure to use more of a big-name producer. And I certainly understand that."

In the eyes of Rise Against, Stevenson's role was irreplicable. Once they were left in the hands of Richardson, they felt like kids stubbornly resisting their first day at a new school. Richardson could sense the hesitancy and tried his best to quell their anxieties. "Every time you work with a band, it's like they're giving you the right to look after their baby," Richardson explains. "You have to get them to trust you, because it's difficult. I'd be the same way if I were in their shoes."

The greatest obstacle between them was a musical language barrier. Richardson didn't possess the same cultural touchstones that had immediately endeared Stevenson to Rise Against. "Once you live in that punk bubble for so long, you think everyone gets it and grew up on the Ramones and Jawbreaker and Op Ivy," says McIlrath. "With Garth and Dean [Maher], the engineer there, we realized, 'Oh, these guys don't listen to those bands and they don't speak our language.' They were the nicest fucking people and loved our band and treated us with respect, but it was clear to me that these guys were not part of the tribe."

"Garth is a super-awesome dude. He just didn't get the band. It was a rough go," adds Principe. "We were under a lot of stress to maintain the sound of the band. He kept trying to get us to do goofy things. A few times, he tried to get us to slow songs down. It just sounded like we were intentionally slowing things down. I'm glad we stuck to our guns, but it was definitely an uphill battle."

The guys had a hard time settling into Richardson's production approach. To ensure perfect tuning and timing, he insisted on recording one measure at a time. "We punch it in chord by chord by chord, which can be very taxing," he says. "It's long, tedious work. But if you want to compete against the world, you kind of have to be the best at it."

The band felt the methodical process was smoothing the rough edges they wanted to maintain. They'd picked up yet another guitarist, Reach the Sky's Chris Chasse, right before the recording session, and the drawn-out process was a draining initiation for the new member. "Each song took twelve hours," Chasse would later gripe to *Rolling Stone*. "It wasn't us," Principe added of the album's sound. "It was very polished, and it seemed robotic."

There were times when McIlrath was hitting his stride in the studio, only for Richardson to tell him to pack it in for the day. "I think the first indication that it wasn't the right fit was that he started tracking vocals for Tim and would cut him off after twenty minutes, like, 'Oh, he's not ready to sing today, we'll do it tomorrow,'" remembers Principe. "Tim, especially back then, took an hour or two to warm up. He'd cut him off before he was warmed up. He would literally shut down the studio and go play Frisbee golf."

"I did have a nine-hole Frisbee golf course on my property," says Richardson. "You have to work very deeply. So basically, when it got too tense I'd say, 'You know what, guys? Let's go play nine holes.'"

Despite Rise Against's frustrations with Richardson's style, or perhaps fueled by them, the Vancouver sessions produced an angry batch of songs. The agitated and anxious tone was fitting for the time, as every news station was covering the United States' increasingly deadly military occupation of Iraq. The album's lyrics saw McIlrath kicking against the Bush administration with rage and fury. Imagery of blood became a reoccurring theme as he implicated the government for being complicit in murder. For the album's cover, which featured a blaring speaker, the band hired artist Shepard Fairey, who would go on to design Barack Obama's iconic HOPE campaign poster.

Of the twelve songs that would make it onto the record, two of them had already been released. "Give It All" had appeared on the first volume of Fat Wreck Chords' *Rock Against Bush* compilation series, and, with its breakneck pace and anthemic chorus, it made a fitting addition to the record. "Swing Life Away," on the other hand, was a stripped-down acoustic ballad that was less of a natural fit. McIlrath had written and recorded it on a four-track with the help of his friend Neil Hennessy, drummer for the Lawrence Arms. The track had debuted the year before on Fearless Records' *Punk Goes Acoustic* compilation CD, but was included on the record at the encouragement of Ron Handler. "I hadn't heard a song that heartfelt and emotional," says Handler. "I thought it was another side of the band that people need to hear."

"Swing Life Away" was a short little tune that clocked in at less than two and a half minutes. Richardson didn't think it had enough meat on the bone to be a usable single, so he tasked McIlrath with adding a bridge that could stretch it out by a minute or so.

"I grabbed this acoustic guitar and went out to his porch on this beautiful island outside Vancouver," remembers McIlrath. "I'm playing it, trying to write that part. I look over and everyone's in the window staring at me. I was like, 'Man, they must think I'm so cool. They think I'm a cool songwriter and they know they're witnessing an important moment.' I walk back in and they're like, 'Dude! That's Sheryl fucking Crow's guitar. Nobody touches that!' And I was like, 'Ah, sorry, sorry! I had no idea!'"

By the time the new version of the song was ready to be laid down, production had to be moved to Gravity Studios, in Chicago, so that McIlrath could be near Erin, who was in her ninth month of pregnancy. "I was in the middle of recording 'Swing Life Away.' She called in the middle of a take to say it was time to head to the hospital, and I told the guys I had to go," says McIlrath. "They knew that once we had the baby, the studio would shut down for a couple days, at least. They were like, 'If you give us four more takes, that will give us enough to work on for the next two days.'"

McIlrath's hands were trembling and the same thousand-yard stare returned to his eyes as he stood in front of the microphone.

Richardson started recording, and McIlrath fought back the shakiness in his voice. He thought about Erin going into labor and remembered the promise he'd made to her that it would all work out. He closed his eyes and imagined the face of his firstborn child as he sang lines of hope and devotion: "If love is a labor, I'll slave till the end."

After a few takes, the frontman finally insisted that he had to rush to the hospital. "We kept him until he absolutely had to leave," remembers Richardson.

"It was probably only another fifteen minutes, but that was too much time to stay," laughs McIlrath. "When Erin found that out, she was so pissed." The next morning, the couple welcomed their first child into the world—a girl, Blythe Elizabeth McIlrath.

$ $ $

Rise Against was scheduled to play an afternoon set on Warped Tour in Hershey, Pennsylvania, the day their major-label debut, *Siren Song of the Counter Culture*, hit stores in August 2004. Although the band was assigned to the festival's smaller stage, it seemed like a positive release-day omen that a large crowd had gathered before their set. As the band worked through their set list, though, it became obvious that something was off.

"I remember getting up onstage and there were all these kids in front. And I was like, 'Holy shit, the word's getting out!'" remembers Principe. "Then I realized they were just waiting for Fall Out Boy, who were playing after us." This was especially funny to McIlrath, who had previously played in a Chicago metalcore band called Arma Angelus with Fall Out Boy bassist Pete Wentz.

"That day was symbolic of all the days that would follow," says McIlrath. "The record came out and nothing fucking changed. Nothing felt different, the crowds didn't get bigger, the records didn't sell any more than Fat Wreck Chords would've sold."

Rise Against was slipping into the dreaded "band's band" territory, getting name-checked within the punk scene as the band that *should* make it big but would probably never get their due. "It felt very easy to root for them because they were easygoing guys," says

Wentz. "Seeing them play sold-out shows in Chicago gave us hope that there was a path for us to do the same."

Even fanzine writers took mercy on Rise Against's major-label jump. *Razorcake*'s review of *Siren Song* was uncharacteristically encouraging for a punk zine, stating, "I wish the band luck and hope they get the support they were looking for. If not, I hope they don't give it up because they are a good band."

For several months after its release via Geffen Records, *Siren Song* largely remained stagnant. Rise Against's core fan base bought the album, but beyond that, the band didn't see much additional benefit to having a bigger label behind them. Geffen continued to shuffle its leadership and the band did their best to stay in touch with their ever-changing contacts there, calling regularly or swinging by the Santa Monica office whenever they were in Los Angeles. "Luckily, Geffen had an amazing team. We made it a point to hang out and get face time as much as we could. I felt like if they saw our faces, they wouldn't forget us," says Principe. "But I felt like we were just a tax write-off for them. I think they could care less about us."

In a way, the band got the creative freedom they'd wished for while making *Siren Song*. No one at Geffen ever hovered over them in the studio or pushed them into directions that made them uncomfortable. In fact, aside from Handler's suggestion to include "Swing Life Away," the band didn't have much interaction with their label until they handed in the final product. "We finished the record and delivered it. We never gave them demos," says McIlrath. "I couldn't tell if we had creative control or if no one gave a shit."

As long as Rise Against had their van and their fan base, they didn't need much else to support *Siren Song*. Christopher Martin booked them enough tours to keep them chugging along on the road, and their new manager, Missy Worth, had a solid relationship with Geffen co-president Polly Anthony and handled any other needs. Beyond that, they didn't seek much assistance from their label. "We were a touring machine," says Barnes. "We weren't the band that needed to call the label and ask for things. We were completely self-sufficient punk kids driving around in a van. So we just got back in the van."

Long stretches on the road failed to inspire the same sense of excitement in Rise Against as they once had, though, especially for McIlrath, who now had an infant waiting for him back home. Days on Warped Tour started to feel like monotonous trudges through blacktop parking lots; international tours no longer gave McIlrath the sensation that he'd lucked out and won a contest. "It felt really unremarkable. It felt like someone let the air out of the balloon," he says. "But at the same time, it didn't get worse. It just felt like a continuation."

Ten days before Christmas, Rise Against flew to Japan to play two nights at Astro Hall, a three-hundred-cap club in Tokyo. Being on the other side of the world made McIlrath feel like the band had run out of road. "Only 150 kids came each night," he says. "I remember thinking, 'These shows aren't even paying for the hotel rooms. This isn't a business model that works. If I could make this much money selling cars, why would I not be home for my family?'"

But as 2004 came to a close and a new year began, Rise Against's luck started to turn in their favor. Impressed by how much organic momentum the band was able to garner as touring workhorses, Geffen put more resources into pushing *Siren Song*'s singles. "Give It All" started to get more play on rock radio stations, and the band was given a budget to film a video for it in Chicago. But it was the decision to release "Swing Life Away" as a single that April that would change the course of the band's history.

To the members of Rise Against, it seemed like an odd strategy to push the lone acoustic song from an aggressive rock album, especially one that had been on shelves for eight months. "It was our last-ditch effort, ace-up-our-sleeve, pull-in-case-of-emergency kind of thing," says McIlrath. "Everyone was nervous about the implications of releasing a song like 'Swing Life Away' with our band name on it. It was weird. We weren't even playing it live. But the record wasn't doing well and the label was excited, so we said, 'What's the worst that could happen?'"

"The label really believed in them," says Geffen's head of rock promotion, Gary Spivack. "We wanted to separate them from bands like Bad Religion and Pennywise and Alkaline Trio, because they were so special. 'Swing Life Away' was our attempt at putting them at another level, and not just another straight-ahead, credible punk rock band. That was the goal."

Spivack credits the song as being the band's secret weapon that gave them an advantage over their peers on the airwaves. It allowed him to book sessions for McIlrath at local radio stations where he could drop by and play his pleasant acoustic song for morning shows, opening them up to a broader audience. "Punk bands weren't doing that back then. They *couldn't* do that," Spivack says. "Maybe Billie Joe from Green Day or Jim from Jimmy Eat World could pull it off, but few other bands could."

The song and its accompanying music video took off in a way the band never could have predicted. It was slotted into regular rotation on rock radio and MTV2, and almost immediately it connected with a new audience far outside the fringes of punk.

"Swing Life Away" was inescapable that summer. Its acoustic strumming could be heard pouring out of speakers in grocery stores and coffee shops across the country. High school seniors quoted it in yearbooks and lovestruck couples swayed along to it at proms. Fans stopped McIlrath on the street to show him its verses inked on their ribcages and forearms. They told him anecdotes about playing the song at graduations and funerals. He received a wedding invitation from a fan and flipped it over to find its lyrics printed on the back.

The song's popularity helped Rise Against crack into the Billboard 200 list for the first time, with *Siren Song* peaking a year after its release. The August 20 issue of *Billboard* reported that the album had reached "the pinnacle on Top Heatseekers." As sales of *Siren Song of the Counter Culture* accelerated, Rise Against got a kick out of the idea that "Swing Life Away" was their punk rock Trojan horse. A casual listener who picked up a copy of the album thinking they were getting a dozen acoustic rock songs would instantly realize how mistaken they were as soon as the opening track kicked off with a loud blast of distorted guitars and Barnes's pounding drums.

"I was always entertained by the thought of someone buying that record for 'Swing Life Away' and unwrapping the CD in the Target parking lot and putting it on in their car and the first song is 'State of the Union.' Maybe they'd almost wreck their car. I always found that amusing," laughs Barnes. "But maybe the soccer mom that bought the record for 'Swing Life Away' got turned on to some heavier music."

Within two years of its release, *Siren Song* had sold nearly 400,000 copies domestically, and it would eventually go on to be certified gold. "To me, none of it seemed real," says Principe. "Yeah, okay, it went gold. Well, what does that mean to a guy sitting in a van driving to Omaha? It's not like we were living in mansions. When something is slow and steady, it doesn't have the same effect as when something skyrockets. It didn't go to our heads. I think we were humbled and were just waiting for it to go away at any moment."

$ $ $

Rise Against's van became the butt of jokes among their friends. As the venues the band could fill grew in size, so too did their stage production. But instead of upgrading to a bus to accommodate their expanding equipment needs, the band clung firmly to their beloved little van. It wasn't uncommon for Rise Against to go on tour as a headliner in their van while the opening act followed behind in a bus.

"All of a sudden, they had a trailer that was longer than their van and a dude named Wild Card traveling with them," remembers the Lawrence Arms bassist Brendan Kelly. "I was under the impression it was because they were punk kids who just didn't know how to even get a bus. It's kind of like when your ceiling leaks and you finally say to yourself, 'Boy, I need to do something about this,' and you just grab a bigger bucket to put under it."

"If you ever get bumped up to first class on a plane, once you know how good it is, you never want to go back," McIlrath reasons. "So I looked at it like, 'If we move up to a bus, there's a good chance we won't be able to stay on a bus forever. I never want to take a step down, so let's just keep the van and trailer forever.' We had to get a bigger and bigger trailer. It was dangerous. It was stupid. We were loading it with the kind of shit you'd load into the back of a semi. We once put our guitarist's car in the back of the trailer; that's how big it was."

Every time someone suggested they finally ditch the van, Rise Against countered that there was no book about Black Flag called *Get on the Bus.* The book was called *Get in the Van,* because punk bands toured in vans, not fancy buses. They even got to pay homage to Black Flag by covering their song "Nervous Breakdown" for the 2005 skateboarding biopic *Lords of Dogtown,* a responsibility they treated with great reverence. But the reality they were hesitant to accept was that their celebrity was elevating by the day. They were no longer a little Chicago band being billed on flyers as "ex-members of 88 Fingers Louie." Fame had found Rise Against, whether or not they were ready to embrace it.

With a growing profile came a growing list of daily obligations —more interviews, more radio gigs, more fan meet-and-greets. As the frontman, McIlrath bore the brunt of it and started getting autograph requests wherever he went. For the most part, he was happy to oblige, though he always insisted on taking the path of least embarrassment. "Sometimes I'd walk out of a hotel to go to a radio station and they'd have a limo pick me up," he says. "I just had my acoustic guitar, so I'd be like, 'Fuck this, I'm not getting in that limo. I'll get in a cab or walk over there, but I'm not getting out of this limo when I pull up.' I thought it was lame. My manager had this really fancy Mercedes and she'd drive me to the Troubadour and I'd make her drop me off around the corner."

Although the band was uncomfortable with their newfound VIP status, they did enjoy the fresh sets of ears their expanding platform afforded them. No longer were they playing exclusively to punk kids who shared their political beliefs. When they scanned the front rows of their audience, they now frequently saw the types of guys who looked like they'd come straight from football practice. And if those guys wanted to take their shirts off and mosh to "Give It All," like they'd seen on MTV, that was fine with McIlrath, but in between those songs, he was determined to force-feed them the band's "sugar-coated bitter pills."

Sometimes Rise Against played in predominantly conservative Republican areas in the middle of the country, and at those shows they were often met with hostile reactions when they preached messages of political dissent, environmentalism, and animal rights, or implored their audiences to take an anti-racist and anti-homophobic stance in their community. The reaction to Rise Against's anti-war rhetoric was particularly incendiary in the towns with military bases, where cars were decorated with American flags and SUPPORT THE TROOPS bumper stickers. Sometimes, McIlrath saw his words lead to shoving matches and fistfights in the crowd. In more extreme cases, the band dodged cans that were thrown at them or were called faggots or pussies. McIlrath felt empowered by the combative atmosphere and enjoyed going into battle each night, as Stevenson had warned him. It was as though the band had grown into their name.

"When we show up to a punk show and I say I'm against the war in Iraq—huge fucking surprise that the guy from Rise Against is against the war in Iraq. I'm not saying anything shocking. You're preaching to the converted," says McIlrath. "But when I went to the Jingle Bash of Omaha to open up for fucking Limp Bizkit or something, and I started saying that the invasion of Iraq is a crime and George Bush is an asshole, you're not preaching to the converted anymore. You're actually polarizing that crowd immediately and they're yelling shit at you. That made it so much fun, to take the stuff I learned from the punk and hardcore world and actually put water where the fire was and say things that were visibly causing friction in these audiences that just came to have a good time. If you came to a show because you just wanted to have a beer and sing along, it was not what you paid for."

Meatheads throwing up middle fingers were merely a by-product of Rise Against's anti-war posturing, though. The band's real aim was to reach the kid in the back who was attending their first concert, and to ignite their punk rock awakening. "Rise Against was that entry band to political punk rock, and that's where you do it, at the Omaha Twisted Christmas or whatever," says Kelly. "That's where you go out and say 'Fuck George Bush!' And people say, 'Wait, did he just say *fuck the president*? I'd never considered those words together before!' And the next thing you know, that person might be listening to Crass."

Rise Against jumped at offers to play international tours and festivals to spread their message around the world. They tore through Europe and Canada, returned to Japan, and played Reading and Leeds festivals in the UK. They made their way to Australia twice within a year, once for Taste of Chaos and once for Big Day Out. At the latter, they played in front of thousands, many of whom had come to see System of a Down, and McIlrath introduced "State of the Union" by announcing, "This next song goes out to someone that we all know. His name's George fucking Bush, and this song is a fuck-you to George Bush and his fucking war!"

They returned to Warped Tour in 2006 but got upgraded to the larger stage, and the crowds that gathered there were waiting for them, not just passing time until Fall Out Boy came on. A cover story about them in *Alternative Press* lauded them as "the undeniable stars" of Warped Tour that year, "routinely playing to some of the biggest, most enthusiastic crowds."

When Rise Against released their follow-up album, *The Sufferer & the Witness,* with Geffen that summer, the band finally caved and retired their trusty van in favor of a bus. But while they were sad to leave an old friend behind, they welcomed another friend back into the fold by returning to the Blasting Room to again record with their mentor, Bill Stevenson. After days of recording, McIlrath now had battle stories of his own to trade with Stevenson. He told the producer about getting pelted with bottles onstage and being threatened by the crowd, and how it felt like going to war every night. And they had a good laugh about how ironic it was that a major label had helped deploy him to the front lines. *The Sufferer & the Witness* would go on to be certified gold within two years.

"It's weird for a guy from a punk and hardcore world to be talking about how powerful major labels are, but it worked for us," McIlrath says. "It made me believe that you can write great songs, but if you don't have a giant machine to push them to people in the right way, they might fall on deaf ears. We'd released 'Give It All.' It didn't change our lives. We'd released 'Swing Life Away.' It didn't change our lives. We gave those songs to this giant building in Santa Monica and it *changed our fucking lives*. That's when I never looked back. I knew why I'd signed."

CHAPTER 11

AGAINST ME!

New Wave

Sire Records (2007)

LAURA JANE GRACE'S first punk rock show didn't look the way she'd imagined. Everything was bigger. The stage was big, the crowd was big, the bodies in the crowd were big, and it was the loudest thing she'd ever heard.

It was September 25, 1994, at the Edge Concert Field, in Orlando, Florida. Green Day was ripping through the final show of a summer-long conquest of the United States, and the band was at the peak of its popularity. *Dookie* had hit number four on the Billboard 200 list the day before, the highest position the album had ever reached.

The thirteen-year-old Grace had recently purchased a copy of *Dookie* at the recommendation of the owners of Offbeat Music, a record store in Fort Myers where she would kill time by poring over the selection of punk albums. She still hadn't given the cassette a proper listen, but she knew the hits. Its singles were inescapable for suburban teens like her, and videos for "Longview" and "Basket Case" were on constant rotation on MTV.

But what she'd seen on her television screen didn't prepare her for the magnitude of witnessing the band in person, where the trio became larger than life. Grace was particularly drawn to frontman Billie Joe Armstrong. She watched in awe as he commanded a sea of fans like a god. If he wanted everybody to jump up and down, they would. If he told them to "sing along, motherfuckers," they'd do that, too. At one point, he dropped his pants to moon the crowd, and the sight of his bare ass only made them scream louder.

Grace and her friend Dustin Fridkin shoved and squeezed their way to the front in their homemade punk attire. They'd both painted their hair green with spray-on dye and spiked it as best they could. Grace wore an army T-shirt she'd swiped from her father, a stoic military officer, and scrawled the Dead Kennedys' logo on the front with a black marker. A passerby pointed at it and gave her a thumbs-up, which made her smile before she quickly remembered that she was punk now, and needed to maintain a Sid Vicious sneer at all times.

When there was no more room to move through the crowd, the two realized they were standing at the perimeter of the much-fabled mosh pit. They peered in to see bodies flying in every direction. It was too loud to speak the words, but their eyes told each other that it was now or never. They locked arms and rushed in. Immediately they were swallowed by the whirlwind of muscles and shaved heads, thrown around like two rag dolls, getting the wind knocked out of them as they dodged flailing limbs from every direction. The pit kept spewing them out, but they kept charging back into danger.

After Green Day finished decimating Orlando, the two teens hobbled away battered and bruised. They couldn't say they'd had fun, really, but they could boast that they'd survived their punk initiation, having stepped into the pit and lived to tell the tale. The two sauntered across the long field and plunked down across the street from the entrance, where they waited for a ride from Fridkin's father. They caught their breath in the humid Florida air while their ears hummed and streaks of green dye ran down their faces. Grace reached into her pocket and pulled out her ticket stub, which was damp from sweat. It was then that an idea hit her like a boot to the head. A spark had been ignited inside her, and she turned to Fridkin and spoke the words that would map out the rest of her life.

"We're starting a punk band."

$ $ $

Grace didn't find punk rock so much as it found her. As the misbehaving teenager of divorced parents, trapped in the swampy suburban confines of conservative Naples, Florida, the tall and lanky Grace was destined to be drawn to the rebellious genre.

Her father's transitory army job had never let her feel grounded in one place or connected to kids her age. After he and Grace's mother went through a bitter split, Grace lashed out by running away from home, experimenting with drugs and alcohol, clashing with local police, and skipping school before dropping out completely at sixteen.

There was also a war going on inside her for which she didn't have a name. Although she had been born into a male body, she felt a confusing sense of identification whenever she saw pretty actresses on television or in magazines. The confusion only intensified as her hormones raged through her adolescence, and the only momentary solace she found came from trying on her mother's dresses in secret. It would be years before she learned the term "gender dysphoria" or heard a person described as a transsexual. All she knew was that she felt different from other kids, and punk rock, with all of its spikes and studs, became her armor to shield herself from the outside world.

After cutting her teeth on punk's commercial darlings, like Green Day, Rancid, and NOFX, she graduated to more underground anarchist bands she found by studying zines like *Maximum Rocknroll,* which she'd picked up in the unlikeliest of places. "I bought my first issue of *MRR* and my first issue of *Profane Existence* at Barnes & Noble, because that was the only place that had them in Naples," she says. "You couldn't get it with any consistency, but every once in a while they'd have a random copy in there."

She shaved her hair into a mohawk, stitched a bunch of Crass patches into her pants, and tried her hand at playing music. She started a couple of bands with Fridkin and other budding punks, which typically lasted only a few practices before fizzling out, but it was a demo tape she recorded on her own at the age of sixteen, under the name Against Me!, that would stick. She's not sure how exactly she arrived at that name, but when imagining the psyche of a teenager at odds with the world, it's not much of a mystery. Recorded on a four-track in her bedroom on Christmas Day, the songs were scratchy and tinny. Grace maxed out the levels as she channeled her teenage angst into a full-volume screech over her acoustic guitar. The cassette's six songs were far from perfect, but they marked the first output she had released into the world and she was proud of them.

Grace eventually combined forces with another local misfit teenager named Kevin Mahon, whom she convinced to play drums even though he didn't own any. The two made do with whatever they could find, be it a hand-me-down floor tom or a cement bucket salvaged from a dumpster. Cymbals weren't necessary; anything that could produce a rhythmic thud would suffice. The duo talked their way into opening slots at local gigs and earned their punk stripes in the spring of '99 when they left Florida for a monthlong trip up the East Coast, a tour that saw them spending more time begging strangers for spare change at rest stops than playing shows.

They continued to cobble together a few more cassette and vinyl releases under the Against Me! moniker, either with their own resources or with the help of pen pals they'd made at small anarchist labels like Crasshole Records and Plan-It-X Records. Print runs were typically limited to a few hundred copies, and were accompanied by photocopied lyric sheets full of the type of imagery and messaging that could be expected from teenagers at the start of a political awakening. An insert folded into one EP read, ALL POLITICIANS ARE DIRTY FUCKING MONSTERS.

Their sound changed the day they recruited James Bowman, a former high school classmate of Grace's who owned an electric guitar and a Marshall amp. Bowman's electrified power, combined with Grace's acoustic strumming, made for a unique pairing, as if a punk band were covering a folk singer's songs in real time. In addition to his guitar work, Bowman could also deliver a clean-cut croon that counterbalanced Grace's abrasive wailing. "Their music was different," Bowman remembers of Grace and Mahon. "I grew up playing in a couple bands. One was a spiky-haired street-punk band. I played with some other friends in a grindcore band. But this was different and special, and that's what drew me to it."

With money she'd saved up working at an auto shop, Grace bought a red Ford Econoline van with a skull and crossbones on the front, above stenciled letters that read HERE COMES ARMAGEDDON. Eager to see more of the United States, she enlisted Fridkin to play bass and took Against Me! on the road as a four-piece. Like most tours arranged with the resources in *Maximum Rocknroll*'s tour guidebook, *Book Your Own Fucking Life,* chances were good that most shows would be a bust, but the ones that actually happened brought in audiences that nodded along to their music and left with copies of their records. Against Me! finally felt like a real band.

While driving back from the last show of the tour, the band was rear-ended by a semi on the highway near Atlanta, causing their tires to blow and the van to flip off the road. Their tour manager, Jordan Kleeman, tore his ACL, but they were otherwise grateful to be in one piece. They couldn't say the same for their Econoline and their equipment, though, which were a crumbled hunk of twisted metal. Hobbling home with no vehicle and no gear, Against Me! took a break for a while after that, during which Mahon decided band life was not for him.

Against Me! remained dormant as Grace settled into a punk house in Gainesville, a college town with a prominent activist scene. It was in that community that she met Warren Oakes, a hippie punk with a big, scraggly beard, who would replace Mahon and reignite the band. It took some time for Grace to adjust to a drummer who actually played with cymbals, but soon they were able to write three new tunes together and retrofit older Against Me! material to Oakes's style.

When they were ready to make their first full-length album in December 2001, they followed the track most bands in Gainesville took: they recorded it on a shoestring budget at Goldentone Studios, in town, and released it with the support of No Idea Records, an indie label that worked primarily with local acts like Less Than Jake, Twelve Hour Turn, and the prolific Hot Water Music. Within the album's first ten seconds, which featured twangy, spaghetti-western guitar work over a marching-band drum line, it was clear that Against Me! was paving their own path in punk rock. Their sound had more of an edge than traditional acoustic-driven music, it didn't rely on repetitive hooks the way pop-punk did, and even though Grace was outright screaming at times, its clap-alongs and gang vocals gave it a friendlier appeal than hardcore.

They titled the album *Against Me! Is Reinventing Axl Rose* and landed on a cover design by Grace that featured a giant cutout of the Guns N' Roses frontman. Grace would explain the Axl Rose reference in a four-page interview in *Maximum Rocknroll:* "The basic idea behind it is to deconstruct the rock star, keeping the music on the level of a person-to-person basis and not having any sort of elevated levels."

The tearing down of the rock star ego was the ethos that drew people in and lit a fire in the hearts of those who heard it. "I don't really believe in instant classics, but there are a few exceptions to this rule," began one glowing review in *Punk Planet*. "It takes a lot to excite me anymore, and for the first time since I was 16, I want to follow a band around the country from show to show."

After years of overblown, commercialized punk in the nineties, *Reinventing Axl Rose* proudly dragged the genre back to its austere roots. The title track's lyrics read like a DIY manifesto, dreaming of a utopian scene in which bands played for "nothing more than a plate of food and a place to rest" and arenas that were "just basements and bookstores across an underground America." But while the album was steeped in anarchist philosophy, it didn't browbeat the listener with heavy politics, and instead managed to be fun and inviting. It even included a breakup song, "Baby, I'm an Anarchist," which arrived at the conclusion that radical anarchists and status quo liberals make for lousy romantic partners. It also helped the twenty-one-year-old Grace become something of a punk scene heartthrob.

Reinventing Axl Rose's stripped-down take on punk rock made the genre accessible to a new generation, the way the Ramones' three-chord approach had done in the seventies. It made it so accessible, in fact, that as Against Me! rose in prominence, a slew of new bands cropped up that heavily, and sometimes shamelessly, borrowed from their style. The band's sound became so popular that the phrase "like Against Me!" turned into fanzine shorthand for any band that put hoarse singing over an acoustic guitar. Against Me! may not have invented folk-punk, but they definitely popularized it.

No Idea didn't have much trouble selling *Reinventing Axl Rose*'s first pressing of 1,100 LPs and a couple thousand CDs. Mail orders kept rolling in as fanzine praise and word-of-mouth buzz spread the name Against Me! around the country. The label went through repress after repress, and the LP would eventually go on to be the Florida label's all-time bestselling release. But despite its growing reach, Fridkin left the band shortly after it was recorded to continue his academic pursuits and was replaced by Andrew Seward.

Seward lived in Murfreesboro, Tennessee, and played bass in Kill Devil Hills, a gruff hardcore band that was on the verge of breaking up. "I knew it wasn't working out," Seward says. "On our last tour, we'd played with Against Me! and we listened to *Reinventing Axl Rose* all the time in the van. You could feel the energy of the songs. The recording is so obtuse; it sounded like nothing else out there at the time. I'd never done anything like this, but I drunkenly emailed Laura one night, saying, 'If you ever need a bass player, I'd join your band.' She responded and said that Dustin was going back to college in Sarasota and if I moved down to Florida, I could be in the band. I was down there in two weeks."

The burly, scruffy Seward injected a hype-man energy into Against Me!'s live show. He wasn't the frontperson, but he stood center stage when the band played and riled up the crowd with his bouncy dance moves and ear-to-ear smile. With this lineup—Grace, Bowman, Oakes, and Seward—Against Me! caught a groove together. They'd all discovered punk in their own ways, but they bonded over the kinetic energy they shared onstage, not to mention the partying that followed.

A copy of *Reinventing Axl Rose* made its way from Gainesville to San Francisco and landed on the desk of Fat Mike Burkett at Fat Wreck Chords. He, too, was immediately struck by the band's originality. "Their first couple records had that sound—the crazy snare, the out-of-tune vocals," says Burkett. "They were kids trying to pull off these great songs. It sounded like a great songwriter with a band that couldn't really pull off the songs. And *that* is punk."

He phoned the band while they were on the road and offered them $25,000 to come aboard at Fat for their sophomore album. Grace accepted on the spot and bullshitted her way through questions about their next record, claiming it was practically in the bag, when in actuality they hadn't written a single note.

The jump from one indie label to a slightly larger indie label might seem inconsequential to casual music fans, but to some within the highly opinionated world of punk rock, Against Me!'s move was sacrilegious. Because Fat Wreck Chords had a few lucrative releases under its belt, the label might as well have been ExxonMobil to broke crusties in the folk-punk scene. "It was still the time where *everything* was selling out. If anybody had success, fuck them," says Seward. But Against Me! was too excited to consider how anyone might react or the repercussions they might face. All they knew was that someone was paying them enough money to conquer the world.

"We were still everyone's darlings on No Idea Records," says Grace, "but once we were on Fat Wreck Chords, that's when the backlash came."

$ $ $

Against Me! as the Eternal Cowboy was released by Fat Wreck Chords in November 2003. Its cover looked like a defiant inverse of Bruce Springsteen's iconic *Born in the U.S.A.* album: instead of a close-up of the Boss's blue-jean butt, the record featured a black-and-white photo of Grace's torso in the same pose, but shot from the front. With one thumb hooked on her pocket and the other hand gripping a guitar, a middle finger subtly draped across the fretboard, her body language issued an open challenge. Her face was cropped out, but her stance was confrontational, as if she was daring anyone who picked it up to say it wasn't the greatest punk record ever made.

The eleven songs that made up *Eternal Cowboy* were an appropriate snapshot of the band's rambunctious identity at the time. It was a party record, its catchy choruses built for singing and clapping along in sweaty, beer-soaked basements. The short window in which it was written, as well as the influence of cocaine, had made for a speedy batch of tunes, with five of them not even cracking the two-minute mark. The songs were so fast, in fact, that when the band listened back to their recordings, they realized they hadn't even laid down twenty-five minutes' worth of material and sneaked a few extra seconds of space onto the ends of some tracks to push it there.

The length of the album didn't matter much to Against Me!, though. The way they saw it, they now had eleven new rounds of stage ammunition. Their first opportunity to unleash *Eternal Cowboy* on the world was a package tour in the winter of 2003 with three Fat Wreck labelmates: Rise Against, None More Black, and Anti-Flag. As the headliners, Pittsburgh's Anti-Flag had handpicked Against Me! after being blown away by their show at the local venue Roboto. The performance was so raucous that, as bassist Chris "#2" Barker recalls, "it felt like the floor was going to give out."

"Against Me! had an agenda that was akin to Fugazi in its purity, just in its inability to bend towards what other people thought would be successful. That's why I wanted to be around it," he says. But it became immediately obvious to Barker and the rest of Anti-Flag that they'd gotten more than they bargained for when they invited the Florida punks along.

Against Me! was not accustomed to a tour with a pecking order or guidelines about their operation, and they immediately bucked against the edicts set forth. "We showed up the first day and their tour manager gets everybody in a circle and starts handing out laminates," remembers Bowman. "He's like, 'These are $20 each if you lose them,' laying down all the ground rules for the tour. The way we'd always toured, it was a group effort. *For-fucking-ever,* we split our guarantees evenly with everybody playing the shows. So that just set the precedent. Those are the rules? Well, fuck you!"

For Grace, it wasn't just the urge to rebel against the rules of the tour that motivated her; she also saw a nightly opportunity to make sure people remembered the name Against Me! "My mentality going into it, being a juvenile asshole, was that our aim was to make as many fans on this tour as possible. We were in a battle. We were fighting the headlining band," she says. "The best way to get inside their heads and fuck with them is to break them down psychologically and make them seem uncool. So that's what we did."

And so the pranks began. Against Me! and their crew relentlessly tortured any competition for the spotlight. As the most senior band, Anti-Flag bore the brunt of the green room sabotaging. Barker remembers, "They were pissing in our Gatorade bottles and putting peanut butter on our door handles while we were onstage."

Grace cops to being the ringleader of the mischief. "I did put peanut butter on their door handle," she admits. "We also bought a pickled pig's hoof in Florida and we hid it in one of their duffel bags. We stole their tour rider book and passed it out to people. While they were onstage in Montreal, we let all the fans that were out behind the venue into their dressing room. Warren would stage dive naked while they were playing, just to get in their heads, psychologically. We did terrible shit to them."

"And then once we'd start egging each other on, it'd raise the level of mayhem," adds Seward. "We were wild. We were being immature drunks and we didn't care about the rules."

"It was our first tour where it seemed like there was an unnecessary amount of tension," remembers Rise Against frontman Tim McIlrath. "Every tour we'd done, everyone got along and we were all in the same boat. Against Me! got out there and it seemed like they'd decided they were not in the same boat. They were in a different boat, and they wanted that to be known."

Being the victors of daily games of psychological warfare only bolstered Against Me!'s confidence, which they channeled into their set every night. They played with bravado, like a band hell-bent on leaving a decimated stage in their wake. They'd all taken to wearing black, which made them seem like a menacing wrecking crew, and every second of their set was spent making sure any band that had the misfortune of following them cursed their name. "We had twenty minutes," remembers Seward. "It was just: 'Go! Go hard! Don't talk between songs! Don't even say the name of the band!'"

Their behavior didn't make them many friends on the tour, but Grace maintains that it helped them in the grand scheme of things. "I think it made us seem like a dangerous band," she says. "We came out of that tour with the most buzz out of any band. Rise Against played it slow and steady and very smart, just inch by inch. But I was just going for bigger grabs and trying to make larger gains."

One person who took notice of Against Me! was Tom Sarig, a former record-label A&R rep turned artist manager. Sarig's interest in the band had been piqued after he read a fawning review of *Reinventing Axl Rose* in a fanzine. After seeing and meeting them on the North Carolina stop of the Anti-Flag tour, he immediately recognized that not only were Against Me! the stars of the tour; they were the stars of the entire punk scene.

"They were really rough—like, not businesspeople," Sarig remembers. "They were young kids from Gainesville and they didn't know what the hell they were doing, but they were incredible. I thought a lot of the punk music of that era was just okay. Fat Mike had a whole label of those kinds of bands that I thought were good but nothing special. But [Grace] had something really, really incredible. [She] was a superstar. [She] could've been a Billie Joe or a Joe Strummer."

After the tour, Sarig met with the band in Florida and explained what a manager could offer. "He flew out to Gainesville and took us out to dinner at the Top, which is where we worked," remembers Grace. "We were all stoked. We looked big-time in front of our friends. Some old guy was taking us out to dinner at the restaurant we all worked at. We heard his pitch out, and I was genuinely impressed with the bands he worked with."

Sarig had managed Lou Reed, Blonde Redhead, and riot grrrl icon Kathleen Hanna's post–Bikini Kill project, Le Tigre. But while he talked a big game and dropped the right names, Against Me! turned him down. They figured they didn't need another voice telling them how to run their operation. Plus, they had the backing of one of the most reliable labels in punk, money to pay their meager rents, and enough tour dates lined up to keep them on the road for months. What else could they possibly need?

$ $ $

There's a saying that goes: "If you want an audience, start a fight." That was the approach Bill Florio took when writing his monthly column in *Maximum Rocknroll*. "It was half truths and half shit I made up, just to see what would happen," he says. "I got a broader audience for my shit-talking."

Florio, a New York native and bassist for punk rabble-rousers the Shemps, had been tasked with penning *MRR*'s popular gossip column by the zine's founder, Tim Yohannan. Cancer had claimed Yohannan at the age of fifty-three, in 1998, but Florio was proud to carry his torch of punk scene vigilance into a new millennium. As far as stirring up shit went, Florio was as effective as he was merciless. He identified the most serious bands and provoked them in hopes of getting a reaction. If the bands got mad, he counted that as a win, and if they threatened to kick his ass, that was worthy of a victory lap. His name became notorious after starting public feuds with the scene's most aggressive hardcore acts, like Sick of It All and Earth Crisis.

If anyone were to ask Florio *why* he poked these bears, he would counter with *why not?* "My whole thing was: you're either in a band or you write for a zine, and those people are against each other," he says. "I was on the zine side, and I was there to fuck with bands."

At some point in 2003, Florio attended a show where there were "three shitty folk-punk bands" playing, a trend that took him by surprise. "I'd never really experienced that," he remembers. "All these people came to see this shit and I was like, 'What the fuck is going on?'" A friend informed him that the burgeoning folk-punk movement was largely attributable to the rising popularity of a band from Florida called Against Me! Once Florio heard that, he knew he'd found his next target.

On April 15, 2004, Florio brought a box of stink bombs to a free show that Against Me! was scheduled to play at Pratt Institute, an art college in Brooklyn, New York. He attached dozens of them to plastic roses and passed them out in the crowd as Against Me!'s set began. People dropped them on the ground, and as they got trampled, the room started to stink of rotten eggs.

"It was a mess of a show," remembers Grace. "There was also this kid there, Frank, who had slashed our tires after a show in Long Island. He'd come to fuck with us again. There was a confrontation out front that was ugly. It was an eye-opening moment for me, because I remember being in this kid Frank's face and being like, 'What the fuck? You slashed our tires! Pay for our tires!' Which isn't gonna happen. Why even say it? What, he's gonna bust out his wallet and pay for the tires? And then I remember looking over and seeing another punk pick up a brick. And I'm like, 'What, this kid is gonna brain me with a brick now?'"

Against Me! drove off that night reeking, annoyed, and feeling scorned by the punk scene. Florio, on the other hand, got exactly what he wanted. Not only had he made a new enemy; he'd also picked up fresh material for his column. In the October 2004 issue of *Maximum Rocknroll,* he devoted an entire page to trashing his new favorite punching bag. After making a few cracks about the band's sound, likening it to "James Taylor with curses," he derided them for doing package tours, like the one they'd done with Anti-Flag and Rise Against, and accused the setup of being a pay-to-play scheme that took opening slots away from local bands. He half joked about forming "punk rock terrorism squads" to disrupt package tours and advised readers that if one came through their town, they should "fuck it up. Dump Clorox in the merch box, throw pizza at the bands, grease the stage—we shouldn't just sit back and let them buy and sell punk rock like your admission is a commodity."

The band was at the airport, returning from a tour of Australia, when Fat Wreck Chords' publicist, Vanessa Burt, called to tell them about the column. "Maybe I shouldn't have even called her," says Burt. "In hindsight, we shouldn't even have invested our emotions in it. Bill Florio was just an agitator." She read it to Grace over the phone, and with each word the frontwoman's blood boiled hotter. Grace was familiar with Florio, having read his zine *Greedy Bastard* as a teenager, and she found his condescending punk purism enraging.

"It was infuriating to me, because I'd seen behind the curtain on their end," Grace says of *MRR*. "When we did that interview with them, we were taken to their super-fucking-swank headquarters and offices that had a fucking tranquility garden in the center of it and everyone's typing away on these really nice-ass computers and there's a wall-to-wall record collection. And it's San Francisco, so how much was the rent in this fucking place? Meanwhile, we were living in Gainesville, paying two hundred bucks a month to live in these rooms in shitty student ghetto houses."

After the column ran, Against Me! started noticing Bill Florios cropping up in every town. Wherever they went, irate punks would be waiting to start trouble, confront them about their touring ethics, or vandalize their van. One tag on the door read, REMEMBER WHEN YOU MATTERED?

The band perpetually found themselves on the defensive. If the DIY punk community was going to turn on them, then they were ready to turn on it right back. But the harder they leaned against the skid, the more they lost control of the situation. "Looking back at it now, [Florio] was doing the same thing we were doing to Anti-Flag—punching up," Grace says. "If I would have just ignored it and kept my head high, I think it would have had way less of an effect. I self-perpetuated it and manifested it in a lot of ways, because I let it get to me."

Against Me!'s star was rising so rapidly that their influx of new fans bumped up the size of venues they could fill in the span of a few short months. Yet, despite their success, they were too prideful to ignore the handful of vocal and militant critics. "I was defensive of everything," says Seward. "We were like a gang, in a way. 'Don't fuck with my friends.'"

But while Against Me! faced hostility on the ground over petty scene politics, there were more substantial conversations happening about them above their heads. Major labels had begun hearing tales of punk's hottest band and started reaching out to them. One by one, A&R reps called, inquiring about their plans to release a third record. With more questions than they could field, the band reconsidered the benefits of having an organized manager and hired Tom Sarig, who immediately got to work rounding up the interested parties.

"Pretty much every major label chased them hard," he remembers. "Every label wanted to fly them to New York or L.A. to have meetings." Sarig played the labels off one another. When he heard from one interested party, he used it to leverage the attention of two more labels, which grew the intrigue surrounding the band exponentially.

"Tom Sarig was really good at that," says Grace. "He was creating a bidding war." Sarig set the band up with reps from just about every label: Universal, Virgin, Warner, Island, Epic, Sony, and Capitol. For a band as cocky as Against Me!, the attention felt flattering but also deserved. "In everything we were doing, it was like, 'Of course they're interested. Of course this is coming to us. We're the chosen ones.'"

"[Grace] was anointed from an early age of being this hero out of Florida, and was so unique and special," says Sarig. "[She] was the Jesus of that No Idea Records DIY punk scene in Gainesville."

At first, Against Me! found the notion of taking business meetings comical, and viewed any label delegate they met as another target for their pranks. But while they laughed it off as a farce, to maintain their punk cred, deep down there was a part of them that thought, "Why not us?" After all, Rise Against had just left Fat Wreck Chords to sign to DreamWorks, and Anti-Flag was talking to majors about doing the same. Tons of bands they'd played with had made the jump over the previous couple of years and Against Me! believed themselves to be better than all of them.

"I was so conflicted," says Grace, "because on the outside I was making fun of it and pretending I wasn't interested, but on the inside I was like, 'This is an opportunity and I should pursue this and exploit it.'"

At the height of their major-label attention in the spring of 2004, Against Me! spent a month on the road with the British band No Choice and the notoriously rowdy Planes Mistaken for Stars. "I wouldn't have wanted to be in their shoes," says Planes frontman Gared O'Donnell. "I can't imagine how conflicting it must have been for people to hold this brass ring in front of you when that's really not what you're about. But at the same time, we were all getting old enough that we had to worry about paying bills."

During that tour, Against Me! filmed a documentary entitled *We're Never Going Home.* The film, released later that year by Fat Wreck Chords, captured the band at a crossroads: they were on the verge of making the most crucial decision of their lives, yet they were still unable to avoid the trappings of juvenile tour mayhem. The documentary showcased the nightly rampage that constituted Against Me!'s lives, where steamy, free-for-all shows blended into raucous hotel after-parties. Every evening was a blur of empty beer cans, shirtless arm wrestling, and regrettable tour tattoos. "We were just kids, traveling around playing music," says Bowman. "You do drugs and drink and hang out and party. That's what you do."

Much of the alcohol being guzzled on the tour was charged to the Universal Records company card, as the label's vice president of A&R Tom Mackay and his assistant, Maureen Kenny, tagged along in an attempt to woo the band. For years, punk fans had heard lore about their favorite bands being picked apart by A&R vultures, but *We're Never Going Home* was one of the first authentic peeks under the hood of the courting process. "I think that they're all genuinely sweet people," Oakes said in the documentary, speaking of the Universal reps. "As far as having a business relationship, free drinks don't really change my thoughts about that, they just make me drunk."

"The band would open their throats to the major-label wallets," says Sarig. "As far as getting completely wasted goes, they weren't shy to that."

In addition to running up bar tabs with Universal, the tour saw them taking in days at baseball games and nights at strip clubs with other label suitors. "It started with some dinners and bars, then it progressed to packages showing up at the house full of, like, Ben Sherman bags and supplies to go on tour. It got kind of aggressive," says Bowman.

"I remember visiting labels in L.A. and getting so many fucking CDs and box sets," says Seward. "They asked if I needed a bag and I said I needed two. I was just clearing off the shelf. My wife was like, 'Why do you have all these?' And I was like, 'Because they were free!'"

Comped tabs and free swag were nice perks, but ultimately, the number on the paycheck was all that really mattered to the band. "We've had someone say, 'I'll give you a million dollars to make a record,' and it's fucking crazy," Grace said in the documentary. "And it's so far from anything we ever wanted to be as a band or anything we ever wanted to stand for." On paper, the offers actually hovered in the high six-figure range, which was still more money than the four punks from Florida could even comprehend.

While major-label dollar signs floated around the band, Fat Wreck Chords remained a reliable presence in the background. Although the indie label couldn't pony up anywhere near the sums that the majors were throwing at them, Burkett offered them a respectable $250,000 to stay on board. It was a more substantial amount than most bands would ever see from the label and ten times what Against Me! had pocketed on *Eternal Cowboy*.

"I told Rise Against they should go to a major. I told Anti-Flag they should go to a major. I told Against Me! they *shouldn't* go to a major," Burkett says. "I thought they were turning down a career as a respected, independent band that could go for thirty years. I told Laura, 'If you go to a major, you might get big, but you're gonna lose that specialness that NOFX has, that Fugazi had.' I really thought they were *the* band. Their sound, it excited everybody."

And when it came down to it, that's what Against Me! decided: They were sticking with Fat. Fuck the majors.

$ $ $

If songwriters are meant to write about what they know, then Laura Jane Grace had a problem. When she pulled her head out from the fog of *Eternal Cowboy*, which saw the band at the center of a nearly two-year-long party on wheels, she discovered there wasn't much substance underneath.

"I got really fucked up on drugs while we were touring for *As the Eternal Cowboy*," she says. "A lot of that came with the Fat Wreck Chords scene. There was just a lot of fucking cocaine going on at Fat Wreck Chords at that period of time. It was not major-label people giving us cocaine. It was indie-label people giving us cocaine."

She kicked drugs and alcohol to write songs for Against Me!'s third record. In her sobriety, she realized most of the memories that had stuck with her over the past several months entailed soul-crushing conversations about things like "market share" and "target audience" with the employees that suddenly made up the band's "team" —managers, agents, accountants, lawyers. So when she picked up a pen and paper, that's what came out.

The album, entitled *Searching for a Former Clarity*, saw Against Me! shifting away from the fun, carefree spirit that had radiated from *Eternal Cowboy*. It was a bitter record on which Grace griped about the music industry drudgery that had poisoned her relationship with her art over the previous year. Many of the songs' lyrics read less like artistic expressions and more like peeks into Against Me!'s accounting files. On "Unprotected Sex with Multiple Partners," Grace gave detailed breakdowns of the band's cash flow: "It's three points on production / fifteen percent to management / ten percent to the agent / five percent to legal representation." The business-speak lyrics were a far jump from the anarcho-punk politics of *Reinventing Axl Rose* and from the drunken nights and slurred rhythms captured on *Eternal Cowboy*.

Maybe it was the chip on their shoulder from all the major-label flattery, but Against Me!'s relationship with Fat Wreck Chords soured during the course of making *Former Clarity*. Even before its release, in September 2005, the band started to feel at odds with their label as Burkett picked apart their vision for the record, particularly its cover, a grainy black-and-white photo of a Florida palm tree.

"They thought I was being too arty with *Former Clarity*," says Grace. "Mike didn't like the cover art. He wanted the name bigger, he didn't like the track listing, he didn't think there was a real single on the record. All the shit that people told us the major labels would do was happening at an indie. So even before it came out, I had such a bad taste in my mouth."

"I signed a fucking band; I didn't sign an artist!" Burkett says of the cover. "If I'm gonna give you hundreds of thousands of dollars, help me sell the fucking records! It wasn't the gray palm trees—it was that you could barely read the name of the band. It was so small you couldn't read it."

The famously blunt Burkett was not shy about voicing his opinions, and the debate created friction in their relationship. "I've seen it time and time again—bands putting out great records with a terrible cover, and they don't sell as well. That's when a band should listen to a label president. I've put out four hundred records, and I've seen it all before," he says.

Former Clarity had a strong release that saw Against Me! making their debut on the Billboard 200 list at number 114 and selling fifty thousand copies within a year. They also performed "Don't Lose Touch" on *Late Night with Conan O'Brien,* with O'Brien introducing them as "the pride of Gainesville, Florida." Still, the band couldn't shake the feeling that they'd made the wrong decision in sticking with Fat. With all of the talk of singles and the pressure to market their album properly, it felt as if they'd lost the freedoms that punk was supposed to afford them. It felt a lot like they'd signed to a major. So, since they were already making major-label concessions, they figured they might as well make major-label money.

Sarig once again corralled A&R interest after *Former Clarity*'s release, reignited the bidding wars, and watched the price tags soar even higher. Mackay was still heavily in pursuit of Against Me! for Universal, but ultimately he couldn't produce enough zeroes on the check. "Tom Mackay flew something like fifteen people to come hang in Atlanta and shoot pool, and was heartbroken when we turned him down," remembers Grace. "But they only came up with around 750K. Warner offered us over a million dollars. Plus, it was a two-firm deal, which meant they had to do the second record no matter what."

Warner's hefty offer came courtesy of Sire president Michael Goldstone and Craig Aaronson, the A&R rep who had pulled numerous bands into the major-label system, including Jimmy Eat World, the Distillers, and My Chemical Romance. Warner chairman Tom Whalley had a reputation for seeking out headstrong bands driven by a steadfast point of view, which made Against Me! an ideal candidate. The band was particularly drawn to Warner's Sire Records imprint, which had been home to everyone from Madonna to the Ramones.

After nearly two years of being very publicly pursued, Against Me! finally gave in and accepted an offer of $1.5 million from Sire. Since the band still owed Fat Wreck Chords another album, their move to another label should have been a breach of contract, except that there was no contract to breach. "It was a handshake agreement with Fat. Mike had asked us for two records for what he gave us for *Searching for a Former Clarity*," says Grace.

"They never actually signed it, but they took the money, which makes it a binding deal," says Burkett. "My lawyer said they had to give us a record, because they took the money." Although his attorney advised him to sue the band, he says, he was adamant that his label not get embroiled in lawsuits with any band. To meet somewhere in the middle, Fat Wreck Chords got a live Against Me! record out of the band's departure.

"At Fat Wreck Chords, we normally don't work very hard," Burkett says. "But with Against Me!, we gave them a lot of money, which means we spent a lot of time on the record, because we thought we were getting their next record. We spent more money marketing that record than any record ever on the label. So, yeah, people at the label were super bummed."

If employees at the label felt betrayed, certainly Against Me!'s hypercritical fans would, too. News of the signing soon overloaded comment sections across the internet as punks raced to point out the hypocrisy in light of *We're Never Going Home*. "They'd just released a fucking video where they said they were gonna stay with Fat Wreck Chords, and then six months later they're on a major. You can't have it both ways," says Burkett.

But unlike Thursday, My Chemical Romance, Rise Against, and other bands that had made the major-label jump before them,

Against Me! didn't see the point in releasing a lengthy explanation to their fans asking them for their continued support as they took this leap into a new phase of their career. "I thought those manifestos were full of shit," Grace says. "They weren't saying what they were really interested in." The band didn't really care anymore if people thought they were selling out. It was what it was; take it or leave it. The only mention on their website was a quick item sandwiched between housekeeping updates about new merch and tour photos that read:

> SUBMITTED FOR YOUR MESSAGE BOARD
> DISAPPROVAL!
> Against Me! has signed to Sire Records. Expect a new album in
> 2007! For real.

Grace, especially, felt she had little to prove and nothing left to lose. "I already felt like a pariah around town. I didn't feel welcome in places," she says. "You walk into Leonardo's by the Slice, the pizza place that everyone goes to, you walk into Burrito Brothers, you walk into the Top, and everyone looks at you and they know who you are and they have an opinion about you, and I could feel that. I was sensitive to it. It made me uncomfortable. But all that fueled me, too. Like, 'Fuck you all. I'm gonna do it.'"

Her social anxiety was further exacerbated by her on-and-off relationship with sobriety, as were the underlying feelings of dysphoria she kept in secret. Although her band was skyrocketing, she was privately hurting. Her inner demons were starting to eat away at her as she found as much difficulty in kicking her drug habits as she did with her compulsion toward cross-dressing behind the locked doors of hotel rooms. There was a looming darkness waiting for her when she looked ahead. At twenty-five, she had all but accepted it as an inevitability that she would one day join the infamous list of famous rockers who'd perished by the age of twenty-seven.

"At no point was my secret end goal to get all this money and buy a mansion," she says. "It was: '*I will be dead*. I will be dead by twenty-eight. I'm not going to live very long. I'm going to run this into the ground. I'm going to explode this, because there's no other way it'll survive. The only thing that's going to keep us going is this constant inertia and constant momentum.' That's it. Just run it into the fucking ground, and I'd rather have the explosion."

$ $ $

"Humble" was not a word that was ever used to describe Laura Jane Grace. Whenever friends and supporters tried to slip her the occasional piece of career advice, she would hear them out. Ultimately, though, Against Me! was her band, and she knew what was best for it. It wasn't until she met producer Butch Vig that she found someone worth listening to.

"You have A&R people throwing out the biggest producer names at you—Chris Lord-Alge! Rick Rubin!—with no knowledge of whether or not any of those people were interested," says Grace. "But the second Butch's name was said, I was like, 'Yes! We want to make a record with Butch.'"

The fifty-year-old Vig had arguably been more responsible for shaping the sound of rock music throughout the nineties than anyone alive. His production credits included albums by the decade's most celebrated acts, like the Smashing Pumpkins, L7, and Sonic Youth. But the crown jewel of his résumé was Nirvana's era-defining *Nevermind,* which catapulted him into an elite tier of super-producers. In addition to his work behind the boards, Vig was also the drummer of the band Garbage, which gave him an edge of relatability over his studio peers.

At the urging of Aaronson, Vig checked the band out at their Milwaukee stop on Warped Tour during a week in which Vig happened to be visiting his parents in Wisconsin. "I liked them right away," Vig remembers. "I thought they could be the new Clash. I loved their passion, I loved what they were doing with their songs, stylistically. It was punk rock, but there were songs that had some shuffle grooves and different little things they brought in that reminded me of *Sandinista!*"

Vig swung by the band's bus after their set to introduce himself. A couple of hours and a case of Miller Genuine Draft later, they agreed they were a perfect match and made plans to create the band's major-label debut together. Vig left Grace with the suggestion that she write as many songs as possible. Grace took the advice to heart and, over the next several months, sent him demo versions of more than two dozen tracks, which he then helped refine. "All the suggestions I gave, she was open to them," he says. "I'd say things and she'd trust me enough to at least try them. That doesn't always happen with artists."

When Against Me! was finally ready to record their Sire debut, *New Wave,* in October 2006, they relocated to Los Angeles's Oakwood Apartments, or the Cokewood Apartments as they were often known in the biz, the same complex Nirvana had lived in while recording *Nevermind.*

Bowman couldn't help but laugh when he saw the swanky setup at Hollywood's Paramount Recording Studios, which had produced platinum records and Grammy-winning hits by everyone from the Jackson 5 to Bob Dylan. He thought about how far the band had come since the slapdash recording session for *Reinventing Axl Rose.* "Our first record was recorded in one day. We actually played too fast and rerecorded it the next day. It was 740-something dollars for that whole experience," he says. "Now we're in this crazy studio and making a record in the most polar opposite way from how our previous records were made."

Vig didn't care much about how Against Me! had made *Reinventing Axl Rose* or the criticism their fans hurled at them anytime they'd dared to take a step up since then. "I kind of threw it out the window, because I wanted to make a big, widescreen-sounding record," he says. "There's a point where I think you have to take a leap of faith as an artist if you want to get to a bigger level. Punks, like anybody, are sometimes so narrow-minded and conservative in their viewpoint that they don't want a band to grow at all, or be anything other than what they were when they initially discovered them. Every record I've done, there's been someone saying, 'Butch Vig ruined that band.' I don't care. I'm making the record with the band that we want to make. I told James and Laura, 'You have to stop going on the fucking Punknews.org forums!' It was just hate, hate, hate. They'd get on there and write these passionate responses. I was like, 'Close the fucking computer! You're gonna drive yourself crazy.'"

The three months in the studio with a scrupulous producer like Vig exposed a weak spot in Against Me!'s operation. Oakes's rough-and-tumble approach behind the kit had contributed to the band's lovably sloppy charm at their live gigs, but under the unforgiving studio lights, it became clear that his skills were not up to snuff for a big-budget record.

"The drums were a bit of a problem on *New Wave*," remembers Vig. "I knew that in the rehearsals. I wanted them to at least start with a click track so we could keep the tempo, but it didn't always stay there." Guitar and bass sessions were often rushed to accommodate the additional drum time. "When you're taking a whole day just to get one drum track, and you're two weeks in and all you're doing is drums, you start to get a little panicky."

Bowman is less tactful in his recollection: "The fact of the matter was, Warren was not a very good drummer. There's audio proof of it. Sure, he had charisma, but as far as technical skill, he just couldn't do it."

Aside from the extra days expended on drum tracks, another weak spot Vig noticed as the album came together was that it lacked a standout song. Many of Grace's lyrics were dense airings of personal grievances. On "Up the Cuts," a song she describes as being "the self-examination to make that decision to sign to a major," she penned a wordy response to *Maximum Rocknroll*'s cynicism. To give the album a bit more variety, Vig gave her a specific piece of homework to inject it with something more upbeat.

"I felt like the record could use some breadth," he says. "At one point I suggested, 'You should write a song like "Walk on the Wild Side."'" That suggestion prompted Grace to write "Thrash Unreal," a song whose heavy lyrical content about a young woman whose youth spent partying leads to a drug-addicted adulthood is offset by the cheerful *ba, ba, ba's* of its chorus. "It's a totally different vibe, sonically, but there's a spirit of a journey in that song that's not unlike Lou Reed's lyrics."

The last song recorded in the *New Wave* sessions was "The Ocean," a bass-heavy number with a quasi-Caribbean beat. During one of Grace's vocal takes, Vig was struck by the peculiarity of one of its lyrics: "If I could have chosen, I would have been born a woman / My mother once told me she would have named me Laura."

"I'll usually get a lyric sheet so I can take notes when she's singing," says Vig. "I was looking at the lyrics to 'The Ocean' and I said, 'Hey, what is this song about?' And she said, totally elusively, 'I was sitting on a beach in France, smoking a doobie, and these words came to me.'"

$ $ $

All eyes were on Against Me! when *New Wave* was released by Sire Records, in July 2007. The band was being watched closely by industry insiders eager to see if the year's most high-profile gamble was going to pay off, as well as by a punk scene that wrung its collective hands and waited to find out if the band would crash and burn. But the eyes that were locked onto Against Me! the day they posed for their first photo spread in *SPIN* magazine were far more menacing.

The photos were taken in Paynes Prairie, a state park near Gainesville, during the worst drought the area had experienced in more than a century. "I was leading the way down this trail where we were doing the photo shoot," says Brian Bumbery, the band's publicist at Warner. "The water was really low, and when the water's low, the crocs come up. We got to this clearing and there were ten alligators in the water and all you could see were the eyes staring at us."

Despite the ominous foreboding, the magazine's reception to Against Me! was exceptionally warm. The accompanying four-page feature rolled out the red carpet for the band. It declared *New Wave* to be "the best rock album in ages" and described it as "the rare album that's as likely to appeal to 14-year-old budding pissants as it is to pushing-40 Fugazi nostalgists."

"I think some of their success was timing," posits Brian Raftery, who wrote the article. "*New Wave* came out toward the end of

[George W. Bush's] second term, and the communal pent-up anger of that era made a song like 'New Wave'—an apolitical call to arms, but a call nonetheless—feel all the more welcome."

While punk websites and zines picked apart Vig's slick production and debated the merits of Against Me!'s career choices, mainstream outlets gleefully latched on to the record as their token punk pick. In addition to the *SPIN* feature, esteemed critic Robert Christgau gave the album four out of five stars in *Rolling Stone*. It earned a sturdy B+ rating from *Entertainment Weekly*. And across the pond, *NME* called it the band's "best album to date."

"It was an absolute landslide in press," says Sarig. "It was *SPIN*'s number one record of the year. Brian Bumbery, who was one of the best publicists in music, got them an unbelievable amount of positive press."

"The goal was to get people to see them live if we could. Once you saw that, it was undeniable," says Bumbery. "The sweat was dripping from the ceiling."

In addition to print features, the band practically played the entire album across the late-night talk show circuit—"Thrash Unreal" on *Conan*, "Stop!" on *Letterman*, "Up the Cuts" on *Leno*. Against Me! was a publicist's dream—a fiery punk band with a rebellious streak and an outspoken but charismatic frontperson. "They fucking had it all. The music was solid, the live shows were solid, they were just incredible," says Bumbery. "People were receptive because they wanted a band to champion. I think that was a time when a lot of people, especially young and emerging artists, were really playing it safe. Not them. They were like, 'This is who we are. We may have signed to a major label, but we're not changing.'"

The mainstream exposure roped new crowds into their shows, which now saw them headlining bigger venues than they'd ever played. The band embraced their new stature, successfully translating their basement-show energy to rooms filled with more than a thousand people each night. On the surface, the band might've seemed like they were in control, but behind the scenes, they were making more compromises than they cared to admit. As the band's leader, Grace endured long days of photo shoots and interviews, and did so with a smile in hopes that a positive attitude would trickle down to the rest of the band. The filming of the music video for "Thrash Unreal," however, pushed them to a breaking point.

Grace was unable to sell the label on her treatment for the video, which leaned heavily on the idea of her cross-dressing. My Chemical Romance's Frank Iero also wrote a treatment that got rejected. They instead settled on the director's vision, wherein the band performed in a basement below a swanky party. As the tuxedoed partygoers above them—Vig made a cameo as one of them—dumped barrels of red wine into the floor's vents, the band members were showered from the ceiling.

"We were being completely fucking soaked in 'wine,' this dyed food-colored water," says Bowman. "I remember it being a super-long day and being soaked in this shit. Then they called lunch and everybody just left and we were standing there, dyed pink, soaking wet, and it's fucking freezing." After getting drenched more than half a dozen times, their skin had a fuchsia tint to it that wouldn't scrub off. Seward had to take his contacts out, because all he could see through them was red.

"Laura brought the first cut over to my house and we watched it," Seward remembers of the video. "I was like, 'Oh, yeah . . . it's great.' But I was thinking, 'No, it's not.' I liked Laura's concept better."

As a single, "Thrash Unreal" didn't have the explosive selling power the label had hoped it would. It spent twenty weeks on the Billboard Alternative Songs chart, peaking at number 11, but it largely failed to cross over to general audiences the way Green Day's "Longview" had reached Grace a decade prior. Grace wasn't exactly surprised, as she'd never found "Thrash Unreal" to be a natural fit for the airwaves. "There's a fuck ton of words to it," she says. "The chorus—'No mother ever dreams that her daughter's gonna grow up to be a junkie'—that's not an immediate radio grabber."

In its first year, New Wave would sell 107,000 copies. Sarig remembers hearing mixed feedback about New Wave from his contacts at Warner. "They were definitely pleased as far as the acclaim the record got, but they were moderate on the sales," he says. "It definitely didn't sell what we'd hoped it would sell, but they definitely weren't dumping the band, either. They had a lot of money sunken into them. The other thing was that they truly believed [Grace] was going to change the world."

Grace was highly invested in hearing about sales numbers, poring over weekly reports when they came in, and she knew the slow trickle wasn't enough to cut it. The pressure was starting to feel heavy on her shoulders, and she kept thinking of something she'd heard years before: "I remember Chris from Anti-Flag telling us, 'Major labels want you because you've already proven you can sell that first 100,000 records. That's what they want to see. Now you have to transcend that and sell a million records. They don't want you to sell 250,000 records, they don't want you to sell 500,000 records. They want you to sell a million records or else you're fucked.' I knew that if we didn't hit it on the first record, the interest on the second record would be next to nothing."

$ $ $

Against Me! had been hit by a truck once before, and it turned out that promoting a major-label debut was like a slow, drawn-out version of that. By the time the band was ready to record *White Crosses,* their second record with Sire, they felt run-down and disoriented from the long, crushing two years they'd invested in *New Wave.*

Some bright spots had certainly peeked out of the darkness. The band had played to their biggest crowds to date, on an arena tour opening for Foo Fighters. They'd planted a punk flag in the sand at dozens of music festivals like Lollapalooza, Coachella, and Reading and Leeds. And even though they were still pissing off unappeasable purists, they were now hobnobbing with celebrity fans. Among them was Bruce Springsteen, who would praise Against Me! as "vicious-sounding" and "soulful" in his memoir years later. But pressure to sell records, combined with a relentless touring schedule and hefty doses of alcohol and narcotics, was pushing Against Me! into fights with disgruntled ex-fans, fights with management, fights with the press, and fights with one another.

In an attempt to salvage the band, Grace tried shaking things up. She first fired Sarig and brought in new management, a decision she hoped would inject new energy into their operation, but which ended up resulting in a lawsuit. The case accused the band of a breach of management contract and maintained that Sarig's company was "entitled to an amount not less than $1,240,000." The case would eventually be resolved, but not before draining the band financially and emotionally for more than a year.

Additionally, the band had a rocky split with Oakes once Grace decided he had to go. After months of feeling at odds with her drummer, she convinced Bowman and Seward that new blood needed to be brought in. "It's been a long time coming," read the May 1, 2009, entry of her blog. "Warren's heart hasn't been in this for a while now." They replaced him with George Rebelo, drummer of the legendary Gainesville band Hot Water Music. It wasn't a permanent solution, but since Against Me! was being held together by duct tape, it'd have to do.

The band returned to Los Angeles in August 2009 to again work with Butch Vig, but the experience didn't hold the same hopeful excitement as *New Wave* had. "They weren't as naive and wide-eyed," Vig remembers. "But the studio was sort of a calming oasis as they were being sued. They were worried about losing everything, but in the studio, we'd close the outside world away and focus on the songs."

White Crosses was released in June 2010, and although it ended up charting higher than *New Wave*—hitting number 34 on the Billboard 200 list—the traditional sales model continued to be ravaged by the internet. A leak of the album surfaced on file-sharing websites three months before its release and was downloaded more than seven thousand times, cutting into sales at the cash register. (Some suspected that Grace herself leaked it, since she was encouraging fans to download it, an accusation she still denies.)

The album was the band's last-ditch effort at translating their sound to a mainstream audience, and its hooky songs sought to bridge the gap between punk and radio rock. *Revolver* described it as "the most polished and pop-inflected album of Against Me!'s polarizing punk career," and the *Village Voice* noted that Grace came off like "a reformed punk anarchist who has mellowed enough to embrace major-label compromise."

The record's lead single, "I Was a Teenage Anarchist," was sonically catchy, but thematically unrelatable to the average radio listener. It saw Grace reckoning with the activist politics she'd been fed as a punk youth, asking, "Do you remember when you were young and you wanted to set the world on fire?" It concluded: "The revolution was a lie!"

The dismissive lyrics rubbed some fans the wrong way, including former tour mates Rise Against, who would pen a song the following year called "Architects," which fired a shot squarely at Grace when it asked, "Don't you remember when you were young and you wanted to set the world on fire? Somewhere deep down, I know you do." When asked about it in an interview, Grace countered, "What's Rise Against's revolution? Is their revolution that a bunch of people are gonna start coming out to their shows and make them really rich? Because that's been done a million fucking times before."

Snippy comments like that were emblematic of Grace's headspace during *White Crosses*' release. She was on edge, at the end of her rope, and out of ideas. Over the course of two album releases, she felt she'd done everything Sire Records had asked of her. She'd answered days' worth of interview questions, she'd filmed music videos she wasn't crazy about, and she'd gritted her teeth through talks of radio singles and chart positions—none of which had made Against Me! the next Clash, like everyone had hoped. Grace was fed up with the whole thing, so when the band was called into Warner's Burbank office for a meeting at the end of September, there was only one thing left that she could think to do. "I went in there with the intention of pissing on the desk," she says. "I was gonna stand up and I was gonna piss on the desk. I'd decided that in my head that's what I was gonna do."

But when the band and their management walked into the meeting, she was unsure at whom to direct her ire. Much of the staff had turned over since Against Me! signed with the label nearly five years earlier, leaving her looking at an unfamiliar set of faces. Tom

Whalley had just moved on from Warner, and CEO Lyor Cohen announced that Rob Cavallo, who'd signed Green Day to the label in 1993, would be stepping in as chairman. There were layoffs and personnel shake-ups as Warner, along with the rest of the music industry, scrambled to adapt to shrinking sales. "I didn't even know who we were talking to," remembers Seward. "All our people were gone."

Grace recalls, "There was this new person who was head of production, who didn't work on *New Wave*. I remember she had a little balcony, and when we walked into her office she was outside chain-smoking a cigarette and quickly put it out and came in."

There was an uncomfortable air in the meeting as the Warner staff danced around difficult topics. "They were saying stuff like, 'The music industry is going through some *changes* and things are being *restructured*,'" remembers Bowman. "I was kind of zoned out, but I remember feeling like, 'Hmm, I think we're getting fired.' It felt like being called into the boss's office."

Grace, on the other hand, understood exactly what was happening: Against Me! was being deprioritized. Warner's contract provided the label with the option to release the band's next record, and she knew then they would not be taking it. The label's weak attempts to placate the band only came off as more insulting. The staff suggested that other *White Crosses* songs be pushed as singles and, ironically, were keen on one called "We're Breaking Up."

"I just went off," says Grace. "I was like, 'You're telling us to make "We're Breaking Up" a single? Well, it's not a fucking single!'" She got so worked up shooting down bad ideas and cutting through bullshit that she'd forgotten her plan to drench the desk in urine.

"When we walked out, I remember thinking, 'Wow, the music industry is in trouble, I guess,'" says Bowman. "And then Linkin Park was sitting in the waiting area to come in and have their turn. That's when I realized: 'Oh, they're not getting fired today. *We're* the dead weight. I get it now.'"

"I walked up to Linkin Park and I said, 'You all have more fucking sway here than we do. You fucking get these dickheads in line!'" says Grace. "They were totally stunned. I didn't wait for them to reply; I just stormed out."

A tense meeting spilled over into a tense car ride. Everyone in the Against Me! camp sat in silence as they processed what had just transpired. The only words Grace remembers anyone saying was what their manager uttered at a red light, to no one in particular: "I have been passed the poisoned chalice."

Things went downhill quickly from there. Grace recalls being hit with a swift one-two punch from their management shortly afterwards: "It was in the same phone call. They were like, 'Warner's gonna let you go. Also, we're gonna let you go.'"

In what seemed like the blink of an eye, the band that had been hailed as the saving grace of rock music was left with no label, no management, no money, no full-time drummer, and no hope. "It felt like the world was against us," says Seward.

The band was staying at the Garland hotel, in Los Angeles, scheduled to leave the next morning for a tour of Australia, followed immediately by a European tour that was not expected to net them a profit. Grace could barely stomach the idea of getting out of bed, let alone flying around the world, so she called her bandmates up to her room. She told them that Against Me! had hit the end of the line and it was time to put it to rest.

The next morning, Bowman, Seward, and Rebelo headed to LAX, got drunk at the airport bar, and flew home. Grace decided to rent a car and make the journey solo. She took a last look at Los Angeles as the interstate carried her home. Three days later, she was back in Florida, where Against Me! had started, and where it now came to an end.

$ $ $

The members of Against Me! regrouped in Florida and, although their future looked grim, Grace decided to hold the band together after all. The frontwoman forced herself to view the collapse of the band's professional relationships not as dead ends but as new beginnings—a complete restart. It wasn't that she'd suddenly found a renewed sense of optimism; it was more that she was about to turn thirty and had devoted her entire life to the band since she was a teenager. She wasn't sure what else to do.

For all the chaos and drama surrounding the band's split with Sire, the aftermath was surprisingly painless. As a peace offering, the label handed them their album in full. "To Craig Aaronson's credit, God bless him, they gave us *White Crosses*," says Grace. "Just fully gave us a record that cost them half a million dollars to make. All the assets, all the rights to the songs, all the videos—just gave us the record as a parting gift. Meanwhile, there are shady indie labels I'm still asking for an honest accounting statement."

The downshift was not without its collateral damage, though. Band members continued to cycle in and out as Grace and Bowman struggled to maintain a steady lineup. Barely holding on—financially, practically, and mentally—the two cobbled together Against Me!'s sixth record. After several contentious experiences with record labels of all sizes, they launched their own label, Total Treble, as a means of distributing it.

Released in January 2014, the album was called *Transgender Dysphoria Blues*. Even without the push of a major label, it ended up being the band's highest-charting release on the Billboard 200, at number 23, though it still failed to break into mainstream radio or outsell their previous records. It did leave a more significant cultural imprint, however. *Transgender Dysphoria Blues* became a landmark album for punk rock, as its songs saw Grace openly and honestly addressing her gender dysphoria for the first time.

Grace became a trans pioneer, helping push the conversation about gender into the national conversation. The more her message caught on among kids who felt the same confusion and frustration over their own bodies, the more new fans Against Me! found themselves playing to. Their crowds suddenly looked a lot more diverse. The gender-fluid newcomers weren't strictly punk rockers, and they weren't much concerned with the band's history of "selling out." They didn't care if Against Me! was on a major label, or any label at all, in fact. All they knew was that when they looked up in awe at the band onstage, they saw Laura Jane Grace, a person they could aspire to.

In 1994, a thirteen-year-old Grace had watched Green Day from a field in Florida, dreaming of one day being the rock star who could command an endless sea of faces, like frontman Billie Joe Armstrong. Her band never quite reached that same level of fame, but it had a similar influence on the generation that came after her, igniting the spark in young listeners that would map out the rest of their lives.

Grace still has her ticket stub from that show in Orlando. The words GREEN DAY have faded away over the years, but they've been replaced by autographs from the three band members, who signed it on a 2017 tour that saw Against Me! warming up their crowds every night. Armstrong took up the most space, writing: "To Laura Jane, double names 4ever, Billie Joe."

"You have that most cliché of dreams as a kid: 'I want to be a rock star,'" Grace says. "The bands I was listening to when I was eight years old, I wanted that to be me. I wanted to be on that stage, I wanted to be on MTV. Even when I found punk, if I really looked inside myself, I had that desire to play music on that scale and reach that many people. That came before punk rock. That was my desire as a musician. That was my dream. It was messy, and it was complicated, and there was more dirtiness in it than I ever could have speculated. There are a lot more compromises you have to make along the way. But at no point did I give up on that dream, even to this day. To me, selling out would be saying, 'I don't have what it takes.' Fuck that. I'm gonna keep swinging for the fences, until I die."

EPILOGUE

AGAINST ME! MIGHT be the last punk band a major label ever cuts a check for a million dollars. In a way, their release from Sire Records marked the end of an era in the music industry. For more than a decade after Green Day kicked open the door in 1994, record companies were willing to take high-risk gambles on promising bands from the punk, emo, and hardcore worlds, dumping resources into them in hopes that they might develop into the next breakout stars. But by the time the Florida band made their exit, it was clear that the well had run dry.

It's not so much that Against Me!'s failure to cross over into the pop world marked an official end to the major-label experiment with punk. It was that, by the time they left Sire, the industry itself looked unrecognizable from what it had been in its golden years. As the digital revolution wreaked havoc on the business, fewer and fewer opportunities could be afforded to bands of their kind.

The walls had been caving in on the music industry for a while. Through the early 2000s, the rise of online piracy cut into sales numbers and reduced profits. For a while, it appeared that record labels were doomed to become a thing of the past. Eventually, though, the industry figured out how to make it work to its advantage and started to treat the internet less like a threat and more like an opportunity. Record labels and tech companies began working in tandem to capitalize on digital sales and streaming music, reversing a hemorrhaging business model.

The business on the whole stabilized around 2012. Global music sales finally saw an uptick after many years of watching lines plunge on just about every sales chart. It wasn't a big increase. In fact, at 0.3 percent up, it was just about the smallest victory to pop open champagne over. "Still, even if it is not time for the record companies to party like it's 1999," the *New York Times* noted, the figures did "provide significant encouragement."

But even as the ship righted itself, the structural damage had been done, and there were casualties. For starters, the CD was dead. After several unsuccessful attempts to stop the bleeding of online piracy with updated compact disc technologies like DualDisc and DVD-plus, labels finally conceded that it was a losing battle and let the format die off. The concept of the album itself was becoming a thing of the past as well. The modern, content-hungry streaming model primed listeners to consume singles and individual tracks, diminishing the significance of the full-length release. Physical music in general became so antiquated that vinyl LPs began to be marketed by retailers like Urban Outfitters as retro relics of a bygone era.

The landscape of the music business changed as a result of these seismic shifts, too. The Big Six were no longer the Big Six. They'd joined forces, disbanded, or eaten one another for survival in the industry's leanest years. Universal Music Group absorbed PolyGram, rendering them the Big Five. Then Sony Music and BMG merged and reduced them to the Big Four, and later Universal also consumed EMI. Sony BMG, Universal, and Warner now constituted the Big Three, if it was still even worth viewing these companies as industry titans.

As the industry shrank and consolidated, the nature of record contracts also evolved. In order to keep seeing as many zeroes on their advance checks as they did in the lucrative nineties, big-name artists became more amenable to signing 360 deals, which gave labels all-encompassing cuts of earnings, on everything from touring income to merch sales. And while that split may have made sense for A-list artists with the selling power to rake in millions, it left behind rookies and midsize artists who depended on those elements as primary sources of income.

The role of A&R scouts changed as well. The ease of new music discovery on the internet relieved the burden—or perhaps the fun— of the job. No longer were A&R reps as invested in the old-fashioned, hands-on work of unearthing and developing embryonic rock acts out of the underground; they could now simply crunch numbers to predict whether an investment would be worthwhile. Scouts began trusting data over intuition, and analytics over gut feelings. Dedication to artistry was superseded by commitment to a brand.

On October 29, 2014, Craig Aaronson, the A&R rep who'd played an integral role in many of the stories in this book, died of cancer at the age of forty-nine. During the time frame documented within this book, Aaronson had ascended from mailroom clerk at Capitol to the president of Sire, and along the way he provided support and opportunities for numerous bands to succeed with him. It's hard not to view his passing as a bookend on the traditional role of a record-label A&R rep.

As for the concept of "selling out," the heated debate largely faded from punk circles. To sell out, there has to be someone looking to buy. And after 2012, major labels were less willing to spend money on bands in this vein. The industry instead turned to its reliable sellers in pop, hip-hop, and its new cash cow, EDM. Only proven acts from the punk world that had been grandfathered in, like Blink-182, Green Day, and Jimmy Eat World, wielded any clout within the major-label system. And thanks to the interconnectivity of social networks, the DIY ethos permeated music subcultures. Bands no longer needed the help of major labels—or any label, for that matter—to reach listeners around the world. Anyone could record an entire album in their bedroom in the morning and have it available online by the afternoon. The mainstream and the underground once again seemed incompatible. After the internet rebalanced the system, the industry looked more like it had before the nineties, when the two worlds were separate and the lines were drawn in black and white.

So it does seem likely that Against Me! will be the last punk band that deposits a hefty check with a major-label logo on it. Then again, if history has proven anything, it's that culture moves in cycles. No one who survived the birth of punk in the late seventies could have predicted that, nearly twenty years later, a band like Green Day would come along, put their own spin on the genre, and carry it to even greater commercial heights. Sex Pistols frontman John Lydon certainly didn't foresee it or welcome it. Ever since Green Day broke in 1994, punk's ornery elder statesman has never been able to resist taking jabs about the trio in the press. "I look at them, and I just have to laugh," he told the *New York Times* in 2018. "They're coat hangers, you know. A turgid version of something that doesn't actually belong to them."

What Lydon failed to grasp is that punk belongs to no one and everyone. It is nebulous and malleable, a reaction to the world around it and a response to what came before it. It perseveres eternally, and only occasionally does mainstream interest circle back around to catch up to it. Although the genre has largely retreated into the underground, the albums documented in this book reached audiences of millions and planted countless ideas in the minds of young listeners. An entire generation gazed up at singers like Laura Jane Grace, Gerard Way, and Brody Dalle and were inspired to go home and start their own bands. So perhaps punk's next form is already on its way. Some thirteen-year-old with a sticker-covered guitar might right now be in a garage in Denton, Texas, or Peoria, Illinois, or Macon, Georgia, writing an album that could one day flip the world upside down.

AFTERWORD

As MENTIONED IN the introduction, this book was never intended to be a comprehensive history of every band that made the jump from an indie label to a major in the fertile post-Nirvana rock boom. Scores of worthy stories had to be cut, for a variety of reasons. For every band that had a chapter devoted to them, another unfortunately fell by the wayside. For every Jawbreaker, a Jawbox. For every Thursday, a Thrice. For every Against Me!, an Anti-Flag. Members of these bands do make brief appearances throughout the chapters as knowledgeable firsthand witnesses, but their own experiences deserve to be expanded upon somewhere. The paperback edition of this book seemed like a fitting place.

This additional section comprises interviews with members of bands who either signed to major labels or turned down the opportunity to do so during the period this book documents. While there is some variation in their stories, it is remarkable how many similarities shine through. The most common sentiment among these accounts, now that time has passed and the dust has settled, is regret over not taking more time to enjoy a rare, fleeting moment in the music industry.

JAWBOX

Immediately after *Nevermind* became a sales phenomenon in 1991, major labels frantically combed through scenes that they hoped were harboring Nirvana's successors. Washington, D.C., seemed like prime real estate to scour. After all, the city was where Nirvana drummer Dave Grohl had cut his teeth years earlier as a member of the punk band Scream. The problem was, Scream and many other bands local to the D.C. area were part of the Dischord Records family, a community that famously operated with a proudly independent ethos. Dischord, co-owned by Fugazi's Ian MacKaye, had little interest in doing business with corporate America. But while Fugazi and many other Dischord acts could not be bothered to hear the pitches of major-label A&Rs, two bands were bold enough to test the waters. Shudder to Think signed to Epic, and Jawbox signed to Atlantic. Jawbox's major-label debut, *For Your Own Special Sweetheart*, hit shelves a week after Green Day's *Dookie* in February 1994. Jawbox may not have hit the heights of rock megastardom that Green Day did, but frontman J. Robbins says they never expected to. The members of Jawbox fully recognized that there were deliberately obtuse elements of their music that would prevent them from ever reaching mainstream audiences. For them, the goal was always to expand the limits of what the band was capable of, and if major labels could provide the resources to do that, they were willing to give it a shot.

What do you remember about the pre-*Nevermind* rock scene?
J. Robbins: I worked at Dischord and was such a fanboy. I ended up being the person who responded to letters. I was working at the Dischord house when Dave Grohl came back, right before the release of *Nevermind*. I remember him playing an early cassette of *Nevermind* for Ian. I heard "Smells Like Teen Spirit" from the other room and I

remember thinking, "Wow, Dave's new band is pretty good!" Dave was someone who everyone knew in D.C., and it was interesting to see him ascend to rock superstardom but also continue to be the guy he was. He was "one of us." So, at that time, to see someone familiar come out of the scene and become something else in the eyes of the world, it was almost symbolic, because people in D.C. who had grown up being inspired by the punk music scene there were very concerned with the idea of authenticity. I really was. I had nothing but disdain for the concept of rock stardom. The idea that someone wanted to be a superstar was ridiculous. What was really important and valuable was what came from the grass roots—people expressing something unique to them. It wasn't about ambition; it was about communication. That was a lesson I learned from going to punk shows in the early eighties—the underground scene had an adversarial relationship with the music business.

How was that view impacted by the success of Nirvana?

There's this ideological aspect of it, which, especially when you're younger, can be very black-and-white. I've gone through a personal journey about it, because I no longer see things in that way. Jawbox was a very hardworking band, and we wanted to continually expand our horizons. We were not actively seeking to be picked up by a major at all. But my theory is that, like any corporation, major labels look for something that's already successful that they can absorb and exploit. Corporate culture looks at everything as an opportunity to make money. If something is off in the distance making money and the corporation doesn't have their fingers in it, well, they'd better get on it. Nobody knew Nirvana was going to be that huge, and then all the labels were like, "Oh shit, oh shit, oh shit!" They knew Nirvana was from a scene where there were lots of other good bands. I think they rushed to throw money at things they didn't understand. If you're throwing money at bands that are successful, you don't have to look far before you find Fugazi, and Fugazi was having none of it. So the next best thing for them would be to take a band from Dischord that would be the next tier, and that was [Jawbox] and Shudder to Think.

Were you open to signing to a major label?

I think we were against the idea, but it kept getting put in our face. And the circumstances under which we signed were very favorable. When you have people knocking on your door over and over again, and you've been a touring band as long as we had, you start thinking that if you had more resources, you could go to new places. But a big part of it for us was the recording—being able to spend time in the studio. Every time we'd made a record, we had to do it from start to finish in five days. If some of the singing was shitty and the playing was loose or we were out of tune, you just had to roll with it. So the idea that we could just relax in the studio and not feel rushed—that was a huge draw, probably the main enticement of the major-label idea. And then also, the idea that we had been working very hard and wondered what it would be like having a label that was interested in actively promoting the band and reaching new people.

Having grown up with that staunchly independent Dischord ethos, did you feel like you were crossing any ethical lines by going to a major?

We had interest from a bunch of labels, but the two that were really wooing us were this guy Michael Goldstone at either CBS or Columbia, I forget, and the other person was Mike Gitter [at Atlantic], who we had known for years through the hardcore scene in Boston. He'd been a hardcore kid, he did a zine, he was in bands, we knew all the same people. In our mind, he was not a music industry person. He was a punk guy we knew and liked. He loved music and had to make a living. And almost everyone we ended up working with at Atlantic, they had been college radio DJs or programmers, they were all music fans. See, the real problem is not with the individuals. It's a structural problem with, dare I say, capitalism. It's the exploitative system where the profit motive comes first, and that's just ingrained in the system. So the people who rise to the very top of that system are, more often than not, not people I can relate to. So Goldstone was fun to hang out with and he had cool stories and all, but Gitter was Gitter! We already knew him. He was our friend. We trusted him. If we were going to sign to any major label, how could it not be with this guy?

But we still agonized over it, because the DIY ethos under which we operated was super important to us. It was central to the way we ran the band. The fact that anyone cared about our band was extremely meaningful to us, so we wanted to respect those people. That human connection is one of the most beautiful things there is. So we were politically resistant to the idea, but practically, we felt like we were bumping our heads on the ceiling of what we could achieve on an independent level. So when Gitter became interested, we made what we called our list of impossible demands. We said, "If they meet all these demands, we'd be foolish not to sign."

What was on the list?
We wanted to control the budget, we wanted to pick the producer, we wanted final say over the artwork, final say over all the musical content. We didn't want to become a widget and be transformed by this change into something a label would consider more palatable. We just wanted to be who we were and use their resources to achieve more. We also wanted to be able to release the vinyl ourselves. So we gave them this list and they said yes to it. It might have just come down to timing. We might've just been in the lucky two weeks when the labels were all just going, "I don't know what any of this means, but if we pass on it we might lose a lot of money."

And do you think it intensified after *Dookie* exploded?
I mean no disrespect to Green Day when I say this, but the essence of what they did as a band was very easy to distill. It's an extremely simple and recognizable sound that is very easy to repeat. That's why there are so many pop-punk bands—because it's easy. And that's not a diss in any way, because it's still hard to write a good song. But that sound was what connected with people enough to make them huge, and then it was very easy to find lots more examples of that. Nobody in their right mind should have ever imagined that Jawbox was gonna have a hit record. It was just never that kind of band. We

were a weirdo band. The things we liked about music were things that make music difficult for people. Whereas Green Day, their songs are quite simple and tuneful. It hits you all at once. You don't have to chew on it.

LESS THAN JAKE

Like Jimmy Eat World, Less Than Jake was approached by Capitol Records when they had only one independently released album and a handful of EPs to their name. The Gainesville, Florida–based ska band was young, inexperienced, and flat broke when they signed a deal with the label at the end of 1995. They ended up releasing two albums with Capitol—1996's *Losing Streak* and 1998's *Hello Rockview*—before internal personnel shake-ups at the label led to their unceremonious departure. And while frontman Chris DeMakes knew it was unlikely that Capitol could make radio darlings out of his scrappy band, he also saw an opportunity to exploit the corporate machine, even if it put him at odds with his bandmates.

You said earlier that Less Than Jake and Jimmy Eat World had the same A&R guy at Capitol. I'm assuming that would have been Craig Aaronson?
Chris DeMakes: Yes.

How did he find you?
So there was a scout underneath Craig named Loren Israel. Loren had heard a song of ours. Loren called all over at southeast United States record stores and finally found a ten-song sampler cassette at some store in Atlanta and said, "Look, I'll give you my credit card number over the phone. I need someone to overnight this to me." The guy at the record store was like, "What the fuck are you talking about?" Loren gets the cassette and he dubs the four best songs on it for Craig. A week or two later, he got a phone call. It was Craig, hysterical, like, "Dude, dude, the song that says 'soundcheck,' who is that?" And Loren was like, "Yeah, that's that band I keep telling you about, you dumbass. That's Less Than Jake."

So he wanted to sign us. That would've been March of '95. I came home from delivering pizzas in Gainesville and saw my answering machine was blinking. There was a message from someone saying, "Yeah, I'm looking for the band Less Than Jake. My name is Craig Aaronson, I'm an A&R rep for Capitol Records." And I'm like, "Who the fuck is yanking my chain here? Is this one of my friends being a dumbass?" Lo and behold, it was real. Craig chased us around the United States on tour that whole year before finally signing us in November of '95. He was just the biggest champion of the band.

How old were you then?
I was twenty-one.

You and Jimmy were on a very similar track. They'd put out just one self-released album and Craig tracked them down when they were eighteen, nineteen. In the same way, too—Loren tracked down a seven-inch they were on with Christie Front Drive.
It was crazy, because we were starting to see the inner workings. We had no idea how any of this shit went down. These scouts and these A&R people, at the end of the day, yeah, it was about units and sales and numbers and all that shit, but most of the guys I met loved music. They eat, breathe, and sleep music 24/7/365. They were constantly looking for talent. Who is the next unsigned, unknown band? We were out in L.A. and getting scouted, Craig took us to a Dodgers baseball game. That's back when you'd get wined and dined on the Capitol card. We got taken to Universal Studios, Magic Mountain, we were eating at fifty-dollar-a-plate restaurants.

Did you get the free-CD tour of Capitol?
Oh, that was every time we went in the building. We'd raid the building and walk out with backpacks full of shit. [*Laughs*] We stayed at some place called Shutters in Santa Monica. Ozzy was there; he was recording *Ozzmosis*. We saw him wandering around a couple of times. It was insane, every kid's dream. We lived it on every level. Jimmy was right there. Then they got dropped from Capitol, Craig got a job at Warner Bros. Then of course *Bleed American* blew up,

which kind of sucked for Craig, because he hadn't had a bona fide hit. He'd go on to have hits with My Chemical Romance, Avenged Sevenfold, and a number of other bands. But Craig re-signed us at Warners in 2002. So we had a couple of major-label runs, and they worked out great for us. I'm sure you know, but Craig passed away in 2014. My son's middle name is Aaronson.

Oh, no kidding. That's so sweet. I also wanted to ask you: This conflict where people were afraid of being called sellouts, like a punk faux pas— did that ever factor into your thinking when Capitol was interested in you?
Well, I mean, we had a song called "Johnny Quest Thinks We're Sellouts," which was kind of a tongue-in-cheek thing before we even had Capitol knocking on our door. I hated it. My band wouldn't even let me do interviews in the nineties, because my position is: Is Michael Jordan a sellout? He just signed a ten-million-dollar contract with Chicago. How's that different? He made ten million because he's fucking worth it. I want to live in a mansion in Beverly Hills sandwiched between Ozzy and Jon Bon Jovi. Fuck you.

So you didn't have any punk hang-ups?
Not me! Our band did. We wrestled with it. We were getting courted by Capitol, and those guys were sending letters to Fat Wreck Chords, wanting to get signed. I was like, "What? I like Fat Wreck, but this is apples and oranges. It's Madison Square Garden versus the Viper Room. It's not even in the same league. Why are we not going for the gold here?" It wasn't just our band; I think most bands in the punk world were so brainwashed that they had to act a certain way. I never called myself a punk rocker. I was just some dude in a band who liked punk rock.

I don't mean to keep comparing you to Jimmy Eat World, but there is a big parallel there. They told me that once they went to Capitol, the people there didn't understand how to market them. Any gains they made were off their own hustle.
Three years before, the label was pushing men who looked like women and the eighties hair poof. Then Nirvana hit, a short four

years before we got signed. They didn't know what to do with us. Loren Israel was probably the closest thing there to a punk rocker. He liked the Clash and the Undertones. No disrespect to anyone there, but they were pen pushers. They were crunching numbers, trying to sell records. Then here comes this ragtag band from Gainesville, Florida. We were crass as hell. We were young and wouldn't shower for days and smoked a ton of grass. We were kids. But even though we were young and partying, our band was *on it*. We knew what we wanted to do, so we marketed ourselves.

So I can totally relate to what Jimmy was saying. [Capitol] would come up with ideas sometimes that were like . . . I remember we showed up one time and they had a stylist. I'm wearing my shorts and my Operation Ivy shirt and there was this woman there wanting to put makeup on us and she had shiny clothes with studs on 'em. We laughed this woman out of the building. In hindsight, we probably could've sold a few more records if we'd just worked with the brass a little more. But we were not putting that shit on. That, to me, was selling out. Being on a major and playing arenas—that wasn't selling out. But being who you weren't—that was. If you listen to those records on Capitol, those records are who we were.

Did Capitol help you with radio singles and things like that?

The record doesn't sound great. How could you get that record on the radio? It's a punk record. I don't say that disparagingly against myself. But if you listen to a track like "Here in Your Bedroom" by Goldfinger or Rancid's "Ruby Soho," and then you listen to *Losing Streak*, I think there are songs on it that are as good as those songs, but we basically made a $100,000 demo. In terms of getting the songs on radio, Capitol tried, but I think out of the thirty bands in '96–'97 that they were trying to get on the radio, we were probably number twenty-nine.

Number thirty was Jimmy Eat World.

[*Laughs*] Yeah. And we knew it, but we didn't care, because we had the machine behind us. We had our CDs in Tower Records and we were making money. We were selling out every place we were going—

eight-hundred- to one-thousand-seat venues. Selling merch that we couldn't stock fast enough. A lot of bands get on majors and they're disappointed their tour support ran out and they're not on the radio. Thank God it wasn't a 360 deal like it is today, because we were making all the door money, all the merch, and that was where the money was. So anything else we could get from Capitol was gravy.

How long did you stay on Capitol?

We got signed in November of '95 and we made *Losing Streak* in '96 and *Hello Rockview* in '98. We made a third record for them in the spring of 2000 called *Borders & Boundaries*. Right before the making of that record, Craig Aaronson and a few marketing people had left. The label was getting restructured. Gary Gersh, the president of the label, left. Craig followed Tom Whalley over to Warner Bros. Depending on who you talked to, we either got dropped or we left of our own volition. We wanted to leave. We didn't want to be there anymore. We knew the writing was on the wall. So we took the record and went to Fat Wreck Chords.

Was that legally complicated?

No, not at all, because we were an afterthought at Capitol. It wasn't like the Foo Fighters or Green Day were leaving. We weren't keeping the lights on. There are a couple songs that are hits among our fans, and if they'd have gotten pushed at radio properly, they could've been hits on radio. But because it went to Fat Wreck Chords, it had *punk cred*! [*Laughs*]

Looking back at the experience, are you glad with the decision to do two records with Capitol? If you could go back, would you do it again?

Oh yeah. I wouldn't change a thing. I wouldn't change anything about my career or my life. The only thing I wish I could go back and redo, and I've talked about this with Hoppus, is that I wish I could go back and soak in the moment more. It went by so fast. It was such a blur. Things were happening so quickly. And the things I thought were important back then turned out not to be important.

And isn't that just life, right? [*Laughs*] I'm glad we didn't have one hit in the nineties, because I don't know if I'd be talking to you now. After almost thirty years, people still want to see the band play. And what a great position to be in.

When you have a hit single or a fan-favorite album, it seems hard to come down from that with grace. You know you won't hit that peak again and it's all downhill. The artists that seem to have the best careers are the ones that did pretty well for a long time.

Yeah. A lot of weird things happen with huge success. Look at Blink—the last fifteen years of their career have been all over the place. It's not just three guys in the band when you get to that point. There's lawyers, there's managers, there's label people, there's the T-shirt people, the truck drivers. It's an organization that's bigger than who you are. And to keep that together is enormous.

ANTI-FLAG

On paper, Anti-Flag seemed like the least likely candidate for a major-label signing. Their songs were forcefully critical of the police state, American imperialism, and the military-industrial complex. Everything about them was unmarketable and unfit for the mainstream. Even their name was problematic in a post-9/11 world. And yet, all it took was hitmaker Rick Rubin showing interest in them for all that to change. When the legendary producer took a liking to the Pittsburgh punk band, numerous other labels suddenly had their curiosity piqued. But at the time, Rubin and his label, American Recordings, were in transition. In 2005, his distribution deal with Island Def Jam (part of the Universal Music Group) expired and he was shopping around for a new deal to handle his roster, which included a diverse lineup of artists from Slayer to Johnny Cash. The members of Anti-Flag found themselves caught up in a label bidding war that sought to obtain not only their band but Rubin himself. It was a rare and unlikely opportunity that bassist Chris "#2" Barker says they proudly rode for all it was worth before ultimately turning Rubin down to sign with RCA.

When you put out *The Terror State* on Fat Wreck Chords [in 2003], was that when major labels started showing interest in Anti-Flag?

Chris Barker: Before *Terror State* came out, Rise Against had signed to DreamWorks. Their A&R guy was this guy Ron Handler. Ron came out to a handful of shows when we took Rise out for our *Terror State* tour—Rise Against, Against Me!, and Anti-Flag, for three months across America in 2004. Their guy came to a bunch of shows and saw we were for real. He expressed interest in wanting to buy *Terror State* from Fat. We had no interest in doing that at all and squashed that relatively quickly. At the same time, unbeknownst to us, Tom Morello—who was the executive producer on *Terror State* and has been the band's mentor since [Rage Against the Machine] took us on tour in 1999—he was playing the record for Rick Rubin. Rick called me one day and said, "Hey, I got your number from Tom and I'd like to see you play." That was really it. It was really important to me, specifically, that we do it. I was really into what it meant to have Rick Rubin like your band, almost to a fault.

Were you a fan of his work?

Yeah, Beastie Boys in particular was a thing that connected me to my cousins and my brother and the people who were older and cooler than me. But I'm the only one in the band who really cares about pop culture. Rick took note of that and would play it up. He'd text me when he was in the studio with Justin Timberlake because he knew that would get a rise out of me. At that time, he was working with Metallica, too. The other guys in the band didn't give a fuck about that. It was very exciting and it led to every major label wanting to sign us.

So he wants to see you play, and so you set up a show?

Yeah, I had to champion the idea to the rest of the band pretty hard. In 2003, our records on Fat did very well and we were consistently selling 200,000 records. But I convinced the guys that this was a valuable thing to do. Rick Rubin is at his peak enigma—you don't see him before the show goes on, and then somehow, first song, he just appears in a booth and is nodding his head. He has a great fucking time, the show is great. He comes up the stairs first and he tells us, "Guys, that was a fantastic show, I think you're a great band, I would love to sign you to American and produce your next album. There are a bunch of people who are gonna come through this door behind me and try to sign you. My recommendation is that you make your record with me. See you later." And we said, "Cool, can we walk out with you? Because it's really important to me that you know we did this show for you. Not so that everyone could come to see Anti-Flag play." If I remember correctly, it was me and Justin [Sane, guitarist] and this guy Dino, who was Rick's assistant and running American at the time. We walk to the back door and it has an alleyway that leads to the main road. We get down to the steps and a car just pulls up as soon as we get there. It was unbelievable to me. It was like a James Bond movie, like he'd hit a magic button. He didn't call anybody, nobody reached out, the car just pulled up and he got in it. We went upstairs and all these people we'd never even told we were playing the show walked in the door one after another, from Sony, Universal, Island Def Jam, on and on.

Obviously Rick saw something in your band, but when you were dealing with these other people who seem to be driven largely by hype, did they know anything about your band? Were they knowledgeable about what you stood for?

We were delegating our interactions, but I was just so all in on Rick that it was in one ear and out the other. To varying degrees, people would know specificities about the band or what our agenda or goals were. It was apparent the ones that were there only because they were like, "If this band gets signed and then at the next meeting our boss says, 'Hey, why didn't you try to sign this band?'" they had to show that they went and tried.

So if Rick had not kicked this off, and these labels were suddenly interested in you, do you think you still would've made the jump to a major?

No, because we wouldn't have had the leverage we had with Rick. If you go in knowing what you want, and somehow have the leverage to do it . . . that's ultimately how we got a two-record deal from RCA, how we were able to maintain our vinyl rights, how we maintained the same royalty rate we got from Fat, why we got mechanical royalties on thirteen songs when the industry standard is ten.

So Rick really wrote you a golden ticket.
Rise Against ended up on Universal because DreamWorks went under or got sold or something. They ended up with this woman Polly Anthony, who passed away a few years ago. They conglomerated so much work in trying to bring American to Universal that they saw us as a major coin. They offered us the fucking sun and the moon. The contract came in and Rick Rubin said, "I won't do this deal. I can't let you guys sign this deal." And we were like, "Well, this is the deal we want. It gets us you. This is what we think we should do." And he said, "Well, I'm out if you sign this deal."

What was the line in the sand for him?
What he told us was, "You need to sell a million records for this deal to be a success, and I don't ever want to be in a situation where any amount of sales is a failure. I'm looking out for your career. You will be done at the end of this. You'll do one record and then they'll leave you." He knew the music industry was on its last legs. The writing was on the wall. But what was interesting was that we immediately left the room with that contract and gave it to Matt Marshall at RCA and said, "If you match this, we'll sign with you today," knowing Rick wasn't gonna do it anyway. So we used this bargaining chip that didn't exist to get RCA to write us that contract. We signed it and it was over. So the fork in the road was: Get a more traditional major-label deal with far less money, far less control, but you get Rick Rubin, or we dupe this label into thinking Rick Rubin was giving us all this shit he really wasn't.

Were you confident about your band then? Or did it feel like you were getting away with something?

Pat [Thetic, drummer]'s confidence in these situations is un-fucking-believable, because he doesn't care. He doesn't play music because he likes the drums or he likes rock 'n' roll. He plays music because he wants to meet people and communicate his ideas. For me, I like rock 'n' roll and when people clap for me. My ego is there, though I try to keep it in check. A great example was, we met with Jimmy Iovine around this time. Jimmy's office is literally behind a bookcase. You pull the book and the door opens. I believe it was "Hollaback Girl" that was jamming in the room; it was about to come out. He turns the music off when we enter and he says, "Oh, that's the new Gwen Stefani. It's gonna be a hit. Sit down, boys." A very major-labelly old-money guy thing to do. We sit down in the nice leather chairs and the guy comes in and pours us all drinks. He proceeds to ask us questions about what the band is about and what we stand for. While we're answering, he stops and says, "I know, like Bono and U2. Let me play this for you." He goes to the stereo and plays us the "unos, dos, tres, catorce" song, which also wasn't out. He cranks it up. Justin puts his little earplugs in. Pat raises his hand to Jimmy and goes, "Turn it down, please." [*Laughs*]

But this is the only time I'll speak ill of Rick, which purely comes down to finances. He had (International) Noise Conspiracy at the time. He had their record done, and he was trying to find a new home for American so they could release it. So it was frustrating that our friends spent two years or whatever making that record and they couldn't get it out. And the most powerful guy in music is the one who recorded it! We were getting these little horror stories about having one song on a mixing desk for a week. That means that a studio, which could cost anywhere from $500 to $1,000 a day, they've got to mix one song for a week.

Our biggest record is *For Blood and Empire*, which is the first major-label release. There are a handful of songs on there that did really well. But one of my good friends that I play hockey with, he loves Rick Rubin and his production. He will remind me once a year, "Could you imagine if Rick Rubin had produced 'This Is the End'? Your life would be different!" Maybe it would. That part is so far out of my control.

What did you see as the band's ceiling?

In the past, any time we'd gotten interest from the mainstream, the answer that came back was "We can't do anything with this; you're called Anti-Flag." We were very aware of the glass ceiling involved in what we're doing. Every record we do, people still try to take our songs to radio. And I'm like, "Just give me the money and I'll go buy fucking scratch-off lottery tickets with it." [*Laughs*] They always go, "We can't say the band's name on the radio without people calling and being like, 'You commie sons of bitches!'" It's a major hindrance. It doesn't hurt us that bad on satellite radio, which has shown us love, but it wasn't played on MTV like *American Idiot* was.

Were you worried about being perceived as selling out? How did you think your fans would react to a band called Anti-Flag signing with RCA?

What a lot of bands consider backlash in terms of reactions from the punk rock audience, whether it was Jawbreaker fans refusing to attend their shows or Against Me!, who I saw firsthand have their tires slashed or have people protesting outside the shows because it was $15 instead of the usual five, a lot of those things were self-inflicted by the rules that were set up by the band. It's very difficult to have your favorite band tell you they want to play for "a plate of food and a place to rest" and then you have to spend $20 to see them play. I understood that. Against Me! was our generation's Fugazi, and I think that's what hurt the heart of that scene—this underground network of venues that were thriving because Against Me! lifted a whole scene up, because their songs were so fucking good. So when that was happening, I felt bad for them. We were on tour and they were being jerks to us, but I still felt bad. I understood they were lashing out at us because of the growing pains of what was going on.

But I also have to look back on what we endured as a band. We would play shows where people would pull guns on us. We'd play shows where the security guards would turn around and spit on us while we were playing. We were a band called Anti-Flag playing shows post–September 11. It was really fucking difficult, and it was scary to be anywhere in the South in 2002. So whenever there were crust-punk kids in the parking lot playing Against Me! songs and changing their lyrics to be about how shitty they are, it was like, "That's okay! We'll take that." The reason I bring that up—the angry Against Me! fans—that happened at a venue called Trees, in Dallas. Three years prior, we'd played that venue with the Dropkick Murphys and the stage was covered in glass beer bottles that were being thrown at us. I'd gladly take the kid who's outside and is just a little mad. This was violent.

So, overall, the major label experience was net positive?
Oh yeah. I truly believe it's why we're a band today. I think a lot of our contemporaries that had that early-aughts success but didn't [sign to a major], it was hard to go back to being in a band and play smaller shows. The cool thing for us was, there were no peaks.

MURDER BY DEATH

Eyeball Records released debut albums from a trifecta of exciting new bands in the early 2000s. Thursday and My Chemical Romance, of course, would eventually end up setting sail for major labels, but the third band, Murder by Death, carved out their own distinct path. While they never felt comfortable signing a proper contract with a big label, they did accept a distribution offer that would help get their records widely released but would also allow them to maintain their artistic autonomy. As a result, Murder by Death never hit the commercial peak that some of their peers did, nor did they ever get much critical praise. Their wholly unique blend of gothic punk and macabre Americana largely flew under the radar of industry tastemakers. But the band never crashed and burned under the weight of inflated expectations, either. Instead they've enjoyed a decades-long career over which they've maintained complete control, as well as a cult following. It's a route that frontman Adam Turla says has had its successes and its struggles.

I get how My Chem and Thursday got hooked up with Eyeball Records, being from Jersey, but how did your band, from Indiana, get connected to them?

Adam Turla: It's kind of wild. Our seventh show we ever played was at this anarchist bookstore. Thursday was supposed to play a show in Indianapolis; it might've been their first tour. The show fell through, like everything did in 2001. We said they could jump on our bill and we'd give them our money, because it was only like sixty bucks or something. Geoff really liked our band, and we thought they were great. He gave me a burned copy of *Full Collapse* that they'd just finished recording. We owe a lot to Thursday in the sense of them pushing us to take our band seriously. It was our seventh show and they were saying, "You should make a record, and you should put it out on this label." That gave us a lot of confidence.

Eyeball became a bit of a hot spot after Thursday and My Chem went major. Did you ever get sucked into that world?

There was a little bit of it. We had the fortune of becoming friends with those guys when we were really young and playing those formative shows with them. We got to watch as My Chem and Thursday made bigger and bigger moves, and we'd open those gigs. And we'd see the shows be well attended or see industry people around suddenly. We were coming from such an indie and punk world that we rolled our eyes at a lot of industry stuff, because we never dreamed anything would ever happen for us. We're this weird band that's not part of any scene. Eyeball and other people would say, "You guys are going places." And we'd always be like, "Eh, are we?" But we certainly had some courting and people sending us cases of whiskey.

But we never found the label we thought would let us do what we want and take us seriously as outsider artists that we saw ourselves as. At least Thursday and My Chem could be put under the broader banner of the emo or punk worlds. They had a sound other people were already emulating. They just defined their sound in a clear way. But for us it was like, "Hm, I don't think there are a lot of people starting gothic cello indie bands." So I think we didn't take it seriously when there was big talk around us. All we wanted was to be able to do it and not be broke.

Do you think the offers were genuine?

We got it all. We did get some legal offers, but for us, the labels that we imagined would know what to do with us, those never seemed to work out. What ended up happening was, probably through My Chemical Romance, who I'm sure said nice things because they're good dudes, we ended up in 2005 signing with ADA distribution, which was through Warner Bros. That's how we put out *In Bocca al Lupo*. It was the same thing Lucero did. It was the Triple-A baseball of major-label deals. They weren't gonna put their best guys on it. They just gave you a budget and let you market how you wanted to. They financed your creative ambition.

Our best bet was always gonna be: Are we gonna be a cult band that gets popular or not? We understood that. We knew our limitations, we knew our strengths. It happened—not in the way I thought it would—but it definitely happened. We've been way more successful and had way more longevity than I ever dreamed of.

Do you think doing a big major-label signing the way My Chem or Thursday did would've impeded that progress?

I think I would've been a pain in the butt. I was so adamant about making this weird record that didn't sound like what anyone was doing at the time. In 2005, there was no Americana scene. Heavier music like screamo was big. The indie stuff was just starting to creep out, like Death Cab for Cutie and whatnot. That stuff was so much more . . . what's that word? Like, kinda cute . . .

Twee?

Twee, yeah! Exactly. All the indie that was getting big in 2005 was kind of twee, and we weren't that. We'd come up playing with punk bands. And with the name Murder by Death, we couldn't be twee people. So who would even know what to do with this record? It was a pure creativity explosion, for better or worse. Our progression was so gradual because we've never had "a moment."

Time seems to have proven that to be the better path, no?

It's hard to say. You can't really know for sure.

DASHBOARD CONFESSIONAL

It's no coincidence that new life was breathed into the punk and emo scenes around the time the internet became more commonplace on home computers. These traditionally disconnected communities were able to easily congregate on message boards and chat rooms in the early 2000s. The problem was, interest in this music was often growing too fast for those involved to keep up with the demand. Vagrant Records was a relatively young independent label at the turn of the century that was flush with rising acts, including Alkaline Trio, the Get Up Kids, and Saves the Day. Their stacked roster would have made for a hefty workload for any small label, but it was the addition of a solo acoustic act that really stretched Vagrant to its limits.

Chris Carrabba, who went by the moniker Dashboard Confessional, toured relentlessly to support his first album with Vagrant, 2001's *The Places You Have Come to Fear the Most*. He grinded away and saw his celebrity within the scene begin to rise as a result. It wasn't hard to figure out why. Carrabba had clean-cut good looks, arms full of colorful tattoos, and an arsenal of heart-on-sleeve sing-along anthems. After a year of building an audience within punk and emo circles, Carrabba was given the rare opportunity to perform on *MTV Unplugged* in 2002, and he crossed into the mainstream almost immediately afterwards. *The Places You Have Come to Fear the Most* and its follow-up, *A Mark, a Mission, a Brand, a Scar*, both went gold for Vagrant.

But the overwhelming success of Dashboard Confessional and other Vagrant acts pushed the indie label into some uncomfortable positions. A 2002 issue of *Punk Planet* detailed how Vagrant's founders, Rich Egan and Jon Cohen, were begrudgingly entering into problematic partnerships with larger labels and distributors to meet market demand, which only served to embroil them in legal battles and contract disputes. But even as major labels lined up to sweep the extremely marketable Carrabba away to a more stable home, the songwriter remained loyal to his Vagrant family for many years. Eventually, Vagrant partnered with Interscope so they could shoulder some of the workload and responsibilities, which Carrabba says offered him the best and worst of both worlds.

When you joined Vagrant, it was a hot time for the label. They had Saves the Day, the Get Up Kids, Alkaline Trio. Can you tell me about the vibe of Vagrant during that era?

Chris Carrabba: I was pretty close with many of the bands that were signing to Vagrant in seemingly rapid succession. I was a huge fan of Face to Face and those other bands. The vibe I got was that it was a label willing to go left of center in an already left-of-center genre. I'm sure you remember those days, when you'd buy what a label put out because they were a purveyor of taste.

The logo meant something.

It did. And Vagrant had this feeling that it was us against the world. That's speaking strictly as a fan. It seemed like if they believed in a songwriter, they were willing to put their backs into it. Many of their bands seemed like they'd be the outlier on any other label.

After your first album with Vagrant, *The Places You Have Come to Fear the Most*, came out, it seemed like things took off pretty quickly for you. Can you tell me what you remember about that time?

It really wasn't overnight. It was a slog. The first week of record sales is important, and I remember being told that there weren't that many sold. It really was a longer campaign for the ball to start rolling.

What do you think most helped propel it?

Touring and Napster. Before I was on Vagrant, my first record, *The Swiss Army Romance*, was on my great friend Amy [Fleisher Madden]'s record label, Fiddler Records, then she sold it to Drive-Thru. I didn't really have distribution. If you were curious about it, you couldn't find it. That's what Napster did for everybody. It made everyone a distributor of the bands they loved.

That's funny, because most music industry people will talk about Napster with such bitterness.

Well, I also recognize that it destroyed the commerce of it all. But I personally had no tools by which I could reach anyone. It was like a college radio station, a copy of *MRR*, and a distributor all rolled into one. I'd play a show sometimes and, because of Napster, the people there would go home and download the record that night and send it to their friends, and then I'd show up in some other town four hours away the next night and be shocked to find people were singing my songs.

A year after that first record with Vagrant came out, you did an *MTV Unplugged* session, which seemed to be something typically reserved for legacy artists. How did you get that prestigious opportunity as a newer artist?

The creator of the show is a guy named Alex Coletti. Alex is nothing if not a huge music fan. He's constantly at shows digging for new music. So he found himself at my show at that place in downtown New York that had a Volkswagen inside.

Wetlands.

Wetlands, yes. He came and said hello. He said, "I have this show called *MTV Unplugged*." I remember he said it like that, too, as if anybody wouldn't know what that was. It disarmed the bigness of it. He said when he created it, he envisioned the audience singing along, like they were doing at my shows. He asked me to do it, and was kind of putting his career on the line. I jumped at it, and it happened pretty quick. We were talking about overnight success earlier, and after that it went pretty fast.

It seems like one of the biggest hindrances of an indie label is that they are often unable to get their artists on the radio. But you were unique in that you were getting radio and MTV play. How did those doors open for you and not some of your peers?

It's such a good question. I've considered it but still don't have the answer, other than saying that the people at Vagrant were able to build some relationships at some of these places like MTV.

But even so, it seemed like you had a different kind of celebrity than your peers. I'm thinking specifically of your famous *SPIN* cover the following year. You kind of became this emo sex symbol.

There were so many things we said no to. There's a long history, as you can attest to, of things working awkwardly for indie rock and punk rock acts. There was an ethos, there was a rule book, and we followed them all. We said yes so sparingly to things. It felt risky. I don't think I noticed until later the sexiness of it. I don't perceive myself that way. To be frank, I didn't have a lot of confidence. But then I learned how to make it work. I've watched the WB, I could figure out how to do smoldering eyes. [*Laughs*] So I took risks. None of it was hubris. I was green and didn't realize the riskiness of it. As a kid from the scene, I was change averse.

What were you most worried about? Losing cred?
Not my personal cred, but the trust you build with a word-of-mouth success story. I didn't want to trade on it or disappoint them. It was a personal thing. I didn't want to let anybody down, but I also wanted to succeed with music. I believe both can be done, but just trying isn't a failure.

What are the growing pains of having a rising celebrity?
Well, haters, for one thing. There were plenty of people who didn't like what I was doing. But the actionable nature of dislike—"How can I make sure this guy knows I don't like him?"—that was new to me. I didn't love that. I also didn't love the responsibilities thrust at me and my peers. I think the same things were happening with New Found Glory and My Chem, where you were being made to feel like you could break this out for everybody and wouldn't that be fantastic, but also don't fuck this up for everybody, because that will ruin everything you care about.

Something I learned recently was that your celebrity at that time was such that you needed bodyguards.
I want to be careful to not call them bodyguards. They were two guys who were heads of security. Security wasn't something we thought we needed until we started butting up against really violent bouncers that were beating on the kids that were moshing in a feel-good way. You don't really mosh to Dashboard, but you might bounce

around a little. I remember being in San Diego, watching a security guy choke out a seventeen-year-old kid, and thinking, "Oh my God, we gotta find a way to protect these kids." It was that coupled with the size of our fan base growing so quickly. I literally couldn't get in or out of the club without being shepherded. There was also a period where I couldn't go to the movies, I couldn't go to the mall, I couldn't go to the grocery store. I'm always happy to stop and chat, but to make no progress throughout the day became difficult.

I'm sure also that due to the nature of your music, these interactions were probably quite personal.

Yeah, you'd be right about that. And I don't mind hearing it. I know a lot of people say it makes them feel uncomfortable. General interactions with people is something I feel comfortable with. The specifics of people telling me how they feel about my music, even if it's for difficult reasons—I'm also comfortable with that. But there was just a period of a year and a half or two years where I just couldn't function without feeling weird about it. It wasn't like I was Gwen Stefani, where, when I'm home from the road, I couldn't walk down the street. It was specific to being on the road. I'm sheepish about talking about it. I was never comfortable with it.

I assume that with how fast you were growing, people from major labels must've taken an interest in you. Is that the correct assumption?

That is the correct assumption. It was all the people you'd think—Interscope, Atlantic, MCA, Geffen, DreamWorks, Warner Bros., Sony. You name it. Just about everybody put in a call to have a lunch or dinner.

How did those meetings feel?

I'm pretty suspicious of that stuff. I came up under the assumption that you won't be Green Day, you will be Jawbreaker—the two best bands in my opinion. If Jawbreaker couldn't break out on a major—and neither could Jawbox or the litany of others who tried—it just seemed like: *This will ruin you.* But I don't think that's true [now]. I do wish I'd had slightly less trepidation. I might've taken more risks in my career, but also I probably would've been treated as poorly as those who were treated poorly. But I came from a world that was like, [*Majors*] *don't want to help you, they just want to take it from you.*

So much major-label support seems to come down to how well that first single does or doesn't do. But Vagrant seemed to have more of a familial vibe that would have supported you no matter what.

My arc on Vagrant is what it is—it was success, and then more success, and more success. All of it from the benefit of their team's hard work. When the radio single possibility came around, they were looking at it as a lotto win. They were still going to work on the whole record, whether we got [radio play] or not. And if we did get it, they felt like they couldn't lean too far into it, because we couldn't count on another one, whereas that's what's expected everywhere else.

When you became Vagrant's bestselling act, did that change the dynamic there at all? Was there any jealousy directed toward you?

Oh, probably. I did feel a bit set apart. Some of it was on me. What do they call it—new money guilt? But compared to the major labels, I felt like I was being cared for in a way that wasn't defined by who had sold how many records. It was being part of this thing where we're all looking out for each other. Maybe some of that was naive.

There was a moment where emo crossed over into the mainstream, and a lot of the artists did well, but very few of the records actually went gold. Your second record with Vagrant, *A Mark, a Mission* . . . , was one of the few to pass the half-million mark. What did having a gold record feel like from your perspective? Did things change for you?

I'll tell you, it felt great. It felt really great. I don't want to say I did it without compromise, but I made a huge effort to not compromise. But I'm also aware it probably would've sold more if I'd compromised on some things. So there's some of it where I think I should've pulled out the stops and lived in the moment I was in, and not the moment I was afraid of being in. Your second question about if it changed things for me—it was more of a reflection of how things were changing for me. It was evidence that we were a big band.

A hypothetical: Say at this time you could've gone gold for Vagrant or platinum for a major label. Which would you have taken?

At that time, I think I would've chosen gold with Vagrant. What's that saying? You gotta dance with the one who brung ya. I think after a while, Vagrant understood: *This kid's not leaving. We're gonna have to figure out how to buoy this success story.* I think they were coming up with plans instead of sitting by. They were modeling themselves after Sup Pop and Epitaph, and I believed they could [become that], and I think I made the right choice.

Eventually you did enter a deal with Interscope. How did they come into the picture?

Vagrant was pretty candid with me: "Your growth has now gotten to the point that we can't do this without assistance and still be able to service the other bands." I'm guessing on the details, but they wanted to possibly do a co-ownership with Interscope, or certainly a distribution component. They were telling me that as I was getting offers from all of these labels, including [Interscope]. So I figured: If I could find a way to be on a major label but still work with these [Vagrant] people, I think I could see a road for avoiding the pitfalls.

That was when Jimmy Iovine was heading Interscope. How was that relationship?

Our relationship, frankly, was great. I have a lot of personal affection for Jimmy, so I did feel good about who I was working with at the top. But I still felt as uncomfortable in that system as I thought I was going to feel.

What was uncomfortable about it?

Well, it was pretty clear to me that radio was now a necessary piece of the puzzle. And it was also clear to me that their head of radio did not think I had any radio songs. So it was either that I was going to have to prove them wrong or prove that we could have a successful record without that piece, and I think we succeeded at the latter.

Say you could go back to 2001. Dashboard has just signed to Vagrant. What advice do you give a young Chris Carrabba?
That's a great question. I would say . . . There may not be harm to come by allowing yourself to enjoy it.

Enjoying your moment can be challenging, too, though. Active appreciation is very difficult.
It is. But here's my encouragement: With some frequency, go out with your people—your close people—and go: *Isn't this great?*

THE BRONX

Joby Ford, founding guitarist of the Bronx, once claimed that his band landed a manager after their first show and had A&R reps scouting them as early as their second. The Los Angeles–based band's rowdy punk sound and riotous performances netted them immediate label attention, and they soon had more interest than they knew what to do with. Ultimately, it would be Island Def Jam who persuaded them to come aboard. But by the time the band's major-label debut, *The Bronx*, was released in the summer of 2006, Island Def Jam was in transition and didn't put much effort into promoting it, Ford says. The band and the label released only one album together before parting ways. Although the Bronx's major-label tenure was brief, the band did manage to squeeze their contract for every last dollar and purchased a studio, assuring that they could continue to make music, no matter what label would be releasing it.

It seemed like the Bronx got on a major label pretty quickly. You did that one record with Ferret and then went to Island Def Jam. How'd that happen?

Joby Ford: We'd made a record and Island Def Jam basically paid Ferret to cover the cost of Ferret putting it out, because it was already done. So they signed the band for record number two. I had never been in a signed band. None of us had. It was crazy. The band I was in previously, before I started the Bronx, was this band called Letdown. There was this club up on Santa Monica called the Garage. My buddy booked the Tuesday night punk night. So we'd play once or twice a month. We were so bad that we were the last band on a Tuesday and it's 11:30. There are two people in the club, we start playing, and by song two they're gone. The bartender waves his hands and says, "Guys, guys, guys. There's nobody here. What do you say you pack it up and everybody goes home early?" [*Laughs*] And I went from nights like that to being . . . I think we got twelve different offers from labels [for the Bronx].

Wow. So what do you attribute that to?
Just fucking around, pretty much. We made some demos—this was early on in using the internet for music, kind of the Wild West then. There was this guy we knew who worked for a record label— I think Jive Records. And so we sent him this three-song demo we did. Then he contacted a guy by the name of Jonathan Daniel, who manages Fall Out Boy and Weezer. At the time, I think he managed Gilby Clarke. He came in and liked the band. He was like, "Let's put you in the studio with Gilby Clarke." I was like, "What?!" This all happened within a week. So all of a sudden we had this management deal, and he was the one who ramped it up. We played this show at the Troubadour, opening for this band called the Dragons, who eventually canned their guitar player, who would end up joining the Bronx. So [Daniel] basically put all these A&R guys in the room together and we had a good show, and that's how he got bands signed.

But we used to fuck around. We'd get these emails and we never took anything seriously. We'd get emails from labels and reply in Morse code. We were just fucking around. But in those days we got so many free records, and that's all we cared about. "If we're gonna take a meeting with you, we need the Who's box set." And they'd send it to you!

Did you keep them or sell them?
I kept them.

OK. Because I've talked to so many people who said they'd go to the Capitol Records building and then sell the box sets at Amoeba.
Oh yeah, there was some of that going on. But I never asked for anything I didn't want. They'd throw that stuff at you all day long. This one dude from I think Roadrunner, he was like, "Send me the rock"—that's what they called [our music]. So I told him to give us his FedEx number to send him a CD. So he gave us the FedEx number and we filled the whole FedEx box full of rocks. Just that kind of stuff. Looking back, we were maybe trying to build a lore.

Were you doing that type of stuff because you weren't interested in the offers? Or was it a deliberate way to make yourself seem cool?
I don't know. We were just jerks. I never thought we'd get a record deal, or that eighteen years later I'd still be playing my guitar for a living.

Why did you decide to go to Island Def Jam eventually?
We liked their roster of bands. It seemed like the right place to associate with at the time, and then a year later everybody got fired and they got a new president. When our major-label debut came out, it got shelved.

Which one got shelved?
Our second record. Nobody at the label did anything.

Oh, so it was released, it just didn't get a marketing push.
Oh yeah, it came out. But at that point, Island Def Jam turned into a pop label. L.A. Reid was there. People trip out when I tell them this, but the Bronx and the Killers got signed at the same time, by the same

guy. We used to play a lot of concerts together, which blows people's minds, because they obviously have gone on to be this huge band. They'd take our mariachi band on arena tours. We did a Christmas song together. After all these years, we still talk.

Going to a big label is a big decision as it is, and then suddenly your people are gone. Was that scary?

Probably. But then I had this idea. I think we spent like $275,000 on our second record. Like, a stupid amount of money. And then on our third record, they owed us more because of the way the deal was structured. So I told them, "Look, if you guys give us X amount of dollars, I can buy a studio." [*Laughs*] So they bought us a recording studio. Or they gave us the money and we found stuff on Craigslist. But after our A&R guy, Rob Stevenson, got canned, then we had two A&R guys and nobody knew what was going on. So I asked to be let go and they said, "Cool." So Island Def Jam paid for our second record, which they didn't really work on, they bought us a recording studio and we recorded our third record, and then they let us go. I was like, "What is going on here?"

It seemed like a time when they were just cutting their losses. Geoff from Thursday said the same thing—that they were on the hook for another record with Island, and he went in there just man-to-man with L.A. Reid and asked to be let go, and they parted on a handshake.

Yeah, that's the kind of money that was being thrown around in those days. Looking back on it, I think that was the end of it. It was an interesting experience. I'm glad I got to make one of those big-budget major-label records that I'll never get to make again. At the time you're like, "Of course I'll have the ahi tuna delivered. Can I get a bottle of whatever?" [*Laughs*]

In the nineties, when more bands were doing deals with major labels, there was this fear of a backlash over selling out. Is that something you guys worried about?

Of course, yes, because we grew up in those times. The reason there was such a backlash and people were turning on bands for selling out is because everybody was making a lot of money—independent bands. SST artists were moving tons of records. Early Epitaph stuff, those records were selling millions of copies. But then the band goes and does a commercial, and that just made them look like they were total sellouts. Now, I think if you got a sync in a commercial or a movie, people are like, "Yeah, all right!" It's almost championed now.

When you went to Island, did you hear from your fan base? Were people pissed?

Yeah, of course. We'd played a handful of shows and got picked up, whereas some bands had been struggling for years. We were on tour with Thursday, actually, and Piebald was opening. The street teamers would come up and plaster the whole club with posters promoting your release back then. And I was like, "Man, this is getting a little intense." But Travis [Shettel] from Piebald goes, "I wish someone would do that for our band." He was kind of pissed at me. It was just stuff like that. If I had to go back, I'd probably do the same thing. Those were good times.

CAVE IN

Cave In formed in the Massachusetts suburbs in 1995 and spent a few years carving out their place in the Boston hardcore scene among other heavy up-and-comers like Converge. The scrappy group of Methuen teenagers worked out the kinks in their style over a few stray releases with local indie label Hydra Head Records. Then, in 1998, armed with a newly solidified lineup—lead guitarist Stephen Brodsky, rhythm guitarist Adam McGrath, drummer J.R. Conners, and bassist Caleb Scofield—they put themselves on the map with *Until Your Heart Stops*, a debut album so heavy it shook the ground throughout New England. It was an entirely original onslaught of chaos that patched together monstrous chugging riffs and flashy metal shredding, and it was glued together with deep, full-throated roars that hit like a sonic boom.

But two years after practically revolutionizing the hardcore genre with *Until Your Heart Stops*, Cave In surprised everyone with their follow-up, *Jupiter*, a musical 180 that did away with the bellowing growls and cratering riffs that hardcore kids had come to love. It was more mellow and spacey, and lacked the crushing breakdowns that could soundtrack a stage dive. Although *Jupiter* may have left fans divided, major labels were intrigued by Cave In's new, more marketable sound. The band eventually signed with RCA Records for the release of 2003's *Antenna* and spent two months in Los Angeles's Cello Studios with producer Rich Costey, trying to shape their evolving musical identity into something that might be a smooth fit for the radio.

Cave In didn't really live up to their commercial potential on *Antenna*. After its first single, "Anchor," failed to connect with radio listeners, RCA wasn't able to justify pouring more resources into the album or funding their follow-up. The band retreated back to Hydra Head for their next record, *Perfect Pitch Black*, a Frankenstein's monster of contrasting elements from the two markedly different eras of Cave In. The band has soldiered on as an indie operation in the two decades since its major-label days, releasing one genre-bending album after another. Bassist Caleb Scofield, whose bone-rattling bass tones and battering-ram vocals helped make Cave In a destructive force, tragically died in 2018, but his bandmates keep his memory alive every time they get onstage, playing with an intensity that sounds like they're trying to punch a hole through the earth.

You made a pretty drastic shift in your sound on *Jupiter*. Can you tell me what effect that had on Cave In's audience?

J.R. Conners: I remember people fucking hating us. I remember playing the Palladium and being spit on, having shit thrown onstage.

Adam McGrath: It was pretty polarizing. People were big fans of *Until Your Heart Stops*. Even people close to us said they weren't really sure about what we were doing. But we were confident in doing our own thing. When we had that new lineup with Caleb, we felt like that was a really solid group to push forward with. I certainly think we lost fans, but I also think we gained some. And there were people who came with us for the entire time. It also opened up new doors for us to play different types of gigs. All of a sudden we were playing with Jets to Brazil or Neurosis or Rainer Maria or Rival Schools.

When did bigger labels start taking an interest in you?

AM: On the tours we did for *Jupiter*, people started sniffing around. We'd start to meet different characters in the city of Boston who'd claim they were part of the music industry, or that they were lawyers who could get us connected to certain people.

When you met with A&R reps, did they understand what you were about?

AM: We were so young, and were just trying to feel these people out. There were some that were really nice, and there were some that were looking at us in business terms and had no idea what we were about. We were always trying to find their mistakes—the things in their careers that didn't work out—because they always wanted to talk about the things that did work out.

Stephen Brodsky: Yeah, it was only their success stories. They tried to bury everything else. At one meeting, the dinner was pretty chill, but by the end of it, this person started getting ramped up about how much he wanted to sign the band. He sort of went on this spiel, and at the end of it he said, "I'll go over the cliff with you guys! We'll go over the cliff together!" That stuck with us and ended up being used later in our song "Trepanning."

Which labels were interested?

AM: We talked to Virgin, Capitol—there were a few. There was still a bit of that money around where they were buying us dinners and taking us to the record store and saying, "What do you guys need?" or "What do you guys need for jeans?" Just stupid Hollywood stuff you'd see in movies. I believe we were choosing between Capitol and RCA, and it was so strange. They flew us from Boston for this meeting with Capitol. They said they really wanted to meet with us. There was a gentleman we met at the Chelsea Hotel, and I remember the dude sat down with us and he fell asleep. [*Laughs*] The vibe wasn't that he was bored with us, it was that he worked too hard or partied too hard or something. That meeting was supposed to show us how much they wanted us, but he fell asleep and it was weird.

JC: We also started hearing that Capitol was doing a big shuffle and a lot of people were leaving. But RCA seemed solid. Capitol seemed really shaky.

What about RCA ultimately won you over?

SB: Our A&R, Bruce Flohr. His success stories were Foo Fighters, Dave Matthews Band—not necessarily a band where we loved their music, but it was obvious that the band had something going on where they were selling a lot of records and had people coming to see them.

JC: He'd also signed the band Hum, which was one of my favorite bands.

SB: And he was at the label for fourteen years, he was the head of A&R, and he was this really cocky dude.

AM: And I felt like he was going to let us do what we wanted to do, even though I don't know if we even knew what we wanted to do at the time. He was always saying, "We need a 'Black Hole Sun.'" We were Methuen kids getting wined and dined in Los Angeles. We'd do demo nights with pretty big producers. We recorded with Mark Trombino at Sunset Sound, in the room where Van Halen recorded. I saw the room Prince used and the Doors used, and the Rolling Stones. There was a basketball hoop outside, and [Flohr] was like, "If you get this basket, I'll give you $500." And I got it in and he gave me $500 out of his pocket!

Were you worried about getting backlash from fans about going to a major label?

SB: I think we'd already gone through that with *Jupiter*.

JC: I remember feeling like "We already have fans who hate us and love us. What does it matter at this point?" I always remember that quote from Jason Newsted, who said, "Yeah, we sell out. We sell out every place we play!" It became a joke to sell out. Who gives a fuck? I also remember thinking, "Let's try this. If it goes somewhere, it'd be fucking cool. If it doesn't, we were a band long before this moment and we'll continue being a band long after it. So why not take the chance on trying?" As a kid, you can't help but picture being on a major label and all this stuff happening, you know?

SB: And I'll say this about Boston: Boston, for a long time, was an underdog town. You've got this place where the Red Sox just can't seem to win the World Series. It's generations of people waiting for this thing to happen. So I seem to remember that when word got out that we were going to sign to a major, people were actually pretty supportive, especially the older guard in Boston. They were just happy that something cool was happening to a band from around town.

How was the experience of having a major-label budget and resources when making *Antenna*?

JC: We got a practice space in L.A. for pre-production and we were really killing the songs—trimming them and cutting them up and changing them from what they were initially. I remember playing the songs over and over and over, to the point where you don't know what's going on and the song doesn't feel like it once did.

Why were you changing them so much?

JC: I'd say to make it more commercial. The label was trying to get five-minute or six-minute songs down to three and a half minutes. I thought it was a good idea, to see how concise you could get something.

SB: On one hand, it was exciting to see how streamlined the sound of Cave In could be. But then there were times when we'd come into the space to play a song and say, "Wait, which version of this song are we doing?" It got so blurry and convoluted that the seed of whatever the song was—the magic that had birthed it—we were two, three, four, five, six arrangements away from that. It was very disorienting at times.

AM: It was a cool experiment, but looking back, some of what makes us special as a band was lost in that process. Not completely—

I think there are some good songs on *Antenna*—but in doing the arranging and rearranging, something got lost.

Did that process ever make you remorseful about signing to a major? Or did you welcome the feedback?

SB: I think it made us more sensitive as far as who we were going to pick for a producer. We were like, "Who is going to be the answer to this weird problem we have where our identity is at stake?" We were in over our heads a bit. We looked to producers to answer that. We were presented with some interesting options as far as people to work with, and in the end I think Rich [Costey] made a really good record and helped us problem-solve.

JC: We were a band that was used to recording a record in a weekend or two. And then all of a sudden we were in this studio for almost two months. You're showing up every day and not a whole lot is getting done, but you're busy the whole time.

SB: You get really good at *Grand Theft Auto*.

Did you ever feel like you had too much time?

SB: We started to wonder why we had so much time in the studio. We started to wonder if certain things were done just to eat up studio time so everyone could get paid. There was also a lag at the very beginning where we got into Cello Studios, in this massive live room that's the size of a small fucking basketball court, where they'd done "California Dreamin'." And then Rich has this idea to set up the fucking drum kit in the vocal booth, which is the smallest room in the goddamn studio, because he wanted a trashy drum sound. We tried that for about a week and then Rich was like, "Eh, yeah, I guess this doesn't work." We also got 80 percent of the guitars all tracked, and then Rich comes in one day and is like, "Guys, I discovered this amp, the Diezel. We've got to redo all the guitars on the record with it."

JC: They had a drum tech in there with like fifteen different snares and three different drum kits. We were like, "We don't need all this shit." But they were like, "This is how it's done."

What was your reaction to the finished product?

SB: I got really emotional, actually. Hearing everything so pristine and clean and layered, after months of working on it—to finally have it finished and to sit back and hear it all without wanting to change anything about the arrangement of the songs, I just felt really emotional. It choked me up a bit.

And what did the label think of the record?

AM: It's hard to say. Around the time the record came out, Bruce Flohr had one foot out the door. There were some people there that kind of liked it, but there was a transition happening. Once "Anchor" dropped, it was pretty much dead after that. The whole time, I thought there were better songs we could've put out there first as a single. But they were like, "No, we're gonna give 'em a little taste with 'Anchor,' and then it's gonna open the door for 'Inspire.'" But we never got to "Inspire."

SB: Their whole thing was playing the long game, but none of us realized that there actually was no long game. "Anchor" was the song where Bruce came to visit us in the studio and was listening to it and he was jumping up and down like a little kid, like, "That's the song! That's the shit I wanna hear!" But the whole campaign felt like it ended before it started.

Aside from the radio, was the label doing much to promote the record?

SB: There was this street team—I think they were called Streetwise. They partnered up with RCA to do street promotion. We came up with this packaging idea where we did two or three CD singles. One of our friends was working as a bike messenger in Boston. They came to this area in Government Center and noticed that all these fucking Cave In CDs were just strewn about and littering the ground all over downtown Boston. Were they giving them out to people who were just chucking it? Or were the people on the team just tossing them? We didn't know. It was hard to see what was happening.

AM: Bruce was saying that the single wasn't doing well in Boston, and if you're not getting traction in your hometown, that's not a good sign. And my attitude the entire time was that "Anchor" was the worst song on the record. I couldn't believe we were using "Anchor." But like I said, Bruce had one foot out the door.

How did it feel when your A&R left?

SB: The band was signed in 2001 and our record came out in 2003. There was this two-year honeymoon period, and a lot changed in that time. With Bruce gone, it became very evident that he was the biggest reason we'd signed to the label. We hadn't formed any strong relationships with anyone else there. We weren't assigned a new A&R person, I think because there was a big price tag on our heads. They'd spent so much money getting us signed, making the record, all the promotional stuff, tour support. And then when the record tanks, whoever is going to A&R that project has to assume the responsibility of this giant debt that's accrued to some degree.

AM: When Bruce left, there was no identity to the band. There was this sense that we needed to look busy. We were staying busy playing these weird shows. We played a show with Ben Folds Five, which was weird. We played these weird college shows. It was this illusion of looking busy. We'd play Minneapolis and then be back in Minneapolis a month later.

JC: We'd tour in the States, then go to Europe for a month, come back and play the same places. We did that back and forth for a year and a half. They'd be like, "You're drawing less people." Well, yeah, no kidding.

How did your relationship with RCA unfold from there?

AM: Clive Davis took over RCA, which was a big deal. And we'd failed with this record, so we had this finger waved at us, like "Do better next time."

SB: And it sucks, because we were like, "We did everything you asked us to do!"

AM: So they wanted to show our second record to Clive Davis. I didn't even know who Clive Davis was at the time. So we started doing demos, which became *Perfect Pitch Black*, and they fucking hated it.

SB: They were like, "Wait, you're bringing back the Cookie Monster vocals? This is a step backwards."

AM: People started abandoning ship. Our lawyer quit. They knew the writing was on the wall. They knew we didn't want to be on the label anymore. Was it self-sabotage on our part? I don't know.

SB: We were reconnecting with ourselves and starting to form a new musical identity that was a merging of the things we'd picked up in the *Jupiter/Antenna* era and bringing in that *Until Your Heart Stops* energy and making something completely new. To them, it just seemed like a complete step backwards. I don't think anyone put up a fight about Cave In needing to get dropped from RCA.

Looking back, is there anything you wish you'd done differently?

AM: One thing I do wish now, especially with Caleb being gone, is I wish I'd enjoyed myself more. I wish I'd soaked in more of the sun in Santa Monica, I wish I'd gone for a run every morning on the beach.

SB: There are times when I look back with a bit of a sense of heartbreak, wishing things could've gone a bit differently. But I also understand that things had to go the way that they did for me to have that perception. That's just the weird conundrum of life.

CURSIVE

Less than two years after their tour with At the Drive-In, Cursive grappled with their own struggles on the road. By 2002, the Omaha band had run themselves into the ground supporting 2000's *Domestica* and were forced to cancel the remainder of a summer tour after frontman Tim Kasher suffered a collapsed lung. While home, they began channeling their exhaustion into a new record, which would become 2003's *The Ugly Organ*. The album caught them at their songwriting peak and would often be hailed by critics and fans as their unimpeachable masterpiece. But while it put up extremely impressive sales numbers for their independent label, Saddle Creek, Cursive never took the next step by jumping to a major label. In fact, not only did they remain indie; they were never even approached by

A&R reps, Kasher claims. And while many of the band's peers got poached by the majors during those years, Cursive stayed a beloved indie rock holdout.

I'm very surprised to hear you say that Cursive never had the opportunity to do a record with a major label.
Tim Kasher: I think we never came off as very sellable, although many other bands didn't come off as accessible and got picked up anyway. But I do recall that when we were touring *Ugly Organ*, there would be rumblings and people coming out to shows. That chatter about the Saddle Creek family and how fiercely independent we all were and had built our own label ourselves—there was a certain intimidation. I don't know if intimidation is the right word . . .

You seemed not for sale.
Exactly. And the truth of it is that we weren't for sale. I think maybe that extended past us and people were answering for us, almost. Like, we weren't even asked, but we'd hear about this or that label that was excited, and if we ever were open to it, they'd want to be involved. But that's as close as it got. It might be because Robb [Nansel] from Saddle Creek was saying we weren't interested.

Do you think if you had gotten the opportunity to do a record with Atlantic or Capitol, one, would the band have been interested, and, two, how do you think Saddle Creek would've taken that?
Saddle Creek would've been fine with it, because ultimately that doesn't really matter; the thought would've likely been we should all maintain some sort of friendship over that. If it's a decision we wanted to make, then it's a decision we wanted to make. But we were all pretty fiercely independent at that point. I do remember, when those conversations would come up amongst the band, the rare times it was brought up, we were just totally disinterested.

Why?
Because we were so into Merge and Dischord that we were really proud that we had our own ecosystem going, so there wasn't a need.

Here's a hypothetical. Say you could sell 200,000 copies of your record on Saddle Creek, versus selling 700,000 on Atlantic. You'd take the former?

No. But at the time, yeah. Fifteen years ago, the gray area of major label/independent that existed . . . nobody really cares [now]. It was such a huge deal growing up, and that's what your book's about. Conor [Oberst] has had this attitude for years of "Why does it matter? Who cares?" It took me years to catch up with him. [*Laughs*] I just kept sticking with this DIY ethic. It ultimately just doesn't matter. Unless you're really gonna release it yourself and sell it out of your own van and not touch any of the greater system, you're just using the system or the system is gonna use you. So what does it really matter?

THRICE

Thrice's and Thursday's major-label stories run parallel to each other on opposite coasts. Much like their New Jersey counterparts, Thrice was signed to Island Def Jam during the era in which the label was dipping its toe into the genre of post-hardcore, under the management of Lyor Cohen and Julie Greenwald. A&R rep Rob Stevenson took a liking to the band after witnessing the passionate following they'd amassed in their hometown of Irvine, California, as well as the respectable sales numbers their second album, *The Illusion of Safety*, did for their independent label, Sub City, an offshoot of Hopeless Records. Also like Thursday, Thrice released two major-label albums—2003's *The Artist in the Ambulance* and 2005's *Vheissu*—before pop mogul L.A. Reid took over the company, at which point it became obvious that Island was no longer a tenable home. The band started work on an over-the-top, four-part concept album, which they hoped, perhaps subconsciously, would get them released from their contract. And it worked: Island Def Jam let Thrice go, and the band retreated back to the indie system, where they've remained since. And while Thrice didn't exactly become a household name, drummer Riley Breckenridge believes that their brief stint on a major label helped elevate their profile high enough that they could maintain a musical career for years to come.

How did interest from larger labels come about when you were on Sub City?
Riley Breckenridge: Before we put out *Illusion of Safety*, Rob Stevenson, who ended up being our A&R guy at Island, came sniffing around a bit. He came out to see us play at Chain Reaction. We were playing on absolutely any bill we could get on there. We felt like the house band. We'd be on emo night, and punk night, and ska night, and O.C. hardcore night. We never really fit in anywhere, but we'd slowly gain fans from all those different scenes. So when we finally got to start headlining there, the shows were really fucking great—packed and enthusiastic. Somehow Rob had caught wind of that.

Was it just Rob or were other labels taking interest?
Rob was definitely the first one. We had a good first week of sales for a label like Sub City. It seemed like stuff was snowballing for us, at least on a local level. After Rob started sniffing around, as it usually plays out, all the other dudes started creeping in. It was everybody—Capitol, Columbia, MCA, American. I remember we went on tour with Anti-Flag and Against All Authority in February 2002, two weeks after our record came out. What I remember most about that tour was that after we soundchecked, we'd have to go to a meeting. Every night. We were always getting whisked away to a dinner with some dude who wanted to sign us. I remember talking in the van every night, like, "This is really weird. It doesn't feel like a real tour."

Did you have a mixed bag of A&R meetings?
Yeah. We could tell Rob was really interested, because he was there from the get-go. He'd come from New York hardcore and knew Gorilla Biscuits and CIV and had signed Rival Schools. So we knew he got it. But there were meetings we took with guys we knew didn't get it. They didn't understand the music, they didn't understand where our heads were at as a band, they didn't understand what kind of people we are. So there were some weird, weird meetings.

Do any stick out to you as the absolute worst?

The worst that I can remember was we went to a meeting at Columbia. I don't remember the guy's name, but I remember him making us wait for a long time. When his assistant finally took us back to his office, he had *The Illusion of Safety* playing on the stereo in his office and was like, "Oh, oh, I didn't know you guys were coming in here!" So he pulled that move. We sat down with him, and part of his pitch was "Are you guys familiar with the band Refused?" And we were like, "Yes, of course." And he was like, "Have you heard of the band Crazy Town?" And we didn't say this out loud, but we were like, "Yeah, they're fucking terrible." And he was like, "Did you know Crazy Town covered Refused? Check this out." And he played us the "New Noise" cover, and we were all sitting there in the office, the craziest douche chills, as he's blaring this. Instantly I was like, "This meeting is over."

What were you looking for when you were taking these meetings? What was most appealing to you as a bartering chip?

We were taking the meetings because the interest was there, and it seemed silly not to. From the beginning, our whole mentality was never "We're gonna be rock stars! We want to be in the biggest band ever!" Our whole thing was "We want to take the next tiny step up the ladder." So if the next rung seemed like a logical step, we were open to it. That they were interested at all was enough for us to take the meetings. We knew we weren't going to change. We wanted to do what we were doing but get more people to hear it somehow. So any label that was interested in further facilitating what we were doing was appealing to us.

Were you guys worried that you'd get blowback from your fans by going to a major label?

No. Just because we'd been catching shit for everything, from the get-go. Once we signed to Sub City, we got shit from people. Once we started messing with tempos that were not the forbidden Fat Wreck Chords beat, we got called sellouts. Once we wrote songs that were heavier in the melodic sense, we were selling out. So it wasn't a concern, really.

It's funny that fans refuse to accept their favorite artist changing or growing in any way.

Yeah. We still get it. We'll be playing some mellow newer song and people are just screaming the name of a song that came out twenty years ago.

So did you guys meet Lyor Cohen?

Yeah. That's the reason we signed with them. I grew up listening to a lot of eighties hip-hop, so it was like, "Oh shit, Lyor Cohen. EPMD, Eric B. & Rakim, LL Cool J, Run DMC—this dude is a behemoth in music." And he's such an imposing figure. I remember we were at some dinner talking about how we were gonna roll out *Artist in the Ambulance*, and it was a civil conversation. And then he slammed his fist on the table and said, "We will crush them!" And we were like, "Fuck yeah! This guy's into it!" And Julie was enthusiastic and a really caring person. She'd ask me about my family. Lyor had the drive and Julie had the compassion. It was a really good fit. So when they bailed, it was like, ah man, we took all these meetings to figure out the best situation for us, and now we're stuck with somebody we would never have chosen.

How was the experience of making a big-budget record?

I cannot remember the dollar figure, but the budget was somewhere near what [Thursday] had. We did *The Illusion of Safety* with Brian McTernan, so when it came time to do *Artist in the Ambulance*, we were like, "We want to work with Brian again, full stop. No negotiation. We had a great time with Brian, we just need more time." Brian ended up getting Michael Barbiero to engineer the record. He'd worked on Metallica's . . . *And Justice for All*. He's a mega-producer. We went to Bearsville Studio, in upstate New York. The number of gold and platinum records on the walls there was staggering. Fucking mind-blowing for a bunch of twenty-year-old kids. We did drums and bass in Bearsville for two weeks. Then we went to Brian's studio in Beltsville, Maryland, for six weeks.

Did you ever worry about having too much time?

I think it was too much time to be in the studio. What we did not have a lot of time with was writing. We were touring on *Illusion of Safety* and everything was going well. Then for some reason the turnaround they wanted was a very short amount of time, and we didn't have shit written. I remember getting home from tour and feeling the most insane pressure to come up with a major-label debut in a couple months. Everything felt rushed. We had these ideas of expanding our scope sonically, but we couldn't experiment in writing enough to actually do it.

Did you meet L.A. Reid when he took over the label?

The clearest memory I have of meeting L.A. Reid is very similar to Geoff Rickly's story in the book. We were playing the second single from *Vheissu*, called "Red Sky." It's kind of a ballad, almost like early Coldplay. We had a meeting with him. The four of us went into his office, which is just lavish. The fanciest desk, animal pelts on the cabinetry. He had some scantily clad assistant walking in and out, handing him lip balms and shit. And we were playing that song extremely loud on his fancy speakers. I don't even play our records for my family or friends. It's just uncomfortable. I think he was pretending to like it. It was an instance where we were like, "This is not the right spot for us." We loved Rob, but everyone above him did not get it.

What were you not getting from the label that you'd hoped you would get?

Hard to say. We took this step, trying to play the game with as much comfort ethically as we could, and we're in this and it's just not working. We thought we could make the record we wanted to make, for better or worse. At least for us, we weren't clicking the boxes that people needed. We realized we played the game, but it wasn't where we needed to be. We're not gonna write singles, we're not gonna work with cowriters, we're not gonna work with the hotshot producers. We don't want to keep fighting against the label that wants to turn us into "rock band." So maybe we made a mistake.

How many albums were in your contract?

I think we had three and an option. So, following *Vheissu*, we made a twenty-four-song, four-EP concept record.

Which labels just love.

They love 'em! Any label, even indie labels. [*Laughs*] They were all themed around the four elements, and they're themed sonically as well as lyrically, and it was out there. I think maybe, even though it wasn't discussed, we were like, "This is how we get out. We make a fucked-up concept record and the label's gonna be like, 'What the fuck is this?'" And that's exactly what happened. I think Rob, in a way, thought, "If they write twenty-four songs, there's got to be at least one single, right?" And there wasn't. But I think he fought for us for as long as he could, and once we got to that concept double album or whatever, he was like, "Yeah, I can't keep fighting these battles. This is not worth it for me anymore."

So how did you get out of your deal?

There were some legal battles to get the rights to that record. We were also in a weird spot as a band. Dustin [Kensrue, singer] and Teppei [Teranishi, guitarist] had kids and it seemed like interest in being a full-time band, where we were touring 280 days out of the year, was wearing on them a bit. But thankfully we were allowed to keep that record. And we started talking to indie labels. Vagrant came around and was like, "Just give this to us and we'll put it out."

Were the growing pains of those major-label years difficult?

I just remember being exhausted and stressed out all the time. Every show seemed like it was make-or-break. "So-and-so from this station is here" or "So-and-so from this retail whatever is here." I'm a pretty anxious person, so if the stakes are high, it messes with me. I remember feeling exhausted and really stressed and not eating a bunch. I lost a ton of weight, not sleeping. But also being so blown away that any of it was even happening.

If you could go back and give yourself any advice, what would it be?
I'd tell myself to enjoy it or calm down. But how do you calm down when you're in the midst of all this stuff? There's no time. When you have downtime, you just want to sleep.

Looking back at it now, is there anything you'd do differently?
I don't think so. It gave us a big boost. It got our music out to more people and laid a fan-base foundation. Obviously that fan base has dwindled, but the people who have stuck with us for the last twenty years, they understand what they're gonna get from us and they know where it's coming from and that it hasn't changed since the beginning. So the jump to the major was helpful just to get our music to more people's ears. And the fact that we're still doing this now is just insane to me.

ACKNOWLEDGMENTS

First and foremost, I owe the biggest debt of gratitude to my editor, Kate Napolitano. When I shopped this book around to publishers, I felt the same reticence the bands in it must've felt when talking to interested record labels. But when I walked into Kate's office, I saw the Bikini Kill sticker on her notebook and her necklace that read OUT OF STEP, and that was it for me. For two years, she and I worked so intensely on this book together, like it was a secret between us. Although it belongs to the world now, I'll always cherish that time, when it was for no one but the two of us.

Thank you to my agent, David Patterson, who took notice of my writing before I was ready and waited patiently for years as I came up with a book idea. I hope it was worth the wait.

Thank you, once again and eternally, to Laura Jane Grace. Writing a book proved to be a lonelier experience without her.

Thanks to my parents, Lucy and Wayne Ozzi, who afforded me the perfectly good education I squandered to write about rock bands for a living.

Thanks to Dan Mulhall, my oldest friend and pro bono lawyer, who looks over all my contracts for no money down. (Wait, I got that all screwed up. It should read: "No, money down!")

Thanks to Jaime Boulter for rescuing me from a flaming car that was parked on the deck of a sinking ship.

Thanks to David Anthony. I'm sure there have been ways in which he's helped me, but I can't think of one at the moment.

Thanks to Chris Norris and Mark McCoy, whose effortless creativity inspired me and whose misanthropy cut me down to size.

I'm heavily indebted to Amanda Fotes for lending me the stunning photo that graces the cover of this book. I hold dear many memories of screaming in Geoff Rickly's face, and her shot captures the energy of those evenings perfectly. (And thanks to Geoff for all the mornings I woke up with a hoarse voice.)

The sincerest of thanks to Natalie Zea, Travis Schuldt, and Reygan, who took me in, treated me like family, and lent me the most serene place to write this book while the world literally burned around us.

All of the love in my entire heart goes to my nieces, Victoria and Ashley. If for some reason you two are ever reading this: See the world, raise hell, and be kind!

A small army of people lent support that has carried me not just through the creation of this book, but through my entire "career." I'm surely forgetting people, but a special thanks to these kind souls: Kim Taylor Bennett, Jeremy Bolm, Brendan Kelly, Annalise Domenighini, Trey Smith, Lauren Denitzio, Anika Pyle, Chris Farren, Tim Barry, Vanessa Burt, Benjamin Shapiro, Ciel Hunter, Lisa Root, Jonah Ray, Tim Kasher, Dessie Jackson, Alex Winston, Chris Gethard, Kyle Kramer, Greg Barnett, Jeff Rosenstock, Augusta Koch, Andrea Domanick, John Hill, Colin Joyce, Rob Pasbani, Mike Yannich, Lindsay McMullen, Kyle Kinane, Laura Stevenson, Mike Campbell, Kevin Devine, David Castillo, Brian Fallon, Dan Faughnder, Christina Johns, Josh Epple, Kayleigh Goldsworthy, Alex Robert Ross, Emma Garland, Shirley Manson, Kerry DarConte, Sarah Tudzin, Keith Paras, Luke O'Neil, Hilary Pollack, Steph Godshall, the Milas family and the entire Wolfpack, and everyone in PUP, the Dirty Nil, and Murder by Death.

I will forever be grateful to every person who made time to talk to me for this book and trusted me to tell their story.

And thank you to Annie Flook. For everything.

WORKS CITED

BOOKS

Anderson, Chris. *The Long Tail: Why the Future of Business is Selling Less of More*. New York: Hachette Books, 2008.

Arnold, Gina. *Kiss This: Punk in the Present Tense*. New York: St. Martin's Griffin, 1997.

Azerrad, Michael. *Our Band Could Be Your Life: Scenes from the American Indie Underground 1981–1991*. New York: Back Bay Books, 2002.

Barker, Travis, with Gavin Edwards. *Can I Say: Living Large, Cheating Death, and Drums, Drums, Drums*. New York: William Morrow, 2015.

Blink-182 with Anne Hoppus. *Blink-182: Tales from Beneath Your Mom*. New York: MTV Books, 2001.

Boulware, Jack, and Silke Tudor. *Gimme Something Better: The Profound, Progressive, and Occasionally Pointless History of Bay Area Punk from Dead Kennedys to Green Day*. New York: Penguin Books, 2009.

Bryant, Tom. *Not the Life It Seems: The True Lives of My Chemical Romance*. New York: Da Capo Press, 2014.

Caress, Adam. *The Day Alternative Music Died: Dylan, Zeppelin, Punk, Glam, Alt, Majors, Indies, and the Struggle Between Art and Money for the Soul of Rock*. Montreat, NC: New Troy Books, 2015.

Diehl, Matt. *My So-Called Punk*. New York: St. Martin's Griffin, 2007.

Givony, Ronen. *24 Hour Revenge Therapy*. 33 ⅓. New York: Bloomsbury Academic, 2018.

Grace, Laura Jane, with Dan Ozzi. *Tranny: Confessions of Punk Rock's Most Infamous Anarchist Sellout*. New York: Hachette Books, 2016.

Grubbs, Eric. *Post: A Look at the Influence of Post-Hardcore, 1985–2007*. Self-published, iUniverse, 2008.

Haydn, Reinhardt. *My Chemical Romance: This Band Will Save Your Life*. London: Plexus, 2008.

Lawrence, Grant. *Dirty Windshields: The Best and Worst of the Smugglers Tour Diaries*. Madeira Park, BC: Douglas & McIntyre, 2017.

Livermore, Larry. *How to Ru(i)n a Record Label: The Story of Lookout Records*. New Brunswick, NJ: Don Giovanni Records, 2015.

Prested, Kevin. *Punk USA: The Rise and Fall of Lookout Records*. Portland, OR: Microcosm Publishing, 2014.

Shooman, Joe. *Blink-182: The Bands, the Breakdown, and the Return*. Church Station, UK: Independent Music Press, 2010.

Sinker, Daniel, ed. *We Owe You Nothing: Punk Planet; The Collected Interviews*. Exp. ed. New York: Punk Planet Books, 2007.

Small, Doug. *The Story of Green Day*. London, Omnibus Press, 2005.

Spitz, Marc. *Nobody Likes You: Inside the Turbulent Life, Times, and Music of Green Day*. New York: Hachette Books, 2007.

Winwood, Ian. *Smash! Green Day, the Offspring, Bad Religion, NOFX, and the '90s Punk Explosion*. New York: Da Capo Press, 2018.

FANZINES, MAGAZINES, NEWSPAPERS, AND WEBSITES

AbsolutePunk
Addicted to Noise
The Advertiser
Alternative Press
AV Club
BAM
Big Cheese
Billboard
Blender
Book Your Own Fucking Life
Boston Globe
Buddyhead
Chicago Tribune
Cleveland Scene
CMJ New Music Monthly
CMJ New Music Report
East Bay Express
The Economist
Entertainment Weekly
The Face
Flipside
Fracture
The Guardian
Guitar World
Harp
Hits Daily Double
Hollywood Reporter
Kerrang!
LA Weekly
Lookout
Lollipop
Los Angeles Times
Maine Campus
Maximum Rocknroll

Melody Maker
MOJO
MTV News
My Letter to the World
New York Post
New York Times
New York Times Magazine
NME
Omaha Weekly
Palo Alto Weekly
Phoenix New Times
Pitchfork
Punknews
Punk Planet
Q
Radar
Razorcake
Revolver
Rock Candy
Rolling Stone
Rubberband
San Francisco Chronicle
SPIN
Thrasher
Trust
Uncut
VH1
Village Voice
Washington Post
Zips & Chains

FILMS AND VIDEOS

Berg, Amy J., dir. *An Open Secret*. Disarming Films, 2014.
Burghart, Jake, dir. *Against Me!: We're Never Going Home*. Fat Wreck Chords, 2004.

Irwin, Tim, and Keith Schieron, dirs. *Don't Break Down: A Film About Jawbreaker*. Rocket Fuel Films, 2017.

Kaplan, Greg, dir. *My Chemical Romance: Life on the Murder Scene*. Reprise Records, 2006.

Pedulla, Steve, dir. *Kill the House*. Grey Sky Films, 2007.

Redford, Corbett. *Turn It Around: The Story of East Bay Punk*. Capodezero Films, 2017.

OTHER SOURCES

Driven: Green Day. VH1 Television, 2005.

Green Day: The Early Years. Spotify, 2017.

Ryan, Kyle. Rise Against, Oral History. In *Rise Against Career Vinyl Box Set*. Universal, 2018.

INDEX